Aiken:
Senate Diary

Aiken:
Senate Diary
January 1972—January 1975

George D. Aiken

The STEPHEN GREENE *Press*

Brattleboro, Vermont

Woodcuts by
Charles H. Joslin

Library of Congress Cataloging in Publication Data
Aiken, George David, 1892–
  Aiken: Senate diary, January 1972–January 1975.
  1. Aiken, George David, 1892–   2. United
States—Politics and government—1969–1974.   3. United
States—Politics and government—1974–
E748.A193A33   328.73'092'4   75–41870
ISBN 0–8289–0275–5

    76 77 78 79 80 6 5 4 3 2 1

Contents

Sixteen pages of photographs follow page 182.

A Note

ON New Year's Day of 1972 I started to record at the end of each week, for my remaining three years in the United States Senate, the manner in which a Senator observes the events of the passing days, how these events can change their appearance from week to week, and how the attitude of a Senator can change with them.

The result of my evaluations and impressions can only loosely be called a diary since I omitted many small events that did not seem to be part of the picture I had undertaken to convey. None of the entries in the resulting twenty-seven loose-leaf volumes has been revised in the light of hindsight, for to have done so would nullify what I attempted, which was to set down the factors that week by week were the basis of my judgment at the time.

This personal record spans the end of our involvement in Vietnam, our reconciliation with Russia and China, the Watergate affair, the resignation of President Nixon, and the first few months of Gerald Ford's Presidency. Although I noted how I felt and what I did as a Senator during this crucial period in our country's history, what I have set down is not a "now-it-can-be-told" revelation. I hope passages will not be taken out of context and magnified to sensational proportions.

The complete record for the three years contains something over four hundred thousand words, far too many for a single volume that can be easily read or handled. At my request, therefore, Ralph Nading Hill, fellow Vermonter, noted historian, and my good friend, has reduced the total to manageable proportions. He accomplished this by eliminating passages that were repetitious or were not germane to the over-all record as presented in book form for the general reader. For this I am grateful.

GEORGE D. AIKEN

Putney, Vermont
January 1, 1976

vii

Foreword

LATE in December 1974 the dean of the United States Senate sat down with his Democratic confidant, Mike Mansfield, to the last of twenty-one years of breakfasts they had shared in the Senate dining room. Their fare was nothing less than the future of the country. Much of what they discussed through the years very likely became the law of the land.

George Aiken's retirement to his Vermont orchard left the Capitol's supply of agrarian morality sadly diminished, if not depleted. A ponderous government forged by pressure groups makes it unlikely that an old-fashioned populist with abiding faith, not in mobs but in individuals, will again achieve his kind of influence at home and abroad.

He acquired this influence because he did not seek it. Since no posse ever conducted him into the Senate or pursued his power after he got there, he could be everybody's man because he was nobody's man but his own. Of course it is, or at least was, true that to be elected Senator from rural Vermont, with its homogeneous population, it was not necessary to become the hostage of pressure groups, to make promises impossible of fulfillment, or to become politically indebted to fund-raisers. This was demonstrated by the amount the Governor, as he prefers now to be called, spent in the last Senatorial campaign in which he was opposed: a grand total of fourteen dollars and seventy-three cents.

His views, like those of other legislators from the contrary Vermont republic during the past two centuries, are not easily classified. While nominally a Republican he is really a doctrinaire independent, uncomfortable with professional liberals and reactionaries of both parties. He clings to such unfashionable virtues as thrift and balanced budgets. (His wife worked as hard as he did in his Washington office but he took her off the payroll the day they were married, and he regularly returned to the Treasury a goodly proportion of his office allowance.)

The Capitol knew no more articulate critic of bigness—big government, big business, big labor; and one whose heritage was an autonomous Vermont farm would regard as a disaster the trampling, in the stampede to the federal trough, of the self-reliance that built this society. Yet he has always been in the forefront of costly legislation for the farmer, for the sick and the aged and the needy. He is an ardent free-trader and fought hard for the development of nuclear energy. Peace remains his foremost concern: his early protest against the Vietnam war—"Just say we won and get out!"—became a nationwide maxim.

The following diary is the culmination of a public life that led from the Vermont House of Representatives to two terms as Governor and six in the United States Senate. Although it was dictated at the end of each of more than one hundred fifty busy weeks, the diary has all the features of the most precisely considered material. And unlike the pronouncements, spoken or written, of many politicians these days, it is all in the Governor's own words.

RALPH NADING HILL

1972

January 1, 1972

THIS IS the first day of the New Year 1972.

Up here on Putney Mountain five miles from town, eight inches of new snow are piled upon a foot of old snow and crust, the temperature a little below zero, but mostly sunshine and no wind.

L.P.A. [Lola Pierotti Aiken, Mrs. George D. Aiken] has gone to church downtown—now 10:30 A.M. She is an old-fashioned Catholic who hasn't gone "mod" as far as her Church is concerned. She has also learned not to be afraid of winter roads and high snowbanks.

Looking off to the east we can see a twenty-mile stretch of the New Hampshire hills east of the Connecticut River. Mount Monadnock dominates the view now that the leaves are off the trees. On clear nights the lights of New Hampshire homes blink at us from the distance, while during late summer and early fall mornings we look out from our vantage point of fourteen hundred feet elevation in full sunshine over a sea of fog filling the Connecticut Valley.

Two hundred years ago this mountain was covered with virgin forests, and just to think of the work, the courage, and endured hardships of the early settlers cannot help but give one a mixed feeling of pride and guilt. Pride that this land was cleared and this country was built by those ancestors of ours who had the courage and faith which prompted them to leave the oppression and tyranny of their mother countries to face hostile elements in America in order to be free. And a touch of guilt at the volume of complaints we receive when the luxuries of modern living fail to arrive on time or the vacation trip to exotic countries has to be passed up for one reason or another.

New Year's Eve was cloudless, the moon was full, glistening on the snow so that one could almost read a newspaper out-of-doors through most of the night. The effect of full moonlight shining through the white birches with a background of pine and hemlock is indescribably beautiful, conveying the Glory and Power of the Infinite in a manner never heard from podium or pulpit.

¶ IT WAS IN THIS SETTING that I tried to reflect on what the old year had wrought and what the effect might be on the people of this Earth.

3

The year 1971 may be recorded as one of the most momentous of all time: an era of change—almost a metamorphosis—in the public pulse and thinking of America, and possibly of the world itself.

Only three years ago the big news in our country was the demonstrations by millions of young people, and the destruction of property by fire and bomb, sometimes undoubtedly for profit but mostly in protest to our war in Eastern Asia, a war which we could never win in a military sense, a war which a majority of Americans considered immoral on our part and which was costing us the lives of some three hundred of our youth every week. At that time, the armed forces of the United States totaled some 3,400,000, of which 860,000 were stationed in Eastern Asia—543,000 of them being in South Vietnam.

Crime was increasing at an alarming rate, and it was not simply crime on the streets but crime that was no respecter of the levels of society, for the same instinct which prompted a youth on the street to snatch a handbag also prompted the respected members of an industrial board to snatch the resources of smaller developing nations even at the price of human distress and loss of life if considered necessary.

The people protested and members of Congress were deluged by letters and telegrams from those back home whose patience with the executive branch and Congress had become exhausted. Although some of these communications were patently political, the great majority were from sincerely concerned citizens. Their voices were clearly heard in Washington by both the President and members of Congress.

Every President with whom I have been associated has wanted to be a good President. In fact, I think each wanted to be the best President the country had ever had, and President Nixon is no exception.

Listening to public demand, he pronounced the Nixon doctrine, which in effect proclaimed that the United States recognized the right of other nations, large and small, to determine their own destiny. This doctrine, while concededly difficult to enforce, nevertheless met with general public approval. The President also began withdrawal of military forces from Eastern Asia and this, too, met with a favorable public response: the size of our armed forces was materially reduced.

When the President took office in 1969 it was freely predicted that the opposition party, having a sizable majority in both Houses of Congress, would be unco-operative with the President and would undertake to embarrass him, even to the extent of hampering him in the ordinary conduct of good government.

This prediction has not come true. Congress, with its committees headed largely by its older and more experienced members, has given the President an unexpectedly high degree of co-operation without which our nation would have been in a vastly more difficult situation militarily, economically, and socially than it is today.

Of course, there have been some efforts to embarrass the President in his work, efforts to prevent the President from making his own appointments—for whose work he would be held responsible—or by enacting legislation which the President in all good conscience would have to veto. However, the old political custom of enacting legislation that sounds good but that its promoters know full well the President will have to veto, has been employed only sparingly.

Actually, it has been many years since any President has had the wholehearted co-operation of Congressional leadership which has been enjoyed by President Nixon. Reviewing briefly the extent of co-operation between Congress and the President, we find that seven instances stand out:

One. The President asked for new tax laws, and the Congress agreed, providing for a heavy reduction of taxes over a three-year period.

Two. He asked for short-term authority to control wages and prices, and Congress agreed.

Three. On August 15, the President imposed a temporary 10 percent surcharge on many imports from all countries; the Congress and the public generally approved.

Four. In December, the President announced an agreement with major producing countries which included a proposed devaluation of the dollar; Congress generally approved.

Five. From time to time the President announced increased withdrawal of troops from East Asia; Congress approved, but said, "Go faster." About 600,000 troops have been withdrawn in the last three years.

Six. The President recommended reduction in over-all United States troop numbers; Congress, by reducing Defense appropriations, went him one better. (United States military strength has now been reduced by about a million men.)

Seven. The President announced his intention to visit China and consult with the heads of other nations either at home or abroad; Congress approved.

Not all of the President's recommendations were as well received, however. With the White House controlled by one political party and the Congress firmly in the control of the other, this was not surprising

—nor, on the whole, should it be disturbing. Disagreement occurred especially on four items:

One. The President nominated four judges for the United States Supreme Court, and the Senate rejected two of them.

Two. The President's request for high foreign-aid appropriations was sharply cut by the Congress. In the light of subsequent events, this action was probably sound.

Three. The President's request for revenue-sharing with the states has not been approved—and is not likely to be agreed to in anywhere near the shape which he first recommended. Some form of revenue-sharing, however, is desirable and will doubtless be worked out between these two branches of government.

Four. It is in the fields of health, education, welfare, and environment that the most deplorable situations exist. The quest for political advantage in these fields has at times been outrageous, and recommendations for legislation have ranged from reactionary to ridiculous. Those members of Congress who, to paraphrase Gray, "have let ambition mock their useful toil," have made such far-reaching proposals that no self-governing nation could adopt them and still call itself a democracy.

Absenteeism and utopian promises can be regarded as the weakest spots in the record of the First Session of the 92nd Congress.

And one wonders, What is it about failure to perform a lower assignment properly that qualifies one for higher office? And why is it that people who as private citizens are respected for their integrity, so frequently have their credibility questioned once they assume, or seek to assume, higher public office?

¶ THE SECOND SESSION of the 92nd Congress will be meeting soon [January 18]. There will, of course, be problems of legislation. But 1972 being an election year, the problems of human behavior will be of most serious concern. Welfare, the economy, protection of the environment, foreign aid, and what we call national security will likely go on the auction block to see what party, what branch of the government, or what candidates for high offices of government can bid the most for the Election Day support of the beneficiaries of these programs.

Paradoxically enough, out of the maze of unkeepable promises, uncontrollable desires, and some downright dishonesty there will probably come a faintly better world.

¶ LOOKING OUT at the New Hampshire hills across the valley, I feel very small indeed. I know I am bigger than the viruses, the insects, the bees and the birds, but I have had nothing to do with this arrangement. In my dictionary the two biggest words are "Infinity" and "Eternity"; my mind cannot adequately define these words but I do know that nothing is infinite but Infinity and nothing is eternal but Eternity.

Now I must come back to Earth for a brief stay.

L.P.A. is reading *Gone with the Wind* and the telephone is ringing —either a call from my Washington office, or some constituent has a problem.

[*The diaries break for the weeks ending January 8 and January 15, 1972, to resume in the third week of January with the convening of the Second Session of the 92nd Congress, in Washington, D.C., on the eighteenth of the month.*]

[*United States Senate*]

Week ending January 22, 1972

EVEN BEFORE the Second Session of the 92nd Congress convened on Tuesday, January 18, the Secretary of Agriculture [Earl Butz] had announced a decision reversing a previous plan which would have resulted in reducing the number of food-stamp recipients. His decision, prompted partly by political motivation, will be approved by many and assailed by some who would like to outbid the Secretary in soliciting votes for the coming November election.

On Thursday, President Nixon delivered his State of the Union message to the joint session of Congress. His message was widely televised, and on Friday certain Democrats employed television to tell the world how wrong he was about practically everything. In my opinion their rebuttal was a flop and the President was a hands-down winner in this debate.

On Friday he sent a message to the Congress urging prompt legislation for control of the dock strike which is severely handicapping the United States economy and playing directly into the hands of other countries. I believe that the Congress will generally approve of taking action in this field, but no doubt the President will be assailed and charged with recommending oppression against working people.

Secretary of the Treasury John Connally stated that it was high time that industry and labor get busy doing something for themselves, and not depend on the federal government to do everything for them. I think Secretary Connally was right in making this statement. Although for thirty years I have supported the cause of labor, organized and unorganized, I feel that there are many labor leaders in this country who are altogether too big for their britches and whose principal motive is to promote their own ambitions at the expense of the membership of their unions and of other factors of our economy. Labor leadership has changed drastically since the days of Phil Murray, John L. Lewis, John Edelman and others who were sincerely dedicated to the cause.

On the international scene, the action which will have the deepest and possibly the most adverse effect on the United States, at least temporarily, was the entry of Great Britain and other countries into the Common Market of Western Europe. The result can be to force greater economic isolation on the United States and Canada, and possibly on other countries of the Western Hemisphere. While the United States was going heavily into debt last year, Great Britain was showing a favorable balance of payments of $2.5 billion, according to newspaper reports.

Although industry has become international of late years, and the United States has become a nation of investors whose income is partly derived from profits made in other countries, there are still many times more working people in the United States than there are investors in foreign enterprises. I fully expect that there will be an increased demand for retaliatory action on the part of the United States against those countries who patently seek to handicap the United States economy in their own interests.

I am opposed to isolating the United States from the international economic field, but under the circumstances I am also opposed to relegating our country to a weak position in the economic world.

Actually, what is taking place will in the long run result in a better understanding and a broadening of production and trade throughout the world.

¶ I HAVE NEVER SEEN so many incompetent persons aspiring to high office and apparently well financed in their efforts to achieve it. Some of the subcommittees of important Congressional committees appear to be used largely for the promotion of the aspirations of this or that member of Congress. These subcommittees are granted large appropriations which will be used to a great extent to promote the political aspirations of the subcommittee chairman. I would be inclined to oppose these appropriations in the Senate were it not for the fact that in the executive branch of government there are many agencies and subagencies which can legally use appropriated funds to insure the re-election of the President.

Congress has passed a Fair Election law which the President will probably sign, but it will not be very effective in making candidates honest.

Week ending January 29, 1972

ANOTHER WEEK has now passed and Congress as yet can show no record of accomplishment. The entire week has been spent debating and voting on amendments to the EEOC [Equal Employment Opportunity Commission]. I have opposed all efforts to weaken the proposed legislation, although I have my doubts that any legislation can force an employer to hire personnel which is inefficient or which he doesn't want. Labor unions have supported the proposed legislation, but on the other hand some labor unions themselves have been as discriminatory against minorities as any of the industrial groups have been.

¶ SECRETARY OF AGRICULTURE Butz appeared before the Senate Committee on Agriculture and Forestry on Monday in opposition to legislation which would almost completely have nullified agriculture legislation enacted by Congress in 1970. Supporters of this legislation, two of whom are members of the Agriculture committee and are also candidates for the Democratic nomination for President, were apparently most concerned with getting the farm vote in the next November election. They did not make a very good case, and, much to my surprise, on Wednesday, January 26, the committee killed the bill by a 10-to-4 vote with Presidential candidates Humphrey and Mc-Govern being joined by Senators Young of North Dakota and Curtis of Nebraska in support of the bill.

I had expected we would have a majority of only one or two. Young's vote was understandable, since the principal crop of North Dakota is wheat and the wheat price is down somewhat below previous years. Senator Curtis had apparently made a commitment to the wheat-growers of his state earlier, and, I think, prematurely, because Nebraska is also a livestock-producing state and the market price for meat animals, cattle and hogs, has now reached the highest point in over twenty years.

9

Because of the very heavy crop of feed grains, cattle and hogs are being fed to heavier weights than usual, thereby sharply increasing the income of livestock producers. There will be a political reaction to these high prices, however. The retail prices for meats will increase rather sharply and consumers will get mad.

¶ ON MONDAY, too, the new Secretary General of the United Nations came to Washington. I had lunch with him at the invitation of Secretary of State Rogers. The Secretary General, Kurt Waldheim, also had coffee with some of the Foreign Relations committee members that afternoon. Mr. Waldheim appeared quite practical in his views, but was worried lest the United States cut down sharply on its contributions to the U.N. or possibly leave the organization. In the latter case he felt that the U.N. itself could not long survive. I agree.

To complete the record for Monday, January 24, it should be noted that President Nixon sent his new 1973 Budget message to Congress. The amount of his over-all recommendation was startling, almost stunning, to many members of the Congress. I had stated some time ago that the President should not attempt to outbid the Democrats in seeking favors from the voters since the Democrats were professionals in this field and he probably couldn't outbid them anyway. However, it looks as if he has done this.

Although he asked for an increase in the appropriations for national defense, he did in one respect reverse the trend of the two previous Administrations and requested a much larger amount for domestic and humanitarian programs than for military expenditures. The new totals ask for 42 percent of the budget for domestic programs and 32 percent for the military. In a political sense the President may have gained a point, since the Congress will either have to cut down on his recommendations for welfare and other domestic purposes, in which case the Democrats are likely to be blamed, or increase the President's recommendations as they have done in the past, and such action would be almost ridiculous.

In the long run, with the national debt approaching $500 billion and everybody in most all positions of life demanding more money and lower taxes, one is justified in worrying over the future of our country and its government.

However, I well recall that when I came to the Senate in 1941 I was told by competent political and economic leaders that when our national debt reached $50 billion the country would collapse.

It didn't.

¶ TUESDAY: The President exploded what might be termed another blockbuster by divulging the terms of proposals which had been made secretly to the North Vietnam government for ending the war in Indochina. I can support his proposal and commended him for it the next day, although it is doubtful that North Vietnam will accept, since that country insists that we overthrow the government of South Vietnam as a condition for ending the war. Should North Vietnam ever get control of South Vietnam I dread to think of the slaughter that would take place.

There will be opposition to the President's proposal to spend $2.5 billion for reconstruction work in North Vietnam the next few years. This will be based largely on political grounds, but as an economic measure we must not forget that during the years from 1965 to 1968 it was costing us approximately $2.5 billion a month to carry on the war, and therefore possibly including North Vietnam in a list of countries receiving our aid in return for ending the war may be a good investment proposal.

I, along with half a dozen other members of the Senate and the same from the House, attended a preview of the President's proposal at the White House. Lola and I then went on to a dinner given by retired Admiral Lewis Strauss, a small dinner attended by admirals and judges and their wives and a few other interesting personalities, but no others from either the executive or legislative branches of government. It was an excellent evening, but if one does not look out he will find that if he accepts many of the invitations to receptions and dinners the results will be devastating not only to his health but to his work as well.

¶ WEDNESDAY: Senate reaction to the President's proposal on North Vietnam was generally good. The Senate Committee on Agriculture, as I have stated, turned down the proposal to emasculate the present farm program. The Senate droned on with proposed amendments to the EEOC bill.

There was another dinner in the evening and entertainment, given by the Washington Press Club. It was an invitation affair attended by many social and political dignitaries. This is almost a must with many members of Congress, and Lola and I attended. The entertainment was provided by Senator Frank Church of Idaho, who included in his speech some sentences that would have been better received out behind the barn, and by the President's righthand assistant, Henry Kissinger, who oozed conceit from every pore.

¶ THURSDAY the Senate droned on.

Under Secretary of Agriculture Phil Campbell and other officials from the department met with the Republican members of the Senate Committee on Agriculture to explain the President's Agriculture

11

message, which Congress is due to receive soon. None of us like it, since it appeared to be an effort to downgrade or even eliminate the U.S. Department of Agriculture. Just who thought up this proposal is a mystery. I am satisfied that the Department of Agriculture did not propose it, and that in their hearts the topflight officials—and lower officials, too, for that matter—would be strongly opposed to it.

We are told that one of the slogans of the Defense department is "If it works, it's obsolete." I am afraid that someone has told the President that this same slogan or formula should apply to the Department of Agriculture, because as I understand the President's proposal the programs that have worked best for a long time are due for a downgrading. Congress will not agree. Someone has persuaded the President to make a political error. Agriculture is still by far our most important industry.

¶ On Friday, the Senate droned on some more.

A cloture petition on the EEOC bill has been prepared and will be voted on next Tuesday. I don't think it will carry, and also I think if we are going to accomplish anything in this Congress and avoid the appellation of a "do-nothing Congress" which President Harry Truman applied to the 80th Congress, we will have to set aside some proposed legislation that is more political than humanitarian and get down to business.

Week ending February 5, 1972

Congress has now completed a third week of this Session and the Senate has passed its first bit of legislation, the Foreign Aid Appropriations bill for 1972. I hope no one mistakes this action as indicating progress on the part of the Congress, because it was actually last year's bill that was passed, and we haven't even started hearings on current legislation yet.

The ranks of members of Congress ambitious for higher office seem to be growing, although some of them try to keep their hopes covered at least for the time being. They are not very successful in this respect, for when one is bitten by the Presidential or Vice Presidential virus bug, he breaks out in a rash that soon becomes evident.

Absenteeism in the Senate has been very high most of the week, with thirty or more members absent at times. Of course those who are looking to re-election campaigns next fall have a bit more reason for being absent than the host of unqualified members who get the idea that they would make good Presidents.

The urge for travel to other countries, while not as strong as at other times of the year, is also clearly evident. One instance of this lies in the proposal that the usual British-American Parliamentary Conference, which is not even authorized by the United States Congress, should have two sessions this year, one to be held in Bermuda with members of the House of Representatives, and another contemplated for the last week in June at Ditchley in England with members of the United States Senate.

Also, the news media on Friday, February 4, carried a story that members of the Senate Foreign Relations committee and the House Foreign Affairs committee are planning a visit to China soon after President Nixon gets back from his visit to Peking, which is slated for February 21. Whether this proposal represents an effort to take away from the President credit for any gains which may be made in the relationship between the People's Republic of China and the United States, or whether it is an undertaking to embarrass the President by accumulating criticism of the results of his visit, or whether it is simply the urge to go somewhere to some foreign country, I am not sure.

Certainly some of my colleagues seem to be concentrating their efforts to embarrass the executive branch of our government as much as possible. In any election year we must expect some of this, of course, but this year these efforts are being carried so far that they appear to be almost an effort to embarrass our country as well as President Nixon's administration.

Right now there are altogether too many candidates and others who are going too far in taking the position that Hanoi is right and the United States is wrong. They completely overlook the fact that North Vietnam slaughtered an estimated 200,000 people after the French evacuated Dien Bien Phu in 1954, and undoubtedly would have killed as many more had the United States not seen fit to transport the refugees, nearly all Catholics, to South Vietnam where they would have at least temporary security.

¶ THERE HAS BEEN no executive meeting of the Senate Foreign Relations committee as yet this year but I understand there will be one next week. However, since it is called for February 9, and the Senate goes out for nearly a week on that day, I doubt that a quorum will be present. Some members of the committee staff are getting pretty high-handed, and, like some members of other Senate committees, they seem to feel that they rather than the elected members of the Senate should determine policies.

¶ THE AGRICULTURE COMMITTEE, which had slated a hearing for January 31, canceled the hearing since Senator Humphrey withdrew his bill on which the hearing was to be held.

Farm prices and rural conditions have always been a problem. Other sectors of our economy have much better incomes than the farmers, but it is difficult to enact permanent and effective legislation for the good of American agriculture, since we are confronted with such imponderables as weather, labor strikes, and plant disease.

Although agriculture is still the most important industry of our entire economy, the number of farmers has been undergoing a steady reduction for nearly thirty years. The operations of single farm units have been growing steadily larger. A generation ago one could get into the dairy business for a few thousand dollars, and it is now estimated that it will cost over $200,000 to get into milk production from scratch. Whereas thirty-five years ago the price of milk to the farmer was about one dollar per hundred pounds, it is now well over six dollars.

When the price was at its lowest, I urged farm people to organize and join co-operatives in order to strengthen their position in the market. But as in a corporation, when the farm organization gets too large the members have little to say about its policies and management, while the elected officers are in a position to co-operate with other organizations which may or may not have any connection with agriculture.

Much publicity has been given this week to the fact that the Justice department has brought antitrust charges against the Associated Milk Producers, Inc. It is possible that such suits will also be brought against milk-bargaining co-operatives in the Central West and East, since it is estimated that about 80 percent of all the milk sold is now controlled by three large co-operatives. Charges were also made that the Southwest Dairy Co-operative made large campaign contributions in 1970 to candidates for office who would look favorably upon its proposals.

I have very strong suspicions, although I cannot and will not undertake to prove them, that a considerable part of the money contributed to political campaigns came from sources other than the dairy farmer. The temptation to trade influence is very strong, and although it may not be detected for a while it can eventually get the trading partners into serious difficulty.

President Nixon sent his Rural Development message to the Congress on Tuesday, February 1. Whoever prepared it had evidently never milked a cow or dug a potato. There will be no votes in this message for President Nixon next fall. The Democrats will use it to the limit.

¶ NEXT WEEK we go back to the EEOC bill. I doubt if it can become law unless modified by an amendment similar to that which was proposed by Senator Dominick some days ago. Although I voted against the Dominick amendment, I have a great deal of sympathy for the right of an employer to hire his own help and not be obliged to employ those who could be a liability to his industry.

There are two sides to this question, however, since many employers of the past have ruthlessly exploited those who worked for them and would doubtless do so again if opportunity and law permitted such action.

Week ending February 12, 1972

THE FOURTH WEEK of the Session has gone by with little change in operation. Some thirty members of the Senate are absent most of the time and the only legislation to pass both Houses has been a bill designed to bring a temporary end to the Pacific coast dock strike, which has now gone on for some months. Whether the President will sign this bill or not remains to be seen.

Politics have prevailed almost to the point of hypocrisy. As an example, one prominent Democrat is loud in his advocacy of getting food to the refugees in East Pakistan, now called Bangladesh, while at the same time expressing great sympathy for the dock workers, who are preventing the shipment of such food. Although it is assumed that the dock strike is causing the greatest loss to American agriculture, it is my opinion that labor itself may be a greater loser than the farmer.

As I recall, Harry Bridges, leader of the dock strikers, came to the United States from Australia, and even back in World War II days was not friendly to the United States. With election coming up next fall many members of Congress are reluctant to offend organized labor, or at least the top officials of organized labor, and therefore do not support some legislation which might be beneficial to the laboring man himself.

This same attitude applies to the legislation which has been before the Senate almost from the beginning—the EEOC bill. One might think this bill was the most important legislation of this year to hear some of its advocates speak for it, but I know of no proposed legislation that has stirred up less interest among the public. The labor leaders are for it and therefore it may pass in some form, but even if it becomes law I seriously doubt its effectiveness in making the leaders of industry more kind and conscientious. Unless champions of the labor leaders show greater willingness to compromise than they have done so far, I will likely change my position in support of the EEOC bill.

¶ WE HAD committee work during the first part of the week. Foreign Relations handled considerable routine agenda. The principal argument in this committee came on the proposal to send a member of the staff to Harvard University for training. Under new rules adopted a year ago, any major committee and both the Majority and Minority Policy committees can send staff members to college for further training.

While getting this training (which could well include an advanced degree, since major staff members are college graduates anyway), the beneficiary can receive full pay from his committee—about $35,000 a year; all expenses while at college; all annuity benefits and health benefits; and if he wishes to come back to Washington once a week he can do so with the funds provided for consultation purposes. There is no limit on the number of staff members that can be sent and no limit on the length of time they may be gone. The only restriction is that the money for this additional educational expense must be approved by the Rules committee of the Senate or House, as the case may be.

For $35,000 a year, staff members should be adequately trained for their job before being employed by a committee. However, there are those who can't resist getting more and more and more. With Senator Mansfield, I strenuously objected to spending money for college educations for staff members, and I told the Foreign Relations committee that to proceed with such a plan could lead to an unconscionable scandal in the near future. The committee agreed to eliminate the college education for one of the staff members, but did include $50,000 for the study of computers and pay for consultants.

One member of the committee who is running for re-election this fall stated that he did not have enough help and needed more staff assistants. The total amount of funds requested by the committee will permit the hiring of two or three more professional staff members provided that the full committee approves of such action.

¶ I UNDERSTAND that we will soon give consideration to the President's proposal to increase the price of gold, which will have the effect of devaluing the dollar. As I don't know much about the valuation of currency, this seems to me to be an idle gesture, since the dollar is already worth only a fraction of what it was thirty years ago.

¶ ON FEBRUARY 10, at the suggestion of Dr. Pearson and at the urging of L.P.A., we went to Williamsburg, which in pre-Revolutionary days was the capital of the Virginia colonies. We visited the Governor's House and the Old Dominion Capitol, where the House of Burgesses sat, theoretically made laws, and even joined in the Revolutionary War after the farmers of New England had already forcefully defied the British government.

If one complains about class distinction in the United States today, he should see Williamsburg and then realize that class distinction today is a lot less than it was two hundred years ago. Members of the House of Burgesses were wealthy plantation owners who depended on slave labor to work the land, and not only property but prestige appears to have been handed down from generation to generation. Although the Virginia colonies did join in the fight for independence from the British Empire, they carried on much of the old country's policies and practices for several generations to come.

Jamestown, settled in 1607, was the first capital of the Virginia colonies, but its wet land was conducive to disease, and the capital was moved to Williamsburg and eventually to Richmond, where it is now. It is possible that many of the settlers in the Jamestown colony were afflicted by chronic diseases, and this may have caused Captain John Smith to order that "he who won't work cannot eat." What a time he would have with the food-stamp program of today.

¶ ON FRIDAY we left Williamsburg for Newport News, where one of the largest, if not the largest, shipyard in the country is located. In effect, we left the past and headed into the future. Much of the work now being done at the Newport News shipyard consists of constructing and renovating submarines, carriers and other ships for a nuclear navy. Being a member of the Joint Committee on Atomic Energy, I was naturally interested in the progress being made there. Admiral Rickover had been quite insistent that L.P.A. and I visit the shipyard. To a great extent he was responsible for the progress which has been made in developing our Navy of today, particularly the submarine fleet, which has probably been more responsible for preventing a third world war than any other factor of our defense establishment.

The president of the Newport News Shipbuilding Company came

to Williamsburg to pick us up, but on arrival at Newport News he left us to attend a meeting of the port authorities of Virginia. We were then taken in tow by the vice president of the company and the supervisor of construction work in the yard, as well as by Admiral Rickover's assistant stationed there. Also, the driver of the car, named Watson, was a great help to us. One thing I noticed about the shipbuilding company was that many employees, from top officials down, are members of the third or fourth generation that have carried on this work.

At Newport News, L.P.A. was very apprehensive about whether she had the nerve to descend the ladders from the conning tower into the depths of the submarine, but as I found out ten years ago when I went on the trial run of the *Skipjack,* the first of the all-nuclear attack fleet, going down those ladders doesn't scare you at all when you have to do it, and once inside the submarine one feels very much like being in a house with no windows. L.P.A. took it all in step and stride, had her picture taken in the bowels of the nuclear submarine *Nathanael Greene,* and I presume by this time has already made a complete report to Admiral Rickover.

In spite of the efforts of the oil industry to keep the Navy on a fossil-fuel basis, it is now quite apparent that the day of the oil-burners is over except as emergency propulsion units; and that from now on nuclear-powered ships will constitute the Navy of the future.

Week ending February 19, 1972

LEGISLATION droned on with little accomplished.

The big news of the week was President Nixon leaving for China on Thursday the 17th.

Although I was supposed to leave Wednesday afternoon with the United States parliamentary group for Ottawa, it seemed more important to go to the White House at 9:15 A.M. on Thursday for a final briefing with the President, Secretary Rogers and Henry Kissinger. Eleven members of the Senate and seven members of the House attended this briefing session and when it concluded all the Congressional leaders announced support for the Presidential trip, even Chairman Fulbright of the Foreign Relations committee.

L.P.A. and I then left for Ottawa, arriving in time for lunch with the United States–Canada delegation where I met many of my old Canadian friends.

It was in 1958 that the Right Honorable Roland Michener, then Speaker of the House of Commons (later Governor General) and Speaker of the Senate Mark Drouin met in New York with Congresswoman Edna Kelly and myself to make plans for the interparliamentary meetings by the two countries. We have now concluded the fourteenth of such meetings and I believe they have been very much worthwhile. Back in 1947 I introduced the first International Wheat Agreement at a meeting in Washington attended by representatives of many countries, including Foreign Minister Sharp as head of the Canadian delegation.

Friday morning the official session started between the representatives of the two parliamentary bodies. I sat in with the group whose discussion centered around the aid programs.

¶ L.P.A. AND I arrived home in Putney just before the biggest blizzard of the winter, to find that our house had been broken into and a great many articles carried away. The people who broke into our house were probably motivated by the same instincts that prompt a big corporation to overthrow the government of a small country and pre-empt its resources.

¶ WE HOPE for more legislative action next week, and it is about time.

Week ending February 26, 1972

THE SIXTH WEEK of this Session has now passed and we are finally getting down to work. On Tuesday the Senate by a large majority, 73 to 21, applied cloture to the EEOC bill which had been dragging since our return to the new Session in January. Surprisingly enough, the bill passed the Senate that very afternoon. What its fate will be in Conference with the House, no one can foretell at this time. Actually the EEOC bill was largely a political gesture and will doubtless be as difficult to enforce if it becomes law as the Honest Election bill, which the President has signed. Human nature being what it is, we can't make people honest and good simply by passing a law. I am sure that many candidates are already busy planning to circumvent the election expenditures legislation, and, as I have previously stated, I am equally certain that it will be difficult to require employers to hire people they do not want and who would likely be liabilities to their industries.

Immediately following action on the EEOC bill, the Higher Education bill, S. 659, was placed before the Senate. It has been under consideration by the Senate during Thursday's and Friday's sessions and, under a unanimous consent agreement, is expected to receive final action on Wednesday, March 1. Many amendments have been offered to this bill, but the main issue appears to be the busing situation.

People all over the country, regardless of race, creed or color, are objecting to having their children transported many miles from home and from their own school districts primarily in order to mix them with children of other colors and races. After all, they seem to think, and I agree with them, that the reason for going to school is to get an education so that these children can take their useful places in national and world affairs later on. The busing programs in many instances have badly damaged the community spirit, and parents of all kinds and colors are no longer able to follow the work of their children in school as they could before the busing craze came into vogue.

Political candidates promoted racial integration in schools thinking it would help them secure the votes of members of minority races at election time, particularly the black vote. It has developed, however, that parents belonging to minority races seem to put a good education for their children ahead of the requirement to mix the races. Political candidates are now back-tracking from their earlier position and trying to find a way out of their predicament.

Senators Scott and Mansfield offered an amendment which, while not very strong, would have placed the whole problem in the hands of House and Senate conferees after the bill is passed. I voted for this amendment because I feel that we should get this proposed legislation to Conference, and I do believe that the small number of conferees involved will be able to work out a satisfactory solution.

While the Scott-Mansfield amendment carried by a vote of 51 to 37, its effect was undone on Friday, the 25th, when an amendment offered by Senator Griffin carried by a vote of 43 to 40. This amendment would prohibit court action to enforce busing to achieve racial integration in communities which might feel that busing is undesirable. The vote on the Griffin amendment provided a striking example of the fact that consistency is not required of members of Congress. Only the week before, most of those who supported the Griffin amendment taking jurisdiction away from the courts, had supported the Dominick amendment to the EEOC bill which retained the jurisdiction of the courts in the field of employment.

Personally, I feel that if the courts are to have jurisdiction over employment, they should also have jurisdiction to act in matters affecting education. This is just another instance of one branch of government undertaking to usurp the jurisdiction of another branch. During the time I have been in the United States Senate I have seen each of the three branches of our government—legislative, executive, and judicial—undertake to usurp the Constitutional power of one or both of the others. I grant that the federal courts, including the Supreme Court, have recently shown indications of usurping the Constitutional authority vested in the legislative branch, and we are all well aware of the efforts of the executive branch, from time to time, undertaking to legislate and to interpret laws according to its desires.

However, the fact remains that while one branch or the other may gain the upper hand, such superiority does not last, and even now the Congress is undertaking to recover its Constitutional authority relative to international treaties and agreements. Considerable progress is being made in this direction.

¶ I HAVE been insistent that our Committee on Foreign Relations take up those matters which we are required to act upon as soon as possible, and then if there is time remaining, members of the committee who have political aspirations could have time devoted to their vote-getting proposals as decided on by the full committee. Since the Majority Party outnumbers us in the committee, they would likely do this anyway.

Chairman Fulbright has now set dates for hearings on State department authorization for appropriation, for the USIA [United States Information Agency], and for the Military Aid program, which will consume most of the months of March and April. So at last we are getting down to work, and I earnestly hope that we will come closer to getting required legislation out on time than we have been doing the last few years.

¶ NATURALLY there has been intense interest in the President's week-long trip to China. Political candidates appear disgusted because this trip has been taking the headlines away from them. Reporters who accompanied the President to China appear to be disgruntled because they don't have big stories to send home every day, since both President Nixon and the Chinese officials have not been feeding them good stories. But I believe the American people are showing interest, tolerance, and restraint, and are hoping for a maximum degree of improvement in our relationship with the countries of Asia.

President Nixon is expected to arrive home Monday evening. Tuesday morning I have been invited to the White House to hear his firsthand report. I expect now it will be far from announcing a full restoration of our relationship with China. Nevertheless, I feel that it

21

will be somewhat broader and go farther than we anticipated when he left on his journey on February 17.

Certainly the President's trip has not been helpful so far to the many candidates who would like to succeed him in the White House.

Week ending March 4, 1972

SEVEN WEEKS have gone by since the Congress re-assembled on January 18, and business is beginning to pick up. President Nixon and the White House, however, were in the limelight for most of the week.

Sunday evening L.P.A. and I went to the Sulgrave Club where a party was held in honor of Burton Wheeler on his ninetieth birthday. He was a powerhouse in the Senate just before the outbreak of World War II, and strongly opposed the entrance of the United States into that war. However, when the Japanese bombed Pearl Harbor and sank a good share of our Pacific fleet, any further opposition to our entry to the war was futile.

Monday night about a dozen members of the Senate went out to Andrews Air Force Base to meet President Nixon, who was returning from his trip to China. Several thousand people turned out for this occasion and many others who would have contributed to the crowd were unable to reach the base because of a traffic jam on the highway. The welcome to the President was very warm, the only dissension, apparently, coming from a very small group of reactionary war hawks. The President addressed the crowd briefly, setting forth the main points of agreement between himself and Premier Chou En-lai and also the items of disagreement.

On the next day, Tuesday, February 29, twelve members of the Senate and nine from the House went to the White House to listen to further discussions by the President, Secretary Rogers, and Henry Kissinger concerning the trip to China. The President was obviously tired, as testified by the fact that he started to speak to us at 10:00 A.M. and kept talking for about one and a quarter hours, a rather unusual length of time for President Nixon to speak. As a matter of fact, when one is very tired and starts to speak, one finds it difficult to reach a stopping point. Incidentally, I will say that this observation would not apply to President Lyndon Johnson, who could usually speak for a couple of hours without stopping and apparently without getting tired.

President Nixon did not give us any more real basic information beyond that which has been carried in the joint news release by Premier Chou and himself. He discussed personalities and apparently was convinced of the integrity of the top Chinese officials. There appeared to be very little dissension between the President and the Chinese on the method of procedure. If they agreed on a subject they agreed; if they disagreed, they disagreed completely. According to the President, they agreed that they would not undertake to dictate to other countries.

President Nixon indicated that he had told the Chinese that we intended to withdraw our military forces from other countries just as fast as we could safely do so, and that under the Nixon doctrine he felt that each country should make its own determination as to its type of government and the conduct of its internal affairs. Of course, they disagreed strongly on what form of government was best. China wants communism and our country wants what we choose to call democracy.

The President reported to us that Chou En-lai was apparently the keenest and ablest head of state he had ever met, that discipline among the Chinese people was meticulous, that crime seemed to be under control. Since the United States and China are fairly comparable in the matters of geography and resources, I have often wondered what type of government we might be functioning under here if we found ourselves with their population of 800 million people. I hope we do not have to face that situation for a long time to come.

An interesting feature of the President's visit to China was the fact that he brought back an invitation for Senators Mansfield and Scott to visit that country. Inevitably this invitation promptly aroused envy and protest among other members of both the House and Senate, but after all it was in line with the strict protocol exercised by the Chinese, since the United States Senate is the government body that is supposed to pass on all international agreements and treaties, and Senators Mansfield and Scott are the leaders of their respective parties in the Senate.

On Wednesday our Senate Committee on Agriculture and Forestry met in executive session and after considering a few lesser items discussed what is called the Egg bill. The price of eggs is inordinately low at this time and the producers wanted legislation to reduce production of eggs. It appeared to me, as it did to others, that they wanted the other fellow to take the reduction, because the bill as written was so full of loopholes that it would have been almost inoperative. I doubt if under our form of government the production of eggs can be regulated by law, because it is so easy for one to get in and out of this business in such a short time.

Anyway, we didn't get anywhere and we will take the matter up this coming week. However, politics being what it is and candidates for election and re-election being what they are, there is no telling what may happen.

¶ WEDNESDAY AFTERNOON the Higher Education Authorization bill was passed by the Senate. It authorizes an expenditure of $22 billion, a lot of money, to be sure. During its debate of several days on the Senate floor, the educational matters of the bill were given very scant consideration and nearly all attention was focused on the busing problem. I supported the Scott-Mansfield amendment, which was finally approved by one vote, because I felt it essential to get this bill into Conference as soon as possible. The House bill contains much stricter anti-busing legislation, and although I voted for the Scott-Mansfield position I hope that the anti-busing provisions of the bill will be made much stricter.

¶ AFTER DEALING with the Higher Education bill the Senate approved three conference reports dealing with United States contributions to three international banking systems.

The Administration's request to increase the value of gold from $35 to $38 an ounce was almost unanimously approved. This means that the value of the dollar is decreased, but the value of the dollar has been steadily decreasing for the last twenty-five years. I am not enthusiastic about the use of gold as the basis for our currency, but inasmuch as it is accepted by most countries we have to go along with it.

The conference report on foreign aid appropriations, which was previously passed by the House, was approved by the Senate 45 to 36. However, opposition to foreign aid seems to be growing. There appears to be a lot of dead wood in the personnel that administers this program, and it is a general feeling that much of the money appropriated is a subsidy to American industries to help them get business in other countries.

Much of the opposition to the conference report was due to the fact that military assistance to other countries was considered excessive. The answer to this, of course, is that if they don't get military equipment from us they will get it from somewhere else. Western European countries, notably England, Sweden, and others, have long been the source of arms supplies for other nations.

¶ The Friday session of the Senate was not a happy one. There were difficulties in getting a quorum of the Senate at all. Forty-two members were absent. Except for two or three cases of illness the members were out on the road playing politics, many campaigning for their own re-election and others taking part in the campaign for the nomination and election of a President. Most of the Congressional candidates for the Presidency have, in my opinion, eliminated any possible excuse for voting for them next fall. I still can't see what there is about neglecting their duties that qualifies them for higher office.

Week ending March 11, 1972

NOT MUCH legislative action by the Congress this week, but a lot of work in committees and a lot of politics.

On Wednesday, the 8th, the Senate approved an increase of $20 billion in the national debt limit, making it $450 billion. Later in the week this action was approved by the House and Senate conference committee, so now we have broken another record.

In the early part of the week much interest was directed toward the New Hampshire primaries. Eleven candidates were competing for delegates to the Republican and Democratic conventions. President Nixon won the Republican vote without much effort on his part. Some of his opposition tried to make something of the fact that his portion of the whole vote was only 69 percent, as compared to 76 percent four years ago. They neglected to point out, however, that this year there were two other Republican candidates also on the primary ballot, whereas four years ago the people of New Hampshire had no one else to vote for.

In the Democratic primary, instead of carrying the state by an overwhelming majority as had been expected earlier, Senator Muskie received only 48 percent of the total, with 37 percent going to Senator McGovern and the rest of the ballots divided among the lesser hopefuls. My opinion is that the large increase in Senator McGovern's vote was largely an expression of disapproval for Senator Muskie's ill-timed effort to discredit William Loeb and his newspaper, the Manchester *Union Leader*. He was very foolish even to notice Mr. Loeb at all, and the Democratic voters of New Hampshire were apparently quite resentful.

I am inclined to think that Muskie is now out of the race for the Democratic nomination for President, and that the ultimate decision at the convention to be held the first week in July will lie between Senators Humphrey and Kennedy. Of the two there is no question in my mind that Senator Humphrey is much better qualified, but he has the fault of not being able to say No to those who make requests of him, and a good President should always be able to say No. At the present time it appears to me that President Nixon would easily defeat any Democratic aspirant who has been mentioned so far.

¶ BACK IN the Senate we took up Senator McGee's Voter Registration bill. As it is written I certainly do not like it, since it is an open invitation to the dishonest registration of voters. On Thursday the bill's supporters, largely Democrats, were defeated 44 to 37 in an effort to prevent its being referred to the Judiciary committee, where it presumably would be buried. Not wanting to take any more risks, the advocates of this bill prevented any further vote on it, and the Senate recessed until Monday, March 13.

Had all absentee Democrats, largely candidates either for the Presidency or for re-election to the Senate, been present, supporters of this bill might have won by one or two votes. I suppose now they want to get past the Florida primaries on Tuesday, March 14, in the hopes that some of their errant candidates may see fit to come back to the Senate and attend to the business for which they were elected by the people of their states.

¶ THE FOREIGN RELATIONS COMMITTEE met in executive session on Wednesday. I was in attendance at another committee meeting, and no quorum was present at the Foreign Relations committee meeting. Nevertheless, they took up some executive items, among which was a Resolution to insist upon the immediate recognition of Bangladesh as a nation. As was my right, I later objected to the acts of the committee taken in that meeting, and another executive meeting was called for Thursday afternoon. At this time it was agreed that the word "immediately" should be stricken from the Bangladesh Resolution, and that, if reported favorably, the Resolution would lie on the Senate calendar until we have received assurance that all Indian troops had been withdrawn from Bangladesh.

Inasmuch as our government expects to recognize Bangladesh soon after it ceases to be occupied by another country, I raised no further objection to the Resolution.

The motivations of the Resolution on Bangladesh, which was proposed by Senator Hollings and supported by Senator Church and others, were purely political. Realizing that the Administration intended to take this step anyway, the supporters of the Resolution

26

apparently hoped to get ahead of President Nixon and take credit for the action. Any political gain which they may have anticipated appears to have gone down the drain.

¶ THE AIR IS FULL of politics with the Democrats groping for issues. The progress in improvement of world relations made by President Nixon leaves them little hope for making any gains on the issue of the Indochina war or in the international field generally. The campaign is likely to become more personal in the months ahead, and as an indication of this the Democrats are making the most of a charge that the ITT [International Telephone and Telegraph Corporation] has offered a substantial sum of money to the Republican Party in return for a favorable decision on an antitrust case which was pending before the Justice department.

As a matter of fact, ITT has apparently made enormous profits and has acquired one of the larger hotel chains of the world. Included in this chain are two big hotels in San Diego where the next Republican convention will be held, and a third hotel which will be completed before convention time. It is always customary for the people in the hotel and other businesses in a city where a national convention is to be held to contribute heavily to the cost of such a convention.

I understand that the three ITT hotels in San Diego were each expected to put up $100,000. Had there been no antitrust case pending, this offer would probably have gone unnoticed since the hotels in Miami, where the Democratic national convention is to be held the first week in July, will undoubtedly contribute heavily to the cost of that convention. I understand that ITT in effect lost its antitrust case before the Justice department, and that the Republicans have received no money as yet and under the circumstances probably will not.

The effect of the Democratic charge, however, has been that the appointment of Richard Kleindienst, who had already been unanimously approved by the Judiciary committee to become our next Attorney General to succeed John Mitchell, has been held up pending the completion of hearings relating to the ITT charge.

It appears that the pots and the kettles have engaged in a very strenuous battle, because it is now charged that the national Democratic Party owes the American Telephone and Telegraph Company approximately $1.25 million which had been pending since the last national election in 1968, and which apparently the Democratic Party had no intention of paying.

The term "dirty politics" is likely to be heard very frequently between now and November, but so far as I can see the situation is no worse than it has been in the past. Candidates are, however, watched more closely than they used to be, and any deviation from the straight and narrow path is promptly picked up, enlarged upon, and exploited by the opposition.

¶ FRIDAY NOON, at the urgent request of the White House, I went down to the signing of three bills, each carrying a new contribution by the United States: one to the Inter-American Development Bank for $900 million per year for 1972 and '73; another to the International Development Association for $320 million per year for three years; and the third to the Asian Development Bank for $100 million for 1972. Only a few people were there, including Secretary of State Rogers and Secretary of the Treasury Connally, as well as the heads of the banks themselves. Altogether something like $2,860 million of United States credit is involved.

The ceremony was very short. The President signed the bills and then said, "That's it." I told him that was about the right length of a speech for the occasion and the ceremony broke up only a few minutes after it had convened.

¶ ONE OF THE interesting features of the week was the start of hearings by the Senate Foreign Relations committee on the authorization bill for State department expenses. The State department had been exempt from requiring special authorization, but last year, 1971, the Congress voted to require authority for State department appropriations, just as for nearly every other department or agency of government. Hearings began Wednesday with Secretary Rogers testifying, and continued Thursday and Friday with the heads of other agencies within the State department. The hearings have gone smoothly. Senator Fulbright, our chairman, has been in an exceptionally good mood and no members of the committee have been inclined to harass Secretary Rogers or his assistants who have appeared before us. Members of this committee like Secretary Bill Rogers very much, and I think this feeling is reciprocated.

Members of Congress, and particularly members of the Foreign Relations committee, are resentful over the apparent efforts of a White House group headed by Dr. Henry Kissinger to downgrade Secretary Rogers and the State department. The thirst for publicity appears to be the overwhelming characteristic of Mr. Kissinger, whereas one of the main traits of Secretary Rogers may well be described as modesty.

¶ FRIDAY EVENING L.P.A. and I attended a small dinner at the Canadian Embassy given by Ambassador Marcel Cadieux and his wife, Anita, who are our very good friends and very good company. The dinner party was small—only eighteen of us in all including Secretary and Mrs. Rogers and Assistant Secretary of State and Mrs. Joe Sisco. It was more like a family affair, and it is at small gatherings like this that one can really talk and learn. The only other members of the diplomatic corps who were there were Ambassador and Mrs. Frank Corner of New Zealand.

It was brought out again at this dinner party, as has been mentioned frequently by the Senate recently, that the State department ought to have an Assistant Secretary for Canadian Affairs instead of lumping Canada in with the Western European countries. After all, Canada has the same problems with Western Europe that we do, and Canada is probably the closest to the United States of all nations. We have everything in common and, although we have competition and disagreements, one might say that they are more in the nature of neighborhood disagreements than international disagreements. Mexico, our other close and important neighbor, can hardly object, because we do have an Assistant Secretary of State for Latin American Affairs, and the Mexicans are well covered by this subdepartment.

The Foreign Relations committee has hearings booked up till the first week of May, and if we all tend to business and don't have too much truancy, we should have most of the necessary work of the Congress completed before the end of the fiscal year, June 30.

Social security and welfare legislation will take prolonged discussion, but even that ought to be handled and out of the way by the first week of June, and appropriations bills can be acted upon soon after.

Week ending March 18, 1972

THE PAST WEEK started off uncomfortably for me. Sometime late Sunday I acquired an intense pain in a region where the backbone and the hip bone come together. It may be I got it from coughing too hard, or maybe that wasn't the cause, because it seems to be a common ailment and no one seems to know for sure what causes it.

On Monday, Senator Fulbright was gone for the week and the State department kept crowding me to get some agreement between the House and Senate conferees on the bill, which had passed both Houses, to extend the operation of Radio Free Europe and Radio Liberty. The Senate had voted to extend the period of operations for fiscal 1972 only, with an authorization of $35 million. The House had voted to extend it two years with an authorization of about $74 million for the period. Two conferences had brought no results, and in the meantime these programs, previously financed largely by the CIA [Central Intelligence Agency], were running out of money.

I was told they would have to give all their employees, some twenty-seven hundred of them, dismissal notices on March 13th unless authorization for further continuance was promptly forthcoming. I had proposed earlier that the Senate agree to the House proposal of $36 million for the first year and that the House accept the Senate proviso for extension for 1972 only. All day long I had telephone calls from people interested in the programs and from United States government officials.

State department kept trying to get the Senate conferees to say that we would hold hearings on a new bill extending the programs which would be sent up by the executive branch of the government. I assured them that we undoubtedly would do that. President Nixon went on the air appealing for continuance of the programs, but all the time advocates of the program were trying to get me to get the Senate conferees to yield just a little bit more by giving assurances, which we could not do. Finally at four o'clock I told them just where they could all go: unless the House conferees signed the report that night, I said, I would wash my hands of the whole matter.

At five o'clock I received a phone call advising me that all members of the House conference committee had signed the report endorsing the proposal which I had made some time before. Senator Fulbright, who was out of the country, was contacted Tuesday morning, and he recommended that the reluctant Senators Symington and Church also sign the conference report, which they did. I filed the report with the Senate the same day, but since the House has to act first and the House cannot act on a conference report until three days have passed, final action will not be taken until next week.

In the meantime the State department has advised us that it will discuss the situation with our European friends and allies to find out if they will help share the cost for continuing the programs. Since these programs are largely for the benefit of Western European countries, they ought to make a contribution. We will just have to wait and see.

¶ THE ELECTION BILL for voter registrations by mail continued to be discussed all day Tuesday, and on Wednesday was laid to rest by a 46-to-42 vote in the Senate; had all the Democratic candidates for President been present, it might have passed by one vote. As written it was a thoroughly bad bill, lending itself to extensive corruption through collusion between election officials and unscrupulous partisans. At any rate we won't be registering all the inhabitants of our cemeteries this year.

¶ ON WEDNESDAY the Committee on Agriculture and Forestry met to consider various rural development bills, one of which I had introduced on behalf of Chairman Talmadge and myself and which sixty-nine other Senators had asked to co-sponsor. I had hoped that we might develop some worthwhile agriculture legislation this year, for it is important to keep up our production of farm commodities, not only for the purpose of providing plenty of food for our own people but also because of the large demand for American farm products all over the world. We had hoped to export about $9 billion worth of farm products this year but the dock strikes on the East and West coasts will undoubtedly prevent us from reaching this goal.

We didn't finish consideration of the proposed legislation, and another session of the Agriculture committee was called for Friday afternoon to continue deliberations. Since a quorum was not present on Friday no action could be taken, and further work on the bills will be postponed until March 20.

My hopes for a worthwhile bill are not very high at this time because various undesirable amendments have been slapped onto it. I fear that the bill is submerged in politics. For the first time in over thirty years all the Democratic members of the committee voted together and in my opinion put politics ahead of a good agriculture and rural program. Senator Talmadge had the proxies of four absentee Democrats, although it was noticeable that he did not have the proxy of Senator Ellender, the former chairman of the committee who, while considered parsimonious, had been an excellent chairman. He had only six members on the staff of the committee. I understand that the number has now been increased to seventeen, the increase being largely to serve a subcommittee headed by Senator Hubert Humphrey, who at present seems to be the leading candidate for the Democratic nomination for the Presidency.

¶ ON THURSDAY the Joint Committee on Atomic Energy started hearings on a bill relating to the licensing of nuclear power plants. The day before, preliminary consent had been given to the Vermont Yankee Plant to begin operations at 1 percent of its capacity. Two bills have been introduced, theoretically at least to speed up the licensing of these plants in order to avoid shortages of electric energy in many parts of the country, including the New England area.

One bill, sponsored by the AEC [Atomic Energy Commission], sadly enough contains a proviso which might permit the electric-utility industry to get out from under the antitrust law which I had succeeded in getting approved less than two years earlier.

If they once could get out from under the antitrust provisions, I suspect they would make short work of many public and co-operatively owned electric systems. I fear the result of this would be a sharp increase in the cost of electricity to the consumers. Actually, I think we are due for some increase anyway; I am, however, just as much opposed to a monopoly in the electric-power industry as I ever was. The Atomic Energy Commission had no good reason for inserting such a proviso into the new bill, and I doubt if the committee will accept it.

Another bill, sponsored by Congressman Hosmer, a House member of the Joint Committee on Atomic Energy, is just as workable as far as licensing procedures are concerned, and does not carry the obnoxious proviso relative to the antitrust laws.

The lawyers for some environmentalists are working as hard as they can to block the development of nuclear energy. I do not know just whom they are working for but I am sure it is not wholly in the public interest, and in the meantime I firmly believe that they are taking a large number of well-meaning conservationists and environmentalists to the cleaners. But then that is nothing new. There always have been lawyers looking for unsuspecting and gullible clients.

¶ FRIDAY AFTERNOON L.P.A. and two of the girls from my office inveigled me into going to New York City—something I had made a rash promise to do some weeks ago in one of my weaker moments. Anyway, we went. Leaving all pending legislation behind us and taking the pain in the lower regions along with me, we arrived in New York about four o'clock. We went up on what was called a Metroliner, thereby making a fairly liberal contribution to the Penn Central Railroad. It so happened the Secretary of Transportation, John Volpe, was also in our car, and I had the chance to talk with him for quite a while.

Friday evening I was taken to a play called *No, No, Nannette*. This show originated over a generation ago. It was quite a drawing card at the time and still is.

On Saturday afternoon I was taken to a show called *Follies*.

The impression which one of my age gets from both of these shows is that he is not a spring chicken any more, for both plays, while entertaining, emphasized the generation gap, which may or may not emphasize the joy of being older. However, while watching the *Follies* I thought back to the first high-level Broadway show I ever saw. It was in 1909. My senior class was graduating from the Brattleboro, Vermont, high school and all thirty-six of us, with two or three teachers, came to Washington and stopped in New York City on our return. It is unnecessary to say that costs in those days were somewhat different from what they are today, otherwise I wouldn't have come to Washington.

But during the stop in New York we were taken to a theater where Maude Adams, one of the great actresses of that day, was appearing in a play called *What Every Woman Knows*. Did I enjoy that play? I went sound asleep. I did, however, enjoy another play which some of us saw in Washington. It was called the *Call of the North*, and it depicted the ruthless dealing of the Hudson's Bay Company with the Indians and with their competitors in Canada. I didn't go to sleep watching that, and even today I find that the practices of the Hudson's Bay Company still prevail in some parts of the world. Even though they don't send their opposition out into the woods with no food or shelter to die of exposure, they have other more effective methods of dealing with their competition.

But what I did remember about this trip was our visit to the White House. William Howard Taft was President at that time, and he shook hands with each of us individually. If a President today undertook to emulate President Taft, he certainly would not be able to do anything else, considering the thousands and thousands of students who come to visit Washington every day.

Week ending March 25, 1972

SPRING came again on Monday, March 20, with beautiful weather, but the political climate in Washington did not change much during the week. If anything, it threatened to become stormier and nastier.

The Foreign Relations committee began hearings on the USIA that were conducted throughout most of the week. The Director, Frank Shakespeare, was quite evidently ill at ease in appearing before the committee.

Testimony by various officials of this agency indicated that the radio programs, especially in Eastern Europe and in particular the RIAS [Radio in American Sector], which was established as part of the cold war mainly for the purpose of influencing East Germans, were not proving to be of much advantage to the United States. Although we

33

are still paying over half the cost, amounting to some thirty-odd million dollars a year, the control seems to have shifted to the Germans. A year ago I had complaints that some of the programs over this system were not complimentary to the United States and that Russia is no longer much concerned about their effect.

The distribution by USIA of American publications throughout the world, while seeming erratic to some members of the committee, incited less concern than the radio programs did. Hearings are continuing but no action on the bill to authorize funds for the coming fiscal year is likely for probably another month. USIA's request for funds amounts to slightly over $200 million for the fiscal year 1973, and the prospects are that the amount may be cut somewhat by the Foreign Relations committee.

Of course an authorization does not mean that the full amount will be appropriated, and under Senator Ellender, Chairman of Appropriations, it is quite likely that those parts of the USIA program considered as part of the cold war against communism may be further reduced.

¶ On Tuesday afternoon there was a short meeting of the Committee on Agriculture and Forestry in Senator Mansfield's office. A large and pretentious bill was voted out favorably. I voted to report the bill to the Senate floor, although I have strong disagreements with some of its provisions, principally that part which would establish an entirely new banking system for the purposes of rural development. We already have this field pretty well covered, and I am not inclined to favor a new banking system which would create more jobs and more power for more people without materially improving the lot of the farmer. Anyway, I do not expect the House will accept this proposal.

Possibly modifications may be made on the floor of the Senate itself when the bill comes up two or three weeks from now. But there are a good many provisions in this bill which would be a great help in enabling more people to live in our rural areas, where they want to live and where they ought to live.

On Wednesday, Secretary Rogers appeared in executive session before the Foreign Relations committee. Chairman Fulbright started to take him to task for a report that he would refuse to testify in a public hearing regarding the promotion policy of the Foreign Service. When the Secretary announced that he certainly was willing to appear in a public hearing, the debate on this subject ended and the committee turned its attention to other proposed matters without any decisions being made.

Late in the afternoon the Prime Minister of Turkey, Nihat Erin, met with some of us for coffee. Naturally he wanted us to know that Turkey wanted more modern arms than they now possess, but since he also indicated that his worries were largely internal rather than inspired by fear of the communist countries, his arguments did not appear to impress the members of the committee that were present as much as he would have liked.

There are ample signs of political desperation among some of the Democratic hopefuls in the Senate, and they seem to be grasping at personality straws, one such straw being Ambassador Arthur Watson, our representative in Paris, who was reported to have overindulged on an air flight from London to the United States and therefore was not fit to represent us in further negotiations with representatives of the People's Republic of China. However, inasmuch as at least one member of the Foreign Relations committee confessed that he, too, had overindulged on a plane, and since Secretary Rogers assured the committee that Mr. Watson was not carrying on any negotiations with the Chinese and would not be our representative in such matters, this issue seemed to subside, at least for the time being. Whether true or not true, it will undoubtedly be frequently referred to between now and election time in November. But should Senator Kennedy become the Democratic nominee for the Presidency, as is quite possible, I feel that the Watson episode will take a back seat to the Chappaquiddick Bridge.

¶ ON THURSDAY MORNING Secretary of Agriculture Butz came up for breakfast with some of the members of the Senate Agriculture committee. Mr. Butz is proving to be a very serious problem for the Democrats. Some of them are now trying to say that he is the enemy of the consumers, in spite of the fact that although he has succeeded in raising farm prices somewhat, reports show that a smaller percentage of the consumer's dollar is now spent for food than ever before. Even so, it is worth noting that much of the food that is purchased now is virtually prepared for the table, and the cost of this prepared food cannot be charged against the farmer, as Secretary Butz points out.

As an example, I noticed on a restaurant menu in New York that two eggs were priced at 80 cents, whereas the egg producer received only approximately 6 cents for those two eggs. However, that doesn't prevent the producer from being charged as responsible for the 80-cent price in the restaurant.

Anyway, on Friday the Senate voted on a bill which theoretically would have increased the price of eggs to consumers which everybody agrees is now below the cost of production. The bill was decisively killed, which only proves that the big feed manufacturers are better campaign contributors than the egg producers, and that the city consumers cast more votes than the smaller number of poultrymen. Egg production, like other phases of agriculture, is now going into the hands of the big outfits, which now have flocks of over one million laying-hens, according to reports. The big grain companies have virtually secured control of the broiler-chicken industry in the United States, and it now looks as if they are taking over the egg-production industry also.

One may wonder why these people are so interested in acquiring an industry where the price received is not equal to the cost of production. The answer is simple. It provides a tremendous market for the mixed feed for poultry flocks. The high prices for the feed increase their profits, and losses on the finished product, eggs, can be deducted from their income-tax returns. In other words, it is good business to lose money on one endeavor if such loss results in a sizable gain in another.

As I say, Secretary Butz is a thorn in the side of the Democrats, but they don't dare to attack him too hard because farmers still control the balance of power in a great many of our Central and Western states. Whether he can keep up the pace until November I would not want to predict at this time, but if he does I will guarantee that the Democratic candidate for President, whoever he may be, will certainly not carry a good many states in the Central West which appeared to be in the Democratic bag only three or four months ago.

¶ ON THURSDAY MORNING I was called on by officials of the Environmental Protection Agency to discuss legislation relating to insect and plant-disease control. Although conservation and wildlife preservation and pure food products are important and desirable, some of their enthusiastic promoters are going so far toward depriving the great majority of the people of an adequate supply of food and the means of making a decent living, that I think they will ultimately defeat their own cause. They just can't seem to understand that you have to work toward a worthy objective step by step and cannot make it safely in one leap.

Officials from Pakistan also called on me in the afternoon. Naturally they want more help from the United States. I told them I don't see any decision in that field likely until after President Nixon gets back from Moscow and legislation relating to foreign aid has been decided upon by the Congress.

¶ ON FRIDAY the senior class of South Burlington, Vermont, high school, about sixty youngsters, met with the Vermont Congressional delegation. They are among the tens of thousands who come to Washington almost every day. I am glad they can come here, but we certainly don't have the time to spend with them that we had years ago when the numbers were fewer and our work was less.

¶ THE FOREIGN RELATIONS committee met again Friday morning and political insinuations again saturated the committee room. Senator Church was insistent that the Foreign Relations committee investigate the reported efforts of the ITT to influence the last Chilean election. He studiously avoided any reference to our big copper companies who, through excessive depletion of Chilean ore and tremendous profits on the same, were largely responsible for the people of Chile resorting to a socialist government.

The Democrats have built up the ITT to make it look as if it were almost the Republican Party itself. However, since the Senate Judiciary committee is at present investigating the affairs of the ITT, cooler heads of our committee, including Senators Fulbright and Mansfield, decided we would not make this investigation a major project. But the committee did agree to authorize a study on the influence of international corporations on United States policies. It also agreed to request from the State department and the ITT any memoranda relating to ITT's influence and attempted interference with the Chilean election. The committee decided not to request such papers from Jack Anderson because, although in his news column he was the one to report their alleged contents to the public, he is at present an official of neither the ITT nor the Department of State.

On Friday the Senate approved the conference report on Radio Free Europe and Radio Liberty, extending the life of these cold war projects for the rest of this fiscal year. There were only six votes in opposition. The future of these two projects is much in doubt at this time.

Week ending April 1, 1972

IT WAS a week of very little legislating but a lot of political talk.

This was just as well, because after going out four nights in succession I probably was not in the best condition for sound legislating. On Saturday night L.P.A. and I attended a reception given by Dr. Pearson, the Capitol physician, for his new assistant, Dr. Freeman Cary, and Mrs. Cary.

On Sunday night we were invited to a showing of *The Godfather,* a picture of exceptionally good acting and photography, but one which would not, in my opinion, be particularly good to show in the school classroom. Every kind of violence was used except poison. Quite a few important newspaper people were there, and I did not feel particularly bad when the picture showed the influence of the underworld over front-page stories which could be slanted to no good purpose.

Monday night we attended a small dinner at the Australian Embassy, where the guests were mostly admirals and other navy men, both Australian and American.

Tuesday at 5:30 P.M. I attended a meeting with about a dozen members of the Foreign Relations committee and Henry Kissinger, President Nixon's chief international political adviser. Kissinger was very frank and better than usual. He made a good impression on the members of the committee, but when asked to comment on the world economic situation he very wisely declined. Because of his political frankness his stock went up sharply from what it had been at the previous meeting.

After the meeting with Dr. Kissinger I went over to the White House to a stag dinner which President Nixon was giving for King Hussein of Jordan. I thought of the moving picture we had seen Sunday night, because if Uncle Sam was ever a godfather to anyone it was to the small country of Jordan, which without our support would probably not be in existence today.

King Hussein visits the United States almost every year and is very well liked. The wonder is that after being King of Jordan for so long he is still alive. I expect that being a direct descendant of Mohammed makes it easier for him among the Moslems.

His present project is to insure a more lasting peace in the Middle East, which would do much to insure us against a third world war. King Hussein also came to the Capitol on Wednesday afternoon for an hour's visit with the Foreign Relations committee and a few other Senators.

¶ THIS WEEK also saw the return of several members of the Senate Judiciary committee from Denver, where they had gone to interview Mrs. Dita Beard, a lobbyist for the ITT. During their interview with Mrs. Beard on the 26th she suffered a heart attack and the committee members hurried back to Washington in what appeared to be confusion as well as frustration. Senator Church has been very insistent that the Senate Foreign Relations committee investigate the alleged efforts of the ITT to influence the Chilean election in order to protect the company's investment there. This committee, having decided to investigate the role of the international corporations in influencing American policy abroad—but not until after the next election—seems to have upset these giant corporations considerably. It goes without saying that they have become a tremendous influence in world economic and political affairs. In some instances their investments have been almost a godsend to small developing nations and in other instances they have very likely overthrown governments and created a lot of bloodshed.

Certainly many of our larger corporations with international holdings have become more powerful than the governments of the countries in which their investments have been made. It is safe to say that an American national corporation, having invested heavily in a developing country, will do all within its power to protect such investment, even to influencing or overthrowing governments and inciting civil war. There isn't much the United States could do to stop such behavior, but we can try to keep it humane, and beneficial not only to the investors in the company but also to the people where an investment is made.

¶ ONE BIT of legislation was acted upon this week. A bill was before the Senate which, if passed, would probably have benefited Northwest Airlines to the extent of hundreds of millions of dollars, a real rich subsidy. The bill was killed by only a small margin. While a lot of people seem to think that the farmers get the principal subsidies in this country, subsidies to the farmer are small compared to the subsidies given to big business.

Last year the Congress enacted two pieces of legislation which I am not proud to have voted for. One was a new tax law ostensibly to help low-income people, but which at present seems to be having the opposite effect. The other bit of legislation enacted last year was supposed to insure clean elections. I almost voted against it because I knew on the face of it that it wouldn't work, but finally went along with the rest of the Senate and voted for it. I would feel better today had I voted against this so-called Clean Elections bill and the new tax law. The national election due next November promises to be anything but clean, and the loopholes in the tax bill and benefits to big business are enabling the corporations to go a long way in their efforts to influence or purchase the election outright.

At this point lack of money seems to be no obstacle for the major candidates of either party.

Week ending April 8, 1972

ANOTHER WEEK without important legislation, but a lot more political talk and some important hearings.

The widespread North Vietnamese attack upon South Vietnam was discussed freely and caused much apprehension lest this effort by Hanoi prove successful. To me it seems quite evident that South Vietnam was unprepared for this all-out attack.

It is also apparent that the attack had a multifold purpose: first, to overrun the South if possible; second, to convince the people of South Vietnam and the world that Vietnamization had failed; third, to make it look as if the United States was insistent on continuing the war; and finally, to strengthen the hand of Russia in the forthcoming visit of President Nixon to Moscow, since it appears that Russia had supplied the North Vietnamese with most of the equipment and matériel essential to this latest drive.

Hanoi has indicated that the United States is using this new drive as an excuse for failing to return to the peace talks in Paris. As a matter of fact, the Paris talks from the beginning have been little more than a show to impress the rest of the world of the virtues of the North Vietnamese. At this time I do not believe that this powerful effort on the part of Hanoi will be successful, and in the long run it may strengthen the hand of President Nixon in handling affairs in Indochina.

There are, however, ambitious Democrats who insist that Nixon wants war, Nixon is planning on war, and that only they can bring peace to that part of Asia, completely ignoring the fact that it was two Democratic Presidents who created this bloody and costly situation.

On Thursday the Senate Foreign Relations committee listened to three representatives of organized labor who recently visited in Hanoi. It was quite evident that none of them was a Republican.

On Friday the committee held hearings on the bill to authorize funds for the Peace Corps. It is quite obvious that the majority of the committee members favors continuation of the Peace Corps, but will also favor its being continued as a separate agency and not included as part of the political conglomeration called ACTION. ACTION is a new name for an organization set up by the present Administration and includes both foreign and domestic programs.

In my opinion it is a mess, since the Peace Corps alone will have to get the approval of eight different committees of the Congress in order to go ahead with its work. Knowing the difficulty of getting two committees of Congress to agree with each other, I feel that the requirement of getting eight committees to agree is not only unworkable but actually borders on imbecility. I realize that every President wants to get the names of programs associated with his predecessors changed, particularly if the immediate predecessor belonged to the other party, but this attitude does not make for better government.

Chairman Fulbright has requested a subcommittee of four members to direct the study of international corporations which is to begin after the November election. I agreed to be a member of this steering committee, and while I seriously doubt the effectiveness of the study I suppose it is necessary in order to appease the public.

¶ DURING THE WEEK we had visits from representatives of local Vermont agencies and commissions. It appears that the Vermont legislature has gone almost hog-wild in authorizing new commissions, which now all scream for federal money to finance their operations, and most of them have appointed, at a salary, of course, someone to serve as contact officer with the Vermont Congressional delegation. Some of these agencies have conflicting authority and responsibility and the work which they perform is bound to be anything but efficient.

Some good may come out of it, but it is certainly disgusting when a state agency receives a generous federal grant and the members who are steering such an agency sit down around the table and try to decide how the money can be best spent with a particular view to how much their own power and income will be benefited. To be philosophical about it, it is apparent that there is not enough productive work to go around, and it is only natural that some enjoy being on a new commission if for no other reason than to increase their own prestige.

From this distance it appears that the Vermont state legislature has been rather irresponsible during its last session, missing the leadership which it had when each town or city, large or small, had a single representative who received a salary of $400 a session.

Instead of saying "What can I give?", too many people in public life today are saying "What can I get?"

41

Week ending April 15, 1972

ANOTHER WEEK of little accomplishment on the part of the Congress.

There was a Foreign Relations committee meeting Monday morning to start marking up [revising] an authorization bill for the State department. Since Congress has decided that the State department should be required to have appropriations authorized just as other departments of government must, we are now starting work on this authorization bill. The outlook is not promising: too much politics in the air, both domestic and international, and too many people with ambitions seek to use this type of legislation to their own advantage.

Also under consideration by the Foreign Relations committee is authorization for the USIA; for arms control, through a commission which is now trying to reach some agreement with the Soviet government; and also authorization for Peace Corps expenditures for the fiscal year 1973. However, not too much has been accomplished, although thankfully the wrangling is not of a strict partisan nature.

¶ IN THE EARLY EVENING I attended a reception for William Driver, past director of the Veterans Administration, and now president of the Manufacturing Chemists' Association. The reception was held in the Dolley Madison Room of the Madison Hotel, which caters largely to businessmen with generous expense accounts. I attended this reception briefly because Bill Driver, when he was Director of the VA, did a good job and was largely responsible, at L.P.A.'s urging, for getting authorization to modernize the VA Hospital at White River Junction, Vermont.

My attendance at the reception for him should not in any way indicate my approval of any of the desires of his organization. Washington is so full of organizations and their paid representatives that I have just about adopted a policy of not attending any of their conferences, or receptions, or dinners, regardless of the type of organization or any previous acquaintance with their Washington representatives, who may have been old friends of mine as members of the Congress. In fact, many members of Congress and many topflight employees of government departments are now working for the very people they used to make laws for and enforce laws on.

However, this is legitimate business, and I do not blame a former member of Congress for taking a position essential to the support of his family and himself regardless of whether such position may represent his own personal opinions or desires. After all, people have to live and eat and keep their families healthy and send their children to school, and being Washington representative for an organization has become one of the most influential industries in our nation's capital and its suburbs.

¶ TUESDAY, the 11th, the Foreign Relations committee continued its efforts to mark up the State Department Authorization bill. I was interrupted in this work by representatives of various interests from Vermont and elsewhere. We made some little progress on marking up the bill, but to tell the truth I am not in favor of some of the amendments or proposals which I vote for in committee. I do so for two reasons. The first is, to get such proposals into a conference committee meeting with the House, where I hope better judgment will be shown than in either committee by itself.

Incidentally, it is an old practice among politicians, particularly among those seeking re-election or election to a higher office, to vote for something they don't believe in and then trust a smaller group of House and Senate conferees to kill such proposals. In that way they can always tell the proponents of a particular idea, "I did what I could for you but that miserable House (or conference) committee just wouldn't accept it." Maybe such action isn't entirely honorable, but it may go a long way toward insuring re-election for a member of Congress.

And another reason why members of Congress sometimes vote for proposals in which they do not believe is to help a colleague in his quest for re-election. If he proposes something which is very popular in his own district, he can then tell his constituents, "I did the best I could for you but it just wasn't enough to get your proposals enacted into law."

¶ L.P.A. ATTENDED the annual luncheon which Senators' and former Senators' wives give for the President's wife and the wives of Cabinet members. It strikes me that she is doing rather more than her share in making arrangements for these luncheons, sending out all the invitations, making decisions as to who should get an invitation and who should not, but apparently she is stuck with the job for another year at least.

While this was going on I was attending the weekly conference luncheon of the Republican members of the Senate. Apparently not much went on at this conference besides the usual roast-beef dinner for two dollars, since I cannot at this point remember what subjects we took up.

During the afternoon we continued the Foreign Relations committee mark-up of the State Department Authorization bill. Also, there was a meeting of the Joint Committee on Atomic Energy relative to power-plant licensing. These hearings and meetings concerning power-plant licensing are rather disgusting and also ineffective.

The utility companies are constantly making efforts to work into any bill proposed a proviso which would exempt them from provisions of antitrust laws. So far I have been able to block such exemption, but no one knows when they may be able to sneak something in.

It is not only United States interests that are seeking monopolies, but international outfits which have very strong representation in Western European countries. I realize that the urge for monopoly leadership and power is very strong in the minds of most human beings, but I also realize that the best interests of our country can be served by preventing such ambitions from being realized, since they would inevitably lead to tyranny in government.

¶ APRIL 12—called to the White House at eight o'clock with other Republican leadership to hear a report on the North Vietnamese all-out attack upon South Vietnam. I think we were correctly informed of the situation by Henry Kissinger and the President himself. Apparently North Vietnam is adopting almost a "now or never" policy and is sending the full amount of its power, backed up by modern offensive supplies furnished by Russia, into South Vietnam in an effort to win a decisive victory and control over that country as far as possible before the President's visit to Moscow, now slated for May 22.

I note the Washington *Post* states that Russia has not been furnishing modern arms or equipment lately to North Vietnam. I do not believe this to be the fact. Russia is not the least bit happy because of our growing better relationship with the People's Republic of China.

¶ DR. JOHN HANNAH, Director of AID [the Agency for International Development], called about legislation which is now pending before the Foreign Relations committee. I suggested to him that the provisions which AID really needs to carry on its work efficiently should be adopted by the House Committee on Foreign Affairs, since the Senate Foreign Relations committee is so jumbled and so afflicted with political ambitions that a conference committee between the House and Senate would be able to deal with the whole subject more intelligently. Dr. Hannah feels that the House will be receptive to many of his proposals, particularly a plan to eliminate much unnecessary and costly personnel from the organization. He agreed that the best thing to do was to let the House get out as good a bill as possible, and then try to straighten things out in Conference.

¶ THURSDAY was a bad day for me, and for the first time since I can remember I did not show at the office. I had too much in common with Achilles, or at least that is where the pain originated, but thanks to Dr. Pearson I was able to get back to the office on Friday.

It appears that I hadn't missed much but squabble between members of the Foreign Relations committee, and the work of trying to write up a State Department Authorization bill has now gone over until Monday, the 17th.

On Friday the Senate was not in session, but on Friday noon at the request of Senators Javits and Church, Chairman Fulbright had invited twenty-two foreign ministers from the OAS [Organization of American States] to come up to the Hill for coffee with members of the Foreign Relations committee. Unfortunately those who were insistent on the invitation did not show up. About half a dozen of us, including Senator Ellender and five members of the committee, did the best we could under the circumstances. It is getting to be altogether too common a practice for a member of a committee or the Senate to insist on appointments like this and then, failing to show, leave other members of the committee to take the blame.

In the middle of the afternoon the so-called steering committee of four in charge of the study on multinational corporations, including myself, met with four professors from four outstanding universities to discuss possible methods of procedure with this study. There are a lot of intelligent professors in this country, but when they are called in as advisers before a committee which is infinitely more experienced in the work, I usually think of the old saying, "He who can, does—he who can't, teaches." Nevertheless, professors do a lot of research work and are frequently helpful.

¶ SATURDAY EVENING L.P.A. and I attended dinner at the White House given by President Nixon for the foreign ministers and ambassadors of the OAS. About nine o'clock I was tipped off that American planes in force had bombed Haiphong Harbor and that the press would be looking for me after the dinner.

I well recall being with a small group at the White House in 1966 when President Johnson announced a decision to bomb Haiphong and Hanoi. I protested as vigorously as I could over this decision because I felt that such action would only prolong the war, which has proved to be the case. In 1966 we were clearly the aggressors, carrying aerial bombing and its resultant destruction to the country of North Vietnam.

The situation is quite different today, with the North Vietnamese committing virtually every bit of military strength they possess to the conquering of South Vietnam. North Vietnam is apparently adequately supplied with invasion weapons, mostly from Russia, whereas our supplies sent to the South Vietnamese troops have consisted primarily of defensive weapons. I believe that Hanoi committed a serious error and if, as is reported, Russia has been egging them on, then the Soviets are only creating more difficulties for themselves.

Probably we won't know for sure for another two months what the outcome will be but, at this point, I feel that Hanoi has made a serious error. There can be no comparison between the bombing of Haiphong Harbor today and the bombing of North Vietnam under President Johnson.

Week ending April 22, 1972

THE WEEK started off with a political bang with Secretary of State Rogers appearing before the Senate Foreign Relations committee and being promptly attacked over the war situation by Chairman Fulbright. Following Fulbright, Senator Church continued the attack, likening the North Vietnamese all-out invasion of South Vietnam to the Northern invasion of the Southern states during the Civil War. I felt impelled to remark that the Northern states had not killed off 200,000 Southerners previous to their invasion of the Confederacy, as the North Vietnamese had done in 1954.

Senator Symington opposed the Administration moderately, and Senator Spong, the other Democrat present, was quite restrained. I tried to show that the North Vietnamese were not guiltless in this latest escalation of the war, and was generally supported by Senators Case and Cooper. Senators Javits and Percy, as usual, were not wholehearted in support of the Administration's fighting back against the invasion from the North, and when the television networks, particularly CBS, re-ran part of the hearing, they carefully excluded any show of support for the United States, meaning that Senators Cooper, Case and Aiken did not show on the program, whereas the attackers of Secretary Rogers were prominently displayed.

On the whole, the newspapers and the columnists were much fairer than the television industry in presenting the arguments on both sides. Unfortunately, however, some local papers even in Vermont carried as headlines that "Aiken Supports the Bombing." This of course is false, since I strongly opposed bombing by the Johnson Administration in 1966 and do not favor it at this time. I do, however, hold North Vietnam and their Russian backers fully responsible for the latest build-up in the war. Whether they think they can overwhelm the South Vietnamese military, or whether they are undertaking to extend the war until after President Nixon's visit to Moscow in late May, is the question.

I do hope, and have so expressed myself, that the North Vietnamese escalation of the war will be a failure, for actually the war has been dying down, and it appears that nearly all American forces could be withdrawn by July 1, 1972. What will happen now no one knows, but if the bloodshed on the battlefield continues beyond midsummer it will clearly be the fault of the North Vietnamese government and its allies.

Of course much of the trouble stems from the fact that we have a national election in November and North Vietnam has evidently been given to understand that if they can prolong the war until after the election, there may be a Democratic victory and they will receive much more generous treatment under a Democratic administration.

¶ AFTER THE PUBLIC HEARING, the Foreign Relations committee went into executive session. We succeeded in getting out a State Department Authorization bill for fiscal year 1973, a very messy bill with several anti-Administration amendments being approved by the Democrats present. The bill was finally voted out by the committee with the understanding that one last amendment might be considered after this action was taken. This amendment, sponsored by Senators Church and Case, called for the stoppage of all expenditures for the military in Indochina after December 31, 1972, and for the release of all POW's by North Vietnam as a condition for this.

However, North Vietnam has already served notice on us that the POW's will never be released until we accept their terms for the cessation of hostilities. Their terms require a virtual surrender by the United States. We are to overthrow the South Vietnam government and to take out of the country all defense arms which we are now planning to leave with the South Vietnamese government and people. This means that North Vietnam, with its heavy supply of invasion weapons, could take over all of South Vietnam, and there is not the slightest question in my mind but what one of the first actions after doing so would be to execute possibly as many as two million people, many of whom escaped this fate when the United States moved them out of North Vietnam in 1954.

I was the only one to vote against the Church-Case amendment.

47

Senators Cooper and Spong abstained. Senator Javits apparently shifted his ideas and voted for it. Senator Fulbright had proxy votes from Senators McGee and Sparkman, who would have opposed this amendment, but he failed to make mention of it at the time. Senator McGee returned to town Thursday and was quite irate over the situation. He promptly put a stop order on the State Department Authorization bill to prevent its being brought up before the Senate next week as planned. I understand he talked with Senator Fulbright, expressing his displeasure, and secured a promise from the chairman to call the committee into executive session on Tuesday, the 25th, to go into the matter. What the outcome will be no one knows.

I have felt that, although I want to get this legislation out of the way as soon as possible, still we may be wise to delay any action on it until the return of the leadership, Senators Mansfield and Scott, from China two weeks from now. I also feel that we should perhaps not take action until the President's promised announcement on the United States' future part in the war, which he is to make before May 1.

¶ THE OTHER important legislation coming up before the Senate during the week was the Rural Development bill, which was brought up Wednesday and on which action was concluded Thursday. The big issue on this bill was a proposal sponsored by the majority of the Committee on Agriculture and Forestry, but primarily by Senator Humphrey, to establish a brand-new banking system, which, according to Senator Ellender, could before long obligate the United States government for $40 billion or more and also take over or compete with much of the work which is now being performed by other agencies of government.

Like Senator Ellender, I insisted that instead of an enormous new agency we could accomplish the same purpose much more efficiently and at less cost by strengthening existing agencies, particularly the Farmers Home Administration.

After considerable debate on Thursday, we were successful in eliminating the new banking provision in the bill by a vote of 44 to 32. As the Rural Development bill is now written, I feel that we can go into Conference with the House Agriculture committee and perhaps come out with a good piece of legislation, although in this intensely political year there is no assurance of this.

In the minds of many members who are candidates for election or re-election, good legislation seems to be unimportant compared to voter appeal, even if such an appeal is ill-conceived.

¶ IT HAS BEEN a busy week in Washington. Tourists by the tens of thousands, and all week long there has been a steady stream of visitors from Vermont, including classes from several schools within the state. I am glad that they can come to Washington but unfortunately I am not able to spend as much time with them as I would like. My estimate is that probably two hundred Vermonters have visited my office within the week. Inasmuch as my office staff is comprised of Vermonters 100 percent, I hope and believe that all of our visitors have been very well received.

Week ending April 29, 1972

GENERALLY SPEAKING the coming election took the center of the stage this week, with Indochina and Moscow coming into the political picture more and more.

The almost certain exodus of Senator Muskie from the Democrats' Presidential candidacy arena did not surprise anyone, since Senator Muskie has been on the skids for some time. To all appearances it was wrangling among his own staff supporters that brought about his downfall. Some of his supporters were apparently so sure that he was going to win the nomination that they went to work to alienate him from his older friends who had raised money for him and given him a real start toward the nomination. He was what is called in political terms "packaged"—with a few taking him over and wrapping him up and claiming him as their own exclusive property, looking forward to the time when he might be elected President and they would be running the country. This maneuvering, plus Senator Muskie's unfortunate shedding of tears in front of the Manchester *Union Leader* office in New Hampshire, has apparently eliminated him from the race.

In my opinion the same thing happened to Governor Thomas Dewey in 1948, when his election to the Presidency seemed to be so well assured that a few of his promoters took him over and made it impossible for those who really could have helped him to get near him. I personally had spent two days and one night with Tom Dewey along with Professor Babcock of Cornell and Congressman Hope of Kansas, helping him prepare for his western campaign tour of the agricultural states. We might just as well have stayed home, because Dewey was not permitted to use any of the material which we provided for him and which I believe would have guaranteed his election had he been permitted to use it.

Political ambition seems to bring out the worst in people who would otherwise be helpful. Such ambition saturates Washington today, not only among candidates for the Presidency, but also among many of their adherents, who envision great importance and even monetary wealth falling upon them should their candidate be elected President. The war in Indochina has been the vehicle upon which many normally sane members of Congress and of the Democratic Party hope to ride on to glory.

As I have said many times, I felt that the war in Vietnam could be concluded by midsummer and our withdrawal completed with reasonably acceptable terms. It now looks as if there are people who are determined that our exodus from that unhappy region shall not be concluded until after the election, the theory being that the Democratic candidate for President will have a much better chance for election if President Nixon can be charged with failure to end our involvement. I am not sure that their hopes of extending our involvement until after November will be realized.

Although I do not believe that the extension of bombing in the North will have much effect upon the present battle going on in South Vietnam, the news media spread the word that I favored resumption of bombing the North. Therefore on Tuesday I had to set the situation straight before the Senate. With so many conflicting reports being spread, it is no wonder that the people on the whole have been confused.

It is significant that the mail and other communications protesting the renewal of the bombing in North Vietnam was very light compared with what it was four or even two years ago. About half of all the protests I received came in the form of identical letters from students at Johnson State College in Vermont. Toward the end of the week mail on both sides of the issue had pretty well fallen off. There were, of course, many who wrote in who supported the President's position, and even here in Washington some well-known Democrats agreed that he was doing about all he could to bring our involvement to an end.

¶ However, a new element came into the picture during the week. On Monday night Dr. Henry Kissinger returned from a four-day visit in Moscow where he talked with Mr. Brezhnev and other high-ranking

Soviet officials. Tuesday night I joined with several members of the House and Senate in going to the White House to get a firsthand report from Dr. Kissinger. He was obviously tired, a little depressed, and rather touchy when foolish questions were asked of him. But it is perfectly obvious now that Russia, who I believe has planned for and instigated the all-out drive by North Vietnam upon the South, may be having second thoughts on the subject.

President Nixon is going to Moscow on May 22. He hopes for highly satisfactory decisions and results to come from this visit and I hope that his hopes are realized. Russia is in a real quandary at this time. Not only is Russia's arch-rival in the communist world, the People's Republic of China, making headway in developing better relations with other countries, particularly the United States, but Russia is having rather severe economic difficulties. The Soviet government has promised the people of the U.S.S.R. better times, a better diet, better everything—and up to now has been unable to deliver the goods.

The Russian people want meat and high-grade foods rather than a diet consisting principally of grain and vegetables. Russia needs industrial expansion and much more development than the present rate of progress shows. Russian agriculture cannot produce the level of diet which the Russian people have been promised, and the country best able to co-operate with the Moscow government in creating a better life for the people is the United States.

I had reports during the week not only from Dr. Kissinger but from the Secretary of Agriculture, Earl Butz, and later his assistant, Clarence Palmby, who had just returned from Russia. Russia wants our help and co-operation, but she wants the favorable terms accorded to a developing nation, which we cannot give her under our laws. Even if we were inclined to do so, Russia should realize that the American people will not forgive Moscow for encouraging and abetting the North Vietnamese military invasion of the South and I doubt at this time if the American Congress would approve any relaxation in its attitude toward the Soviet government.

And to add to the apprehension of Moscow, Chancellor Willy Brandt of West Germany has so far been unable to get approval of proposals that would put his country on better terms with East Germany and other Eastern European nations which at this time are dominated by the Moscow government. Should Chancellor Brandt be ousted from his position in the West Germany government, I fear that the tension between the countries of Western Europe and the communist countries to the east would be greatly increased, and thus would make it impossible—or at least unlikely—that Russia would be able to lessen the cost of maintaining military forces in some of those Eastern European countries.

I am sure that the leaders of the Soviet government know this. And they should also know that they cannot continue to promote warfare and bloodshed in Indochina and at the same time expect any relaxation of their fears in Eastern Europe, or expect much help from us.

This morning, Saturday, April 29, the radio news reported that a high-ranking Russian official is on his way to Hanoi. If the Russian government so desires, it can bring the war in Indochina to a close so far as we are concerned, although the fighting will undoubtedly continue with its present intensity until after President Nixon's visit to Moscow late next month.

So at this point I am quite hopeful that there may be encouraging developments within the next six weeks in spite of any efforts at home or abroad to continue the present tense and uncertain situation.

Week ending May 6, 1972

THE VIETNAM battlefield and rising distrust of the U.S.S.R. dominated the thinking of the week.

There is a pretty well-fixed belief that Russia is responsible for the escalation and intensification of the Vietnam war. Not only do the North Vietnamese have a very large supply of Russian invasion weapons, but it is reported that Russian ships are clogging the North Vietnam ports in unprecedented numbers. The unloading of these ships is not taking place so much at Haiphong Harbor as at a port much farther south nearer the DMZ [De-militarized Zone between North and South Vietnam].

Since the modern heavy equipment furnished by the Russians requires huge amounts of fuel, it is probable that much of the cargo is gasoline. The big Russian tanks do not travel at 20 miles to the gallon, they use nearly 20 gallons to the mile.

The week has been comparatively quiet on the battlefield. Quang Tri was taken and occupied by the North Vietnamese. It was the first provincial capital to be taken by the North, and its fall had been expected two weeks ago. Now, with the rainy season due any time, it will be more difficult to get cargo inland from the coastal ports. Replenishment of fuel and other supplies is essential if the enemy is to make a full-scale attack on Hue or Kontum, the next probable targets. The rains will also make it more difficult for the United States to furnish air cover for South Vietnam's defenders.

While the United States has increased its air-strike ability during the week there has apparently been no bombing of Haiphong or Hanoi since I spoke in the Senate on May 1, making it clear that I questioned its effectiveness and stating my disapproval.

The fighting over the week demonstrated the uncertain caliber of the South Vietnamese Army. Except for air cover, the Russian tanks and other equipment furnished to the North seemed to be far superior to that which we furnished to the South. It was, however, the leadership of the Southern armies which proved most uncertain. While some of their generals were really good, others were clearly unqualified to lead armies and lost little time in proving it. President Thieu has now made some changes, the value of which will be indicated when the enemy attacks Hue, which is expected within a week or two.

However, it is not the fighting that is going on and the uncertainty of the outcome that concerns me most: it is the Russian attitude. Has Russia gone too far this time? There is conclusive evidence that Russia has planned and timed this new expansion of the war—but for what purpose?

¶ THE U.S.S.R. has been trying to get economic concessions from the United States of America. Russia wants feed grains, machine tools and much industrial equipment. She wants special concessions from us, such as long-time credit and low interest rates. There is no question but what we would have co-operated generously except for the expansion of the Vietnam war. It is difficult to understand the Soviet line of reasoning. Perhaps the U.S.S.R. thinks their recent actions will increase their bargaining power when President Nixon visits Moscow later this month. If so, they have made a grave error.

At a meeting of Republican leaders of Congress, called to the White House on May 3, President Nixon made it plain that he had read my speech to the Senate on May 1 and took my remarks seriously. On being called upon for comment, I referred to what I believed was an increasing anti-Soviet feeling among the public and especially in the Congress. The President then asked if I suggested cancellation of his trip to Moscow on May 22. I tried to make it clear that I do not. He definitely should go unless events of the next few days make it impossible. What I said was that if he brought back from Moscow tentative agreements giving Russia the major benefits of any deals, the Congress would not approve them.

As evidence of the growing disapproval of Russia in the Congress, I can point to two votes taken in the Senate. On Monday, May 1, Senator McGee offered an amendment to the State Department Authorization bill which would restore the full amount of funds asked by the USIA. The amount requested had been cut sharply by the Foreign Relations committee at the insistence of Senators Fulbright, Church and Symington. These Senators opposed the McGee amendment, but it was approved by a vote of 57 to 15. Further, on Thursday, May 4, an amendment to restore funds for the Peace Corps was offered by Senator Tunney. This amendment carried 47 to 9. It was opposed by Fulbright and Church, but Symington voted for it.

I am convinced that except for Russia's part in expanding the war, the votes on these two measures would have been much closer, possibly very close.

Pending at the end of the week was an amendment offered by Senator Stennis to strike from this State Department Authorization bill a committee amendment inserted by Senators Church and Case to cut off funds for military operations in Indochina after December 31, 1972, on condition that North Vietnam release the few hundred American prisoners they now hold. I do not doubt that North Vietnam would release these men if we would turn over to them the country of South Vietnam. It would be a small price for them to pay. But it would also most certainly give them the right to wreak vengeance on those who have opposed them in South Vietnam.

The Senate was strongly opposed to the Church-Case plan, possibly two to one, so the sponsors of the proposal succeeded in putting off a vote this week. They say they want to wait until Senator Mansfield gets home from China next week and get his advice. They would do better to ask for a few weeks' delay themselves. It would not hurt their standing at all, but apparently they prefer to pass the buck to the Majority Leader.

I am strongly of the opinion that the Church-Case amendment and probably the whole State Department Authorization bill should be postponed until after the President's visit to Russia.

¶ A PIECE OF LEGISLATION with which I have been especially concerned is a bill which passed the House giving the AEC [Atomic Energy Commission] authority to issue temporary operating licenses to nuclear power plants in areas threatened with a shortage of electric energy. New England is one area which is expected to experience a shortage of electricity next winter unless new sources of energy can be made available. Senator Anderson and I are the sponsors of this same bill in

the Senate. It passed the House by a voice vote without material opposition. I expect it will pass the Senate, but not without opposition
from the so-called environmental societies.

The principal attorney for these organizations is reported to have
said that they will neither oppose nor support this temporary measure,
but if that is the case, he will have difficulties in persuading some of
his clients to follow his lead. I am still convinced that there is a determined effort under way by a group of powerful interests to get control of all sources of energy in the United States. I also suspect that
these monopoly-seekers are trying to use environmental societies to
achieve their purpose.

Week ending May 13, 1972

SUNDAY, the 7th, Senators Mansfield and Scott returned from China,
and L.P.A. and I went out to Andrews Air Force Base to help welcome
them home. All the travelers looked used up, with Mansfield seeming
in the best shape.

¶ IF SCOTT and Mansfield thought they could catch up on their rest
they might as well forget it. The State Department Authorization bill
was still before the Senate, and Senator Stennis's proposal to delete
the Church-Case provision was the pending business. No one was in
a mood to vote on this in a hurry. The battle in South Vietnam was
on. It was obvious that Russia might be asking for trouble—big trouble—and Congress was not well informed as to the situation over there.
I am not sure that the executive branch was, either. The leadership—
Scott and Mansfield—asked President Nixon to invite us to the White
House for an up-to-date briefing. The invitation was received about
5 P.M., with the two leaders of both House and Senate plus the chairman and ranking member of the Appropriations, the Armed Services,
and the Foreign Relations committees of the Senate, and the Foreign
Affairs committee of the House, invited. We were to meet at 8 P.M.
Before extending the invitation, however, the President had announced that he would go on the air and speak to the country at 9 P.M.

There was no previous consultation with the President involved: he
simply took a few minutes to tell us what he had already decided on
and then left for his broadcast.

What he told us was that he had decided to mine Haiphong Harbor
and all other harbors on the North Vietnam coast, that he planned to

destroy railroads, depots, and highways in North Vietnam in the belief
that crippling all forms of transportation would force North Vietnam
to ask for peace. I was not surprised at this decision, but I felt he was
taking a desperate risk for ending the war. I had heard such decisions
several times under President Johnson and none of them succeeded,
only made things worse. I don't believe that mining the coast and
bombing the interior will work. There is only an outside chance that
it may.

Some members of Congress who attended the President's briefing
seemed shocked. Senator Mansfield was mad and made no bones about
it. After the President left, the briefing was continued by Secretary of
State Rogers, Secretary of Defense Laird, and Admiral Moorer [then
Chairman of the Joint Chiefs of Staff]. I left early and heard the President on the car radio. I believe everybody there felt depressed, but not
as much as I did.

If the President wins with this dangerous gamble, it will be because
during his address he made the enemy the most generous peace offer
yet. His proposals included the following points.

First, all American prisoners of war must be returned; second, there
must be an internationally supervised cease-fire throughout Indochina; third, as soon as the first two points are complied with, we will
stop all acts of force throughout Indochina; and fourth, at that time
we will also proceed with a complete withdrawal of all American
forces from Vietnam within four months.

¶ TUESDAY AFTERNOON Congress recessed to let the Democrats caucus
to decide what to do about the Church-Case proposal and the Stennis
motion to delete it from the State Department Authorization bill.
They were in session three hours and turned down a proposal by Senator Fulbright to declare a vote of No Confidence in the President.
They didn't want the English system, even if Fulbright did go to Ox-
ford; he withdrew his proposal.

¶ THE SENATE WAS still stymied Wednesday. The issue was common
sense versus politics. As the week went on, the political situation
seemed to change. The political polls and other criteria indicate that
the country as a whole supported the President's decision to mine the
North Vietnam harbors. This was particularly true in the Middle
West and rural areas of the country. In the Northeast, and particularly in what are called educational centers, the opposition to the
President intensified. It seemed to be systematically inspired to a considerable extent, although many other people were inherently opposed
to what they chose to call an intensification of the war, particularly

the mining of North Vietnam's waters. They apparently forgot that the North Vietnamese thoroughly mined the waters of South Vietnam several years ago.

The Russians did not respond to the President's mining decision with an outburst as had been expected. Instead they adopted a softer tack. The Soviet Ambassador and high Soviet officials visited President Nixon, and there was little sign of outright hostility in this visit. In fact, they seemed to be looking forward to the President's visit to Moscow beginning on May 22.

Russia wants very much to engage in more trade with the United States and is not happy, of course, about our providing huge supplies of arms and other military equipment to Israel, Jordan, and Turkey. However, since Russia did not explode in anger at the President's decision, it is entirely possible that some rather far-reaching arrangements may be made by the U.S.S.R. and the United States at the time of the President's visit.

¶ THE SENATE APPROVED the Space Authorization bill by a one-sided vote on Thursday afternoon; and it was also agreed that next Thursday, May 16, the Senate would vote on a motion to amend the Case-Church proposal which is in the State Department Authorization bill. Approval of this motion would mean that the Case-Church proposal would be almost identical with the proposal for ending the war in Vietnam which was made by the President.

I don't see how anyone could vote against including a cease-fire agreement in this proposal, but I expect there will be many who will do so either for political or for other reasons. However, I will be surprised if the Senate votes against a cease-fire proposal.

Week ending May 20, 1972

ON THE 14th I gave the commencement address at Green Mountain College in Poultney, Vermont. I have a liking for two-year technical schools and colleges. During our stop in Poultney a small group consisting of a minister, his wife, and a couple of others, came to protest the war. It seems everybody has to engage in a crusade from time to time, and these days it's protesting against the war in South Vietnam. A few months ago it was against generating nuclear power, and what it will be next year no one can predict now. Everybody wants to be important, and that is all right with me. I only wish that sometimes they were better informed on the subjects of their crusades.

I had expected that all of our troops in South Vietnam would be withdrawn by July 1, as indeed they would have been had not North Vietnam, aided and abetted by Russia, launched a full-scale invasion of South Vietnam in early April. So many people write in charging the United States with dividing Vietnam into two countries, apparently ignorant of the fact that at the Geneva Conference in 1954 the United States strongly opposed the division of the countries but was outvoted by the other seven members of this conference.

¶ ON TUESDAY we voted on Senator Robert Byrd's amendment to the Church-Case amendment. The Byrd amendment called for cease-fire in South Vietnam as well as for the release of hostages held by the North. The amendment was approved by a 47-to-43 vote, and Senator Church, who only a week earlier had indicated complete approval of the President's conditions for ending the war, promptly announced opposition to his own amendment. I feel that after he had virtually endorsed President Nixon's proposals on May 9, he got a talking-to from someone.

After voting on the Byrd amendment at 2 P.M. Tuesday, a delegation of Senators and Congressmen and wives and aides left for New Orleans to meet with a large delegation from Mexico, including some two dozen representatives of the Mexican Congress. Our meetings with the Mexican delegates were divided into three sections: political, economic, and social. Mike Mansfield and I were on the political committee. The principal issue was the character of the water flowing in the Rio Grande River. Since the construction of dams in the United States this water now contains so much salt that it is indeed injurious to Mexican crop production, and unfit for other uses as well.

It is a problem difficult to solve, one which exists between many of the states of our own country, not necessarily because of salt water, but because of the tendency of one state to pollute the water of another.

Otherwise most of the problems facing the United States and Mexico are mutual, as indeed are other problems confronting the world these days. In this instance Mexico needs fresh water. That part of the southwestern United States needs electric energy. A few years ago at one of these meetings I joined with the Speaker of the Mexican House, Alphonso Martinez-Dominguez, in proposing an atomic development which would desalinate the waters of the Pacific while at the same time producing power for southern California and Arizona.

An economical method for doing this has not yet been developed, but someday one will have to be.

Like so many of our problems with other countries, the Rio Grande pollution is a problem of a political nature which requires a scientific solution.

[Putney, Vermont]

Week ending May 27, 1972

SENATOR MANSFIELD this week proposed the amendment to end the war in Vietnam which he had offered to the State Department Authorization bill last week, but drawn in a somewhat different manner that also made it more understandable. The first part of his amendment provides that "all United States military forces, including combat and support forces stationed in South Vietnam, shall be withdrawn from South Vietnam no later than August 31, 1972." The amendment provides that no funds shall be expended for any ground forces after that date. I am convinced that had it not been for the invasion from the North in early April our ground forces could all have been withdrawn sometime in July.

The first part of Mansfield's amendment did not require the withdrawal of naval ships or aircraft carriers before the August 31 date. The second part of the amendment provided for the termination of hostilities by all United States military forces—land, sea, and air— under certain conditions not materially different from those proposed by the President in April.

There are those who claim that the United States should withdraw in toto after the opposition promises to release all American prisoners. But the Mansfield amendment, as written in committee, provides that we will withdraw all military forces after the prisoners have been released. This change makes the Mansfield proposal much more acceptable, and the committee agreed to accept it by a voice vote. A roll-call vote would have showed a very sharp division in the committee.

Most of us were glad to attach the Mansfield amendment to the Foreign Aid bill, with the expectation that Senator Mansfield would then withdraw it as a proposal to the State Department Authorization bill so that the Senate could complete its work on the impending major bills. I frequently vote to report out bills which contain provisions to which I am opposed, feeling that through consideration on the floor of the Senate and again in Conference with the House the obnoxious provisions may be deleted.

¶ ON THURSDAY, L.P.A. and I set out for Vermont after taking care of morning mail. The weather remained good for the rest of the week, and on Friday I planted our vegetable garden, the ground for which had been plowed for us the week before.

People in Vermont generally were very much concerned with the political situation, particularly the type of resolutions which had been adopted at the Democratic state convention on May 20. These resolutions, relating to abortion, drug use, and army desertions, had really upset the people, particularly the old-line Democrats, since probably 60 percent of Democrats voting in Vermont are Catholics and could not possibly support resolutions of this type.

¶ PRESIDENT NIXON, in the meantime, is having a reasonably successful trip to Moscow where he appears to be getting along with the Russian leadership very well personally and, to a considerable degree, politically. While the two main items supposedly under consideration—ending of the Indochina war and expansion of trade relations with Russia—did not reach any final agreement, other matters were agreed to, including the limitation of nuclear arms by both countries. The Moscow summit conference may be considered as generally successful.

Personally, I feel that there will be an increase in trade between Russia and the United States as soon as reasonable terms can be agreed upon, and that we will find a way to bring the ground war in Vietnam to a conclusion as far as we are concerned at a fairly early date.

The moderate success of the President's trip to Moscow, coupled with the fragmentation of the Democratic Party in many areas of the United States, is now creating the impression that the Republicans may well capture enough seats to control the Senate next session. I personally doubt this, but nevertheless it could happen.

Being in Vermont for only three or four days really makes the situation in Washington and other world capitals seem pretty depressing. We will have to start back for our nation's capital on Monday.

[*United States Senate*]

Week ending June 3, 1972

TUESDAY AFTERNOON was taken up with floor work on the State Department Authorization bill, which came to a final vote on Wednesday and will now go to a Committee of Conference, where I expect that an agreement with the House on diverse provisions of the bill will be reached during the next few days.

Since Senator Mansfield's proposal for cutting off funds for military operations within Vietnam is bound to create considerable debate and delay, it appeared best to take it up as a foreign-aid military proposal rather than to delay and hamstring the work of the State department. Through the week I received a few letters urging support for the proposal offered by Senator Mansfield. The letters were mostly from people who seem to think its adoption would bring about an end to the war and our complete withdrawal by August 31.

Apparently they do not know that there are conditions carried in the Mansfield proposal which North Vietnam has so far absolutely refused to accept unless we accept conditions they insist upon, such as ousting the present South Vietnamese government at Saigon and disarming the people of South Vietnam. Furthermore North Vietnam has adamantly refused to let the International Red Cross interview the prisoners they hold, in accord with an international agreement which is observed by virtually every other country in the world. So I don't feel that the Mansfield amendment, even if approved by the Senate, would be effective in extricating us from our uncomfortable position in Indochina.

Meanwhile our bombing of strategic places in North Vietnam, such as power plants, bridges, and so forth goes on at an apparently accelerated pace. The South Vietnamese armies have also held back the invaders to a far greater extent than I had anticipated.

¶ THE BIG NEWS of the week, of course, was President Nixon's return from his twelve-day trip to Moscow and other capitals. He arrived back at the air field about 9 P.M. on Thursday and immediately came to the Capitol by helicopter to address a joint session of the Congress. Although about half the members of Congress were not present, presumably being involved in political campaigns of their own, the President did receive an excellent reception and made a forthright report on what had been accomplished on his trip.

No agreement, however, has been reached on two major items involving trade with Russia and the termination of our Vietnam involvement. Although Russia has no doubt encouraged the North Vietnamese invaders and furnished them with modern tanks and other equipment, I am not sure that they could at this point persuade North Vietnam to quit the war even if they wanted to. And I doubt that Russia will want North Vietnam to make the road easier for us so long as we supply those countries in the vicinity of Russia with modern planes and arms and assistance of virtually every description. Naturally Russia wants to involve us as far from home as possible, and Indochina seems made to order for this purpose.

The President reached several agreements in Moscow, some of which could have been arranged without the trip being taken at all. The agreement which created the most interest, however, and which met with general approval, was one that would limit the number of nuclear weapons both on sea and on land. Some of the most outspoken hawks decried this agreement, but by far the greater number of members of Congress approved the effort and will doubtless approve agreements of this type officially.

Friday morning the President had thirty of us from the House and Senate down to the White House where he and Dr. Kissinger gave a full two-hour explanation of the trip, of their agreements and the reasons therefor. I believe he had the wholehearted support of the thirty Congressional leaders present. He told us frankly that the arms agreement reached does not give the United States an overwhelming advantage over Russia. In some respects, indeed, it may be considered that the Russians themselves have an advantage.

But the reason he gave that went home to most of us was the statement that it was this agreement or nothing, and if the arms race were to continue with the full capacity of each nation, there could only be disaster for both countries, and possibly for the whole world in the end.

It was also encouraging to learn that the countries of Western Europe are planning a further meeting with Russia and the Eastern European countries later this fall in an effort to diminish the threat of war on the Eurasian continent. Chancellor Willy Brandt has already been successful in making a substantial start toward improving relations between Eastern and Western Europe. And it is possible, I almost think probable, that a further meeting this fall between East and West will result in more progress in this direction.

I also expect that better trade relations between Russia and the United States will be agreed to within the next few months, although no agreement was reached during the President's Moscow trip. The Russians still owe us some $300 million on their World War II account, but this is only a drop in the bucket compared to what other Western European countries owe. Russia is a hard trader. Compared to us, the Russian people have to live a hard life and they want a better one.

Week ending June 10, 1972

A BUSY but constructive week. For almost the first time this year I am quite satisfied with the progress being made to extricate ourselves from Indochina, to establish better relations with other governments of the world, and to lay the groundwork for greatly improved social and economic progress here at home.

It looks now as if all our appropriations will be taken care of before we recess for the holidays and the Democratic national convention in early July.

¶ THE KLEINDIENST NOMINATION for Attorney General was the pending business before the Senate, and argument continued on this subject until the afternoon of Thursday, the 8th, when he was overwhelmingly approved by the Senate. I have regarded the Kleindienst matter as being political from the start. A resulting vote of 64 to 19 was a sharp reverse to those who thought they might get political advantage by their opposition to his appointment. It was a very unusual vote, where all the Republicans voted alike, and only a minority of nineteen Democrats were in opposition.

I think the Primary elections in four states, which were held on Tuesday, had some effect on the situation, with Senator McGovern showing such strong gains for the Presidential nomination over Senator Humphrey and all others. The country really became alarmed, particularly the Southern states, since they mistrusted not only McGovern's fitness for the position but also his changing philosophy on life. Even *The New York Times* and other so-called liberal newspapers seemed to be terribly disturbed. The Clean Election law enacted by Congress last year apparently is not working well, and in some states, like Rhode Island, appears to have put a minority of the Democrats in control of the party.

Senators Humphrey and McGovern returned to the Senate on Thursday, and I suppose will continue their efforts toward getting the nomination. However, at this time the Democrats appear to be split right down the middle, while President Nixon is steadily gaining strength. The Vietnam war apparently is working out in his favor, and can conceivably come to an end before election time, although I think that is doubtful.

¶ ON MONDAY and Tuesday the Senate Foreign Relations committee held hearings on Radio Free Europe and Radio Liberty. While not enthusiastic about these programs, our committee did vote to extend them for one more year, with the understanding that business and the governments of Western Europe will show an interest in carrying these programs and sharing the costs.

Western European businessmen do not contribute anything to these programs, since any contributions they make are not deductible for tax purposes, as is the case in the United States. However, it was felt that, with further negotiations in sight between the countries of Western Europe and the United States and Russia, it was best not to change the present system of operating these two radio programs at this time. The twenty directors of Radio Free Europe are all members of large international corporations, large banks, and law firms which represent them.

¶ FRIDAY MORNING L.P.A. with her two sisters and nephew, Ted, and myself left for Pascagoula, Mississippi, with urgent work on legislation being pretty well completed. Lola had been asked to sponsor the newest of our nuclear-powered submarines, the *Tunny,* while Admiral Rickover had insisted that I give the principal address. The christening of the ship went off according to schedule and it was really thrilling to see how easily the *Tunny* left the dock where she had been under construction, and slid into the bay which sets back from the Gulf of Mexico.

In my twelve-minute address to the six or seven hundred people gathered there I put emphasis on the value of the nuclear-powered submarine as probably the best deterrent to war we have. But I also pointed out the value of the submarine in exploring the depths of the ocean where there are tremendous resources of food and minerals. Without the preparation for military defense purposes, the ocean bed would be nowhere near as well explored as it is now.

I also pointed out that our nuclear submarines had traveled over twenty million miles without any harm coming to anyone through the release of radiation into the atmosphere. This statement of course will not make happy those among our environmentalists who insist that radiation is about the most insidious killer of all. At times I have very strong suspicions that many of those people who so vigorously oppose the development of electric energy from the atom have an interest in the production of the competitive fuels—oil and coal.

Week ending June 17, 1972

THE CONFERENCE report on the Rural Development bill has now been submitted to the House of Representatives and should be acted upon some time next week. This bill represents a long step forward in our efforts to prevent the concentration of our population in the larger cities. It will provide incentive not only for agriculture generally but also for rural living and the establishment of local industries in areas with less than a 50,000 population. It will triple the amount of grants authorized for rural water and waste disposal. I think this is a very important bill.

The other bill which was finally worked out by conferees of House and Senate was one authorizing appropriations for the State department and the USIA. Some twenty-seven amendments introduced by one House or the other were considered and reconciled or deleted. The one creating the most controversy would have established within the State department a grievance committee similar to those which have been set up in other departments of government.

The grievance committee proposal, strongly supported by Senator Cooper, was finally dropped from the bill not only because there was a question in the House as to its being germane, but also because the House conferees agreed that a bill which would provide the same opportunities for members of the Foreign Service would be considered promptly by the House committee if the Senate would approve it first. The Senate committee on the same day voted to report the measure favorably to the Senate, and results remain to be seen.

¶ ON THURSDAY, 122 members of Congress representing the membership of the Committees on Foreign Relations and Armed Services of both Houses and members of the Joint Committee on Atomic Energy, were invited to the White House to a briefing by the President and Dr. Kissinger on the agreements with Russia. I had planned on

Wednesday to attend this briefing session, but on Thursday morning I read in the Washington *Post* that members of the news media would also be present. Since the presence of the news media would mean a full report on the session later on in the day, I saw no sense in taking time off from my work in order to provide window-dressing for the White House, although I do favor the agreement.

¶ Perhaps the principal interest of the week was created by the announcement of another trip to China by Kissinger and a trip by Mr. Podgorny of the Soviet Union to Hanoi. It certainly looks as if the United States, Russia, and China are trying to terminate our involvement in Indochina. And if they can secure good results it will meet with the approval of most of the people of the world and particularly the United States.

However, we can never be sure what the governments of the world have in mind. I still believe that the ills of Asia cannot be cured in Paris or Geneva, but must be handled by Asia itself with the United States of America, a Pacific country, collaborating.

Week ending June 24, 1972

LOTS OF RAIN, causing severe floods in several states; and lots of non-sense politically, causing a good deal of depression on my part.

With the Democratic national convention due to start in Miami in a couple of weeks, the political situation is increasingly worse, with candidates making promises they never could keep, and which, if kept, would be destructive or at least very harmful to the nation. The Capitol is almost besieged by lobbyists, all seeking special advantages for members of their organizations, and the mail has picked up accordingly, many letters purportedly from different people but in the same handwriting; lobbyists in person urging increased benefits and an increase in the minimum wage, while the letters are opposing a very substantial increase in the minimum wage on the grounds the industries will suffer and the price of their goods will be increased.

The bill before us will provide for the tenth increase in the minimum wage rate since the twenty-five-cents law was established in 1938. And letters we received today are virtually identical with the ones that were written us every time a proposal to increase the rate has been made.

Congress is in no position to deny a very substantial increase in wages, since it was only a little over three years ago that members of Congress permitted their own salaries to be raised 41 percent, and doubled the salary of the President at the same time. It was a major contribution to the inflationary prices of today.

Actually, however, the net cash income of members of Congress did not increase much, because of increases in rents, in taxes, and in everything else which a Congressman has to pay for in the District of Columbia area.

What apparently is on everybody's mind is how he is to live decently in the future after retiring from his present job, either voluntarily or otherwise. And retirement payments for members of Congress and employees of government are based on a percentage of their average salary for the last three years.

The members of the labor unions not only have to consider retirement payments, if they are lucky enough to work for a company that provides them, but also unemployment compensation in the event they are laid off. And the officials of a corporation who used to be in the $5,000–$25,000 salary class now feel that in order to be secure they have to get from $30,000–$100,000, and in hundreds of cases much more than this.

All this is not particularly new, because since the United States became independent costs have risen, on an average, about 3 percent a year. Only during the eight years of the Eisenhower Administration did the country get by without an increase in inflation, and it seems now that we are making up for lost time.

¶ THE OEO [Office of Economic Opportunity] bill was brought up at the end of the week. Although this organization has carried out some very good programs—like Headstart and re-training programs—the bill we are now considering contains provisions which would virtually nullify the more valuable provisions of the Rural Development measure.

We will continue working on this bill next week, after which the Congress will have a two-week recess, reconvening on July 17.

A lot can happen during those two weeks either in the Democratic convention in Miami or in the foolish face-saving war which we are waging in Vietnam.

[Putney, Vermont]

Week ending July 1, 1972

SATURDAY NIGHT, and L.P.A. and I are back on the mountain in Putney. She drove 450 miles from Washington—traffic heavy most of the way with many stalled cars and several accidents en route.

It looks like a poor year for field crops. Even so, New England is not so drowned out by the floods as Washington and vicinity. The garden seeds I had planted on May 28 came up well except for summer squash. Radishes are all ready to eat and potatoes planted only five weeks ago are over a foot high; blueberries look fine, and strawberries are excellent. The small producer with an outside job is doing well, but large producers seem to be having much trouble with rot due to the rains.

It was high time to get out of Washington. The air was sultry with what we used to call cheap politics—actually dishonest politics.

Senator Muskie came back to the Senate apparently a sadder and a wiser man, and seems ready to settle down to being a Senator once more.

Senator Humphrey also came back, apparently reconciled to probable defeat at the Democratic convention to be held in Miami starting July 8. Then the Democratic Credentials Committee decided that Senator McGovern was not entitled to all of California's 271 delegates to the convention, even though it was, in effect, California's law, and took 151 delegates away from him, giving the larger part of those left to Humphrey. This restored Hubert's hopes and off he went again, irrepressible as ever.

Scoop Jackson apparently hasn't given up hope, for he still tramps around the Capitol escorted by the four bodyguards which are furnished to Presidential candidates at taxpayers' expense.

What I thought was most interesting, however, was the expression on Teddy Kennedy's face right after the news of McGovern's setback with California delegates. Teddy was actually drooling, and not in sorrow.

At this time the Democrats do not seem to be split, they look fragmented. However, they may recover by Election Day, November 7.

¶ MIKE MANSFIELD came back to the Senate on Thursday after about a week in the Naval Hospital at Bethesda suffering from an infection. Mike has done a lot of worrying this year over the Congress, the Vietnam war, and other things. Fortunately he plans to get out of Washington and away from it all for a couple weeks, avoiding the Democratic convention in Miami. This should help him.

¶ ON TUESDAY, about a dozen of us from both parties were invited to the White House for breakfast to hear Henry Kissinger's report on the war. At 5:30 P.M. the same day, he came up to Senator Fulbright's hideaway office to make a report on the war and his trip to China to members of the Foreign Relations committee. Twelve of the sixteen members of the committee were present, and Dr. Kissinger made a good impression on them, including Senators Church, Symington and Fulbright, all of whom are prone to criticize the Nixon Administration, with or without cause. Kissinger was neither optimistic nor pessimistic. He hoped Congress would not get too rash, and acted as if he felt progress toward our disinvolvement might be made at an early date.

Meanwhile the war drags on, but our forces are being withdrawn while our casualties are less than those incurred by combatants in Northern Ireland or the Middle East. Of late the total number of Americans killed in Indochina in a year is probably less than the number killed by accident in the United States on a holiday weekend.

¶ THE OEO BILL, parts of which I strongly objected to last week, was pending on Monday. As written, this bill would have given the OEO exceptional powers over other agencies of government that carry on related programs, such as loans for rural housing, rural co-operatives, and small business. It would have practically emasculated the Rural Development bill, which had been agreed to in Conference and is now awaiting action by the House.

I was told that the provisions relating to Rural Development in the OEO bill were proposed in committee by Senator Javits who, although urban-oriented, still has to consider upstate New York. Early in the week Senator Javits agreed to an amendment to the bill which provides that the OEO can only supplement the programs for rural development conducted by the USDA [U.S. Department of Agriculture], rather than have priority over them. Senator Nelson, floor manager for the bill, readily agreed, so I offered the amendment, which was accepted. The bill, therefore, was much more acceptable to me and passed the Senate by a substantial majority.

It is not acceptable to several lawyer members of the Senate, and may not be to the President, since as of tonight, Saturday evening, he has not signed it. If he decides to veto it I am inclined to support him, since I am rather unsure as to its effect.

It was on Friday, the 23rd, that I first tried to alert the Senate to the bad features of the bill, and on Monday, the 26th, we were advised of seven new OEO grants to Vermont. It appears that the OEO people may have read the *Congressional Record.*

¶ THE OTHER BILL which brought on much debate and controversy was one to extend the national debt limit to $450 billion. Unless this limit was extended before July 1, the debt ceiling would revert to the old limit of $400 billion. The government has already incurred debt of about $425 billion, so failure to extend and increase the limit would result in a virtual stoppage of government operation, including the pay to federal employees and officials. By extending the debt ceiling for short periods of time, the Democratic-controlled Congress can hold a club over the head of the Republican-controlled executive branch.

And believe me, the Democrats use this club to the limit. The Senate Committee on Finance, which handles Social Security, Medicare and pension funds, had delayed reporting *House Resolution 1,* passed by the House months ago and carrying a 5 percent increase in Social Security payments. This Resolution, although agreed to by the committee, has not yet been put on the Senate calendar. And since the Debt Ceiling bill was a "must" with only hours remaining, the Democrats used the opportunity to ignore *H.R. 1* and rushed through an amendment to the debt bill.

Senator Frank Church proposed an amendment increasing the Social Security benefits by 20 percent. Although I felt a 20-percent increase was justified in view of increased salaries and increased subsidies to business and most everything else, I feared that adoption of the Church amendment would further delay any action on *H.R. 1* and its Medicare amendments, which are really needed now. Since it seemed to be a now-or-never situation, however, I voted for the Church amendment to the Debt Ceiling bill.

The whole procedure was shot full of politics. The Church amendment provides for substantial benefits (20 percent) to be paid in October—when it is expected the Democrats will try to capitalize on these increased benefits just before the election, whereas the increased payroll deductions necessary to meet the cost will not become effective until after the election.

To add insult to injury, the Democrats also insisted on continuing the increased debt ceiling only till October, thereby getting a chance to play more politics before the November election. There were some who felt that President Nixon might veto the bill and recall Congress from the short recess of two weeks. Nevertheless this morning, July 1, the word went out that the bill was signed. I only hope that this political maneuvering does not further delay action on *H.R. 1*.

The garden I planted five weeks ago looks pretty clean by comparison.

[Putney, Vermont]

Week ending July 8, 1972

WE HAVE BEEN in Vermont a week now, and half of our so-called vacation is gone. Am writing this at six o'clock Sunday morning, July 9th. Like Harry Truman, I have never been able to break myself of waking up about 5:30 A.M. Being raised on a farm is one way to get this lifetime habit.

In the field below, which we cleared from the woods and sowed to rye and grass last year, a big woodchuck is wandering around helping himself to young clover and any other plants which may tickle his palate. L.P.A. and I had gone to Montpelier last Tuesday, and when we arrived back in Putney on Thursday we found that Mr. Chuck and his wife had been in our garden and eaten the leaves off our pumpkins, squashes and beans. Fortunately they hadn't stripped them completely, and I closed the gap in the wire fence, so they may not get in again. Since animals, including woodchucks, are very much like people, they will undoubtedly try to find a way. And since people, including myself, are very much like animals, I tried to bomb them to death on Friday.

The 'chucks, however, were smarter than some people and had dug their holes into the wall of an old farmhouse terrace, and although I sealed both ends of the hole after lighting and throwing a chemical bomb down one of them, there were many airholes through the wall allowing Mrs. Chuck to dig out, so that next day they were ready for more raids—just as an international corporation after perhaps a slight initial setback invades a developing nation and helps itself to the resources.

The tourist and vacation season is on in full swing in Vermont, and because of this the state's unemployment rate has dropped below 5 percent. Nowadays unemployment figures often mean that if you can't get the job you prefer and are best trained for, you don't have to take just any job, but can instead receive a check from the state agency for a livable amount. The money for cashing the check comes from a special tax fund paid by both working people and employers. Like most every other law the Social Security Act is subject to abuses, but on the whole it helps a lot of people to maintain their self-respect.

Vermont was the first state to co-operate with all phases of the Social Security Act in 1935. The Vermont legislature approved the Act in March of that year, but since Vermont had both a Republican Governor and legislature, the Democrats in control of the executive branch in Washington did not record our action until after Iowa, then controlled by Democrats, gave its full approval in September. President Franklin Roosevelt's administration played politics to the limit, and Congress was often called upon to make legislation effective retroactively to cover up their sins and sometimes illegal operations.

¶ SINCE 1972 is an election year we hear political talk everywhere in Vermont, both from natives and vacationers. The Democratic national convention is about to get underway in Miami Beach, and the radio and television are giving its preparations full coverage. Reaction so far ranges from enthusiasm on the part of a few to complete disgust on the part of the many. The enthusiasm comes from what people insistent on labels call the intellectual group (sometimes I think the word "intellectual" is sadly misused), while disgust is freely expressed by business people, farm people, rich people living on incomes, and professional people other than educators. The intellectuals seem to have deserted Senator Humphrey and think George McGovern would be a wonderful President and might even represent the Second Coming. The "conservatives" look with horror on the possibility of his nomination.

At this time it does not look as if any Democrat could defeat President Nixon. He seems to have all the breaks up to now: withdrawal of over 90 percent of our military force from Vietnam; reduction in casualties among the 48,000 left there; the trip to China to start better relations with the People's Republic; the trip to Moscow, where treaties and understandings were reached; higher levels of living among most classes of people, even at taxpayers' expense; improved farm prices. All these things have enhanced his prospects for a second term.

Tonight the White House announced a huge sale of U.S. grain to Russia, the biggest in world history. It was not by coincidence that this enormous sale was announced on the eve of the Democrats' national convention. It will just make things more difficult for them than they are making for themselves. Although terms for repayment for the grain, such as interest rates and credit terms, were not announced, the public at large, especially farmers, won't care too much about the terms. The best the Democrats at Miami can do is to charge the President with trying to raise consumer costs, and right now the consumer won't pay much attention.

During the week, John Mitchell for family reasons resigned as manager for Nixon's 1972 campaign and Clark MacGregor was appointed in his place. Although Mitchell was in my opinion the most efficient Attorney General we have had for a long, long time, MacGregor will be a better campaign manager because he is better qualified geographically, socially, and philosophically.

Republicans still cannot take victory in November for granted. Incidents can sometimes change more votes than issues. The White House must not let its aides accuse Democrat candidates of all kinds of crimes and sins ranging from rape to treason. The public resents such tactics. Clark MacGregor knows this.

¶ INTERNATIONALLY the most encouraging news was from Asia. Prime Minister Indira Gandhi of India and President Bhutto of Pakistan were holding talks which may lead to a more peaceful continent, while the top officials of North and South Korea announced their plans for bringing their two countries into peaceful agreement. Although the Korean War was a United Nations effort, it was the United States that bore the brunt of it and took the losses and paid the costs. For the twenty years since a U.N. truce has endured in that area, the United States has maintained a military force of from 40,000 to 55,000 men. South Korea, in the meantime, has contributed some 40,000 troops to the South Vietnamese war, for which the U.S. has largely paid the costs.

The world is sick and tired of war and now looks to the United States, Russia, and the People's Republic of China to find a way to other means of settling international quarrels. So far France does not seem to have co-operated, apparently seeking equality or supremacy in the nuclear field before joining in this effort.

The United Nations, which the world at one time had great hopes for as a deterrent to war, has generally failed. Only when two parties to a dispute agree to call in the U.N. can it be effective. It is still primarily a place to talk, although some auxiliary agencies have done much good.

¶ IN THE WEEK before us I expect the Democratic convention will monopolize the news media. I expect a rough, possibly disgraceful, session at Miami Beach with political chicanery at its worst. There will be much talk of reforms for party rules and national legislation.

While reforms are badly needed in the tax laws and other fields, talk of reforms is mostly hogwash on occasions like this. It is largely an attempt to change leadership and party controls. Blackmail and bribery cannot be ruled out, and delegates will probably be put on the commodity market for sale to the highest bidder. The Democrats will be lucky if there is not bloodshed in Miami, but I certainly hope the occasion will be more peaceful than that.

At times like these I get very discouraged with our democratic form of government, but then I think, What would be better? And my mind fails to come up with the answer.

Mrs. Woodchuck has now gone back into her hole in the ground and the sun is shining much brighter. Things could be worse.

[Putney, Vermont]

Week ending July 15, 1972

WOODCHUCKS still claim ownership of our home on the mountain, but I have closed holes in the fence around the garden, and pumpkin vines are now growing a foot a day unmolested. On Monday a whopping big porcupine sailed across the field with his big tail in the air like the stern of an 18th Century galleon. Birds galore, with the rat-tat-tat of a woodpecker waking me at five in the morning and the wood thrush trying to put us to sleep with his delightful music just at dark.

¶ THE SOUND OF MUSIC provided by Nature, however, had its harsh, discordant interruptions during the week. The Democratic national convention was on in Miami and except for the opening address by Chairman Larry O'Brien, which was excellent and could be given equally well before the Republican convention, the rest of the week was rather nerve-racking and upsetting.

George McGovern was nominated for President and Tom Eagleton for Vice President. The McGovern campaign had been exceptionally well organized, and had the situation well under control for the entire session. The old-line Democrat leaders were upset, beaten, and generally thrown out of the picture by the new element, which had not been taken seriously by the regulars until a short time before the convention, when it was too late.

It is probably a good idea and good for the country to upset the old guard from time to time. Times do change; each generation wants something different, and each generation proposes some things that are better and some that are worse.

Senator McGovern has shifted positions so much that he has alienated a large segment of the Democratic party voters, so much so that I do not see how he can possibly win in November. However, L.P.A. disagrees with me, thinks that he has a real chance for victory, and that, through perfecting his organization, he may be the next President of the United States.

He promised the convention that within ninety days after he becomes President all the American prisoners of war and all American military people will be out of Indochina. That is a very rash promise, and personally I don't want our participation in the Indochina war to continue until George McGovern is installed as President.

At home in Vermont I find most of the old-time Democrats, particularly the Catholics, either sick to their stomachs or tearing their hair over the outcome of the Miami convention.

¶ SATURDAY AFTERNOON is hot, but we have to leave—our parole is over. Two yearling deer have paid their respects to us by standing beside the road to watch us go by.

I hope the dogs don't get them.

[United States Senate]

Week ending July 22, 1972

A HOT, sticky, muggy week back in Washington, the temperature in the nineties and air pollution so thick one could hardly see through it for the whole week, the kind of week that warps one's judgment and intensifies one's emotions.

The Democratic convention is over, and many members of that party, both in Washington and at home, seem to be disgusted, disgruntled and belligerent. The Catholic Democrats seem to be very unhappy over the extreme liberality of the party towards abortion and other rather far-out ideas, while many of my Jewish friends resent the efforts to secure their continuing loyalty through the making of promises which they have heard repeatedly over the years. President Nixon has translated our friendship for Israel into practical action rather than continuous promising, until today Israel is probably in a more secure position than that little country has been since its inception.

The news during the week that Egypt has asked all Russian advisors and military personnel to leave the country and go home is, in my opinion, a concrete result of the efforts which have been made by our government over the past four years to restore the world—including the Middle East—to a more peaceable condition. While I am satisfied that Russia has in recent years been anxious to avoid situations which might lead to a broad-scale world war, she nevertheless has invited hostilities between many small nations and has furnished them with the means of committing acts of war against each other. This was exemplified by the April invasion of South Vietnam by the communist forces of North Vietnam, abetted by what allies they may have in South Vietnam. It also was exemplified to some extent three or four years ago when the forces of Syria undertook to overwhelm the small country of Jordan.

Since the visit of President Nixon to Moscow in May, however, there seems to be a definite change in the Russian attitude. The failure of the North Vietnamese to overthrow South Vietnam quickly has been an important factor in the change of the Russian tactics. And it looks now as if the Middle East will likely be spared the fear of bloody hostilities for a considerable time to come.

The situation in Vietnam is somewhat different, with the military effort of North Vietnam being far less effective than what its sponsors anticipated, although I don't foresee the end of fighting, particularly guerrilla raids, in that area for a long time to come. Hanoi is still insistent on conditions which would require the United States to overthrow the present government of Saigon and disarm the people of South Vietnam. These are most unusual conditions and are not likely to be acceptable to our own government in Washington, regardless of the outcome of our November election.

On Friday, July 21, a UPI dispatch from France stated that North Vietnam would not permit the United States military forces to leave South Vietnam until they have overthrown the South Vietnamese government and arranged for the type of government acceptable to the communist regime in Hanoi. While this is only a news report, I strongly suspect it to be true, but I have never read anywhere in history where one nation engaged in warfare refuses to let their antagonists leave the war area.

While there are many varying opinions as to what has prompted the more amicable position on the part of the U.S.S.R., I personally believe it is the intense desire of the Soviets to get busy developing their own resources and building up more satisfying levels of living for their own people. This means that Russia must establish better trade relations with other countries, and the United States is the one country which is best able to co-operate with Moscow in this respect. Russia needs grain, Russia needs machinery, Russia needs all kinds of production equipment, and we are in a position to supply these. And at the same time Russia knows that we are one large country that has no designs on Soviet resources.

¶ HENRY KISSINGER returned from France on Thursday, and on Friday a few of us were invited to the White House to get his report. I can't say that we learned much new from him, but the purpose of his meeting was apparently to encourage a maximum degree of co-operation between the legislative and executive branches of government. I think there is a better feeling towards more co-operative efforts between these two branches of government than there was a few months, or even a few weeks, ago.

¶ I DON'T BELIEVE that much headway can be made in defeating Richard Nixon for re-election, provided that his party political advocates keep their heads and don't start condemning Democratic candidates in a ridiculous and unfair manner.

There are many sound arguments in favor of re-electing the President, but stupidity, arrogance, and unfairness on the part of his advocates could prove to be very costly.

¶ THE SENATE COMMITTEE on Agriculture and Forestry held hearings on a bill I introduced to set aside wild areas in the East where conditions very closely conform to those which existed when the first white man came to America. We have a law now relative to the preservation of wilderness areas, but this law applies only to the areas of public lands which lie west of the 100th Meridian. There is no provision for setting aside areas of wild land throughout the East, where three-fourths of our population resides.

The bill, which I introduced for Senator Talmadge and myself, came under attack by various groups. The opposition of some was inspired by economic reasons, while others sought to put the East under the provisions of the Wilderness Act and the Interior Department.

I believe the Forest Service has done an excellent job since its collision with the Interior department in 1908. I have said repeatedly that since that time the Forest Service has had a reputation to live up to while the Interior department has had a reputation to live down. Of course the Interior department is not that bad now. Nevertheless, I feel that the Department of Agriculture and the Forest Service are more competent to deal with the situation in our Eastern forests, which are mainly privately owned, than is the Interior department, which is primarily oriented to the Far West where much of the land has always been under public ownership.

The testimony of some of the witnesses at the hearing on the Eastern Wild Areas bill bordered on the ridiculous. As an example, a representative of the Sierra Club advocated that in a wildlife area in the East there should be no facilities whatsoever. Upon being asked what should be done in the event of a forest fire in such an area his reply was "Let it burn." Apparently some of the witnesses had been grossly misinformed, since they seemed to think that to set aside a wild area in the East was for the purpose of establishing recreation areas, whereas just the opposite is the purpose. However, the sponsors of this bill don't go so far as to say that the area should not be made readily available to people who desire to see wildlife conditions as they existed hundreds of years ago. I tried to impress on those present that time is of the essence, and if people in favor of true conservation and preservation of area wildlife conditions let rivalry and jealousy control their actions then the purpose which they all claim to endorse will not prevail.

Anyway, the bill is subject to revision—and probably will have to be revised, since no bill of this importance is ever perfect to begin with.

Week ending July 29, 1972

DURING THE WEEK I received a letter from a budding author who expected to write a book all about funny things that happened in Washington and in the Congress. The letter came at the wrong time for me to comply with his request to contribute something humorous, because this has not been a funny week. It has been almost anything else.

The big news was the report that Senator Eagleton, now candidate for Vice President on the Democratic ticket, has had psychiatric treatments for depression three times during the past decade. In the minds of a lot of topflight Democrats and others, this thoroughly disqualifies him from remaining on the ticket.

My sympathy lies with Tom Eagleton. While he had the foresight to receive treatment for his nervous disorders, the fact is that a lot of his critics in my opinion were equally afflicted, but didn't have sense enough to do anything about it. I don't suppose there is one member of the United States Senate who has not sometime during his life suffered from nervous depression, or nervous exhaustion, as it is commonly called. Senator Margaret Smith tells me that she doesn't recall any such instance in her life, but the fact remains that she is a most unusual person, so I have to accept her statement at face value.

But when I recall how happy Tom Eagleton looked on returning to Washington after the Miami convention I feel sorry for him now. His trouble was made-to-order for the news media, and I suspect that he now may have more sympathy for Vice President Agnew, who over two years ago expressed his opinion of the news media in no uncertain terms. I can stand up for the news-gathering people in general, for most of them are sincere and honest and report events as they see them. But, as in every other profession, there are always a few who do not qualify under the high standards set for them by the public involved in other professions and occupations.

I hope that the amateurish manner in which McGovern's Presidential campaign has been carried on so far does not result in ruining the future for the young Senator from Missouri, who does not deserve the treatment he is getting.

¶ LEGISLATIVELY, the Military Procurement bill is still dragging on before the Senate, with amendments relating to our efforts to get out of the Vietnamese war still the center of attention. Here again uncontrollable political ambitions are causing inestimable damage to our reputation throughout the world. Unfortunately we have members in the Senate who would like to see the United States turn tail and run out of South Vietnam, regardless of what the consequences might be.

At least that is the attitude they appear to have, and they support amendments which would appear to write that provision into the law. However, if one analyzes their proposals carefully, one will find that they are practically all unworkable either from a legislative or Constitutional viewpoint. They do, however, impress many people back home, and they are calculated to convince these people that President Nixon, and maybe President Johnson too, are largely responsible for the predicament we find ourselves in in Southeast Asia.

I don't think that any of those who now seek to put the responsibility for our trouble on President Nixon really want to hurt their country, they simply want to take over the reins. President Nixon, in the meantime, is doing very well in the field of international concern. Both China and Russia are far less hostile to us than they were when he took over the White House, even though their attitudes toward each other seem to have gone from bad to worse during the same period of time.

¶ THE SENATE suffered a severe loss during the week in the death of Senator Allen Ellender of Louisiana. He had been a member of the Senate for nearly thirty-six years, being chairman of the Agriculture committee for about half that time. At the time of his death he was Chairman of the Appropriations committee. In the latter position he had tried his best, though usually futilely, to hold government expenditures within reason. We need people like that these days in Congress, where it sometimes appears that a continuing auction is going on, with candidates and their parties bidding against each other for voters' approval by constantly urging higher appropriations for federal programs, regardless of the ultimate effect on the financial status of the nation.

However, the public doesn't seem to be worried too much about the size of the federal deficit, and keeps on writing to the members of Congress demanding larger expenditures and lower taxes. Still, as President Roosevelt used to say, "The size of the national debt should not worry us too much as long as we owe it to ourselves." Maybe he was right. But to one who has been raised in a "pay-as-you-spend" state like Vermont, this policy is a bit hard to swallow.

¶ WE ARE NOT very near the end of this session, and will be back after the Republican convention to continue with more of the same. As of today, thirty pieces of important legislation are still tied up in conference committees.

As I said in the beginning, this week has not been funny.

Week ending August 5, 1972

WHAT A WEEK this has been!

On Monday, Tom Eagleton stepped down as the Democratic candidate for Vice President. Most of the Senate, like myself, sympathize with him, although it is generally agreed that he should have made his health problem known before receiving the nomination. For the rest of the week George McGovern was offering second spot on the ticket to all his previous opponents for first place, and some others besides; very wisely, it would appear, all rejected his offer. Then today, Saturday, McGovern announced his selection of Sargent Shriver to be his running-mate. This is not as bad a selection as some would make it out to be, since Sarge did pretty good work as Director of the Peace Corps, and got by without much trouble as Ambassador to France. However, McGovern's hesitation and difficulty in finding anyone to accept the second spot on the ticket did not help Democratic prospects for November in the least.

¶ FOR THE FIRST PART of the week the Senate worked on the Military Procurement Authorization bill, with the principal activity directed toward what are called "end-the-war amendments."

The main subject was the Cranston amendment, to which the Administration was very much opposed. This amendment not only called for a cut-off of all funds for use in Vietnam after October 1, 1972, but provided for only a local cease-fire agreement instead of a cease-fire agreement extending over all Indochina, as would be necessary if any arrangement is to be effective. And it did call for return of all American prisoners of war held by the enemy and an accounting of Americans missing in action.

In place of the Cranston amendment Senator Brooke offered a substitute which would have cut off all funds after four months, during which time all American prisoners were to be returned and missing Americans accounted for. The weakness of the Brooke amendment was that, while we were withdrawing our forces from Vietnam, North Vietnam could withhold all our prisoners until the last day of the four-month period, and even if the prisoners were released on the last day the North could start the war up all over again almost immediately. With the withdrawal of all funds the United States would be helpless to prevent the slaughter which would ensue.

At the suggestion of executive branch representatives, I offered an amendment which I felt was far more practical than the proposals of either Senator Cranston or Senator Brooke. The amendment I offered was almost like the one offered by Senator Allen of Alabama last week, which was defeated by a 50-to-45 vote of the Senate. It differed, however, in that while Senator Allen's amendment was a "sense-of-the-Congress" proposal, the one I offered called for direct action. It provided for an internationalized cease-fire over all Indochina and the withdrawal of all our forces within four months from the time an agreement could be reached. I offered it as a perfecting amendment. It did not provide a complete cut-off of funds, for the reason that such provision would encourage North Vietnam and its allies to renew the war promptly after we had completed our withdrawal. The amendment I offered was co-sponsored by Senator Allen and eight other Senators.

81

The Nixon Administration, after having looked with disfavor on all end-the-war proposals, finally approved the one I offered, and on Wednesday about one o'clock President Nixon called me to say that he very strongly supported my amendment and felt that it would help bring the end of our involvement in Indochina nearer. He also had asked me to talk with Henry Kissinger, who confidentially discussed his latest private talk with Le Duc Tho in Paris.

I made known the President's position to the Senate, and inasmuch as my amendment was offered as a perfecting amendment to the Cranston amendment, it came up for the first vote on Wednesday afternoon. The amendment which I offered carried by a 50-to-47 vote of the Senate, but when the vote on Senator Brooke's amendment came next, seven of my colleagues who had voted for my amendment also voted for Brooke's, while only three of those who had voted against my amendment also opposed the Brooke amendment. Therefore my amendment was shelved only a few minutes after it had been approved, and the Brooke amendment superseded the Cranston amendment. Things got pretty complicated. Roll call after roll call was held until what appeared to be the final decision of the Senate was to support the Brooke proposal, to which the Administration was strongly opposed.

This was not the final action, however, for Senator Miller proposed one last amendment which stated that our troops would not all be withdrawn until all missing Americans had been accounted for. His amendment was so precise that it created consternation, particularly among the McGovern-Eagleton cortège of Democrats. Of course it would be impossible to account for every one of the more than twelve hundred missing Americans. The amendment offered by Jack Miller was a political ploy intended to put the Democrats on the spot. It worked: Senators McGovern, Eagleton, Kennedy and all the other ambitious Democrats had to vote for it, thereby virtually nullifying the Brooke amendment which they had supported so enthusiastically only a short time before. Only Senator Cooper and myself voted against the Miller amendment, rejecting its political implications just as we had on previous occasions objected to the political ploys of the Democrats of the Senate.

The bill now goes to Conference with the House, and no one knows what will happen there, but I don't worry about it, for no end-the-war provision approved by Congress can work without an agreement with the enemy—and with an agreement we don't need an amendment anyway.

¶ ON THURSDAY the so-called SALT accord [Strategic Arms Limitation Treaty] between the United States and Russia, which was signed by President Nixon and Mr. Brezhnev on May 26, was brought up for action by the Senate. Being a treaty, it required a two-thirds vote for approval, but this did not prove to be difficult since the vote in the Senate was 88 to 2, with only Senators Buckley and Allen opposing it.

However, we still had what was called the SALT *Agreement,* which provided for an interim limitation on nuclear arms by the two countries.

I think the agreement signed by President Nixon and Brezhnev was pretty fair. In some respects one might say Russia was given an advantage and in others that the United States was favored. This interim arms limitation agreement, unlike a treaty, has only to be approved by a majority vote of both Houses of Congress. I had not anticipated material opposition to it until Thursday afternoon, when I learned that Senator Jackson and several of his colleagues planned to offer an amendment which would drastically change the stance of the United States by giving interpretations to the agreement which I, for one, did not believe were intended. Furthermore, the Jackson amendment implied that the Russians could not be depended upon to keep their side of the agreement. It implied that they might be expected to violate it, and at the first sign of a violation the United States would be justified in withdrawing from it completely, even though the agreement itself was to run for five years.

Had this amendment been approved, I was quite sure that the agreement itself would be defeated by the Senate. Senator Jackson had indicated to the press that the Administration, particularly the White House, was firmly behind his proposal. I could not quite believe this, and I called the State department, advising David Abshire [Assistant Secretary of State for Congressional Affairs] that the Jackson amendment jeopardized the entire agreement. This was late Thursday afternoon. On Friday morning Chairman Fulbright called the Senate Foreign Relations committee into executive session to consider what should be done under the circumstances.

Senators Scott and McGee had both been listed as sponsors of the amendment and both advised the committee that they had become supporters under misapprehension of its meaning. The committee decided that the only way to straighten the matter out would be for the President to make a firm, straightforward statement as to whether he backed the Jackson amendment as was reported, or not.

I was delegated to advise the Administration of the position taken unanimously by the Foreign Relations committee. I also advised Tom Korologos, representing the White House, and Dave Abshire of the State department. Later in the afternoon I met with Mr. Abshire and Marshall Wright, his assistant, who asked if I had any suggestion for changing the wording of the Jackson amendment so that it would be acceptable to the committee and to the Senate. I told them quite frankly that this was their problem now: I had simply reported the facts and it was up to the White House to determine what, if any, revision of the language of the amendment would straighten things out. As the situation stands now, on Saturday night, the Jackson amendment will have to be radically revised before it will be acceptable to the Senate. If accepted in its present form it would probably mean sure death to the agreement itself.

I expect that by early next week we will have some decision from the White House. I hope it will be such as to meet with the approval of the Senate. If by any chance the Jackson amendment, as it now stands, were to be accepted by the Senate or the agreement itself disapproved, then I see little hope for future conferences looking to the further extension of peaceable understandings between Russia and the United States. I am optimistic, however, that the President will see the necessity of modifying the Jackson amendment to more conciliatory provisions.

¶ DURING THE WEEK we had our share of social activities. The first was a reception-dinner for L.P.A. and myself given by Ted Jaffe [former head of the Foreign Claims Settlement Commission of the United States] and Florence Lowe [assistant to Nancy Hanks of National Endowment of the Arts in Washington], winding up with a showing of *The Candidate,* a political picture seemingly directed towards helping the Democrats but actually open to an opposite interpretation. Then on Friday we went to a small dinner party at the home of Jack and Mary Margaret Valenti. Jack Valenti was President Lyndon B. Johnson's righthand man for several years, and now represents the motion picture industry in Washington. Only five other members of the Senate—Senators Mansfield, Hatfield, Church, Bentsen, and Saxbe —and a few others were present. I didn't have to be rocked to sleep when I got home that night.

Week ending August 12, 1972

A WEEK in which politics and legislation have become more mixed and smellier than ever.

The Democrats finally nominated Sarge Shriver to second place on their ticket. Whether this was good or bad remains to be seen, but high-level Democrats of the past seem to be leaving the ticket in droves. John Connally's taking charge of the "Democrats for Nixon" drive was not too surprising, but when Leonard Marks, past Director of USIA and close friend of Lyndon Johnson, became treasurer of the organization, eyebrows went up by the millions. And now that Tom Watson of IBM, who previously has been one of the largest contributors to the Democratic party, has joined up along with a score of other large contributing businessmen, it doesn't look too good for the Democrats' campaign fund. However, there seems to be money enough for almost any purpose these days, so I guess they will get by all right even if they have to run up big bills as in the past.

At the present time it looks as if the Republicans could coast to victory in the November 7th election provided the leadership can hold their overly ambitious—and, in my book, irresponsible—assistants in check. The raid on the Democratic headquarters at the Watergate a few weeks ago smells to high heaven, and the political world apparently believes, as of today, that this despicable and fruitless act was planned within the headquarters of the Committee to Re-elect the President. While complete proof has not been shown, there is a general feeling that it will be shown before election time, and will be costly in terms of votes for Republican candidates.

I don't believe that this incident alone could be materially effective, but in times like these it frequently happens that an incident can change more votes than a bona-fide issue. On the other hand, issues presented by Democratic Candidate McGovern have, in many instances, been so irresponsible as to alienate a lot of rank-and-file members.

On Tuesday, Clark MacGregor, director of the Committee to Re-elect the President, spoke to the Senate Republicans' luncheon meeting. He was just chock full of statistics and tossed them all over the place attempting to show how efficient the Republican Administration is. I wish MacGregor would understand that during a hot election campaign very few voters are impressed by statistics, charts, and graphs. The public is not too much concerned with the size of the national debt or with saving a million dollars here or there: the public wants to know "What's in it for me?"

The Democrats, now that Sarge Shriver, assisted by his wife, Eunice Kennedy Shriver, is running in second place, will undoubtedly resort to glamour as an appealing argument for victory for their team. And there are millions of voters who are far more impressed by glamour than by graphs.

With further regrets I have noticed this week that the Administration seems to be making pretty free use of the taxpayers' money to enhance its prospects of victory in November, although the Democrats always do the same when they occupy the White House.

This came right home to me when I found that the Experiment in International Living, located near me in Vermont, which has probably trained more Peace Corps members and trained them better than any other institution, was being written off as a Peace Corps contracting party. Apparently, being more experienced they were able to underbid nearly all others engaged in this kind of work, but Lo and behold, I find out now that one contract for a VISTA [Volunteers In Service to America, set up to provide trained community-improvement workers for poor areas within the U.S.] training program on which the Experiment bid $417,000 had been given to a comparatively new consulting agency located in Washington whose bid was $1,006,000— 141 percent over the amount of the Experiment's bid. Another contract for Peace Corps trainees on which the Experiment bid $964,000 had been given to an institution in the Virgin Islands for $1,762,000— an increase of 83 percent over the low bid. A third contract for training Peace Corps members for a Latin American country had been given to a Catholic college for only 35 percent over the Experiment's bid.

I don't mind distributing these contracts among worthy institutions that are capable of doing the work, but apparently the VISTA contract was an appeal for the black vote, since the contracting company was organized by blacks; the Virgin Islands' contract was an appeal for the French-speaking vote, although why the Virgin Islands was considered a good place to train people for French-speaking areas I just can't understand. I think it was a straight appeal for more minority votes. The South American Peace Corps contract is, doubtless, expected to influence a few more Catholic votes, which traditionally would go for the Democratic ticket.

I favor giving assistance and opportunity to minority groups, but I don't favor using public funds for political purposes. I have asked an explanation from Joe Blatchford and am waiting, not too patiently, for his response. He is the Director of the Peace Corps. Last week while he was out of town, his assistants concocted several pages of hogwash trying to justify their action. Unless Mr. Blatchford comes up with a good explanation within the next three or four days, I will turn the matter over to the Senate Foreign Relations committee, which handles authorization of funds for the Peace Corps.

It's not only the Peace Corps and VISTA programs that I feel are being used for political purposes now. A small company in Bennington, Vermont, has been trying desperately to get a contract for tabulating cards, and is apparently well qualified to fill such a contract, but was left completely out in the cold while a large contract of which it could have had a share was given to a Minneapolis concern. I may be hypercritical, but I think Minnesota is likely to play a key part in the coming election, and besides it is the home state of Clark MacGregor. I may be too cynical, but I don't like what is going on in some parts of the executive branch of our government.

This is not to say that the legislative branch and even the judicial branch of government do not engage in political maneuvering. I just don't like it, that's all.

¶ LEGISLATIVELY, among other things, the Senate considered the so-called Gun bill. This bill was directed at prohibiting the sale of short-barreled pistols and revolvers which are used extensively for criminal purposes. A couple of years ago when most of this type of cheap firearms was imported from foreign countries and sold for a few dollars, Congress enacted legislation prohibiting such imports, but gun dealers then resorted to importing the parts and assembling them in the United States, thus evading the intent of the law.

The bill considered by the Senate this week applied only to this type gun, which has become known as the "Saturday-night special." It did not apply in any way to shotguns, rifles, conventional pistols, and revolvers commonly used by hunters and for target practice by gun clubs. Nevertheless the word was passed to all gun clubs and sportsmen's clubs to oppose the legislation on the grounds that it would constitute a foot in the door and lead to more drastic legislation later on. I strongly suspect that many genuine hunters and sportsmen were taken in by this argument by the leadership of that element of society which has little respect for law. The bill passed the Senate by a one-sided majority and may or may not be acted upon by the House this year. The Senate overwhelmingly rejected proposals for registration of all firearms and other more drastic measures. In fact the bill, as passed, relaxed some previous requirements of the law to which the legitimate sporting element objected.

The main concern of the Senate this week, however, has been with the request of the President for Congress to approve the so-called SALT Agreement, or Interim Arms Limitation Agreement, which he signed with Brezhnev of the U.S.S.R. on May 26 as a way to a slowdown of preparations by both countries for a possible atomic war.

On Monday, the 7th, a revised version of Senator Jackson's amendment to the agreement was presented. It had been prepared in co-operation with the White House and was expected to pave the way for an early approval of the agreement signed by President Nixon and the Russians. Just as the road to approval appeared to be clear, however, statements by Senators Jackson and Allott knocked the prospects for a loop. The White House then came up with another statement to the effect that while the Jackson amendment was approved, the interpretation put upon it by its sponsors was not approved. The Senate then became involved in a mess deeper and smellier than ever. It appeared that Senator Jackson and his co-sponsors, most of whom seemed to favor unlimited superiority in arms by the United States, had decided that instead of attempting to defeat the SALT Agreement were seeking to nullify it by giving their own interpretations, which seemed to contradict its alleged purpose. If the White House and the President really want the agreement to be approved, and I am sure that the President does, they couldn't have taken a worse route to this end. Senator Jackson repeatedly refers to the fact that the White House approves his amendment while neglecting to say that it also disapproves his interpretation. These repeated allegations only serve to infuriate some members of this Senate who hope to approve the agreement submitted by the President.

In the House the Foreign Affairs committee has overwhelmingly recommended approval without any amendments at all. This is as it should be, and the House expects to vote on the matter next Wednesday, August 16. But in the Senate things have gone from bad to worse. The Senate Foreign Relations committee, by a vote of 11 to 0, with Senator Scott, the Republican floor leader, abstaining, recommended approval of the agreement without any amendments, and recommended against delaying consideration by the Senate; consequently, the resolution of approval was brought up for action on Friday. Although the Senate committee had voted to disapprove any amendments, Senators Mansfield, Cooper, Javits and myself did offer an amendment which would support the President's position as reported to us on June 15. This amendment was offered for the purpose of getting the first vote on the floor and getting it as soon as possible.

Since the President's statement included in our amendment could have been interpreted as being contrary to the Jackson proposal, Scoop Jackson was naturally very excited. After a few short speeches in favor of the agreement, he got the floor and held it nearly all the afternoon. Senator Mansfield tried in vain to get the Senate to agree to a vote on the pending proposals, starting at 6 P.M. on Monday, the 14th, but ran into a snag when Senators Fulbright and Symington refused to give unanimous consent. Since many believe that Senator Jackson's preference is to kill any agreement looking toward a relaxation of the arms race with Russia, it would appear that Senators Fulbright and Symington are playing directly into his hands by delaying a vote until after Labor Day, and possibly killing any prospects for approval of the agreement itself.

Unfortunately many industrial areas of the United States have been built up around arms manufacturing plants, and some communities have become almost wholly dependent on them. Over the years only very few states, if any, have been more dependent on government contracts than the State of Washington, and I have to assume that one of Senator Jackson's motives is to protect the economic position of his own state. Other areas benefit from government contracts too, but not all their elected members of Congress are as ardent in their endeavors as Scoop Jackson is. They believe that while a strong defense posture is necessary for the United States there is no need for an over-kill position in this field. And many of the huge industrial plants could be devoted to other purposes.

As of tonight, at the end of the week, the situation is discouraging. So far as I can see, the White House, through attempting to save Senator Jackson's face, has got itself into a real mess which unless corrected promptly is bound to have some effect on the November election and certainly on any SALT talks proposed for the future.

Week ending August 19, 1972

THE WEEK started off on Sunday with the Vice Presidential candidate, Sargent Shriver, endorsing a recommendation I made for ending the Vietnam war six years ago. He was very complimentary to me on his television program, but I am sure he didn't stir any great amount of enthusiasm in the hearts of the Republican national leadership. However, I'm not inclined to take exception to his endorsing my position of 1966, even though President Lyndon Johnson, at that time, didn't think so much of it.

The Senate met on Monday with the SALT interim arms agreement with Russia the pending business. This has developed into a three-way issue, with one group of Democrats headed by Scoop Jackson, another group headed by Senator Fulbright, and a third group trying to carry out White House desires. Although they deny it, it's apparent to me that Jackson's crowd does not want an effective interim arms control agreement.

Senator Fulbright, representing the Senate Foreign Relations committee, strongly supports the agreement and, strange to say, the White House has bungled the situation to such an extent that we may not approve any interim agreement at all, either when we return to session in September or later on. The President's big mistake was permitting word to go out of the White House that he supported the revised Jackson amendment (which, by the way, has not been formally offered yet) even though the White House does not approve the interpretation which Senator Jackson puts upon the agreement in his amendment. This is an incredible situation and is considered by many a direct slap at members of the Senate who are strongly in favor of supporting the interim agreement and its purpose as outlined by Mr. Kissinger for the President on June 15.

Some of us, including Senators Mansfield, Scott and Byrd, the Democratic whip, Fulbright, and a few others met in Senator Mansfield's office Monday afternoon, Tuesday morning, and again Tuesday afternoon. Most of us were hoping to get a time set for voting on the interim agreement and any proposed amendments to it, but we got nowhere. Jackson wouldn't agree to a fixed time unless it was one which favored his side of the controversy, and Fulbright wouldn't agree to a fixed time for anything but some preliminary votes.

If we could once get action in the Senate on the interim arms agreement itself and on any amendments, and go to Conference with the House, it is entirely possible, even probable, that all amendments would be thrown out in Conference.

At one of the meetings in Mike's [Mansfield's] office I asked Jackson if he would oppose a conference report which discarded his own proposal and he said he would. Later in the meeting, however, he softened a bit and said although he would oppose a conference report of that kind he would not undertake to delay action in the Senate indefinitely.

So that is where we stand now—the "Hatfields and the McCoys" have been remanded to the discard, and the Jacksons and Fulbrights have taken over. This situation is not good for the country.

¶ THERE WAS other work to be done during the week, and on Wednesday I went down to the Agriculture department to attend a meeting of the National Forest Reservation Commission. This commission is composed of two members of the Senate, two of the House, and three members of the President's Cabinet: Secretary of Defense, Secretary of Agriculture, and Secretary of the Interior. The Cabinet Secretaries invariably designate members of their staffs to attend such meetings. Usually two members of the House and Senate are in attendance, but at the meeting on Wednesday I was the only one there from the Hill, since Congressmen Saylor and Colmer were tied up in House activities, and Senator Stennis, the other member from the Senate, was not able to leave the Senate. The meeting lasted about an hour, and I joined with others in giving blind approval to a purchase agreement which had been made by the Forest Service with landowners throughout the country. I don't like this situation. It looks very much to me as if some of the big corporations and other landowners, as well as homeowners, are unloading land onto the Forest Service and making an excessive profit on the sale of the property, or else homeowners (usually wealthy summer residents) are getting the Forest Service to acquire land around them to make sure that no one else will be able to settle in their vicinity. I don't think the Forest Service officials are dishonest, but I do think that in many cases political pressure may be exerted; in others the general public may be demanding the acquisition of forest land or potential forest land at any price. The time is coming, and it may not be very far away, when this situation will have to be looked into carefully and thoroughly either by the executive branch or the legislative branch of government.

¶ IN THE SENATE the Child Nutrition Authorization bill came up for action on Wednesday. Here again we have a program where costs have been galloping upward almost without restraint. And the federal government has been slowly but surely assuming responsibility for the feeding and welfare of children even before they reach the cradle on up through school age. The need is there and the cause is worthy. Like other programs this one is subject to monkey-business in its administration, and members of the Congress are frequently co-operative in trying to get excessive benefits for their state or their district.

¶ WEDNESDAY was really an eventful day. The President vetoed the HEW [Department of Health, Education and Welfare] appropriations bill on the ground that it granted nearly $2 billion more than he had recommended for an already expanded program. The House lost little time in sustaining his veto, and inasmuch as there had been no time to write a new bill since the veto was sustained, money will have to be provided by what is called a Continuing Resolution in order to carry the HEW program over until next month.

On Thursday we had a little bit of good luck, at least temporarily. The Rural Development bill had been before Congress for months. It was finally approved by the Senate last April. The House also approved. We went into Conference with the House, and after eliminating some pretty far-out proposals which had been put into the Senate bill through the urging of Senators Humphrey, McGovern and a few others, brought out a practical conference report. The House approved this conference agreement some three weeks ago, but it was not brought before the Senate for a very good reason.

President Nixon had become extremely critical of the tendency of Congress to expand on the Administration's recommendations for authorization and appropriations. The President himself recommends big increases in appropriations for popular programs, but does not like the Congress to outbid him in this auction for popular favor, which is going on continuously.

Some time ago it was intimated that the President would veto Congressional appropriations which exceeded his recommendations. Although the Rural Development bill was only an authorization, it could eventually involve far larger appropriations than have been made available for this purpose up to now. It was believed that if the Rural Development bill was sent to the White House before HEW appropriations, the President would be under considerable pressure to veto this bill as a warning to Congress, but that if the HEW appropriations bill reached him first he would veto that, and in all probability permit the Rural Development authorization bill to become law.

So, after the House had sustained his veto of HEW, I enquired of Tom Korologos, the President's representative on the Hill, if there were any further objections to our putting the final stamp of approval on Rural Development. He promptly answered No, and I so advised Senator Mansfield, the Majority leader, and Senator Talmadge, Chairman of the Agriculture committee, of the position of the White House. Of course they were very happy, not only because final approval of the rural development program would serve as a delightful bonus to a miserable week, but because they were both strongly in favor of the programs which the bill would authorize and expand.

Consequently the Senate unanimously approved the Rural Development bill, and it was soon on its last mile from Capitol Hill to the President's desk. While it is usually referred to as a bill for developing greater prosperity and higher standards of living for people living in rural areas, it will actually benefit the whole country, urban as well as rural. A lot of people don't seem to realize that most of the wealth of this country is developed in the rural areas and not in the crowded areas and financial districts of the big cities. To be sure, much of the wealth gravitates to the heavily populated areas, but it doesn't originate there.

¶ THE SENATE spent most of Thursday discussing a bill presented by Senator Kennedy which would greatly expand the work being carried on by the National Science Foundation. The purpose of this bill was to provide employment for unemployed scientists and technicians, people who had been employed in the high-salary brackets but are laid off, frequently as a result of their own devices. The Kennedy bill has passed the Senate, but I very much doubt that it will be seriously considered by the House this year. So that is where we are at the end of this week.

¶ THE SUPPLEMENTAL APPROPRIATIONS bill has been approved, assuring funds for government programs until we return next month. The interim arms agreement with Russia is stymied deep in the chasms of partisan politics, and the war continues between arms promoters and pacifists.

Most members of Congress have left for home. Some will go to the Republican convention in Miami, the preparations for which up to now have been as exciting as the second hour of a professor's lecture on the love life of the aardvark.

[Putney, Vermont]

Week ending August 26, 1972

THE REPUBLICAN convention at Miami Beach came and went. Nothing exciting and nothing unexpected happened. The conservative element of the Party—Tower, Buckley, Ford, *et al.*—were in full control. Everything went like clockwork, planned to the second. Nixon was nominated with only one dissenting vote. Agnew was nominated for second place without difficulty and with meticulously planned enthusiasm.

Only Senator Brooke of the liberal wing was given a place as a speaker and that was because of his color rather than his political philosophy. Ed Brooke is pretty adaptable anyway, but being from Massachusetts feels that he has to keep up with the Kennedy brand of liberalism.

As matters stand now I fear that we are in for a bad ten weeks before the November 7th election. President Nixon ought to win in a breeze. Certainly he has made mistakes—his advocacy of the expansion of many so-called left-wing programs in education, health, and social affairs has displeased many conservative Republicans. No one can deny, however, that the world is in a more stable and peaceful condition because of his efforts. Business is much better this year, also farm prices. The fact that our national debt has soared and our balance of foreign trade has become worse will have little effect on the average voter.

We are getting out of Indochina, slowly to be sure, and the Middle East is quieter, but all these things cannot guarantee that President Nixon will win re-election. I think now that he will win and win handily but we must not take this for granted: a single stupid act by a group of his supporters can cost millions of votes. I must repeat again what I have said before: incidents can sway more votes than issues.

¶ A WEEK of almost perfect weather in Vermont, although hot and muggy the last three days. Except for telephone calls from the Washington office and from people with problems, two days on business in Montpelier, news reporters, *et al.*, we might call this a vacation. L.P.A. insists on driving, and in her spare time also paints windows and doors, handles mail which comes from the Washington office each day, gets meals, and does washings and other odd jobs such as typing this weekly report. All I have to do is mow grass, by hand, saw the winter's fireplace wood supply, talk with visitors, chase Japanese beetles, and count the products of the 60-by-60-foot garden which I planted June first.

This poorly cared-for garden shows how well rural people can live and not be hungry. Of course the raccoons may steal all the sweet corn, the beetles may get worse, but all in all it's a pretty satisfying life, especially on evenings like this when the moon is full and the crickets are singing.

[*Putney, Vermont*]

Week ending September 2, 1972

THE WEEK began on a sad note. Last Saturday L.P.A. and I drove to Orleans to attend the funeral of Pearl Keeler. John and Pearl Keeler had been my friends since 1933, when he helped get me elected as Speaker of the Vermont House of Representatives. Up until a few years ago John and I and our friends found time for a few days' fishing each year either in Orleans County or in the Laurentides Park in Quebec. After I came to the Senate two of my colleagues, Senator Willis of Indiana and Senator Butler of Nebraska, frequently went with us. Also, after his defeat for the Presidency in 1936, Alf Landon of Kansas, one of the most conscientious candidates the Republican Party ever had, found time to come to Vermont a couple times for fishing.

John and Pearl became leaders in their community, he holding town office, she in later years active in building the new church, and serving in the state legislature. The Keelers are a good example of the fact that one does not have to have a high formal education to be of service. I have never believed that advanced degrees alone should qualify one for high position or high salaries.

Thursday noon we left for Ely, Vermont, to have lunch with our friends Arthur and Helen Burns. Arthur is Chairman of the Board of Governors of the Federal Reserve System, while Helen makes about the best chocolate-filled cookies one ever tasted. They also had as guests for lunch Ted Jaffe and Florence Lowe, whom we occasionally saw in Washington.

On Saturday we had planned to pick some of the vegetables from the garden to take back to Washington with us, especially the first ears of the sweet corn, which were large enough to eat. An uncanny but coony instinct, however, had told the raccoons that Friday night was the time to raid the Aikens' garden, and they had done a real job— only a few ears of sweet corn remained unmangled. But we did salvage nineteen good cucumbers, a peck of potatoes and four pumpkins.

¶ ON OUR ARRIVAL in Washington at 1 P.M. Sunday, we found the pigeons, headed by one all-white rooster, waiting for us on the front steps of the Methodist Building, where we live. Two weeks have gone by since we left the Capital, two weeks of what most people called a vacation for us—two weeks of hard work, but a different kind of work and certainly a relief from consideration of the ills of the nation and of the world for which, in many cases, we can find no adequate and lasting solutions. At any rate, it is more restful to do something different. And by going back home we get a renewed faith in the democratic system of government and the future of our country.

[*United States Senate*]

Week ending September 9, 1972

THE NEWS of the week was overshadowed by the murder of eleven members of the Israeli team at the Olympic Games in Munich, Germany. The murders were committed by members of an Arab terrorist organization, eight of whom were killed or captured by West German police. The effect of these assassinations was shock and rage around the world, resulting in more support and sympathy for Israel and greater distrust and dislike for all Arab countries, whether or not they were guilty of approving the act. I am sure that the leadership of the Arab nations, with the probable exception of Syria and Iraq, did not approve of the action, although Egypt and Libya likely were sympathetic.

The effect on Israel was understandable, and that country promptly launched retaliatory attacks upon communities in Lebanon, where the assassins were presumed to be accepted or, at least, tolerated. It is my opinion that Lebanon would not welcome these terrorists but is not strong enough to prevent their presence there. As a matter of fact most countries in the world, including the United States, suffer gangster operations which they are unable to prevent.

The desire for revenge on the part of the Israelis was natural, but as a result of their bombing attacks their country is now being charged with the slaughter of many innocent people, an action which has tempered the sympathy for the Israeli government to some degree. The larger nations of the world are naturally disturbed because it is incidents like this which in the past have precipitated world wars. Should a wider war result from this episode, there is a grave possibility that the destruction within Israel would be tremendous. It occurs to me that the Arab assassins might have considered this result in making their plans. I am sure that many prominent Jews do not see eye to eye on the advisability of Israel's taking any action which could conceivably result in more war.

In the Senate a Resolution sponsored by Senator Mansfield expressing sympathy for Israel passed with no dissenting vote. While the fact remains that the United States would undoubtedly go to bat for Israel in the event of a Middle East war, it is most unfortunate that efforts are made, principally by the McGovern forces, to drag Israel into our election campaign. Although it appears that the majority of American Jews have voted for Democratic candidates in the past, President Nixon seems to have a decided edge in their support for this election due primarily to the fact he has already, by his actions, shown his support for Israel, while Candidate McGovern and his associates appear to offer support to the Jews for domestic political reasons. However, I am confident that both Democrats and Republicans in the United States are very desirous of a Middle East peace.

On Tuesday, September 5, the Senate considered five bills intended to strengthen crime-control in the United States. All five of these bills were approved unanimously. The episode at Munich undoubtedly was a factor in these decisions. At least, they were made easier.

Two United States winners who were contestants in remaining events of the Olympic Games were ruled out because of insolent behavior and disrespect for the United States and its flag. They will never again be permitted to compete in the Olympics. Above all else the Games should not be considered in a political sense as has been the case this year. If the trend continues, support for the meeting of the athletes of the world every four years will be greatly weakened.

¶ REVENUE-SHARING and the interim arms agreement with the Russians consumed most of the legislative time of the Senate. Revenue-sharing has developed, as was expected, into a contest between the states, big states versus little states, a contest that has gone on since the establishment of the Continental Congress during the Revolution. At that time the most populous and wealthy colonies thought they should control the nation, but fortunately for us they were overruled by the more sparsely settled colonies, and all of them, large and small, became the thirteen original states of our Union.

One amendment to the Revenue-sharing bill was offered by Senator Kennedy and would have required President Nixon to submit to the Congress before October 31 his recommendations for tax reform. This was nothing but a cheap political trick and the Senator from Massachusetts was slapped down decisively. There are a lot of amendments to the Revenue-sharing bill left, but it looks like the Senate will be through with this and will send it to Conference by next Tuesday, the 12th.

The SALT Agreement, as it is called, is on the other part of the double-track program—still being a contest between Senators Jackson and Fulbright. The Mansfield amendment to this interim arms agreement, which approved the position of President Nixon as stated on June 15, was strongly opposed by the White House for what, in my opinion, was a very unsound reason. Because of the Jackson-Fulbright feud Senator Mansfield was unable to get a direct vote on it; so on Wednesday, in order to get a vote, he moved to table his own amendment. The motion failed 52 to 31, with Mike voting against his own motion. The White House then promptly reversed its position and came out in favor of the amendment, which up to the time of this vote it had strongly opposed. A vote on the amendment was secured on Wednesday, September 6, and it was approved by a vote of 84 to 1—with the White House losing no time in claiming credit for its passage.

In my book it is just too bad that President Nixon and the White House did not weeks or even years ago try to co-operate with Senator Mansfield and other members of the Congress in working out plans to get out of the Indochina predicament and restore peace to a great part of the world. I don't believe that either Senator Jackson or Senator Fulbright will yield from the positions they have taken. So I expect that by next Tuesday or Wednesday the Senate will approve cloture petitions which will permit votes on the interim arms agreement bill and the amendments offered to it before the end of the week. While I will vote No on the Jackson amendment, which in effect demands superiority over the Russians in most every phase of our defense program, I expect it will pass. But with the Mansfield amendment already approved overwhelmingly, the Jackson amendment will lose most of its meaning, and when the bill goes to Conference with the House it is quite likely that both the Mansfield and Jackson amendments will be discarded. This is the proper way to handle the situation now.

¶ COMMITTEE HEARINGS continued throughout the week. The most interesting one that I participated in was the Joint Committee on Atomic Energy hearings on the plans to establish a new experimental project in the TVA [Tennessee Valley Authority] area. This project is designed to bring about more production of nuclear power with less loss of fuel. It is called LMFB—meaning Liquid Metal Fast Breeder reactors. The Commonwealth Edison Company of Chicago apparently expects to run the whole show and apparently has the support of pretty much the whole Atomic Energy Commission. There is no question in my mind but what the Commonwealth Edison Company thoroughly represents the more narrow-minded and greedy element of the electric-power industry, and the officials who testified before the committee gave every appearance of this. In fact they could have stepped right out of a television show.

On the other hand, I thoroughly believe that the big oil companies contribute generously to financing some of the holier-than-thou groups which pretend to oppose the generation of nuclear power in the public interest. I don't trust either of these outfits, and I particularly don't trust the officials who represent them. I concede that most of the membership of the environmental societies is sincere. I don't give the same consideration to all those who represent them.

One practical action came during the week when on Wednesday the Vermont Yankee nuclear power plant at Vernon, Vermont, got permission to operate at 20 percent of capacity until the 28th of February 1973. This was done to guard against an anticipated shortage of electricity in the New England area during the fall and winter, and was made possible by an amendment sponsored in the Senate by Senator Anderson and myself last spring. Of course we were charged with siding with the power companies, and one charge was that the power companies had written the amendment. This statement is of course untrue and dishonest. The legislation Senator Anderson and I promoted simply gives both sides their "day in court" to prove their own case, but apparently certain of the environmentalists don't want the power companies to have their day in court, and in this way are proving that they can be as unscrupulous and dishonest as the utility people themselves.

¶ DURING THE WEEK politics picked up and became dirtier. Executive branch officials now charge the Congress with delaying needed reforms and laws that are good for the people. By doing this they are imitating President Harry Truman, who in 1948 charged the 80th Congress with being a do-nothing Congress and got away with it because the Republicans were so sure they could elect Tom Dewey President that they never bothered to deny the charge. This time, however, Senator Mansfield and other responsible Democrats are not only denying the charge but disproving it. Since the 92nd Congress has done a lot of constructive work as well as making mistakes, I may decide to defend the Congress publicly, since the Executive Office charges reflect on me as well as on the whole Congress.

¶ THERE IS NO QUESTION but what President Nixon is far out ahead in the race for the November 7 election. Candidate McGovern seems to be standing pretty much alone, since other politicians are so sure of his defeat that they are reluctant to stand with him. However, it may be that his courage and willingness to stand alone will turn out to be his strongest asset and may narrow the gap between him and President Nixon considerably before November 7.

Week ending September 16, 1972

ON MONDAY NIGHT L.P.A. and I and a few other members of the Senate were permitted to view the first showing of the new movie *1776*. This documented the wrangling and difficulties which took place among the colonies during the spring previous to the signing of the Declaration of Independence. It was the prosperous colonies against the poorer colonies from start to finish, with New York and Pennsylvania feeling it was their prerogative to run the whole show. Had it not been for Benjamin Franklin of the Pennsylvania delegation the Declaration might never have been written or signed. But Ben Franklin, who must have been considered as a renegade in his delegation, thought in terms of what was good for all thirteen colonies, rather than just his own. And John Adams of Massachusetts having finally been convinced that he couldn't get everything he wanted, including the outlawing of slavery, at one fell swoop, the representatives of the thirteen colonies all finally signed the Declaration of Independence and the United States of America was born.

The significance of this historical movie, which was indeed entertaining, lies in the fact that human traits have not changed to any degree in the last two hundred years. While we have fifty states in the Union now, about half a dozen of them containing our largest cities feel that it should be their prerogative to decide on the rights of all fifty of them.

This was rather dramatically demonstrated when the Revenue-sharing bill was brought up for final action by the Senate. Senators from a few of the larger states wanted to shape this legislation so that their states would be the biggest and the principal beneficiaries of this plan, which provided for the distribution of federally collected funds among all states and localities. As in 1776, the more lightly populated states had a numerical advantage and were successful in shaping the legislation to the needs and desires of their own areas.

Had the New York and Pennsylvania colonies had their own way in 1776, the course of history would have been vastly different. Had a few of the larger states had their way in 1972, the future of our country could no doubt have been changed, too. The Revenue-sharing bill went promptly to Conference, where an agreement was quickly reached. We don't know exactly what was approved, but principally the wishes of the less-populated states were fully protected while concessions were undoubtedly granted to the bigger states. We will know next week when the details of the conference agreement are laid before the House and Senate.

¶ THE OTHER principal measure to be decided by the Senate this week was the interim arms limitation agreement with the Russians, commonly called the SALT Agreement. With the feud between Senator Jackson and Senator Fulbright apparently not coming to an end, Senator Mansfield and others offered a cloture petition which was voted on Thursday morning. This petition was overwhelmingly approved by the Senate, which was really fed up with the rivalry and face-saving tactics of both contestants in this endurance race. With the cloture petition approved, each member of the Senate was allowed to have only one hour's time to discuss the interim agreement legislation and all amendments thereto. Amendments were voted on. Senator Jackson's amendment carried, so he felt that his honor had been vindicated, while Senator Fulbright's honor had really been vindicated with the adoption of the Mansfield amendment last week.

The legislation was approved by the Senate and now goes to a committee of conference. Since the House had approved the agreement with only six votes in opposition, the House conference will undoubtedly go all out for their position which, in my opinion, is the correct one. After all, the amendments offered and approved by both sides, relating primarily to the interpretation of the agreement, amount to very little, for the interim agreement plan, like the SALT treaty, will mean exactly what the President wants it to mean—nothing more, nothing less.

As a conferee I hope we can agree to approve the treaty without any amendments at all, but if necessary I would support an interpretation carefully planned to save the face of all the contestants who have delayed action upon this proposal in the Senate for the last month or so.

¶ WHILE WE WERE having the final debate and vote on the SALT Agreement, things were happening around the world of much greater importance. West Germany and Poland announced the resumption of diplomatic relations after a lapse of many years. The United States and Russia were making much headway on a resumption of full economic understandings, and a French company announced the sale of fifteen million bushels of United States wheat to the People's Republic of China, all of which should have been good news to the world.

But not all news was good. Israel and the Arabs were again engaging in armed conflict: minor to be sure, but nevertheless a beginning which could be expanded into another Middle East war. This was the result of the murder of members of the Israeli Olympic team at Munich. I believe that the United States, the countries of Eastern Europe, probably Russia, and even some of the other Arab states, will do all possible to prevent an expansion of this conflict. I think they will be successful, because in any war of considerable size these days not only the contestants but the rest of the world will be losers.

¶ On Tuesday, the 12th, several states held primary elections, among them Vermont and New Hampshire. My home town of Putney was one of the better voting towns in the state: 50 percent of the qualified voters went to the polls. There are some who are bound to say because of the small vote in the primary we should return to the old method of nominating, that is, the caucus and convention system. That would be a sad retreat for democracy and I doubt that the states will approve any action in this direction. It is indeed disappointing when, as happened this week, only one-third of the qualified voters show an interest in the primary election, but it would be even more discouraging and disastrous to our political system to revert to caucuses, which, as a rule, are not attended by more than 1 percent of the qualified voters of each town.

¶ On Tuesday I had a rather refreshing experience when twenty-seven honor students from around the country, now at American University studying government, some of them employed by members of Congress, asked to confer with me in my office. These young people showed a real desire to learn how to run a good government. Their questions were practical, honest and, I might say, inspiring. They displayed none of the razzle-dazzle tendencies which so many older persons feel is typical of the younger generation. These twenty-seven young people showed a desire and loyalty to good government which some of their elders could well copy.

Week ending September 23, 1972

We are getting bills out of committees these days that would be disastrous if passed as reported by the committees. This is particularly true of the Labor, the Public Welfare, and the Public Works committees, the Commerce committee, and my own Committee on Foreign Relations. Some members of these committees who are running for re-election this year or in 1974 appear to have lost their capacity for sound reasoning as they try to justify positions they never should have taken. Their great desire is apparently to please those people or groups which they feel will support them either financially or by soliciting votes at election time.

¶ MUCH TIME is taken up every morning by fifteen-minute political speeches, usually four or five Democrats making charges against the Nixon Administration, and a couple of Republicans, led by Senator Scott, trying to counteract them. So far this has been an exercise in futility, and I doubt if any votes have been changed. The net result has been to use up to two hours a day in the Senate which should be given to necessary legislation. While these speeches are going on there is no one in the Press Gallery and hardly anyone in the Visitor's Gallery and only two or three Senators on the floor. Of course the Democratic speeches are given to the press in the hope that they will get some favorable publicity.

I would characterize the time taken up with campaign charges and countercharges as a costly nuisance. Although some of the members, particularly Senators Kennedy and Humphrey, seem to have their eyes and ears tuned to the 1976 Presidential campaign, they pretend to be helping Senator McGovern in his efforts to win the 1972 election. Actually they are hurting him badly. Senator Kennedy spent five days on the road with him and in my opinion did Candidate McGovern a great deal of harm, since the crowds that gathered came to see and hear Kennedy, which made McGovern look like a nonentity. It is a wonder this country survives as well as it does while undergoing this unholy ritual every four years, but it always has survived and I expect it will again this time.

¶ THE LAND USE BILL represents a determined effort on the part of its advocates to secure power through controlling the use of all land. Of course the federal government controls a good share of our land area through the Department of the Interior, the National Parks, and the National Forests. But there are those who feel that the federal government, meaning themselves of course, should have control over the use of all privately owned land as well. If these people were all competent, such a policy might have its advantages for the future, but a great many of those who think they should direct the use of the land are terribly incompetent and couldn't possibly make a living by themselves through their own skill and knowledge of the land. Too many of them are living on trust funds or sizable salaries as officials of government agencies, federal, state, and local. Anyway, the Senate amended the Land Use bill to eliminate much of the harm which could have come to our country through accepting the committee recommendations.

I would not criticize too harshly the so-called environmentalists who feel that the use of all land should be put under government control. Most of them do mean well, and the efforts they make go far to offset the other extreme of our society, which feels that industrialists, commercial interests, and developers should have the right to use our natural resources any way they see fit.

¶ THE HIGHWAY AUTHORIZATION BILL this week developed some controversies over whether the National Highway Reserve Fund should be kept for the exclusive work of road-building or whether part of it might be used for other forms of transportation. This developed into a contest between the big-city states and the more rural states, and quite properly culminated in a compromise, with $800 million of the highway fund being authorized to improve other forms of transportation, primarily railroads and airports. The final bill was so written that no reduction can be made in the funds available for the maintenance of interstate, state-federal, and secondary roads.

Representatives of states like Connecticut and New York would have gobbled up much of the highway fund for improved rail service to and about our largest cities. Fortunately the more rural states had the situation under control. The Land Use and Highway Fund bills will have to go to Conference with the House, where errors in judgment and discrepancies will have a chance to be thrown out.

¶ ON WEDNESDAY, the 20th, the Senate Agriculture committee reported out the Wild Areas bill which I had introduced on the behalf of Senators Talmadge, Allen, Sparkman and myself. This bill would provide for setting aside portions of our forest areas which could be kept in a primitive state for the future. The land thus set aside would be in areas where the timber has not been cut for so long that a near-primitive condition already prevails. Under the bill which I introduced, about 15,000 acres in Vermont and over 500,000 acres in the eastern United States would qualify. It is doubtful if action can be completed on the Wild Areas bill this year, but at least we have made a start in what I think is the right direction.

¶ ONE DISTURBING BIT of news came to me during the week. The State of Vermont, which up to twenty years ago operated on a pay-as-you-go basis and had the best credit rating of almost any state in the Union, lost its high credit rating. To my amazement I found that the bonded debt and the provisions for new bonds authorized by the Vermont legislature amounted to $336 million. And the private debt owed by Vermont industries and individuals amounts to as much more. This situation has been brought about by the increase in highway construction—local, state and federal—and by the demand for more and more money for welfare purposes of various descriptions. The situation now is a far cry from the days when I was Governor of Vermont and at the insistence of the state legislature reluctantly borrowed a million dollars to repair damages from the 1938 hurricane at the interest rate of 45/100 of 1 percent. We didn't spend the million dollars after borrowing it, and loaned part of it to the State of New Hampshire at a much lower rate than we were paying.

However, the trend toward greater indebtedness is with us publicly and privately. We are operating both public and private affairs on borrowed money. I don't like it, but I realize that if we are to keep up with other states, other institutions, other industries, and even other countries we have to do things we don't want to do. Very shortly the Congress will have to consider extending the national debt limit to at least $450 billion and possibly more.

Week ending September 30, 1972

A WEEK of wide variety with the Senate concentrating on work it should have done weeks before.

The international situation appears to be changing at a rapid rate. Mr. Kissinger has gone back to Paris supposedly to meet with emissaries from North Vietnam in an effort to bring the fighting in Indochina to a close and bring all the Americans home, including those held as hostages by the Hanoi government. Hanoi has released three of these hostages, obviously for the purpose of using them for propaganda material. It is my opinion that in spite of the sympathy for the North Vietnamese government professed by some people, the attitude of the United States public is swinging more and more to the support of President Nixon and his plans for reducing our involvement in Indochina as fast as feasible.

Also, President Marcos of the Philippines is having his troubles. I was in Manila in the fall of 1965, and at that time it appeared to me that it was only a matter of time before rebellion or possible revolution would break out there. When a few people control most of the resources of an area or a country and most of the people have little or nothing, that is a sure formula for trouble. It is easy to blame the communists for any rebellion which springs up in any country, but usually the cause is that too few people get too much control over resources. And the tendency is to enact legislation and make rules to which the masses are subjected and from which the so-called "upper class" is exempted to a great degree.

¶ TUESDAY the Senate really got down to work and did plenty of it. The Foreign Military Aid Authorization bill was finally approved, with the defeat of all amendments which would likely have made matters more difficult for President Nixon. Senator Fulbright did not ask the House for a Conference on this aid bill and I do not blame him for that, since the last time he asked the House for a Conference the House declined and instead accepted the bill as it came from the Senate.

One of the first acts of the day was to pass the Wild Areas bill which I had introduced. It is doubtful that we can get action on the part of the House this year, but I hope that its passage by the Senate will impress people with the necessity for setting aside unspoiled areas of forest lands in the eastern United States.

The Senate also passed a pesticide bill, the purpose of which is better control of the use of materials which the farm producer has to have to protect his crops from destruction by insects and other pests, including plant diseases. There are many people in this country who disapprove of the use of fertilizers and chemicals for the production of crops, but I hate to think of the food shortage which would afflict us if we depended on only those controls of insect, pest, and plant diseases that are provided and applied by Nature herself. The pesticide bill was the result of close collaboration and co-operation between the Senate Committee on Agriculture and Forestry and the Senate Committee on Commerce. We could use a lot more of this kind of co-operation between committees to good advantage.

The final bill considered by the Senate on Tuesday related to vocational rehabilitation. Again there was little opposition, although there was considerable discussion about how the bill should be written so as not to penalize some states or give unwarranted benefits to others. Of course we never will spend enough money to handle our rehabilitation programs perfectly, but this bill was a definite step in the right direction, and will provide a greater degree of hope to those who, because of physical or mental difficulties, are unable to live a reasonably happy life.

The two major bills brought up on the Senate floor for action were the Consumer Protection bill and *H.R. 1* which provides nearly a thousand pages of amendments for Social Security, Medicare programs, and Welfare. These two measures promise to take up a lot of time, and, along with the busing bill, promise to delay any sine die adjournment.

¶ EFFORTS ARE being made to bring on to the Senate floor political and personal arguments which more properly should be made, if at all, out behind the barn. The situation verges on outright political dishonesty. I got mixed up in one of these occasions on Thursday when I came on the floor just in time to note that Senator Brooke and Senator Cranston were offering what is called the "end-the-war amendment" to a clean-water bill. The Senate had previously agreed that no nongermane amendments could be offered to legislation for the rest of this Session, but Senators Brooke and Cranston, with only three or four of their nonhostile colleagues being on the floor, apparently thought they could get unanimous consent to void the rule and slide this amendment through before their effort could be noted.

If I had not come on the floor just as I did their ruse might have succeeded. Both Senator Ervin, who came on the floor about that time, and I vigorously dissented, and they were thwarted in their attempt to tack this highly controversial legislation on to a completely unrelated bill. I admit that I had difficulty in controlling my thoughts and my language when I observed what I considered to be underhanded actions. I did charge them with undertaking to harass the President in his efforts to get this country out of its unsavory situation in Indochina, and the language which I used in expressing my opinion was not exactly complimentary or of Sunday-school caliber.

I remarked to one of the aides on the floor that the Senate was getting so slimy that we would have to wear rubbers, not realizing that the official reporter took down this remark as if addressed to the Senate as a whole. I also suggested that if anyone wanted to take the part of Hanoi in the war they could go to Hanoi, but if they wanted to stay in the United States they ought to act like Americans. Later on I deleted these two rather unsavory remarks from the official record of the Senate, but unfortunately—or fortunately, according to one's viewpoint—reporters in the Press Gallery overheard them and used them as a basis for their news stories.

These constant efforts by his enemies to embarrass the President have, in my opinion, made the ending of the Vietnam war more difficult, and have encouraged the North Vietnam government to continue with the hopes that Senator McGovern may win the November 7 election and as a result Hanoi will get much better terms than it can get now from the Nixon Administration.

Meanwhile rumors are prevalent, possibly true and possibly planted for political purposes, that Kissinger's conferences with the representatives of the Hanoi government will likely lead to an early settlement of the war.

¶ ON FRIDAY, Senator Mansfield and I introduced a bill which we know should probably originate in the House of Representatives, providing a tax credit for human depletion. By "human depletion" we mean a person's inability to work and earn at full capacity because of physical, mental, or emotional difficulties. We held that since oil wells, mines, and quarries are eligible for special tax benefits as a resource nears depletion, and inasmuch as an industrial concern gets special tax benefits as its machinery gets older, the person operating that machinery should also receive as much consideration as the machine itself. By offering this bill we intended to call attention to the fact that property values get far more attention and consideration in governmental bodies than do human values.

We are not likely to get much in the way of results from offering this amendment, but we did feel it was a good way to call public attention to the fact that in the field of taxation human values are subordinated to the values of industrial equipment and natural resources.

Week ending October 7, 1972

MONDAY the Defense Appropriation bill went through just about as submitted and will now be in Conference with the House. Why does almost nobody vote against the Defense Appropriation bill, when they know that it could well be sheared down, saving tax money without materially injuring our defense establishment or the security of the nation? The answer is that we don't know enough about the details of it or where it could be best reduced. Another reason is that so many of the giant corporations, including those that are well managed and those that are poorly managed, look to the United States government to keep them in business and keep them employing thousands of men and women, almost all of whom are members of labor organizations. The so-called defense corporations and the labor unions exert tremendous power on the Congress. In general the corporations provide the cash contributions for political campaigns, while the principal asset of the unions is the number of votes they can deliver to successful candidates who will co-operate with them after election. It all seems like an enormous waste of money, and it savors of dishonest politics to a great degree, but, paradoxically, out of this system has been developed the greatest and most powerful nation on earth and one in which the individual and the family live at about the highest level of any people on earth.

¶ TUESDAY there was a ceremony at the White House to which I was invited, the signing of the Strategic Arms Limitation Treaty with Russia. A considerable crowd of Cabinet members, legislators, including about a dozen of us from the Senate, and distinguished public officials and citizens watched as President Nixon and Foreign Minister Gromyko of Russia affixed their names to the treaty. Each of those present was later served with coffee and light refreshments and given a pen bearing the autograph of Richard M. Nixon, which the recipient could proudly but erroneously show to his friends while assuring them that was the pen with which President Nixon signed the treaty [SALT] with Russia on October 3, 1972. There was a time when in signing an important bill or document the President would use several pens, making a dab on his signature with each one and then giving them as special favors to those present.

I have several of these pens which I have accumulated over the last twenty-five years, and the thing I notice about them is that the pens used by President Truman were made in my own community. President Eisenhower didn't give out pens, and successor Presidents used the plastic variety. However, these signatures, regardless of the pen used in making them, represent progress of some kind, and take their place in history.

¶ ON TUESDAY also the Senate conferees on the Foreign Aid bill met with the House members and got just nowhere. They met again on Wednesday and still got nowhere. My colleagues in the Senate group are plenty stubborn and plenty determined to reach no agreement that does not, to a degree at least, recover part of the authority and responsibility which the Congress has surrendered to the White House the last few decades. The House conferees are ready to go down the line with the Administration, but it looks as if there will be much difficulty in reaching any agreement between the House and Senate. If that proves to be the case, then the only way the foreign aid program, particularly the military aid program, can be financed would be through a Continuing Resolution which would authorize expenditures at the same rate as last year and no more.

This difference of opinion between the two bodies of the Congress is nothing new. Last year we didn't complete the authorization for fiscal year 1972 until March.

¶ As a member of the Joint Committee on Atomic Energy I listened last Tuesday to AEC Chairman James Schlesinger expatiate on a deal with Japan to provide that country with the atomic fuel necessary for nuclear-power production over a period of years. There is bound to be considerable criticism of this deal, especially from Western European countries, because a virtually unlimited supply of atomic energy for Japan would give that country still further advantage in taking over world markets, particularly the markets of Asia. France will undoubtedly be disgruntled, since the French had hoped to get this Japanese market for nuclear fuel for themselves.

¶ More excitement on Wednesday was caused by President Nixon's veto of legislation increasing the retirement payments for railroad workers by 20 percent. Both Houses of Congress overrode his veto and presumably everybody was happy. The Democrats in Congress like to force the President to veto legislation which rightly or wrongly is designed to give special benefits to any considerable group of voters. So they are happy with this veto; but on the other hand, the President, having given the impression to the country that no increase in taxes would be necessary next year even though he must have known better, can now say that the Congress is responsible for any increase in taxes, thereby taking himself off the hook.

¶ H.R. 1, the Welfare Resolution, before the Senate most of the week, was finally approved with some forty amendments added to it, and has gone to Conference with the House. What comes out of it is anybody's guess. It is unfortunate that consideration of this bill came during the height of the political campaign.

I thoroughly believe that increased benefits, particularly for Medicare patients and older people, are desirable even though they are costly. In so many instances when the question was raised as to what the added cost would be, the question was also raised as to what will be the cost *not* to do it. By increasing the cost of one welfare program it is often possible to hold down or even reduce the cost of another.

The level of income required to maintain a family of four decently varies greatly among the states. These costs are estimates and are largely fixed by state law. Connecticut has a $4,000 poverty level and is closely followed, in the $3,800 level, by Vermont, Minnesota, Massachusetts, and New York. Alabama, Mississippi, and Louisiana fix the poverty level at from less than $800 to $1,200.

The amendment offered by Senator Mansfield and myself, which would permit an old-age recipient to earn up to $3,000 a year without sacrificing any of his old-age payments, was readily adopted by the Senate but will, doubtless, be cut to something like $2,500 in Conference. At any rate this will be a great improvement over the $1,680 which an old-age beneficiary is now permitted to earn, and a substantial increase over the $2,000 per year which was originally considered adequate by the Senate Finance committee.

An amendment by Senator Pell of Rhode Island, which I supported, would also provide for care of the eyes, ears, and teeth under the Medicare law. I have maintained for many years that the condition of these organs has a great deal to do with the happiness of a person. I hope the conferees will retain this provision, but at this time it looks doubtful.

¶ THE PRICE OF WHEAT and the circumstances which brought about an increase of 50 to 60 cents a bushel came in for a lot of political discussion. This increase in price, due largely to an immense sale of wheat to Russia, brought the Western producers out of the slough of despond, and brought considerable dismay to the supporters of Senator McGovern for President. The latter have tried in every way they can think of to discredit President Nixon by pointing out that he favored the big grain dealers and caused the small producers of the Southwest to lose a lot of income for that part of the crop which they sold at a lower price. Since only about 17 percent of the total 1972 wheat crop had been sold before the price increase became effective, this argument isn't resulting in much political gain for the McGovern forces. In fact it seems to have had the reverse effect. Farmers throughout the West appear to be happy with the big increase in the price of grain and the almost record prices being obtained for livestock.

¶ IN THE MIDDLE of the week Senator Jackson offered a Resolution with over two-thirds of the members of the Senate as co-sponsors, directing in effect that business with Russia be cut off until Russia permits all Jews who wish to emigrate from that country to do so without paying excessive exit visas. He ignored the fact that many other countries, including some which are very friendly to us, also have what might be considered excessive charges for those citizens who leave their countries. I was fearful that Senator Jackson's move might result in a drop in the price for wheat, and indeed the price did go down 5 to 6 cents per bushel the next day, but started back slowly thereafter.

The political candidates are competing with each other as to who can do the most for the little country of Israel, and not only because both parties want the Jewish vote. What is of more importance to some candidates is the Jewish financial contributions and fund-raising activities. However, the Jews are very smart people, and I don't believe they relish the idea of being put on the auction block to be sold to the highest bidder. They are fully aware of the fact that the United States will go all out to help Israel in the event that her existence or welfare is threatened by an outside nation. President Nixon proved this at the time when Russia was giving much aid to Syria for the purpose of harassing Israel. But whatever the motive may have been it is fortunate that Senator Jackson's Resolution did not knock down the price of wheat.

¶ ON FRIDAY I went on the Senate floor just as a bill had been called up which would have provided a loan of $20 million to the Railway Express Agency, which is heavily in debt and to all appearances has not been too well managed. This bill, supported by Senators Magnuson and Hartke, would not have required any reduction in dividends to stockholders or in salaries to company officials. Unfortunately the sponsors of this bill had no idea what dividends or what salaries had been paid. I hastily objected to action on the bill at the time and was soon supported by nearly every other member of the Senate present, probably eight or ten in all.

It is my opinion that companies like this should go through bankruptcy, just as smaller business people have to do when their debts become excessive. Further than that, I don't believe that any corporations should be able to call upon the United States Treasury to bail them out of the abyss through the kindness of members of Congress, to whom they in turn may have been very generous during past political campaigns. Senators Magnuson and Hartke agreed to withdraw their request for any action on this bill and it went back on the calendar, where it will probably stay for the rest of the Session.

Week ending October 14, 1972

THIS WAS SUPPOSED to be the last day of the Session, but by eleven o'clock Saturday night any hope the members had that they might start for home for three weeks of political campaigning, or start for other countries for a spell of vacationing and sightseeing—at the taxpayers' expense, of course—was dashed. At least it was dashed for the conscientious members of the Congress. There apparently wasn't a majority of this type, for the House had no quorum on Saturday and the Senate lost its quorum of fifty-one members shortly after noon. I sympathized with the majority of the members of both Houses who played hooky, but decided to stay on till the end.

The last few days of a Congressional Session nearly always bring out the worst traits of the membership.

During these last few days we may expect some members of one House or the other to make proposals which would benefit their states or communities, or their friends, or themselves, by means which would not be considered earlier in the Session. Unfortunately some of the smartest members of the Congress are also the most selfish. During the closing days they make their proposals before the Congress and then, unless their demands are met, bring out a club threatening to block action on legislation that is absolutely necessary and desirable. Certainly the culprits who hijack a plane or kidnap a youngster don't have much on some of the Congressional members who resort to the same tactics.

¶ MANY OF the most important bills passed by both Houses of the Congress are now in Conference.

The Debt Limit bill includes a provision limiting the amount which can be spent for total expenses of the nation during the fiscal year, and, as passed by the House, authorizes the President to decide where cuts in appropriations are to be made. This is obviously a flagrant delegation of authority by the Congress to the executive branch, and demonstrates the weak-kneed character of many members of Congress who, when asked by their constituents, "Why did you cut off the benefits to which we are entitled?" can then say, "We provided your benefits, but that cheapskate of a President cut down on your allowances." The House would have delegated all responsibility for reducing expenditures to the President, but the Senate wisely qualified the wording of the bill, sharply restricting Presidential powers in this respect. A battle royal will develop between the Houses, and within the Houses, of Congress next week.

The Foreign Aid bill is also in a jam. The Appropriations committee reported a Continuing Resolution which would permit this program to continue at pretty much the same level at which it has been operating until February 28. When it came into the Senate, Senator Javits protested that the Resolution carried no funds for Asian Development banks. After I pointed out to him that this item could not

113

properly be inserted in this bill he agreed not to press the matter, but almost immediately started questioning the members of the Appropriations committee in charge of the conference report, Senators Inouye and Brooke. They had virtually no answers to his questions, the conference report got stymied, and up until late Saturday night I had not found out just what the Senator from New York wanted anyway.

Many members assumed that Senator Javits wanted more aid for Israel, since that is one of his chronic demands. But the bill already contains $400 million in aid to Israel, far more in proportion than that given to any other country. Representatives of the State department and AID [Agency for International Development] protested vigorously that any further aid to Israel would result in taking aid away from the Philippines, where, because of a disastrous hurricane and other calamities, assistance is desperately needed. My opinion is that Senator Javits is considerably worried over the prospects for the Overseas Private Investment Corporation, an agency which he had almost single-handedly pushed through Congress, and also over his election prospects in 1974. He is counting heavily on retaining the support of both the banking fraternity of New York and also of the Jewish leaders who are spectacularly good campaign fund-raisers and contributors, and who are also extremely loyal to candidates whom they support.

¶ ANOTHER MEASURE in serious difficulty is the Highway Construction bill, and as of late Saturday night the indications are that this bill will have to go over for the next Congress to consider. Highway construction has been financed on the part of the federal government by special taxes, especially on gasoline, but the highway fund has grown to such proportions that other forms of transportation, principally airlines and railroads, are now asking for a share of it. The House insists that nothing be spent from this kitty for anything but highways. In spite of my supporting a reasonable contribution for other forms of transportation I can understand the attitude of House members who regarded this proposal as a foot in the door—one which could within a few years open it so wide that railroads, airlines, and buslines could really pre-empt a good share of the money intended for highway construction.

¶ REPRESENTATIVES of the United States and North Vietnam are still holding private meetings with growing frequency, undertaking to work out a plan which might insure a reasonable degree of peace for Indochina, and particularly North and South Vietnam. It is quite likely that, except for economic assistance, the United States involvement will be pretty much over before the end of the year. Some think there will be some agreement reached before Election Day. I don't think there will be, and I don't believe that guerrilla warfare and bloodshed in Indochina will end even if we do manage to make a complete withdrawal. I do not see how we can withdraw the arms and defense materials which have been given to the South Vietnamese, since they have already received them and the weapons do not belong to us anymore.

¶ SATURDAY AFTERNOON Senator Cannon of Nevada attempted to attach an amendment to a tariff bill which in effect would have permitted labor unions, government contractors, and other corporations to be more generous with their political contributions. This attempt was blocked by Senator Proxmire and others, including myself. Being offered only three weeks before election this smelled very badly, although it was supported by Senator Dole, Chairman of the National Republican Committee, and supposedly by the leadership of both political parties. Had Congress approved it, we would have come in for much justifiable condemnation by the public. Our so-called Clean Election bill, which was passed a year ago, is in my opinion not a good law but it has the effect of making campaign contributors more cautious, since to be legal the contributions and the names of their contributors have to be made public.

Great appeals and gorgeous offers are now being made to what we call the minority groups. Promises are made which would not and could not be kept, even if the promiser was successful on Election Day. I don't think the majority of the public is taken in by these promises, but there are always enough who believe them to wield the balance of power if an election is close. The proper word for these people is "suckers." They believe what they are told and the unscrupulous candidate, if elected, will give them another line explaining his failure to live up to his promises and vigorously condemning others for the failure.

Week ending October 21, 1972

A WEEK of final decisions—a week of contradictions and controversy, a week of political maneuvering with the question of who gets the benefits and who gets the blame still undecided.

The Welfare Resolution, *H.R. 1,* which has been two years in the making, and which was finally reported and passed by both Houses, contains a little something for everyone and was not fully satisfactory to anyone. Whatever anyone says about the Congress it cannot be said that the more unfortunate and needy people of this nation have been forgotten. Of course the cynics may say that the impending election had something to do with the generosity of the members of Congress, particularly those seeking re-election.

I do believe, however, that most members of Congress are more sympathetic to the poor, the aged, the blind, the sick, and the crippled than they have been previously. Of course these increased benefits cost something, and our generosity will result in an increase of some $200 a year in taxes for low-income workers within the next few years. Much of the one thousand pages of proposed legislation was lost in the process of putting the rest of it through Congress, but there is another session coming and another opportunity to ferret out and correct the errors and omissions of the 92nd Congress.

¶ THE PRESIDENT had asked the Congress to give him authority—in fact he wanted a directive—to cut appropriations enough so that the total expenditure of the federal government for the year would not exceed $250 billion. Constitutionally the authority for raising money and making appropriations rests with the Congress. The Congress indeed delegated to President Lyndon Johnson such authority once during his term of office, but delegating the responsibility of one branch of government to another is pretty risky business. No member of Congress wants his own favorite projects reduced, and if they are reduced he likes to be able to tell his constituents that the President was to blame for withholding the funds or cutting them down.

On the other hand President Nixon, having assured the country that no new taxes would be necessary next year, knows perfectly well that new taxes will be necessary, and wants to be able to put the blame on Congress either for new taxes or for a big deficit in public spending. After a lot of maneuvering the Senate finally decided to increase the debt limit and to knock out the spending limitation, and so on

Wednesday this Debt Ceiling bill was back again in the lap of the House.

The conferees worked on the bill throughout the day and finally submitted a bill carrying a $465 billion debt ceiling but no limitation on spending. Instead they agreed that next session a study would be made by the House Ways and Means and the Senate Finance committees to work out a plan whereby Congress itself would establish a spending limit early in the session.

This is as it should be. Congress should not surrender its appropriation powers to the President, but should carry out its Constitutional duties itself.

¶ A THIRD MEASURE which this week stirred the emotions of members of Congress was foreign aid legislation. Since the foreign aid conferees of both the House and Senate had been unable to agree, the Appropriations committees of the House and Senate reported legislation permitting a continuation of expenditures not to exceed those currently in progress, and not to exceed any authorization previously fixed by the Congress. After our Appropriations committees brought forth their bill (approved by the House), which did exceed the amount actually authorized by about $100 million, Senator Fulbright and those who are dissatisfied with legislation applying to foreign aid programs seized the opportunity to oppose the bill. The Senate, however, shut its eyes to this comparatively minor violation of legislative practices, overrode the protests of Senator Fulbright and others, and approved the bill by a substantial margin.

The fact that there was in this bill some $400 million in loans and assistance to the State of Israel probably had something to do with the sizable margin by which the Senate approved. In this case the executive branch of government wanted a much larger appropriation than was possible under the circumstances, while the Congress had an opportunity to show its devotion to economy.

¶ THE FINAL ACTION of the Senate on Tuesday night—or I should say Wednesday morning, since it was after twelve o'clock—related to what was called the Clean Water bill, which would authorize and commit the federal government to the expenditure of many billions of dollars over the next few years. The President, presumably sensing the opportunity for charging Congress with the necessity for imposing more taxes and borrowing more money during the next few years, had vetoed this bill. The Senate without delay voted to override this veto by a vote of 52 to 12 and passed this hot potato over to the House. The House, by an even larger margin, voted to override the veto, and so the Clean Water bill became law. President Nixon of course expected to be overriden, and will do one of two things: fail to carry out the contracts with the states which the bill requires, or go ahead with the plans and put the blame on Congress for the increased deficit which the act necessitates.

Since Vermont is well out ahead of all the other states in its efforts to control water pollution and, therefore, would stand more to gain through the enactment of this bill with its retroactive provisions and commitments, I naturally voted to override the veto. What else could I do?

¶ On Wednesday night, just before nine o'clock, the Congress adjourned sine die.

The last major bill to come to grief was the Highway bill. The House refused to permit other forms of transportation to cut into the highway fund, and by the time the conferees had reached an agreement, which the Senate accepted, the House members had left that body without a quorum, so no action could be taken and the bill died. Perhaps it is just as well, since the result will be only the slowing-up of contracts until the 93rd Congress can make new appropriations. After all, it is time to go a bit more slowly and watch where we are going.

¶ Thursday we came home to Putney in one exhausting day-long drive. Saturday evening we went to the annual banquet of the Vermont State Grange.

The Grange, a low-key farm organization, is now over a hundred years old, and a good share of its members today are non-farm people —but good people. I have been a member since I became fourteen years old. As compared with other farmer groups, it is less noisy, less provocative and possibly equally effective in the long run.

[Putney, Vermont]

Week ending October 28, 1972

Like all the "best people" hereabouts I'm having a sore throat and chest cold; there are pleasanter ways of achieving status. I've been taking it easy and staying put because, after having served in the U.S. Senate for nearly thirty-two years, I don't want to show publicly how sick I may feel: to appear sick might start a droolfest among those who want to volunteer for my job in the Senate.

I have never believed in stating my future political plans very far in advance of Primary filing-time either, and don't intend to do so now, in spite of the fact that a lot of folks would like to know. To do so would impair my work for the remaining two years of my present term.

Thursday morning Hanoi announced that a peace agreement had been reached and would be signed on Tuesday, October 31. At 10:00 A.M., Dave Abshire, Assistant Secretary of State for Congressional Affairs, called to say that Kissinger would have an announcement at 11:00 A.M. About one o'clock we heard over the radio that Kissinger had announced that an agreement had virtually been reached, though several details were not yet agreed upon. Another meeting with Hanoi representatives would be necessary, he said, and it was unlikely that any agreement would be signed next Tuesday.

The news media reported that nine conditions had been agreed upon, one of which provided that each side would retain the areas in its possession at the time of the signing. Since the Viet Cong and the forces of North Vietnam now hold much of the area of South Vietnam, it was only to be expected that President Thieu would be violently concerned. He was. He stated, in effect, that he would sign no agreement for a cease-fire under the announced terms, thus threatening to demolish any peace agreement at all. I cannot blame President Thieu for his expressions of dismay, chagrin and outward hostility to most everyone, especially the United States. His accession to the presidency of his country, the building-up and arming of South Vietnam's military force, and the fact that his government still rules over most of the people, if not the land, has been made possible only through the assistance of the United States taxpayer, the Navy, and the Air Force as well as United States ground troops, which have been reduced from 543,500 when President Nixon took office to only about 34,000 as of today.

But however much we may sympathize with President Thieu's objection to being downgraded (for that is what it is), the fact is that we cannot let him dictate the policies of the United States. We did not let Chiang Kai-shek do it, and we cannot let President Thieu or the head of any other nation, large or small, determine our policies if we are to survive as a democracy.

¶ THIS WEEK, I got involved in the New Hampshire campaign for the Senate, though not from my own choosing. A few weeks ago, while Luther Hackett, Republican candidate for Governor of Vermont, was visiting me in my office, Wes Powell, who is running against Tom Mc-

Intyre for the U.S. Senate in New Hampshire, also dropped in. Wes asked to have his picture taken with me and as usual I obliged.

On Monday my Washington office received a call from McIntyre's office saying that Wes was using the picture with remarks ascribed to me, but which I never made, as campaign material. Naturally, Tom was not happy about it, but all my office could do was to remind him that not many weeks ago I had my photo taken with Tom McIntyre, too. Well, that's politics—and most anything goes as the campaign nears its end and there is not much time left for effective denials to unfounded charges.

Week ending November 4, 1972

[*Putney, Vermont*]

THE THRUSHES of summer are gone. Goldfinches are putting on their dark winter suits, while juncoes, year-round sparrows and other birds are still in the woods where there is a heavy crop of hemlock and other tree seeds available for their daily fare. Only one chickadee so far, but they will show up before long. Blue jays, those most beautiful sneak-thieves, are stealing and hiding everything they can lay their beaks on.

Birds are so much like people. The blue jay, for instance, after stealing and storing everything he can possibly need, continues to keep grabbing for more, taking it from needier birds wherever he can find it. And like the blue jay, local, national, and international business interests, professional people and intellectuals, some with common sense and some with very little of it, are now trying to elect to office at all levels candidates who they think will help them to get more gravy, or their "front feet in the trough," as we used to say. Even the welfare groups have powerful organizations working for the candidates that will serve their purpose best. Only those who are really in need or who are too proud to ask for relief are voiceless and in the background. Fortunately, their numbers are smaller. And judging from the great amount of birdfeed sold in the stores, the percentage of needy birds is lower, too.

¶ SUNDAY EVENING George McGovern was on a question-and-answer broadcast from Hartford, Connecticut. It was not the George McGovern I used to know, nor has it been all the week. George was always decent so far as I knew, although he was inclined to go overboard in proposing aid to needy people which he was never successful in effecting. As a candidate for President, however, George has been unfair to an unexpected degree, making insinuations, unsubstantiated charges, and impossible promises. He actually acts as if he does not want the Vietnam war to end while Nixon is President, or else he wants it to end in humiliation for the U.S.A.

He is doubtless acting from desperation, for hardly anyone believes he can win the election; or he is taking direction and advice from supporters, financial and political, who care very little about George McGovern. Instead, these supporters appear to be more interested in discrediting the President, and even the United States itself, and to be planning to take over our government in 1976 and to run it for their own glory or profit.

How many persons have downgraded themselves and resorted to vicious and disgraceful tactics in order to obtain high positions in government, justifying such actions by assuring themselves that, having achieved their throne, they will then exercise their own judgment and do more good for their country and their people than anyone else could possibly do? It does not work that way. Once they have committed themselves to the less humane and greedier elements of society, they cannot escape. Unless I am mistaken, George McGovern will regret for as long as he lives some of his or his supporters' actions of today, and try to atone by being more helpful at lower levels.

¶ PRESIDENT NIXON is conducting his campaign in a manner calculated to make McGovern look worse. Naturally quick-tempered and impulsive, the President now expresses himself on television in a dignified and constructive manner, and in public appearances keeps his temper under control. He never mentions his opponent by name, and all the taunts and insinuations by the McGovern forces have not caused him to depart from his studiedly dignified course. I strongly suspect that the assurance of victory on November 7 enables Richard Nixon to resist any temptation to "lose his cool" and attack his opposition with its own kind of weapons. Ignoring a political enemy is, in many cases, about the most effective weapon one can use, and Mr. Nixon seems to be using it with devastating effect.

[*Putney, Vermont*]

Week ending November 11, 1972

THE CAMPAIGN for the election of 1972 came to an end and the campaign for the election of 1976 picked up speed. Senators Brooke and Percy have virtually announced candidacies for the Republican Presidential nomination, while it appears that an office is soon to be opened to promote Senator Kennedy for the Democratic nomination. I cannot see any of these three men occupying the White House. While Senator Percy's influence in the Senate is probably greater than that of Senator George McGovern, he still has a long way to go before he might be regarded as a prime leader, but he sure does seem to ooze desire with every move. Ed Brooke is an astute politician but his ultra-liberal tendencies which at least equal, if indeed they do not exceed, those of Ted Kennedy, would surely lose the solid South and all the Mountain states of the West for the Republicans. As for Teddy Kennedy, I do not believe he will ever be President of the United States of America.

No doubt a horde of other candidates from inside and outside the Congress will soon express in subtle, or not so subtle, ways a willingness to make the sacrifice.

¶ THE ELECTION proved the polls to be accurate, for this time at least. President Nixon carried forty-nine states, most of them by overwhelming majorities, while the Boston *Globe* poll scored 100 percent by predicting that McGovern would take Massachusetts by a 55-to-45-percent margin. The President's success in improving relations with the rest of the world and the withdrawal of most of our military personnel from Southeast Asia paid huge dividends in votes, while the boom in the stock market to the highest level in history for a short time on Friday undoubtedly paid dividends in cash to many, many investors and speculators.

George McGovern was defeated so badly, not only because he and his staff made mistake after mistake—or because of the style of his campaign, which caused millions of voters to recoil in disgust—but because the voters of the United States could not see him as an administrator and would not trust him with the nation's security and welfare. In spite of the weird and eccentric campaign carried on, and in spite of seemingly irregular voting which went on in many communities, the American electorate may have voted more independently than in any previous election. As a party, the Democrats concentrated on governorships and Congressional seats, and candidates for these offices for the most part either ignored their candidate for the Presidency or else actually opposed him. This strategy paid off and, much to the surprise of nearly everyone, the Democrats added one to their list of governors and two to the United States Senate.

When the returns showed that the Republicans had captured four contested seats for the Senate—Virginia, North Carolina, Oklahoma, and New Mexico—I began to have qualms, since I would be in line for the chairmanship of the Senate Foreign Relations committee, and frankly I was not thirsting for the job. When later returns came in, however, and the Republicans had lost Kentucky, Delaware, Iowa, South Dakota, Colorado, and Maine, my qualms went away, and I had very sincere regrets that we had a net loss of two in the Senate.

I never expected the Republicans would take over the Senate, but the losses of Maine, Iowa, and Colorado came as a real shock to me, since, like everyone else, I had expected little trouble for Republicans in those states. The loss of Senator Margaret Chase Smith in Maine was the sharpest blow to the Republicans, and was undoubtedly due to the fact that her re-election was generally taken for granted, and so she stayed in Washington attending to the nation's business at a time when so many others were out on the campaign trail.

The defeat of Senators Jack Miller, Gordon Allott and Margaret Smith leaves vacancies in the Republican Senate organization. There will be plenty of volunteers to fill the vacancies created by their loss. Already Senator Cotton has asked if I aspired to the Republican Conference chairmanship. I told him emphatically that I do not. As an official of the party, I would feel obligated to carry out party policies with which I occasionally disagree. I much prefer to remain completely independent in my voting. After talking with me Norris Cotton immediately announced his own candidacy for the position, arguing that New England should be represented among the officials of the party in the Senate. I will undoubtedly support Norris in the event of a contest, even though we find ourselves on opposite sides of many roll-call votes.

¶ PRESIDENT NIXON, having carried forty-nine of the fifty states, lost no time in making clear that the next four years would be different. He does not have to campaign for re-election. His principal concern now will be his place in history rather than appeasing minority groups, campaign contributors, or ivory-tower intellectuals with their one-track minds and dreams of personal glory.

A reorganization of government is indicated by his request for the resignation of all his political appointees, including those who undoubtedly will be re-appointed to the same or other jobs. But by this means he can eliminate the dead wood which has handicapped him during the last four years.

The place of Richard Nixon in history is what concerns him now, and to insure that place as a great President he will have to offend the public and the Congress time and again. He cannot avoid this if his interest lies in bringing peace to the world while insuring security and a prosperous economy for the United States. Peace in Indochina is his first concern, and I feel that this objective will soon be achieved as far as our country is involved.

And peace in the world, or at least among the major countries, will bring about an unprecedented increase in world production and world trade, and higher living standards for at least two billion people. There will be those in and out of Congress who, while urging, begging, and even threatening for peace in Indochina, will urge our intervention in other parts of the world. The President will resist this pressure.

The welfare programs of the United States, whose number is now almost legion and whose efficiency in many instances is deplorable, need wholesale revision. In attempting to improve the operations of these agencies without depriving the worthy of their just consideration and assistance, the President will be charged with cruelty to the needy, in spite of the fact that the record shows that the really needy people have had far more consideration and assistance during Mr. Nixon's first term than ever before.

The vote on November 7th showed that the great majority of the people will support the President in his efforts to correct the grievous errors of the past, although millions may say they don't like him personally. Well, so what? I have frequently said over the past years that if the Devil himself could bring an end to the Indochina war I would give him full credit.

¶ RICHARD NIXON is concerned with his place in history. To achieve a worthy place in history, Richard Nixon must have the same objectives as ourselves.

Why don't we work together? I believe that the Senate, under the leadership of men like Senators Mansfield, Stennis, and other Democrats and Republicans, will place the needs of the country above personal ambitions or party politics. President Nixon will make his mistakes just as any human being makes mistakes, but the most costly mistake for us all would be the failure of Congress and the executive branch to co-operate in the welfare of all mankind.

[Putney, Vermont]

Week ending November 18, 1972

As LOWELL had written, "The snow had begun in the gloaming/ And busily all the night/ Had been heaping field and highway/ With a silence deep and white." By Tuesday morning "Every pine and fir and hemlock/ Wore ermine too dear for an Earl,/ And the poorest twig on the elm tree/ Was ridged inch deep with pearl."

Snow not only ridged "every pine and fir and hemlock," but every wire of every utility company serving adjoining counties in Vermont and New Hampshire. At 1:30 P.M. on Tuesday the electricity went out, and we were left without power for heating, cooking, pumping water and other conveniences. Only the wood fire in our small fireplace was left to heat our house. Until the power lines were repaired in the late afternoon on Thursday, there was very little reading or writing done at our house after 5:00 P.M. for two days. Fortunately, I had cut a couple of cords of fireplace wood, mostly with a pulp saw, and L.P.A. had put it in the cellar where it was dry.

The experience was very educational for a lot of people. Or at least it should have been. It should have made them think back to the time when early settlers lived on the very sites where people now live in comfort or even luxury, when a log cabin sufficed for shelter, when wood from the forest burning in a stone fireplace was the only source of heat, when an iron kettle hanging over the fire provided the only hot water for the family, and water came from a brook or a well dug just outside the cabin.

Those pioneers didn't have the leisure to read much, except at night —and then only by the light from the fireplace or from the luxury of a tallow candle. And now, when I hear whining and complaining because the color TV is out for a couple of days or the electric stove doesn't work, I feel like putting some people back into those early days for a short time, so they would really appreciate the facilities and luxuries we have today.

One such luxury is the battery-powered radio which has kept us abreast of the news from the outside world.

¶ WHILE THE CONSERVATIVE Republicans seem to blame the White House or even the President himself for their losses in the elections, they also are making it plain that they intend to control the party in Congress with a very tight rein. The boys in the White House have very little regard for the Republicans in Congress, and were concerned almost wholly with re-electing the President and maintaining their own positions. Except for Vice President Agnew they hardly showed any interest in the election of Republicans to the Congress or local offices. If ultra-conservatives exclude all moderate and liberal Republicans from having any part in formulating party policies in the Congress, we will suffer even greater losses in 1974, and probably a complete defeat in the 1976 Presidential year.

[Putney, Vermont]

Week ending November 25, 1972

IN A SETTING like ours in Vermont during the early part of the week it was not easy to think of government and politics, but the news of Willy Brandt's victory in Germany came through Monday morning. I believe this was good news, and augurs better prospects for peace and prosperity for all Europe than would have been the case had Brandt lost.

And Fidel Castro is indicating a willingness to make a start toward re-establishing better relations with the United States by dealing harshly with airplane hijackers who have regarded Cuba as a refuge. While there would be benefits to both countries in restoring much better relations, there would also be problems. Cuba used to be the world's largest supplier of sugar. When relations with our country were severed some ten or twelve years ago, the Cuban sugar quota was parceled out among other sugar-producing countries. Now if we restore a sugar quota from Cuba of anywhere near the old proportions it would likely mean the reduction of quotas elsewhere.

¶ MR. KISSINGER left Sunday for Paris to meet with representatives of North Vietnam. For the first two days the outlook was good, with the representatives of the United States and Hanoi emerging from their meetings smiling and cheerful. But on Wednesday something must have happened: the traders in peace and prosperity came out scowling and sour, and their demeanor was promptly interpreted to indicate that their best-laid plans had "gone a-gley."

To add to the pessimistic outlook, President Thieu launched a full-scale radio attack on Henry Kissinger, using a characterization that was anything but flattering, and applying adjectives like "ambitious" —which was not exactly original with President Thieu. But peace must come, and come reasonably soon. President Thieu was careful not to include President Nixon in his outburst, but blamed Kissinger for everything unfavorable in South Vietnam that has been reported to date.

Assuming that Kissinger is the conceited scamp that Thieu portrays him to be, and that Thieu himself is an apostle of honor and integrity, Mr. Kissinger will win the contest, for regardless of who is right and who is wrong neither the American public nor the Congress will stand for our continued involvement in Vietnam. Nor can President Nixon afford it at this stage of the game.

Saturday evening Kissinger came back to confer with President Nixon and report on the several meetings with Hanoi representatives during the week. Apparently both Hanoi and Saigon are insistent on calling the shots. If they asked me for comment it would likely be, "A plague on both your houses"—and the American public would overwhelmingly support this position.

¶ ON THIS THANKSGIVING DAY there are still those who say we have little to be thankful for. Taxes are too high, snow removal is too slow, electricity was off because of heavy snow, the newly established passenger train from Washington to Montreal was late, and so on.

These people are not really unhappy. What would make them really unhappy would be to deny them the right to grumble. They really love it.

But at times when they get on my nerves, I would like to put them back under the leadership of Governor Bradford or Captain Miles Standish, so they could understand better the meaning of real hardship and the blessings of today's luxuries.

[Putney, Vermont]

Week ending December 2, 1972

A FEW DAYS ago Bill Timmons, one of President Nixon's assistants, advised me that the President would like suggestions to consider for his second term. Assuming that the same request had probably been made of many others, and that there was also a strong possibility that the President would never see my letter anyway, I nevertheless sent him a reasonably short letter on Monday.

Since I regard all Presidential appointments as the President's prerogative and responsibility, I made no suggestions in this field. However, I did make the following four very general suggestions:

First, that he continue the Nixon foreign policies of which the electorate indicated high approval on November 7th.

Second, that he ask for as little legislation from Congress as is necessary, since much of the Congress, with future elections in mind, is likely to be antagonistic anyway; and that he correct errors of the past legislative and executive branches by executive action as far as possible.

Third, that for such legislation as is necessary, he get bipartisan sponsorship. After all, while some Democrats may concentrate on harassing the President, most of them, as well as most Republicans, will put the needs of the country uppermost.

And fourth, that he not try to reorganize the framework of government at one fell swoop, and that he not ask Congress for authority for it. Granting that continuing reorganization is necessary, the plain fact is that if recommendations for a large number of transfers of authority or the shifting of responsibilities are made at one time, every member of Congress will find some recommendation with which he cannot agree and which he will not support, and the whole effort toward reorganization will be weakened. If, for instance, the President should try to tear the Department of Agriculture apart and distribute its functions among other agencies whose only qualifications for agricultural supremacy or dominance is a desire for power, I would oppose the President. However, if he wished to take step-by-step action in improving the work of this department, I would doubtless support him.

In brief, I would support to the limit those agencies within Agriculture or any other department which have done and are doing good work honestly and constructively, and at this time would not consider transferring their function to State, Interior, or HEW, which are the departments said to look most covetously at the functions of the Agriculture department.

¶ ON AN EARLY morning TV program came a description of life in the high-rise apartments of our larger cities. I feel sorry for people who live in those densely crowded conditions of 600 people to the acre. Some 2,000 people now live on Putney's 20,000 acres. The area could, and we will, accommodate many more as regional employment opportunities expand or people from other states find the means to live in Vermont. Of course we can't move the people of the big cities wholesale into rural life, but we can make life better for all who live in either city or country.

The Rural Development Act, passed by the 92nd Congress, would go far in making life better for all. Rumor has it that President Nixon does not intend to let this act function as Congress intended. I hope the rumor is false for, if it turns out to be true, it will have a serious impact not only on the President's second term but also could spell trouble for the Republican Party in future elections.

¶ FRIDAY NIGHT's television news showed many members of the Congress, their wives and their staff associates, enjoying trips to foreign countries with all expenses paid by the government and with liberal allowances for spending-money. When these people return to the United States the customs inspectors will be very lenient as to purchases made abroad.

While I agree that interchange of visits with officials of other countries is helpful and is, in fact, drawing the world closer together, and that some members of Congress regard these trips as a duty and perform accordingly, I have to admit that there seems to be much truth to the charges that some members also use the opportunity to get an all-expenses-paid foreign vacation without personal cost. These pleasure trips at public expense and the criticism given them actually have the effect of making some members of Congress reluctant to take such trips at all, even when by doing so they accomplish much good. In defense of any Congressional culprits I will say that their critics may be motivated by envy and would do the same thing themselves if they had the opportunity.

¶ HENRY KISSINGER goes back to Paris today, December 2, undoubtedly flying in one of the President's four elaborate planes. The cost of operating such a plane is considerably more than the 12 cents a mile allowed members of Congress for using their own cars on official business, but if Kissinger can really contribute toward bringing our Indochina military episode to an end I won't be too harsh about his travel expenses.

[Putney, Vermont]

Week ending December 9, 1972

MONDAY the dairy operators in northwestern Vermont said they couldn't get feed for milch cows, and they were inclined to blame the grain sales to Russia for shortages and higher prices. I took their complaint up with the U.S. Department of Agriculture, which was very co-operative. We found that transportation systems were largely responsible for the milk producers' fears. Plenty of grain is available but railroads make more money by using cars to ship to other parts of the country where return loads are available. Also, speculators would appear to be active, boosting the cost of dairy rations produced in the Midwest and South. On getting the dairy complaints Monday, I promptly contacted the ICC [Interstate Commerce Commission], urging that agency to direct the railroads to furnish the necessary transportation. I feel the ICC will co-operate. Late in the week the Agriculture department promised to take action to ease the feed situation by Monday, the 11th.

Great changes have taken place in dairy industry. Farms have been mechanized and herds are necessarily larger. Costs and facilities and equipment have gone up until a herd big enough to support the family requires an investment of $200,000 or more, compared with the investment of a few thousand dollars a generation ago. Developers here in the Northeast offer such high prices for land that the operator of a dairy farm is tempted to sell out. He can hardly get a good vacation, and there is always the threat of subsidized imports hanging over his head. Extremists among the environmentalists object to the normal use of stable manure and even chemical fertilizers and weed-killers. These extremists don't have the votes that they would like political candidates to think they have, but their voices are shrill and incessant.

Early in the week a reporter called to ask what I thought of the proposal to eliminate the College of Agriculture at the University of Vermont. Since Justin Morrill of Vermont was author and sponsor of the Land Grant College Act of 1862, since Vermont is still the most intensive dairy state in the Union, as well as being the most rural of all the fifty states, and since agriculture is still far and away the most important industry of the nation and the world, I definitely am opposed to downgrading agriculture in Vermont or in the nation.

American agriculture has literally saved the world from famine, and is far more potent in promoting peace among the nations than all the warhawks and munition-makers put together.

¶ THE MOST DISTURBING news of the week was the report that former President Harry S Truman, was critically ill in a Kansas City hospital. Although not the world's greatest diplomat he was one of my favorite Presidents, representing America as the place where it is possible for one to rise from a lower level of society to become head of a great nation. I always liked him, and did all I could to help him during the early months of his Presidential career. He had an uphill fight to get elected in his own right in 1948 when many of the stalwarts of his own

party were so sure he was going to lose that they would not help him.
¶ DURING THE WEEK, President Nixon announced most of the rest of
his selections for next term's Cabinet. The selection of Frederick Dent
of South Carolina for Secretary of Commerce to succeed Pete Peterson
caused some apprehension. Dent is a textile man, and the U.S. textile
industry is pushing hard to close out or sharply reduce imports. If this
should be done, there is a feeling that other of our nation's manufac-
tures would expect the same consideration, and the effect would be to
put the United States on an isolationist trend.

   While I realize that many U.S. industries should have some protection from imports (some of which are subsidized by the producing
country), we have to be very careful not to overdo this form of protection, which, if carried too far, would have disastrous effects upon
our own economy and our own world markets.

   Many American concerns and many American investors have put
well over $100 billion dollars into foreign industries, and they will
not permit such disasters to happen; nor will Congress go all the way
with the protectionists. Nevertheless, there seems to be a lot of ner-
vousness among a large segment of labor and American producers.
The announcement of Mr. Dent's selection has not quelled this apprehension in the least, and the appointment of Peter Brennan, a
hard-shell labor leader, to be Secretary of Labor, does not relieve the
tension.

   But to offset these appointments we find Elliot Richardson named
to Defense, Bill Rogers to State, and Earl Butz to Agriculture—none
of them bearing much relationship to an isolationist. On the whole
the Cabinet will be comprised of conservative and successful businessmen and politicians who worked hard for the President's re-election
and were supported by the electorate. They represent a swing to the
right, but I believe they recognize the facts of life which pertain to
world politics and world economy. If my judgment is wrong, it will be
bad for the Republican Party.

¶ TWO EPOCHAL EVENTS of the week seem to be causing the public
little concern. For one, Apollo 17 left the Earth on Wednesday and
our astronauts plan to land on the moon next Monday, and hardly
anyone doubts that their trip and return to Earth will be successful.
For the other, Kissinger and Le Duc Tho continue their discussions,
looking to an end to the Indochina war. Nearly everyone believes that
our military involvement in that area will soon be over.

   Apparently it is the less important things of life that cause human
beings to get red in the face, blame others for our own mistakes, and
get an exaggerated idea of our own importance.

[Putney, Vermont]

Week ending December 16, 1972

PHONE CALLS to and from Washington continue at the usual rate and three to five personal or business problems come in each day. Ordinarily, if the troubles have not already been taken up with our Washington office, I advise the complainer to put the problem in writing and mail it to Washington. We then advise the people in our Senate office to expect it in the mail, alerting them to the general nature of the problem. Frequently a solution is found before the mail gets there.

The office then telephones the person who has the trouble and reports on the progress made. Sometimes nothing can be done to help my constituent—and sometimes nothing ought to be done, since Vermonters are also human and once in a while, though not often, ask for unreasonable solutions, just as do representatives of big corporations or transportation companies. Normally I do not take such complaints in detail or try to handle them myself, since that would simply be impossible. We have several people in our Senate office, all Vermonters who know the ropes thoroughly, to whom the various problems are assigned.

One great difficulty often confronting a constituent is that he does not know where to go for help. We can usually direct him to the proper person in a state, regional, or federal office. If it is a business problem we can usually tell him who is handling it at the official level and sometimes make appointments so he can present his own case. By knowing where to go, a constituent can save a lot of time and expense. Once in a great while we are asked to show an interest in a matter where a judicial decision is pending. We give a flat No to such requests, because the intervention of a member of Congress in a court case would be unethical and is probably illegal. More than one member of Congress has come to grief through violations of laws which he himself may have approved.

As an example of the problems presented to us, a construction contractor who uses heavy machinery was in trouble. Since L.P.A. was at the hairdresser's and couldn't stop me, I answered the phone myself and took the problem. The man's difficulty was that certain parts of a big machine had broken down at a time when use of the machine was urgent. He could not find a replacement in the United States, but finally located one in Germany. The part was sent by air express to Salt Lake City, and from there it was reshipped by air to him in Vermont. Three days later it had not arrived, so the contractor called his Senator, gave me the shipping number and his own telephone number.

According to him the airline had no idea what became of the shipment and apparently showed little interest in the matter. I reminded my constituent that it is only a few days to Christmas and the transportation lines are congested, but I told him we would see what we could do. About an hour after talking with the contractor, I talked with my Senate office, gave them the problem, told them it was not official business, but to see what they could find out anyway. Within an hour the office called back, said they had talked with the airline, found that non-delivery was caused by weather conditions closing down airports in the Northeast. Consequently air express had piled up in Chicago, but the airline said it would try to find the missing package and deliver it to the Albany airport as soon as possible. The package was found and delivered to Albany that very night.

That is all the airline could do and, considering everything, it was all my office could do. Unofficial business, to be sure, but it shows the extent to which the electorate expects a member of the Senate to help out. For one, I am glad to co-operate on occasions like this.

¶ WHILE THE TROUBLES of constituents continue to come in, as usual the important events of science and history are hardly causing ripples. Kissinger and Le Duc Tho have left Paris and have returned to their respective capitals. Most everybody is too busy getting ready for Christmas to give the Vietnam war much thought. More Americans are killed in one of our larger cities every night than are lost these days in Indochina. The war must end officially before long. The President has practically assured it, and the 93rd Congress will not appropriate funds to continue military action in that area, anyway. If Hanoi acts up, I doubt that we will appropriate for reconstruction in that country either.

¶ OUR ASTRONAUTS on the moon kept up their happy and successful exploration and after three days took off for the trip home, with nobody worrying about their safe return unless it is those in the Command Center in Houston who have to time every action of the astronauts to a split second. Ironically one of the most spectacular and important events of all history must take a back seat to the selection of the right-colored necktie and the right-size shirt to give for Christmas.

¶ NEWER MEMBERS of Congress, especially in the Senate, are trying to get rules of the Congress changed so they can immediately go to the top in committees, with the experienced older members relegated to lower levels. It takes quite a while before we realize how much we have to learn about running a democratic government. In Congress ambition is a potent word, and some who are imbued with an exorbitant amount of it fail to realize how soon they and their policies and pronouncements will be forgotten.

¶ FORMER PRESIDENT TRUMAN is still fighting for life. He does not give up now, any more than he did in 1948 when everyone thought he would be badly defeated in the Presidential election. I hope he wins again this time.

[Putney, Vermont]

Week ending December 23, 1972

WE MAY CALL it a week of shock, dismay, and disbelief.

When it was announced on Monday that President Nixon had ordered a renewal of the bombing of Hanoi and Haiphong Harbor in the heaviest American air attacks of the war, the nation was stunned. Hope for release of American war prisoners was gone; charges that civilians of North Vietnam were bombed and killed horrified millions of Americans who had voted for Richard Nixon on November 7th. The losses of our air force appear to be the heaviest of the war, including the crews of several B–52's, which were supposed to be invulnerable to enemy attack. The question asked over and over was, What has happened to the man we elected as our President on November 7th? Why did he lead us to believe that a peace settlement was at most only a few weeks away? Is he now determined to win a military victory to show the world that we are the strongest nation on earth?

As one who supported Richard Nixon for a second term in the White House, and as one who had freely predicted that our military involvement in Indochina would be over before Christmas, I find these questions to be extremely embarrassing.

I do not hesitate to say that the renewal of the bombings is a bad mistake. President Johnson asked me to the White House, along with some fifteen other officials of the executive and legislative branches, at the time he announced the decision for the first bombing of North Vietnam. Our government then thought that such action would stop infiltration of men and matériel from the North into South Vietnam, force Hanoi to ask for peace, and bring our military operations in Indochina to an early conclusion.

I protested the proposal as strongly as I could, but to no avail. They went ahead with the bombing. Infiltration to the South increased. Our force in the South increased until by the spring of 1969 it numbered 543,500 men. Expanding our military operations simply did not work: it only made matters worse. Apparently the executive branch has learned little from the experience.

One reason I am not able to answer questions with any degree of certainty is that I am not informed of the plans of our government or of what is really going on in the field of military operations. Occasionally when I talk with President Nixon himself at White House dinners or at meetings to which I have been invited as the senior Republican on the Foreign Relations committee, he gives me information which I believe is factual. As for Mr. Kissinger and certain other aides, however, I might as well be on another planet. I have received far more information from top officials and representatives of other countries than from my own.

To the best of my information, Chairman Fulbright is the only member of our committee to whom Mr. Kissinger reports, and I am inclined to believe that such meetings are at my chairman's insistence, and are not good examples of perfect harmony. Personally, Kissinger has not contacted me since August 2nd of this year, when he and his military assistant, General Haig, both called to support an end-the-war amendment which I had introduced in the Senate. President Nixon called the next day, August 3rd, to offer his support also.

My amendment carried in the Senate by a vote of 50 to 47 and then was knocked in the head by a parliamentary maneuver. The House, however, would have nothing to do with the Senate decision, so the whole matter went down the drain, for the time being at least. Incidentally, or otherwise, Mr. Kissinger has not communicated with me since that day.

Still, failure of the executive branch to advise me of any impending action or plans does not bother me too much, because it leaves me free to express my own views, based on what knowledge I may have, without any fear of being charged with leaking secret information.

By the end of this week the losses to the U.S. Air Force were the heaviest of the war, but the loss of prestige to President Nixon was much greater. Unless he can produce an exceptionally sound ending to the war, and do it soon, his credibility, as well as his place in history, may be severely damaged.

North Vietnam has charged that our bombings have wounded many American prisoners in the POW camps. In return the United States charges North Vietnam with violating the international rules of warfare. Hanoi has never respected either the terms of the Geneva Conference or the rules of warfare. I take with a large grain of salt their reports of American POW's wounded by American planes, although I may be mistaken. Hanoi would issue such a report to arouse American anti-war and anti-Nixon sentiment. The rules of the game would not impede them in the least.

However, the American prisoners are like money in the bank to the North Vietnamese. They are Hanoi's stock in trade for bargaining or blackmail purposes. Hanoi cannot afford to lose any of them, and the bombing raids have apparently added at least fifty more Americans to those already held. Only an uncontrollable urge for revenge could prompt them to put the POW's in a bombing area.

Millions of Americans are wondering if an uncontrollable urge for revenge prompted President Nixon to order a renewal of all-out destruction in the Hanoi and Haiphong areas. At this time I do not know what the reason may have been. All I know is that right now the people of America are aroused, and unless a satisfactory explanation is given and our involvement in Indochina is ended very soon, the effect of the renewal of all-out bombing will be too bad for our President, the Republican Party, and our country. Whatever the reason, it is a sorry Christmas present for the people of the United States of America. And unless a reasonable explanation is given, co-operation between the White House and the 93rd Congress is bound to reach a new low.

At present it is doubtful if Congress or the American people will be satisfied with whatever explanation is given them. It certainly looks as if Mr. Kissinger has been outsmarted in his efforts to deal with the North Vietnamese. The slaughter and cruelties imposed on the Catholic population of North Vietnam from 1954 to 1956, the refusal of Hanoi to let refugees even see members of the International Control Commission, which had been agreed to at the Geneva Convention, and the adamant refusal to let the International Red Cross see the POW's at any time, should have warned Mr. Kissinger not to trust Hanoi.

[Putney, Vermont]

Week ending December 30, 1972

I HAVE CHANGED my thinking as to Vietnam somewhat since last week. Then I was in a rather despondent, if not actually bellicose, mood, ready to condemn or distrust more than ever those high officials responsible for the renewal of intensive warfare and bombing in Indochina. But the more I think of that which appeared to be a horrible state of affairs and a sorry Christmas present for the people of America and all the Christian world, the more I realize that if it had to come at all, it came at the right time. The contrast between the observance of Christmas and the renewal of bloody warfare is so great that it is bound to create a deeper feeling for the ending of war than would have been produced at any other time.

¶ THE UNITED STATES of America showed itself at its best on Sunday, December 24th, when the full extent of the earthquake devastation in the country of Nicaragua began to be revealed. The thousands of people killed and thousands of homes destroyed touched the hearts of all Americans. Our government lost no time in getting hospital supplies, medicine, food, temporary housing supplies and all manner of other domestic necessities on the way to the capital, Managua. In a matter of hours after the earthquake, hundreds of Americans were on the way to give aid to this shattered city. This immediate action is characteristic of the United States. When disaster strikes anywhere in the world, we are there. It is safe to say that our country has done more to alleviate misery among the people of other nations than has the rest of the world, at least during the last thirty years.

Right now we are doing more to help the people of Bangladesh than any other group of nations combined. And this in spite of the fact that Bangladesh has called us names and is inclined to co-operate with other countries that hardly ever lose an opportunity to embarrass us or blame us for their troubles. When they needed help, however, they looked to us, and found a badly needed helping hand.

¶ TUESDAY MORNING Harry Truman died. It was not unexpected, but I hate to see him leave. The news media called all day long for my comments. His old friends and enemies alike paid him glowing tributes. Frankly, I don't like eulogies, especially on the Senate floor. Many are inspired by sheer hypocrisy or personal ambition, although many are indeed sincere. I am more than glad that Mrs. Truman insisted on a private funeral attended only by invited friends. A public funeral would have been attended by dozens of hypocritical publicity-seekers trying to show what friends they were of the late President, and trying to get photographed in the most advantageous position.

I considered Harry Truman my friend. We talked the same language and understood each other. He confided many things to me and the White House doors were always open so far as I was concerned. As President he had both courage and humility, a combination of traits not possessed by some of our high officials. He could be hard and he could be kind.

I was a member of the so-called Hoover Commission during 1947–1948 when President Truman appointed former President Hoover chairman of the commission. Herbert Hoover was a good business manager but a poor politician, and from the time he was defeated for the Presidency in 1932 had been maligned and unfairly charged with being responsible for the Depression of the Thirties. I am satisfied that, had Hoover been re-elected, the Depression would have been over long before it was finally brought to an end by World War II.

At the first meeting of our commission Mr. Hoover was a sick man, sick in body and sick in heart. Harry Truman knew this, and by his consideration for and discussions with the former President added several years to Mr. Hoover's life. He became a tremendous worker and his health improved greatly.

This is only one instance in which President Truman showed his sympathy where sympathy was needed. He did not forget his friends; nor did he forgive his enemies—at least not easily.

¶ CONTINUING THE SAD NEWS, on Tuesday Lester "Mike" Pearson died. He was Prime Minister of Canada from 1963 to 1968, and I always liked him. In his younger days he was a hockey coach, but from the time he became Prime Minister up until the time of his death his principal ambition and desire was to restore peace to the world, or to as much of it as possible, and to persuade people of different countries to get along with one another.

When I heard he was sick about the first of the month, I sent him a note of encouragement and under date of December 15th he wrote me that he was going south in hopes that his health would be improved. It did not, and now his funeral will be held in Ottawa on December 31st. President Nixon has asked L.P.A. and myself to attend the funeral along with Vice President Agnew as representatives of the White House. Of course I will go even though I don't like funerals. I expect there will be a lot of formality and a lot of people from all over the world at Mike's funeral, a sharp contrast to that given Harry Truman in Independence, Missouri, on Thursday. I shall miss these two distinguished citizens of the United States and Canada.

¶ IT SEEMS like the Christmas season brought little but bad news until the final day of the week. After stopping for one day our bombing of North Vietnam was renewed at a record pace. Protests from the public continued to increase. Nobody seems to know how many planes we lost, but we apparently did give North Vietnam a hundred more hostages to use for bargaining and blackmailing purposes. Undoubtedly we have been causing tremendous damage to both military and economic installations around Hanoi, but the damage to morale in the United States is probably even greater.

However, about ten o'clock on Saturday a ray of sunlight came through the clouds. The White House announced that the bombing of North Vietnam is stopped as of today, and will stay stopped. Low-level personnel of both North Vietnam and the United States will start discussions in Paris on Tuesday, January 2nd. On January 8th, Mr. Kissinger, Le Duc Tho and company will renew discussions at the higher level.

Who won this ten-day bombing war? This is a question which I think I can answer factually. The White House said we would continue the bombing until Hanoi agreed to renewed discussions; Hanoi said that they would not renew discussions until we stopped the bombing. Did both sides win? Not in my opinion. Both sides lost heavily, and the next meeting in Paris represents a "mutual surrender party" which ought not to have ever been necessary in the first place.

1973

Week ending January 6, 1973

BACK AGAIN IN WASHINGTON, with members of Congress in a variety of moods, some seeking revenge for the outcome of the November 7th election; some vowing to take action to placate constituents in their home states; some with eyes and minds concentrated on the 1976 election; and others, thank goodness, thinking of means to free the United States from its Asian involvement and other problems abroad while stimulating the economy and maintaining high standards of living for the people at home.

Early in the week both Republicans and Democrats held their party conferences in both Houses, with the Democrats seeking much greater Congressional control over actions of the executive branch. This was a virtual challenge for supremacy in formulating policy and carrying on the affairs of our nation, a challenge which the Republican executive branch promptly accepted.

The Republican conference was dominated by a small majority of conservatives, with all areas of the country being represented by its elected officials. The meeting was enlivened by comparatively new members of the Senate, particularly Senators Taft and Packwood, who sought an amendment to the rules so that newly elected Senators could go right to the top while the more experienced, though less politically ambitious, ones could be relegated to lower levels. Also, Senator Buckley of New York is proposing that no one over seventy could be chairman or ranking member of a committee. If applied to the Senate as a whole, such action would eliminate some of the most competent leaders of the Senate, particularly men like Senator Stennis of Mississippi. The outcome of such efforts will not be determined until next week at another meeting of the Republican conference set for Monday, the 8th.

The seniority system of choosing committee chairmen and ranking members of the Minority Party is not perfect, and indeed has been questioned almost since the legislative branch of government was established nearly two hundred years ago. In the late 1950's I was chairman of a subcommittee of Republicans appointed to see if a better method of selecting committee members and leaders could be found. We were unsuccessful in this search for an alternative insisted upon by the younger, more eager members of the party, who had not even been re-elected by their own states as yet. My subcommittee thought that any change would involve us in greater difficulties. But the main objection to permitting members old or new to gain committee posts through the elective process remains the same as it was then, and it is that the change would be dangerous—and very likely scandalous—since campaigns for committee positions would be conducted through pressure practices wherein the vested interests, so-called, and ideological organizations would exercise their full power regardless of expense to get persons they feel they could control into strategic positions in the Senatorial organization.

However, after a new member has been here long enough to be re-elected by his own state, usually his own seniority and his own experience have grown to the point where he no longer believes that overnight pre-eminence is good for the legislative branch or the country.

The Democrats, having a substantial majority in both Houses of the Congress, establish subcommittees to the extent that each new member soon finds himself a chairman with an elaborate staff and political promoters, paid for by the taxpayers, whose business it is to build up his prestige at home so that he doesn't have to worry so much about the next election. Of course the resulting host of subcommittees maintained by the expenditure of millions of dollars is not in the best interests of the country, but even this is better than having a political campaign put on for committee positions by Congressional members.

¶ ON TUESDAY the Foreign Relations committee met with twelve of the sixteen members present, an unusual number for any meeting of this committee. The Vietnam situation is causing concern to all. One or two members seemed to be thinking more in terms of condemning the Nixon Administration than of seeking practical solutions to the whole problem of our involvement. The majority of those present, however, including the chairman, Senator Fulbright, thought we should wait until after the Inaugural on January 20 before becoming actively engaged in legislative efforts to terminate our military operations in that part of the world. If we delay any active effort on our part, the Paris meetings between representatives of Hanoi and Washington would be given a chance to achieve worthwhile results, if not an actual settlement.

Should the Congress undertake to assume the prerogative which the executive branch is now exercising, and should the new Paris conference which is to begin on Monday, the 8th, turn out to be a failure, then the Congress itself might be charged with such a result. Personally I have little hope for any practical or workable decisions being reached at the meeting of Henry Kissinger and Le Duc Tho in Paris next week.

¶ No one seems to know for sure what prompted President Nixon to order massive bombing operations over North Vietnam, but the result of the bombing—aside from the heavy cost to us in loss of planes and possibly as many as one hundred more hostages to North Vietnam—has been to leave Hanoi with a decided advantage at the conference in Paris. Nearly the whole world has condemned the United States for the renewal of the President's apparent attempt to terrorize the North Vietnamese government into seeking a peace agreement which would be more to our liking than any which has so far been offered by Hanoi.

If that was the purpose of the renewed bombing, the result has been a failure, and Hanoi now appears to have the upper hand and greater support from many world powers than was the case a couple of months ago. If, as I believe will be the case, no progress is made towards reaching a settlement by January 20th, the Congress will then become active in trying to find other means to force the President to withdraw from further military participation in Indochina. In so doing, Congress will be taking a calculated risk and a very serious one, for in assuming authority over the Vietnam situation it would also be assuming responsibility for what may happen later. If the South Vietnamese, with all the assistance we have given them, can defend their country against outside aggression and terror, that is well and good. If, however, the Saigon government cannot protect itself, the Congress will be held responsible for the inevitable blood-bath which will follow. Although I am pessimistic over the situation right now, I hope that my fears are unfounded.

¶ Tuesday afternoon Agriculture Secretary Butz called me to say that the effect of decisions concerning disaster loans for farmers who suffered from last year's weather conditions, and also concerning the interest rate to be charged on loans to rural electric co-operatives in the future, has been greatly misunderstood. I think that the Administration was back-tracking and realized that its earlier announcement had been in error.

According to the Secretary, all applications for loans due to disaster conditions would be accepted and processed if such application had been made within sixty days after a disaster status had been approved for any county or area. If an application from a farmer was approved, then loans would be granted.

¶ I HAVE TAKEN THE POSITION that promises made by either the Congress or the executive branch should be kept. The situation right now indicates that Congress and the executive branch may have a violent collision not only in the field of foreign policy but in domestic areas as well, particularly over the many welfare and agriculture programs which are operating.

I can appreciate the President's desire to consolidate many of the functions of government and to hold expenditures within reasonable bounds. We have so many agencies and commissions that a great deal of the funds appropriated for them are spent for administrative costs and too small a percentage of the money appropriated actually reaches those for whom it was intended. I can also appreciate the reluctance of thousands of people now drawing good salaries as administrators of these programs to give up their positions.

As soon as Congressional committees get fully organized and the President has given his State of the Union message and sent his Budget message to the Congress, we may expect a lot of fireworks, with the result uncertain.

This situation is called "democracy at work."

¶ ON SATURDAY a Constitutional provision for operating our democracy was exposed as obsolete and requiring change. A joint session of the House and Senate met in the House to count the electoral votes for President and Vice President. As the vote of each state was opened and read by the tellers, the handful of members present engaged in conversations about almost every subject except the election of the President. It got so noisy that we could not hear the announcement of the tellers or understand what the person three feet away was saying.

The situation was indeed ridiculous, since everyone knew that President Nixon had been overwhelmingly elected by the people on November 7th. Nevertheless, although the wide margin of his election left nothing in doubt, the vote of one elector from Virginia for unknown persons for President and Vice President pointed up a real danger. Had the vote at election time been so close that a deviation of only a few Presidential electors could have changed the results, the will of the majority of the voters could have been thwarted. This situation needs correcting before another election.

146

Week ending January 13, 1973

PERHAPS I SHOULD DESCRIBE this week as a week of thickening storm clouds. While Congress has not got down to work yet and will not be considering important legislation until after the Inaugural ceremony of the 20th, there is a lot of thunder and lightning visible in the distance, and not the very far distance at that.

¶ THE REPUBLICANS finally got their Minority committee members named. In spite of the fact that there have been several hours spent in arguing the respective virtues and qualifications of freshman and senior Senators, the committee appointments wound up just about as they would have had there been no arguments at all. We are ready to have our first official meetings next week, and the need for lightning rods on the part of both the executive and legislative branches is quite apparent.

There are a lot of Presidential appointments to be considered by the committees, and there are many threats on the part of the Democrats to hold up these appointments until the President comes to heel and sends his star officials to appear on demand by committees. Some of these appointments ought to be confirmed without delay for the good of the country, but the feeling against the President is so intense that even if his nominations get out of committee, they may possibly be held up on the floor of the Senate.

In my opinion, the President has invited this situation, not only by ordering the intensive bombing of North Vietnam, and Hanoi in particular, but by arbitrarily ordering the cut-off of farm and rural programs established and appropriated for by the Congress—and, as I understand, without even notifying the heads of departments most seriously involved. Nevertheless, I feel that the first consideration of the Congress must be the welfare and security of our nation. Failing to provide for this in order to get even with the President is not justified.

¶ THE VIETNAM SITUATION is still unsettled, although there are rumors to the effect that an agreement with North Vietnam is near. I hope the rumors are true this time, but having heard similar rumors and outright predictions on the part of Executive officials for the last several months now, I am rather skeptical.

The responsibility for bringing the war to an end clearly rests on the President, and I hope that the Congress does not relieve him of this responsibility by taking it upon its own shoulders. We should insist upon his carrying out the will of the American people as expressed by their duly elected representatives. Early in the week Secretary Brezhnev of the U.S.S.R. indicated that he thought the Vietnam war was about over. I interpreted this statement to represent pressure on Hanoi to agree to a settlement without further delay.

¶ DURING THE WEEK I was visited by several members of two groups of people, one representing Presidential appointees who wondered if and when Congress might consider their nominations, and the other representing foreign countries that had problems which their ambassadors thought I might help solve. They were hoping for the impossible.

Representatives of the Saigon government indicated that they were now amply able to protect their own country if the United States would only get out and not try to dictate to their government. On the other hand, we understand that Hanoi is insistent that we enforce our power against President Thieu's government before Hanoi agrees to release the five or six hundred American prisoners of war whom they are holding as hostages. The reason for Hanoi's insistence lies in the fact that South Vietnam holds possibly as many as twenty thousand prisoners from the North and the Vietcong rebels of the South. We are in the ludicrous situation of having our ally, the South Vietnam government, asking us to go home and our enemies in Hanoi insisting that they won't let us.

I have been working this week on a statement concerning this situation, and unless there is visible progress on the path to peace, at least between ourselves and the North Vietnamese government, I shall probably make my statement to the Senate some time next week.

¶ THE PRESIDENT CONTINUES to order the cancellation of programs established by the Congress. Such action infuriates not only members of the Congress but millions of people throughout the nation who voted for the President—or rather voted against Senator McGovern. Retaliation by the Congress is inevitable, but I sincerely hope that it is selective retaliation.

Receptions and dinners are crowding in on Washington as they never did before. All this is an indication that the economy of the country is getting better. Otherwise every industry or profession and a hundred other organizations wouldn't be able to pay the costs of these Washington parties. Seemingly, the more money that people have and the higher the level of living, the more they ask for.

¶ DURING THE WEEK the President removed a considerable part of the price- and wage-control program, leaving its continuance to voluntary co-operation. He may think that this action is going to hold down inflation to a greater degree, but I don't feel that way. I am sure that prices will go higher, and as prices go higher, so will wages, salaries, and probably dividends. The standard of living is rising all over the world, and as the standard rises, so do all those factors which enter in one's personal and family life. Expansion and extension of international corporations is the order of the day. Distances have become so short and trade so well developed throughout the world that it could not be otherwise. And yet, when our industries and professions get on an international basis, problems and difficulties arise.

The Congress last year authorized setting up a committee to study this trend toward internationalizing business and industry and its effect upon the people. Senator Church is chairman of this committee, which has now requested an appropriation of $650,000 for this and another committee, headed by Senator Symington, with which to maintain a staff of thirty-one persons. I believe this amount to be excessive, but I don't know what the Senate will do about it. I am very fearful that under present political circumstances the excessive demands by Senator Church may be used largely for witch-hunting purposes to discredit the President. I don't like this situation at all, but the President himself has invited it, and there is no doubt in my mind but that the executive branch of government will also use large amounts of money unnecessarily for political purposes. These practices are not new, but at present are the worst I have ever seen them.

¶ THIS MORNING, Saturday, I received information through the press that Kissinger would be returning to Washington today, that he and Le Duc Tho both appeared to be in good humor in Paris, that Kissinger had had official photographers in to take photographs of him and all his assistants, and the assumption is that a settlement with Hanoi is imminent. I have heard the story that peace is imminent so many times over the past years that I can't help wondering whether the new "peace-around-the-corner" report is intended to keep Congress and the public more quiet until after the Inauguration next Saturday.

¶ AFTER NEXT WEEK I expect we will settle down to a spell of domestic warfare to determine whether the three branches of government established nearly two hundred years ago are still adequate for democratic operations, or whether far-reaching changes may be necessary. In the meantime, Americans continue to spend money, either borrowed or earned, in a perfectly gorgeous manner.

Week ending January 20, 1973

KISSINGER is slated to go back to Paris early next week, and there are predictions that before the end of the week some sort of arrangement, including a cease-fire, will be agreed upon.

¶ DOMESTICALLY, grants for disaster loans are beginning to be paid off and checks started being mailed from St. Louis the middle of the week. The Administration has made $350 million available for approved loans and grants.

The President's apparent plan to sharply reduce federal aid to farmers is bound to hit a snag. He seems to think that farm people would do better with less federal support and more reliance on an open market for their products. This has proven true in some instances. With beef cattle now approaching 40 cents a pound, hogs over 30 cents a pound, and grain prices going higher every day, farm income is indeed on the upgrade. What people fail to realize, however, is that much of the increase in farm income is paid for by other farmers. When the prices of grains shoot up, the Eastern dairyman is put in a bind which in some cases can prove disastrous. Agriculture always was an uncertain source of income, and in many instances a farmer is tempted to sell out to developers or other buyers rather than keep on with an uncertain future. Dairy products are beginning to be in an increasingly short supply, particularly those which are used in the manufacture of cheese and candy.

¶ EARLY IN THE WEEK I joined Senator Hubert Humphrey in introducing a bill to continue the low interest rate of 2 percent for loans to Rural Electric Association Co-operatives. With the increasing costs of borrowing money I realize this rate cannot last much longer. But so long as the federal government is expected to bail out big corporations to the tune of hundreds of millions of dollars, I feel that we are warranted in seeking continued assistance at the lower levels.

¶ THE WILD AREAS BILL which I introduced with Senators Talmadge, Sparkman, Allen, and Humphrey has come under attack, with Senator Jackson of Washington leading the opposing forces. This bill, which would set aside certain forest areas in the East, does not permit the extraction of minerals and oil from these nearly primitive areas. In my opinion this is the real reason for the opposition of the so-called vested interests. Not that the areas which we designate in the Eastern forests are rich in minerals and oil, but I think these interests fear that the precedent thus established might extend to the Western states, where fortunes have been made by extracting the natural resources. This is the same old fight that started back in the days when William Howard Taft was President and Gifford Pinchot and Secretary Ballinger engaged in a vigorous fight.

¶ THE INAUGURAL CEREMONIES went off as usual, although the cost to the taxpayer was probably higher. Policemen and plainclothesmen were in evidence everywhere, which was probably just as well since there are many people who feel that their reputation has been made and their sacred honor well preserved, if they can harass or insult the President of the United States in any way.

Vice President Agnew and President Nixon renewed the oath of office which they had taken four years before. The President made a short speech—which was satisfactory to the crowd of thousands, including those who came so late that they were unable to get to their reserved seats. The weather was raw and windy.

The President intimated that an agreement looking to our withdrawal from Indochina would likely be reached soon, and he put emphasis on his belief that the federal government was doing far too much in helping able-bodied people to live an easy life when they ought to be helping themselves. The expression of this sentiment will be much more favorably received throughout the country than would have been the case two years ago.

I hope that the President's feeling that peace in Indochina is near is well founded, and I believe it is. We have carried on this face-saving war for at least six years now, and if Dr. Kissinger can arrive at any arrangement which gets us out of the mess and saves the faces of the parties involved I will have to back away from some of my previous opinions. Next week will tell the story, and I hope it will be a story well worth reading for generations to come.

Week ending January 27, 1973

MONDAY NIGHT LYNDON JOHNSON DIED. The thirty-sixth President of the United States was a powerful, although debatable, character. As Majority leader in the Senate he was dictatorial, and influenced the votes of the Democratic members. Elected Vice President in 1960, he never seemed very close to President Kennedy and the White House. But when he became President after the death of President Kennedy in November 1963, Lyndon Johnson really came into his own. He was the President, and although he had his confidential advisers I always felt that he made his own decisions. I was at the White House frequently when some of these decisions were announced. Some of them were good and some were mistakes.

We worked together closely on all matters relating to public welfare, agriculture, and rural life in general. He was approachable, he could be called almost any time, day or night. He liked to talk over problems which concerned us all. I would describe him briefly by saying he liked to be asked but he didn't like to be told or receive advice unless he asked for it. In agricultural matters he frequently would ask for my opinion, and he was a stalwart supporter of most of the rural programs which I stood for. In the matter of the Vietnamese war we did not agree, but he did not show signs of resentment.

On Wednesday funeral services were held for President Johnson in the rotunda of the Capitol, and on Thursday services were performed again in the National City Christian Church downtown. All the pomp and ceremony which would be expected by the great State of Texas was carried out, with official dignitaries from many foreign countries present, as well as his old staff members and associates in the Congress and in government. Throughout these ceremonies his wife, Lady Bird, and his two daughters stood without showing the emotions which might be generally associated with a bereaved family.

Lady Bird Johnson is one of the strongest characters I ever knew, and it goes without saying that she must have been largely responsible for the success that Lyndon B. Johnson made of his life. I don't mean that she determined government policy or even slanted it. What I mean is that Lady Bird must have been responsible for keeping the emotions of her distinguished husband under control and extending to him the sympathy and understanding which he must have needed during the difficult periods of his life and tenure of office.

¶ MINGLED WITH THE TRAGEDY of Lyndon Johnson's departure and the frustrations of political maneuvering, the country was treated to an epoch of rejoicing. Tuesday evening President Nixon announced to the world that an agreement had been reached with all parties involved in the military conflict in Vietnam and that this agreement would be signed in Paris on Saturday, the 27th, calling for a cease-fire and a cessation of hostilities in that long-troubled part of the world.

On Wednesday morning, in company with other members of the House and the Senate, I went to the White House and listened for over two hours to a more detailed explanation of the proposed agreement given by President Nixon and Dr. Henry Kissinger. Although I had been considerably upset by the prolonging of the war in Indochina and the failure to reach some kind of a peace agreement long before, I now have to admit that the work done by the President and by Henry Kissinger and his associates appears to be a masterpiece of diplomacy.

Certainly it is a victory for us to be able to get out of our Vietnam predicament at all. The North Vietnamese claim that it is a victory for them, since they are not required to immediately withdraw some one hundred thousand troops that they are supposed to have in South Vietnam. As a matter of fact, they have always denied having any troops there at all and therefore could not withdraw non-existent personnel. The world knows better than to believe their story, but the agreement provides a face saving device for them. The South Vietnamese government can also claim victory, for the terms of the peace agreement are apparently similar to those which the Saigon government officials told me some time ago would meet their demands. As for the National Liberation Front (NLF), commonly called the Vietcong, I suppose their victory lies in the fact that during the cease-fire period they will retain the land areas which they have seized and now occupy.

So again I say that if Henry Kissinger is responsible for reaching an agreement satisfactory to all four factions, we will have to tip our hats to him.

The agreement was signed formally by all parties concerned on January 27th, and under its terms our prisoners of war now held by North Vietnam will be returned within the next sixty days. As far as possible all of our personnel missing in action will be accounted for. All our troops will be withdrawn from the South Vietnamese territory, and the cease-fire arrangements will be supervised by a commission and personnel provided by Canada, Indonesia, Poland and Hungary.

I certainly hope that this commission functions better than the International Control Commission set up by the Geneva Conference in 1954 to handle the refugee situation which existed in North Vietnam after the French had been forced to leave that country. I do believe that the new commission representing the four countries I have named will function better. It couldn't do worse, anyway.

¶ APPARENTLY THE SIGNING of the agreement has been disconcerting to some of those who had used the Vietnam war as an excuse—or a reason, they may call it—for harassing and discrediting the President of the United States to the fullest extent.

I happen to know that President Nixon has been determined to terminate our involvement in Indochina almost from the time he took office in 1969. About three months after his first Inauguration, he told me that he intended to reduce our involvement, to bring the weekly casualties down from the three hundred a week which they were running then to not over fifty a week, and to reduce the number of our military personnel in South Vietnam as fast as he could safely do so. It has taken him almost four years to accomplish his purpose, during which time he has been subjected to continuous harassment and abuse.

Some of his prominent detractors do not give up easily. Only yesterday a bill was introduced into the Senate to prohibit the President from sending any military personnel back into Indochina without the consent of the Congress. The bill does not apply to any other country, only Indochina, and its introduction at this time can mean nothing more than that some members of the Congress are telling the world that they don't believe the President of the United States intends to keep the terms of the agreement. I personally believe they are doing a disservice to our country, and that the President has no intentions of ever returning troops to that troubled area.

¶ I BELIEVE that the United States and much of the world may be entering upon a new era, an era of peace and improved welfare and economic conditions throughout the world. No one nation can guarantee this, but if the strong nations of the Earth join forces in saying that we will alleviate hardship throughout the world, that we will create a better economic understanding among the nations, and that we will do all within our power to prevent the outbreak of war in the future, then I shall feel that the years I have put in in the Senate have not been in vain and that, after all, life is worth living.

Week ending February 3, 1973

AT LAST, Senate committees have become fairly well organized and are starting on the work of the 93rd Congress. The Joint Committee on Atomic Energy is completely set up for business with all subcommittees appointed and two new subcommittees established—one on licensing and regulation, and the other an energy committee. As a matter of fact, up to now none of the subcommittees of the Joint Committee on Atomic Energy has amounted to anything more than a means to give the chairman of each some publicity to help him in his bid for re-election. None of them has ever held hearings on its own. It is possible, however, that the two new subcommittees may find some important work to do.

¶ THE COMMITTEE ON AGRICULTURE AND FORESTRY started off hearings with Secretary of Agriculture Earl Butz as first witness. Virtually every member of this committee has taken sharp issue with the President's announcement that some programs applicable to agriculture and rural life will be sharply downgraded or cancelled. I think the President is wrong in claiming authority to cancel programs authorized and financed by the Congress. He is not all wrong, however, because in many ways certain programs could be very much improved and operated more economically. I do not believe that all the positions taken by Secretary Butz are his own idea, but that he has received instructions from the White House to take positions with which he might not otherwise agree.

The agricultural interests of America have very strong grounds on which to base their claim for continuing certain government programs which have been beneficial to farmers. They point out that although agriculture accounts for only 2 percent of the budget expenditures, the Budget Bureau is now insisting that agriculture bear 12 percent of the proposed reduction in government expenditures.

Right now, I feel that Congress will enact farm legislation over the objection of the Budget Bureau, and if such legislation is vetoed, that there will be votes available in both Houses to override the President. The one alternative available to such a situation is a compromise which could result in lower costs and changing practices in some programs.

¶ THE COMMITTEE ON FOREIGN RELATIONS poses the greatest problem at the present time. This committee has a normal staff of sixteen, but actually now there are forty-two members employed by the full committee and its subcommittees. There are indications that even greater numbers may be called for during this Session. A staff of this size is completely unnecessary and should be reduced, although I doubt that it will be. The chief of the committee's permanent staff, Carl Marcy, appears to have a possessive attitude, apparently dominates nearly all the other employees, and does not take too kindly to suggestions for changes in operations of the committee of which he does not first approve. This attitude may result in a vigorous confrontation, not only with other committees of Congress and the executive branch of government, but within the Foreign Relations committee itself.

It is true that under the rules, the committee and its staff members are all supposed to be non-partisan, yet every member of the Majority Party is given a chairmanship of a subcommittee, and no committee meeting can be held until members of the Majority Party decide to hold it. This situation hardly indicates a non-partisan atmosphere.

In spite of this situation, under the pressure of Majority Leader Mansfield, the Foreign Relations committee did report out a half-dozen nominees, including Deputy Secretary of State, the U.S. Representative to the United Nations, and others. These nominees were voted on favorably by the committee on Thursday morning, and on Thursday afternoon the Senate confirmed them all. Failure to have done so would have been harmful not only to the executive branch of government but to our position in world affairs.

¶ PRESIDENT NIXON is using rather strong-arm tactics in his endeavor to maintain the strength of our nation, both politically and economically. I think he has made some mistakes, and I do not expect to support all his recommendations by any means.

There is a quite prevalent belief that to maintain our economy we must unite more closely with Western Europe and Japan. This is easier said than done because competition is still rife among nations. On the other hand there is a developing feeling that to protect our own investors we must adopt a greater degree of isolation from the world than we have had in recent years. To retreat into isolationism would be disastrous. It may be that imports may have to be more closely regulated, but this should be done prudently, and only to the extent necessary to prevent extermination of some of our industries.

¶ THE SENATE, and indeed the whole country, were shocked Tuesday night when Senator Stennis was shot by hold-up men outside his home. This is a sharp reminder that crime is far from under control in the United States. And we are all thankful that John Stennis's condition appeared to be improving at the weekend. We certainly cannot spare him for long at this time. He is one of the most loyal and broadest-minded Americans I ever knew.

Week ending February 10, 1973

THE COMMITTEE ON AGRICULTURE AND FORESTRY reported out my Wild Areas bill without dissension. This promptly brought the lumbermen into the picture in opposition to it. With the price of lumber reaching as high as $900 per thousand board feet it is understandable that they desire to preserve the option of cutting trees wherever such trees would produce marketable lumber.

I assume that the lumber industry much prefers Senator Jackson's bill, *S. 316*, which is much more liberal with the commercial interests, although they probably would prefer no legislation at all. If legislation is held necessary, however, they seem to feel that they would fare better under the Interior department and the Interior committees of the Congress than under the Forest Service and the Agriculture department.

The problems of the U.S. Forest Service are increasing as the prices of land gallop upward. Even in Vermont, land which less than a generation ago could have been bought for $5 or $10 an acre, now costs from $200 to $800 an acre, and land in strategic locations reaches a selling value as high as $5,000 an acre. Although the inflationary trend is applicable to every line of our general economy, it has outstripped itself in the field of land values.

We also have the problem of land use. Too many agencies, state and federal, are seeking control over the use of land, private as well as public. The environmentalists think they should control it. The farmers feel that they should be permitted to use their own land as they see fit. And the commercial interests—which are notable and generous contributors to political campaigns—are working pretty effectively towards retaining what influence and jurisdiction they may now possess.

¶ IT IS IN THE FIELD OF AGRICULTURE that the first confrontation between the Congress and the executive branch of government is taking place. The House voted by somewhat less than a two-thirds vote to continue the REAP [Rural Environmental Assistance Program]. The Department of Agriculture says only 20 percent of the country as a whole is making use of this program. I am sure that the Senate will follow the action of the House, and probably by more than a two-thirds vote. The President will undoubtedly veto the bill, and I doubt that the House will muster votes enough to override the veto.

The action on this program carries an importance which goes far beyond the proper use and improvement of agricultural land. It brings to the front the question as to whether the President can by stroke of the pen eliminate a program which has been authorized and financed by the Congress. This, however, is only one of the many examples which will be brought to the forefront during the term of the 93rd Congress.

¶ THE SENATE FOREIGN RELATIONS COMMITTEE this week reported

out Presidential nominees, largely for embassies in the different parts of the world. These nominees were all approved, as was Caspar Weinberger to be Secretary of Health, Education and Welfare. There were ten votes against Mr. Weinberger, who had just finished a term as Director for the Office of Management and Budget. I believe that the ten votes in opposition were largely politically motivated by those who held him responsible for cutting off funds for many projects which they felt were good vote-getting programs in their own states.

I agree that some of the programs where funds have been cut off by the executive branch were indeed good programs, and I will vote to continue some of them. But on the other hand we have altogether too many different agencies and commissions, some of them competing with each other, so that consolidation in some cases is advisable; and elimination of some others, where administrative costs have far exceeded a reasonable figure, would be desirable. I prefer, however, to take them up one by one as they come before the Congress for renewal or appropriation.

¶ THE QUESTION of staffing the Senate Committee on Foreign Relations also arose again. I thought it had quieted down until Chief of Staff Carl Marcy sent me a four-plus pages long letter which in effect disagreed with the 1970 act giving the Minority members of the committee a share in the staffing of the committee.

Carl's letter promptly brought a response from Senator Javits, who recommended a separate staff for the Minority members of the committee. Although I am entitled to select a member of the permanent staff, I have never asked to do so, hoping that the committee and its staff could be operated as non-partisan in fact as well as in theory. For many years I had little difficulty in this respect. Now, however, it appears that the Minority members of the committee must insist upon sharing in the membership of the staff, although I still believe that most of the staff members are non-partisan in their thinking. Nevertheless, it only takes one or two to upset this practice of non-partisanship, and therefore more representation by the Minority is necessary. It must be remembered, however, that partisanship does not necessarily mean lining up Republicans against Democrats, because the members of both parties on the committee are frequently divided among themselves. As one of the four members of the Personnel committee and as ranking Republican, I have concluded that, in spite of my previous reluctance, I should exercise my own authority and try to make sure that any new members on the staff are competent, fair, and not unswervingly dedicated to political desires.

On Thursday morning I spoke for fifteen minutes on the necessity for co-operative effort in the field of foreign affairs between the executive and legislative branches of government. At present the President has the whip hand. He has made his place in history already if he doesn't upset it within the next four years, while the Congress has made little progress in re-establishing its Constitutional responsibility and authority. As I said in my remarks, the Senate now spends too much time planning for the next election and too many of its members spend too much time and effort running for the Presidency. The result is that Congress is getting nowhere fast.

In my remarks as originally planned, I included one line which read, "The Senate should not be a prep school for the White House." I deleted this line; nevertheless, we have possibly a half dozen members of the Senate today who slant their work in this legislative body with a view to having the positions they take, and the speeches they make, contribute to their aspirations for higher office.

Week ending February 17, 1973

A WEEK of little accomplishment and considerable maneuvering.

On Thursday *Senate Resolution 59*, sponsored by Senator Huddleston of Kentucky, a real veteran with six weeks' tenure as a member of the Senate, was brought before the Senate for action. This Resolution would tell the Department of Agriculture to stop releasing government-owned grain for feeding purposes in disaster areas, to cease the export of grain to other countries, to stop sending government-owned grain to hungry people in other parts of the world—in effect, to disregard the programs and the rules of the game which have been laid down by the Congress itself.

It is a speculator's resolution, and the grain speculators are noted for their generosity to their friends by providing the means for getting votes at election time. This procedure is nothing new. I have been watching it ever since I came to the Senate, and I have had personal friends among many of the grain dealers of the country, although I have never accepted any of their generous offers.

The election records for 1972 show that one grain company alone, through its various offices, contributed $500,000 to candidates for the Presidency, both Republican and Democratic. No one knows how much they contributed to lesser candidates and I, for one, do not question their importance to the grain industry of the United States.

When the showdown on the floor comes, I predict that both Senators from Kentucky will vote with the dealers even though the farmers of their state would be adversely affected by the passage of this Resolution. To cover up their noble impulses, the promoters of the bill now call it a box-car bill seeking to provide greater means of transportation for the farmers, processors, and consumers of America. As a matter of fact, if this were indeed a measure relating to transportation as claimed by its proponents, it should have been referred to the Committee on Commerce, of which Senator Magnuson is chairman.

But Senator Magnuson, coming from the State of Washington where shipping interests are prominent and important, might not look kindly upon the proposal to stop the shipment of government grain to foreign countries. Furthermore, Warren Magnuson has now been a Senator for twenty-nine years and naturally wouldn't be expected to understand the situation as well as those who have now had six weeks' experience in the United States Senate. We will see what happens on Monday next week when a decision will have to be made as to whether Magnuson's committee should be relegated to the background, or whether this Resolution will be re-referred to the Committee on Commerce.

If this report sounds a bit cynical, it is simply emphasizing another human trait which I possess. But although experience in the Congress may make one more cynical, it also has a tendency to create more tolerance—a trait which is not usually too much in evidence among the freshmen members of either House.

But perhaps the main issue lying behind the Huddleston Resolution is this: If this United States Senate urges the President and the Department of Agriculture to disregard the rules and regulations which Congress has laid down and emphasized, do we then have any right to attack the President when he, on his own volition, sets aside other rules and programs established by the Congress?

Week ending February 24, 1973

ON MONDAY MORNING, Robert Rumler of the Holstein-Friesian Association came in with a major and growing problem. His association now handles the export of cattle for various breed organizations of both beef and dairy stock. Their problem right now is to get planes quickly to transport two thousand head of cattle to Iran and Hungary. Ocean shipping is out of the question for this livestock even if it were available, which it is not. Monday being a holiday for all government workers except members of Congress and their staffs, we made a date for Mr. Rumler to visit the CAB [Civil Aeronautics Board] on Tuesday. I haven't heard from him since. I assume that successful arrangements for transporting these cattle may have been made; otherwise I would have heard from him. This is only one example of a situation in which, when we don't hear from people who have come to us with problems and complaints, we assume they have acquired at least a degree of satisfaction, and we make no effort to stir them up again. They are just too numerous.

And Tuesday demonstrated just how numerous they are. First, there were thirty-five people representing the OEO [Office of Economic Opportunity], all lamenting the fact that the President, without asking the Congress, has decided to do away with this over-all organization. Plans are under way, however, for continuing a considerable part of the work which the OEO has done among the poor people of the country. I think that several of the programs initiated under the OEO, such as Head Start, Manpower Re-training, and others, ought to be continued. The type of jobs is changing so rapidly now that re-training appears to be essential to our economic requirements.

¶ THINGS REALLY GOT JAMMED UP on Wednesday. I had to leave one committee meeting before 10:00 A.M. to attend an open meeting of the Foreign Relations committee where Secretary of State Rogers was testifying on the general field of world affairs, with particular reference to Southeast Asia. Because of the Foreign Relations hearing, I missed an executive meeting of the Joint Committee on Atomic Energy and also an executive meeting of the Committee on Agriculture and Forestry. This, however, is not unusual when one has two or three committee meetings at the same time. It is possible to get recorded as present at all of them by simply sticking one's head in the door and asking to be recorded present. This may not be good legislating, but some of my colleagues consider it to be good politics, and they are probably right.

Wednesday afternoon Senator Hugh Scott had five Russian publishers in his office and invited some of us to meet with them. It is not generally known that Russia is one of the great publishing nations of the world, although I believe most of their production is in paperback form. The publishers assured us that they reprint and sell a tremendous number of American novels, and that the old novels written by Jack London years ago are still immensely popular in Russia. This is only one instance of where co-operation in fields of human interest is being promoted between the U.S. and the U.S.S.R. Of course still greater co-operation is expected in the field of space exploration.

To wind up Wednesday, L.P.A. and I attended a reception at Blair House hosted by Secretary of Agriculture and Mrs. Butz. Secretary of the Treasury Shultz was there, as were other members of the Cabinet and righthand men of the President, and Arthur Burns, Director of the Federal Reserve Bank. It was plainly evident to me that differences of opinion exist within the President's own official family and that all is not sweetness and light.

¶ SECRETARY BUTZ has succeeded in raising the price of farm commodities to almost record proportions and is consequently a prime target for the champions of the consumer, many of them self-appointed.

On Monday the Senate acted on a Resolution which would have stopped the sale of government-owned grains in an effort to raise prices. Fortunately the proposed moratorium on the sales was not accepted by the Senate, but prices are still going up due to the fact that all over the world there is a great demand for American food products. When it was announced on Thursday that Mainland China and the United States had agreed to establish formal representation in each other's country, another incentive to raise prices came into the picture because the 800 million people living in China are bound to have a great effect upon world economy, once trading with that country becomes established in far greater volume than it is now. Who would have thought a few years ago that the time would come when the United States would be undertaking to keep peace between the two powerful nations of Russia and China—and yet that is what we are doing and are making ground in that respect.

¶ AFTER TWO OR THREE EIGHTEEN-HOUR DAYS I didn't feel particularly like going out Thursday night and therefore passed up an invitation for a reception at the White House which was called "Peace with Honor." This reception is one of several which will undoubtedly be held and to which all members of Congress will ultimately be invited. I call these "computer parties." Many of my colleagues, particularly newcomers, feel highly honored or neglected when they are or are not invited to one of these big receptions.

¶ So, it was a busy week, too busy in fact—and I wound up Saturday by dictating a good part of the forenoon and attending a dinner for

John Volpe, newly appointed Ambassador to Italy, at the Italian Embassy in the evening. Since John Volpe is a "paisano" of L.P.A., attendance at this dinner was a must. Thirty-six persons sat down to dinner and we had a good time.

Week ending March 3, 1973

STATES AND COMMUNITIES are pretty flustered over how to make the best use of the revenue-sharing funds. Some communities put part or all of it in a savings bank and draw interest. Some thought they could use it to pay off old debts, but were advised that no revenue-sharing money may be used to pay indebtedness incurred before 1972. Inasmuch as an equal amount of federal money will be received for the year 1973, some communities, and I presume some states, will make plans for spending two years' revenue-sharing money rather than just the amount received for the year 1972.

I would not be a bit surprised if there was occasionally a community or a state which would think it smart to obligate the revenue-sharing funds for the next five years, after which the program will theoretically expire. However, it is a safe bet that at the end of five years, instead of giving up the revenue-sharing program, the states and communities will all ask for more and probably get it. It would have been better had the Congress in passing the law designated those areas in which these federal contributions could be expended.

The President's proposal to put more responsibility and some authority back in the hands of the states and communities has created a situation which understandably will not be straightened out for some time to come. His proposals will result in many of the "do-good" programs having more resources than they ever had before. Theoretically, those local programs which are complaining bitterly about a cut-off of funds could get the needed money from the state's revenue-sharing fund, provided of course that the governor and the state legislature had not already promised it for something else. The chaotic conditions which now exist are at least forcing more people to give consideration to the workings of government at all levels than they would have to do if Uncle Sam furnished the whole amount and directed all expenditures.

¶ THE AGRICULTURE COMMITTEES in the Senate and House are continually holding hearings looking to the re-enactment of agricultural programs due to expire this year. The self-appointed champions of the consumer—some self-appointed at very good salaries—are constantly pointing the finger of shame at what they call the "greedy farmers."

The fact remains, however, that the percentage of the average family's total income spent for food these days is probably the lowest in history. But, believe it or not, the cost of eating out in restaurants, which has doubled or trebled—or even more in some instances—is charged up to the cost of food. And a lot of people don't seem to realize that the cost of food stamps for needy people, breakfasts and lunches for school children and needy youngsters, and food contributions to avert famine in foreign countries are all charged up to the "greedy farmer." Nor does the hardheaded businessman who thinks that our balance of trade with other countries should be favorable to the United States, realize that if it were not for the exports of farm commodities for cash, our balance of trade with foreign countries would be little short of demoralizing. Two years ago we exported about $7 billion worth of farm commodities. It is estimated that our exports may reach $11 billion this year.

¶ IN THE LATEST INDIAN UPRISING out in the Black Hills of South Dakota two hundred militants took about a dozen hostages and insisted that the Foreign Relations committee review their treaties with the federal government running back for 150 years or more. Apparently the Indians were about evenly divided among themselves on this question. There is no doubt in my mind but what the Indians got rooked plenty in the old days, but they comprise a pretty small percentage of our total population, and the prospects for recovering all the land and property which once was theirs are pretty slim.

During 1947 and 1948 when I was chairman of what is now called the Government Operations committee, we found that a lot was going on in the Bureau of Indian Affairs which was not very commendatory to our government. There was too much job-making for not-very-well-qualified officials and too little consideration being given to the claims of the Indians at that time.

Anyway, the hostages in the Black Hills were released, and the situation may die down—or it may flare up again. It so happens that Senator McGovern of South Dakota is chairman of the Subcommittee on Indian Affairs of the Interior committee, a subcommittee which had not shown much interest in the protests of the Indian. Maybe the situation was embarrassing to him and maybe he took it lightly, but I seriously doubt that he gained much in political stature by his attitude. Just another case of giving every member of the Majority Party in the Senate the chairmanship of a subcommittee for the primary purpose of building up his own ego and providing an air of national importance when he comes up for re-election.

¶ OVER IN PARIS the meeting of the nations concerned with ending the conflict and improving the economy of Indochina went on. On Tuesday, Hanoi flared up, saying they couldn't go on with the discussions and wouldn't release any more American prisoners of war until certain demands were met. There isn't the slightest doubt in my mind that the South Vietnamese, the North Vietnamese, and the Vietcong are all violating the terms of the cease-fire. There may be a difference of degree in their operations, but I believe they are all sinners.

The action of the Hanoi delegates was, in my opinion, an effort to get the United States to agree to a better deal, but the actual result was to scare much of the world into believing that the cease-fire would be called off and the war renewed. By Thursday, Hanoi had backed down and promised to continue releasing American prisoners until they would all be out by the 27th of March. I strongly suspect that Russia took the North Vietnamese representatives by the neck and told them to behave themselves or else.

The new agreement, or "accord," was signed by the delegates of all countries represented in Paris on Friday. No one expects that the agreements reached will be carefully observed by the North Vietnamese signatories, but the situation may be better—and probably will be better—than would have been the case had no effort been made to improve the situation by endorsing the cease-fire agreement.

One matter which was undoubtedly considered seriously in Paris and which has created quite a little stir in the United States, particularly in Congress, was President Nixon's proposal to contribute materially to the reconstruction of facilities in North Vietnam that had been destroyed by our bombing of that country. Some of the sharpest-beaked hawks took the position that we shouldn't spend a nickel there until they had been beaten into the ground and begged for mercy. The fact that such action on our part would have undoubtedly precipitated another world war doesn't seem to bother them in the least.

Then there are the softest-cooing doves, some of whom took the opposite view. But many of these people for many years have been strong supporters of Hanoi, and apparently anti–United States.

I certainly hope that neither of these extreme views prevails, and I don't believe either will. I spoke on this subject on Tuesday and have had surprisingly few protests so far for my endorsement of what I believe to be President Nixon's plans for the Indochina area. Hanoi dislikes China. Hanoi dislikes Japan. Hanoi, I believe, distrusts Russia, and Hanoi would prefer to have the United States alone helping them to reconstruct their facilities and rebuild the economy which they have lost through many years of warfare. Up until 1961 Hanoi was usually on our side in many international disagreements.

I think it is generally agreed upon by the big countries of the world that the United States should by all means help in North Vietnam in order to prevent the start of another war which might assume greater proportions than the one in which we have been involved for the last twelve years. I expect that Hanoi will say the United States is making reparations for the damage we have caused. The fact is, though, that this country could have reduced Hanoi to rubble at almost any time, but did not do so since such action would most likely have brought other countries into the fray and created an untold disaster for the world.

President Nixon stated on Friday that he would not advocate taking any funds necessary to restore the economy of North Vietnam from those necessary to maintaining all worthwhile domestic programs. I am sure he will not ask for a crash program. I believe that any reconstruction program necessitating our presence in North Vietnam must be continued for many years if we are to achieve the purpose of preventing another war. As far as the rest of Indochina is concerned we could well handle that situation through a consortium or multilateral effort, since many other countries would be willing to contribute for this purpose.

No one can say for a certainty whether this plan that I believe to be the President's will accomplish its purpose or not, but right now it seems to be far preferable to any alternative. I doubt that the President could get the majority support of the Congress for helping restore North Vietnam to the list of approved and accredited nations, but by the time the purpose of his position has been explained and is understood, I think that the Congress will co-operate with him.

Week ending March 10, 1973

As THE WAR IN INDOCHINA died down close to the zero mark, the war in Washington, D.C., kept merrily on, with the White House and Congress continuing to charge each other with full-scale rascality while each laid claim to holiness and credit for the improved economy and better living throughout the United States and the world.

¶ IN SOME RESPECTS hypocrisy was king. This was evidenced in the Senate by a proposal to open to the public the executive meetings of all committees, unless the majority of the committee members (after sitting down to consider and vote on proposed legislation on which public hearings had been held) decided to throw the public audience out into the street.

I would like to see this practice tried, even though I voted against the proposal. I will guarantee that the first to squawk under such a rule would be many of those who voted to approve it. I can just see an open meeting with the members of a committee voting under the watchful eye of the vested interests or of their chief campaign contributors. The pious souls who promoted this ill-fated proposition assumed that only good people would attend the open executive sessions of each committee. This is not the way Washington works, however.

We do have a rule now that executive meetings may be thrown open to the public by a majority vote of the committee members. Also—and I think this is important—the way each member voted on reporting a bill, or on amendments to that bill, is promptly made public. If the bill is important a host of cameras and newsmen are usually waiting outside the committee room door all ready to spread the glad or bad tidings to the public.

The whole open-sessions proposal was simply an attempt to make the public believe that its advocates were chock-full of righteousness.

¶ THE SENATE AGRICULTURE COMMITTEE was busy most of the week holding hearings in preparation to reporting an extension of what, for years, has been known as the Farm Program. All witnesses quite understandably wanted to continue all phases of the farm program which benefited them or the people whom they represented.

The White House, however, having announced the discontinuance of certain agricultural programs that are popular among the rural residents of the United States, found itself to be the target of a widespread uproar which could not be ignored. It is almost certain that the Congress would vote overwhelmingly to continue or re-instate these programs, and there is a strong possibility that, should the President carry out his promise to veto such legislation, his veto would be overridden. Members of Congress naturally want to take the credit for continuing or restoring many popular programs, while the White House—with an eye to some objective which I am not quite sure of yet—wants the people to believe that only the President and the executive branch can be relied on to really serve the taxpayer, the consumer, the poverty-stricken, and the upper levels of society.

Since it is certain that the President will veto many bills which Congress is determined to enact, legislative strategy calls for passage of the most popular programs first. Among these bits of choice legislation is a proposal already passed by the House by a wide margin to restore the grants for rural water and waste-disposal developments, which the President has arbitrarily suspended. This program is one which I sponsored in 1965 and in which I was joined by 92 of my colleagues, and it has proven to be extremely popular and helpful to rural America. If the President can be forced to veto this legislation, there is no question but what he would be overwhelmingly overridden by both Houses of the Congress. Theoretically, such action would then make it easier to override later vetoes, although I am not sure this would be the effect.

The President is not wrong in all his proposed cut-backs, though. His objective appears to be to restore more responsibility and authority to states and local communities.

However, should any of his proposals result in abandonment of worthwhile local projects, he can always make a recovery. He is quite astute politically, and when he finds himself on a bad spot because of some improvident decision, he can say that he never intended to do that unpopular thing, but instead simply meant to transfer its functions to another agency of government where benefits may be even greater, and cost less, than under the present program.

¶ THE JOINT COMMITTEE ON ATOMIC ENERGY held hearings during the week relative to the means of meeting our rapidly increasing demand for energy. What we are doing in this field also concerns other countries and, for the first time, representatives of Japan and Sweden testified before the committee. The rest of the world is intensely interested in the development of nuclear energy, and so are the principal rivals of this source of power, the oil and coal interests.

The world is getting very small, and hardly any nation can live by itself much longer. The upshot of higher living standards throughout most of the world has been the creation of problems which cannot affect one country alone or even one group of countries. We have become tremendously dependent on one another. More co-operation is badly needed, and yet the competitive spirit is stronger than ever. In some countries reciprocity is almost a bad word. Western Europe is highly dependent on America, and yet some of the countries of Western Europe lose no opportunity to squeeze the last penny of benefits from us without giving much in return, and what little they do give is given grudgingly.

Oh well, I suppose we can't blame people or governments of other nations for doing what we try to do among ourselves here at home. But with nearly 70 percent of the people of the world not yet living decently or having enough of the right food to eat, and with the means for destroying civilization rapidly increasing, it is more essential than ever that we sit up and take notice.

Week ending March 17, 1973

CONTINUED POLITICAL MANEUVERING made this week not at all inspiring.

The President has served notice on the Congress that he has no intention of signing many bills which Congress expects to pass. He is pretty insistent that the total expenditures of government do not exceed $250 billion for the year, and apparently most members of Congress are willing to co-operate with him on this limitation, provided that no reductions are made in the programs which are of particular interest to them and to their states.

On Thursday the Republican Policy Committee of the Senate, of which I am a member, considered a proposed Resolution expressing the intent of the Republicans in the Senate to support any vetoes necessary to hold the total expenditures of government to the line. This proposal will be submitted to the full Republican Conference next week, and considerable debate may result, for many Republican members of the Senate can say, "I will support the vetoes that don't affect my position adversely, but I will vote to override those which might put my re-election in jeopardy."

Under an interpretation of this sort any member can vote to override the President's first six vetoes, but vote to sustain others. Considering the makeup and diversified interests of this country this expression of determination to sustain the President doesn't mean much. If it were intended to be binding, as some of the most conservative members would like, the Republican Party in the Senate would promptly become fragmented. No member who seeks re-election is going to jeopardize his own prospects by voting in a manner calculated to please the White House but offend his constituents at home. As a matter of fact, the policy of a good many Democrats and a few Republicans seems to be to disparage the President at every turn and on any excuse, whereas the White House policy seems to be to discredit the Congress and expose its inadequacy and unfitness to the world. Not a good way to run a government.

¶ A REAL REFRESHING NOTE to an otherwise depressing week was a visit to the Foreign Relations committee by Secretary of State Rogers and three of his principal aides, William Porter, Marshall Green and Joseph Sisco. These men gave the committee members an excellent briefing on what was happening in their fields of responsibility. Joe Sisco, who is one of the State department's best workers, told us of the problems, the progress, and the general situation in the Middle East, including how it affects Arabs, Jews and Pakistanis. Progress toward international harmony is slow, but I think there has been some gain in restoring order and a little better understanding between the Arabs and the Jews, although it is not particularly noticeable yet. Here again we have the same old problem of face-saving, which seems as important to nations as it is to individuals. I am sure both sides want to get things straightened out so that progress can be made in the whole area, economically and culturally.

The situation gets complicated, however, by certain members of Congress who never lose an opportunity to launch an attack on the Soviet Union. Although a cease-fire has been agreed to in Indochina, there are those who still persist in keeping things stirred up in the Middle East. Senator Scoop Jackson got about seventy of his colleagues to join in a Resolution which would sharply restrict trade with Russia, just as a better understanding between Russia and the United States is developing and a more tolerant attitude toward the Jews by the U.S.S.R. is beginning to appear. Ostensibly, my Senatorial colleagues condemn Russia for charging an excessive exit fee for Jews who wish to leave the Soviet Union, but Russia permitted over thirty thousand Jews to leave last year, a figure many times the number that used to be permitted to leave annually. And the amount of tolerance is increasing every year.

Frankly, I believe that the leaders of this move to incite more trouble and possibly war in the Middle East, which would involve both Russia and the United States, are prompted by two principal motives. First, as leaders of what some folks might call the "War Party" in the United States, they were defeated in their efforts to keep the conflict in Indochina continuing at high speed until a military victory was won. Their position on Indochina, of course, would have meant a lot more business to the manufacturers of war matériel in the United States. The second reason lies in the fact that if Russia could be taunted or persuaded to give more aid to the Arabs and more trouble to Israel, then these stalwart champions, several of whom have high political ambitions, could rush to the aid of Israel, competing with each other to see who could offer the most, militarily and otherwise, in support of that small independent country.

Why are they so devoted to Israel? In my opinion it is because the Jewish people in America are among this country's most spectacular campaign fund-raisers and staunchest political workers, and certainly could be expected to be most generous in their contributions of support to those who promised the most American assistance to their brethren in the Middle East. I think my ambitious colleagues are making a mistake. Mrs. Meir and other top officials know the difference between real friends and allies and those who are making loud noises and promises for the purpose of getting support for the next election campaign.

¶ AT THE MEETING with the Secretary of State and his aides, Marshall Green, who has been nominated to be our next Ambassador to Australia, covered the situation in Southeast Asia pretty thoroughly. I consider him one of the most capable officials of the whole State department. And then William Porter told us about the prospects for progress in improving U.S.–Chinese relations. While he was speaking, the White House announced that David Bruce, who has been our Ambassador to Britain, France and Germany in the past and is now seventy-five years old, was to be our first representative to China. Unfortunately when this information was released to the public and to the world, I am sure it was not given to the topflight officials of the State department or even to members of the White House staff. It is episodes like this that give credence to what I believe is the ill-founded report that the President seeks to establish a one-man government, or almost a one-man government, in this country. The situation between the executive and legislative branches of government is bad, to say the least. I feel that the Congress is in a more compromising mood than the White House, and I recently told the Republican Policy Committee members at their meeting that instead of trying to ride the Democrats, who have a substantial majority of the Senate anyway, we ought to be trying to convince the White House and the President that the future welfare of this country depends upon at least a reasonable degree of co-operation between our two branches of government.

I don't blame the President for being sore about the things that members of Congress say and sometimes do to the executive branch, but neither do I hold him blameless in his apparent unwillingness even to consider programs which the Congress deems essential to our national welfare.

Week ending March 24, 1973

A WEEK in which a lot of news was devoted to the ITT's [International Telephone & Telegraph Corporation] efforts to influence the Chilean election, and to the bugging of the Democratic headquarters at the Watergate last summer. Our constituency so far shows not the slightest interest in either of these matters, leaving any demonstration of interest to the candidates for re-election or for election to higher office. What our constituency *is* still writing about and talking about is the termination or shifting of federal programs related to health, education and welfare.

The press and the self-appointed champions of the consumer are still concentrating heavily upon the price of food, especially meat, and a few have written in inquiring as to what makes the price high and what can be done about it. If these champions of the consumer would stop going out to exotic and exclusive restaurants for meals costing anywhere from ten to twenty dollars, that would help some. People have more money to spend than they used to have, and they spend it. And more people who used to be called housewives now have jobs and earn money which they can spend to buy more consumer goods, including foods. Another reason for increased prices, and for shortages of somewhat higher-priced foods like the more costly meats, is that they are in greater demand, not only in the United States but all over the world. Countries that didn't used to eat meat at all, like India and parts of the Middle East, now consume beef or pork products.

When people buy all they want and have the money to pay for it, as so many do have, the supply is not equal to the demand. Our exports of food have increased tremendously and show no signs of letting up. Our federal contributions for Food Stamps and such recent programs as Child Nutrition and Care for the Aged have undoubtedly contributed to the higher prices and shortages of some foods that used to be in plentiful supply. The Food for Peace program provides large quantities of food from the United States to those countries where there are still a lot of hungry people. It is estimated that only about two-thirds of the world has enough of the right kind of foods to eat these days.

Figures recently released and printed in *The New York Times* indicate that in the last twenty-five years the cost of food has increased 20 percent, and other living costs have increased 80 percent, while wages and salaries have increased 200 percent. I think these figures alone explain why certain foods are in short supply today and the price of choice items is very high. I am advised that many customers of the chain stores, fearing a further increase in prices or actual shortages, are buying food in large amounts and storing it away for future use. This has its effect on the whole situation.

It has been suggested that price controls be slapped on farm production. This would be a serious mistake, since it could actually reduce the production of meats, and other countries would likely pay a higher price than the limit set for a commodity here in the United States. We already have had the experience of other countries bidding so high for finished lumber or even logs that the cost of materials for building a house has gone up drastically in a short time. If we want to get adequate supplies we have to have an increase in production, not only in the United States but in the world.

Week ending March 31, 1973

I WISH THE PRESIDENT would cut out challenging the Congress and asking the public to support him and oppose the Congress. I know that Congress reciprocates in kind, but all this warfare going on is no substitute for attending to the business of the nation and considering proposed legislation with a maximum of concern and a minimum of partisan ambitions.

The President announced price controls on meat, which in my book was simply a sop to some of the labor leaders who supported him in the last election.

¶ ANOTHER MATTER of partisan interest has been the Democrats' continuing to make hay with the Watergate episode. Apparently the Republican bigwigs never heard of a counterattack: otherwise they could certainly come back and accuse Democrats, some of them pretty well known, of breaking into Republican offices previous to the election of last fall. The White House crew has acted very stupidly, politically speaking, in resisting the demand of Senator Ervin's committee to testify on the subject like other people who would be called upon to testify. The White House should be demanding an opportunity to testify before this committee in order to clear up the situation and exonerate the Administration if, as it claims, it is not guilty.

Unless the bunch at 1600 Pennsylvania Avenue shows more sense pretty soon, a lot of Republican candidates are going to be in very severe difficulties for a good many years to come. It is true the public is showing comparatively little interest in the Watergate affair at present, any more than it is in the alleged efforts of the ITT to interfere in the politics of Chile. But what the Democrats are doing is building up a record with which to tarnish the Republican Party for a generation or more to come. Even the old-line Republicans in the Senate are becoming aware of this situation, and are applying whatever strength they have on the White House to come clean and act as other people would be expected to act. So far, no success. The President keeps aloof at least publicly, apparently having the idea that his own place in history has been secured by bringing peace to the world during his occupancy of the White House. Apparently he isn't worried too much about the success of the party, or the lack of it, after he leaves office.

¶ HOWEVER, his place in history may not be quite as secure as it appears, since he is continuing to authorize heavy bombing in Cambodia after he assured the country two years ago that bombing in Cambodia would be continued only to the extent necessary to protect the American military in South Vietnam. Now the American military in South Vietnam has all been legally withdrawn, but bombing in Cambodia continues. Why does it go on? Secretary of Defense Elliot Richardson says it is to keep the communists from taking over the country, yet he and the White House seem as strongly opposed to the return of Prince Sihanouk to Cambodia as they are to communist control. But I heard Prince Sihanouk, then Prime Minister of Cambodia, give a very strong anti-communist lecture and am satisfied that, had he remained in control, he would have had no intentions of converting Cambodia into a communist nation.

Week ending April 7, 1973

No WEEK PASSES that I do not receive visitors, particularly official representatives, from other parts of the world. Wednesday evening about twenty-five members of the Canadian Parliament came to town for the annual interparliamentary visit with members of the United States Congress. At the opening of the session I told the group that it was only our minor problems that we could disagree about, because all our major problems, particularly our dealings with the rest of the world, are mutual. I think the interparliamentary meeting was very successful this year. The United States is indeed lucky that we have Canada for a neighbor. Of course we compete with Canadians, but we also have the same competition between different states of our own country. Competition, if fairly conducted, is good for us all because it usually produces progress.

¶ LATE THURSDAY AFTERNOON, President Thieu of South Vietnam and some of his top officials came to the Capitol to meet members of the Senate. I have known some of the top Vietnamese officials for a good many years and they have at times been quite helpful in supplying me with information as to their status in the Indochina situation. They declare now that they will not ask us for military support in the future, although they do want economic assistance for some time to come. As far as that goes, most every other country in the world, large and small, wants us to give them economic assistance in one way or another

Week ending April 14, 1973

ON MONDAY AFTERNOON I had a meeting of the Subcommittee on Public Works Appropriations for Nuclear Development. I stayed in the meeting for about an hour, then decided that the best thing I could do for my country was to get a haircut, which I proceeded to do.

While I was getting the haircut, a call from my office reminded me that Senator Sparkman was giving a coffee hour for the Spanish Foreign Minister, Lopez Bravo. I went to the Foreign Relations committee room to help entertain Señor Bravo, but no other member, not even Senator Sparkman, was there. A member of the staff had taken our Spanish visitor to see some other parts of the Capitol, particularly the Senate Chamber, where no one was present since the Senate was not in session. After a while they returned and the chairman of our committee, Senator Fulbright, also appeared. He very promptly started a rather animated discussion—or, it seemed to me, a monologue—with Minister Lopez Bravo, which I listened to for about a half hour; then a call from my office reminded me that I had a four o'clock appointment with folks from home who were particularly interested in the affairs of Honduras, since Honduras was a country which the people of Vermont had set out to help some years ago.

People of about forty five states have dedicated themselves to assisting other people in the Western Hemisphere, and Vermont chose to "adopt" Honduras. The story I got was that Honduras is in rather desperate shape now and suffering from an acute shortage of food.

What my Vermont visitor wanted was a special million-dollar appropriation to help the people down there, and he wanted it outside the regular AID program. I don't know as yet what the United States will do for Honduras, because we don't even know what our regular AID program will be. It will be controversial and possibly long delayed, since the Administration wants to get military aid out of the hands of the Foreign Relations committee, where the majority of the members are opposed to military aid in general.

¶ ON TUESDAY I was invited with eight other Senators and nine members of the House to meet with the President at the White House at 8:30 A.M. for a discussion of a new trade bill for which the President proposes to request Congressional approval. There is no question that legislation relative to trade with other countries is essential, but viewpoints on the subject range all the way from shutting the gates of America to imports from other parts of the world to throwing the gates wide open and letting human nature take its course.

¶ ON WEDNESDAY I had a variety of committee meetings, which I had to leave several times to meet visitors who had been appointed to office by President Nixon and who wanted to impress me with their talents and the need for early confirmation. Hardly a day goes by but what somebody appointed to a major office by President Nixon shows up at my office hoping that I can smooth his path to confirmation by the Senate.

¶ ON THURSDAY the Senate Foreign Relations committee acted with a high degree of unanimity. The National Geographic Society wanted to take a picture of the full committee to be included in a book titled *We, The People,* which is sold by the tens of thousands to visitors to the Capitol. Sure enough, at ten o'clock sharp, sixteen of the seventeen members of the Senate Foreign Relations committee, which usually exhibits a high degree of partisanship on any pretext, showed up for the picture. Senator McGovern was the last to arrive, but he made it and sat alongside his erstwhile rivals for the Democratic nomination for the Presidency last year, Senators Muskie and Humphrey.

At 10:25 the cameras left the room, and then the lone absentee, Senator Case, finally showed up. But he won't be left out of the picture, because a photograph of him seated in the vacant chair will be fitted to size and stripped in to the group picture.

¶ FRIDAY SAW more committee meetings, more visitors to the office, and a luncheon given for several Japanese governors who were making an annual visit to the United States. Only former U.S. governors, including all those who had been or are now members of the Senate, were invited.

I stayed at the luncheon as long as I could and then was called to the TV recording room by the National Broadcasting Company to make some remarks about the White House attitude on the Watergate affair. The only reason I was called was that I had made a casual remark the day before to the effect that if I were a White House employee I would get up to the Capitol and pound on the door until they let me come in and testify to my innocence. It is such casual remarks that get picked up and make news, so I had to go on TV and explain why I said what I did. I also stated to my interviewer that President Nixon might have something up his sleeve which would kick back on his accusers, since Richard Nixon is not exactly an amateur politician. I can't guess what it might be, however, and don't even try to.

Anyway, I paid my respects to the Japanese governors, and late in the day L.P.A. and I went down to the White House to pay our respects to the Foreign Ministers of American Republics to the OAS [Organization of American States] General Assembly.

When we came out, not having had enough foreign relations for the day, we went to the National Gallery of Art to view a display of Russian paintings. The exhibition of these paintings, I understand, was made possible by Armand Hammer [president, Occidental Petroleum Company], who the day before had announced a contract between his company and the Soviet Union amounting to several billion dollars. Armand has always had a soft spot in his heart for Russia, since it was the Soviets who helped him to make his first million through the manufacture of lead pencils.

¶ I SPENT MOST OF SATURDAY MORNING on dictation, half of which should have been done a week ago, and on Saturday night went to the White House correspondents' annual dinner for the President, where everything was normal and the annual ritual was well performed.

Sunday looks like an open day right now, but in this business you never can tell. For next week all I can see on my book are more committee meetings, more foreign visitors, more constituents with complaints or special requests. But also I should mention one other thing. Every day we get letters from folks thanking us for something we have done to make their life a little easier or more worthwhile, and these letters help make this job more tolerable.

Two weeks ending April 28, 1973

TWO WEEKS HAVE NOW GONE BY, two weeks which many people would like to forget.

During the week ending April 21st, with the Senate tied up by Senator McGee's Voter Registration bill, the most interesting and exciting event was the meeting called for the Congressional leadership at the White House on Wednesday, the 18th, for a review of plans to prevent a future energy crisis in the United States. The President assured us that there is no energy shortage now, though unless we plan for the future there could be one which would have a very serious effect upon our nation, especially upon our economy.

Independent oil and gas dealers, including some from New England, feel there is a gas and oil crisis right now. Personally, I think there is a gasoline war on, with the big dealers considering this to be a good time to put the independents out of business. As far as the consumer or user is concerned, the prices of energy, oil, gas and coal are on the way up the ladder at an unhealthy and possibly dangerous rate. I believe the President is right when he now says that the United States should be more self-sufficient as far as energy is concerned and less dependent upon other countries.

The consumption of gas and electricity and petroleum products is growing altogether too fast for our national welfare. People watching the rapid increase of traffic upon our highways believe that the automobile is the greatest consumer of gasoline. The fact is, however, that for years American agriculture has been the biggest user of petroleum fuels; and will continue to be, since the food supply of this country—and of much of the world, for that matter—depends upon the American farmer and processors of farm products.

¶ AFTER THE MEETING on energy a smaller number of members from the House and Senate left the Cabinet Room of the White House to meet with the President and Dr. Kissinger in a smaller room where another subject, which could have a bearing upon our energy requirements, was discussed. Within the last year the Soviet Union has developed into one of the most important customers of such American goods as machine tools and other equipment, and of American farm products, primarily grain. It seems that Russia had a bad crop year and the Russian people appear to be becoming more restive and demanding of their government, particularly for an adequate supply of higher-grade foods. They are no longer happy with the diet of cabbage, potatoes, and rye, but want foods like meat, as we have in this country.

Because of Russian purchases, the unwieldy surpluses of grain in America are dwindling until, though they have not reached the vanishing point, they cannot be used to depress the market price for United States farm products. A year ago American grain producers were in pretty bad shape, but prices have now increased so much that the producers can foresee a prosperous period ahead for several years. In America our machine-tool and other factories are now stacked with orders which promise to keep the industry busy for at least another three years, provided that business with the rest of the world—primarily Russia, and in the future, China—can be maintained or expanded. To insure a continuation and expansion of exports our country has what is called the Most Favored Nation Act, which permits us to extend credit for a longer period of time than is now permitted on sales to countries with which we have had difficulties in the past.

Under our present laws Russia cannot receive credit for more than three years. I understand that Russia is asking for ten years' credit, the same as we allow to many other countries of the world, including some of Russia's neighbors. To give Russia similar extended credit, it will be necessary to include the U.S.S.R. under the Most Favored Nation Act. The President has requested such legislation from the Congress, but is encountering opposition at present from a majority of the members of both Houses. They would block the extension of most-favored-nation status to Russia until Russia permits all Jews living in the Soviet Union to emigrate without paying what is considered in many cases to be an excessive price for permission to leave. Enactment of any such Resolutions in Congress would, as the President put it, not only stop the development of trade in that area, but also would undoubtedly force Secretary Brezhnev to cancel his proposed goodwill visit to Washington, scheduled later this summer. In addition, the President was emphatically opposed to any action which might result in a renewal of the "cold war" with Russia. Any such renewal, instead of liberalizing the restrictions on emigration from the U.S.S.R. to Israel or any other country, would undoubtedly cause Russia to shut down on emigration or make the terms more restrictive than ever. A letter was read from the Soviet government to our government assuring us that the restrictions against emigration of Jews are being removed and will continue to be removed. In fact Jews are now permitted to leave Russia at the rate of twenty-five hundred per month and, according to the Russians, without restriction or payment of high costs.

Senator Jackson, who was present, disagreed with the President and insisted that we should not grant Russia most-favored-nation privileges. The session got very hot and, sad to say, I participated in raising the heat. Senators Javits and Ribicoff, both of whom are Jews, were present at the meeting but had little to say except for Senator Javits's proposal for us to "think it over a while" before reaching a decision—which, under the circumstances, was the best thing to do. I am sure that many members of both the Senate and House who co-sponsored the anti-Soviet Resolutions do not want them brought up for action and certainly do not want them passed.

There is a feeling that renewal of the "cold war" could lead to a hot war involving the use of nuclear weapons, which would result in the virtual extermination of hundreds of millions of people, including a good share of those living in the Middle East. Even if the world did not resort to a nuclear war, a renewal of the "cold war" could be disastrous to the United States. The meeting in the Cabinet Room earlier related to the need for better sources of energy in this country, since there is a growing dependency upon the Arab states which now own and control the largest known supply of petroleum. It is undoubtedly true that if Israel should be attacked by Egypt or any other, or even all, of the surrounding Arab states, Israel could win such a war in a comparatively short time, since she has people far more skilled and far better equipped than the neighboring Arab states do.

But Israel could not win that war if Russia came to the rescue of Iraq, Syria, Libya, and other Arab countries. However, it is believed that Russia will not become further involved and does not desire a renewal of the Middle East warfare—unless adverse economic conditions force her back into actively supporting the Arab states under circumstances which would lead to a widespread war. Should this happen, I understand through non-public information that the Arab oil-producing countries would shut down on the export of oil to the United States, which would undoubtedly result in an energy crisis in our country. This is not likely to happen if the Congress and the executive branch use reason in dealing with the rest of the world. I cannot conceive of the U.S. Congress taking any step that would, as I believe, cause great anxiety among some of the top leaders in Israel, but strange things happen these days.

A disastrous world war, or any renewal of the "cold war," is something that we constantly have to guard against. It would take only one idiot in a high political office in one country to push the button that could result in the virtual destruction of much of the Western world. ¶ ON THE 19TH OF APRIL members of Congress went home for a week's vacation, and returned to the political melee the 28th. It certainly was a change to get away from conditions in Washington. No one ever saw better weather for April than we had in Putney for about a week.

Our neighbors up on the mountain were very helpful. We got our garden plowed by Mike Antonowicz, and we got a lot of broken-down trees cut by Bob Gray and the three boys helping him. This not only improved our view but in the near future will result in having a little more land cleared, which I hope will soon be used for productive purposes. Action around our place was such that L.P.A. said Saturday night that Washington, D.C., was the dullest place she knew.

Week ending May 5, 1973

OUR ARRIVAL back in Washington was warmly welcomed by the pigeons and squirrels who had been fed only haphazardly by my office staff during our absence. They proved once again their close association with human beings: some seemed truly glad to see us back and others just hoped to get more free peanuts. ¶ THE WATERGATE AFFAIR is now becoming the major subject of interest throughout the Congress and the news media, and with the public to a somewhat lesser degree. On Monday evening the President addressed the nation on this subject, proclaiming his own innocence and disassociating his Administration as far as possible from any guilt in connection with the episode. I thought he went about as far as he could in proclaiming the innocence of his Administration. But there are plenty of people, including members of the press and some of the public, who still feel that his talk was evasive and that there is much more which ought to be told.

My own opinion is that in the 1972 election President Nixon did not really want to know how the campaign for his re-election was being conducted, and divorced himself as far as possible from the campaign. Apparently the organization called the Committee to Re-elect the President, comprised of younger, more politically ambitious, conceivably more dishonest, and certainly more stupid people than the Republican National committee, took over the campaign, ignoring the older, more experienced politicians of the party, and got Republican officials and future candidates generally into difficulties. There is no question but what the Watergate episode, which has now been broadened, rightfully or otherwise, to include other questionable tactics charged to this Administration, has injured future prospects for the party, and for the next Republican candidate for the Presidency.

I doubt that Republican candidates for Congress and state offices will be as adversely affected as the next candidate for the Presidency, since voters are more and more showing a disregard for the party label and are voting more for or against a candidate, depending upon what sort of an impression he has made upon them. At any rate, party discipline—and there hasn't been too much of this during the last few years—has become seriously weakened.

¶ THE WATERGATE EPISODE has aroused the lightly slumbering ambitions of many members of Congress who have an itch to be nominated for President or Vice President in 1976. On Tuesday during the period from 12:30 to 2:00 P.M. when both Democrats and Republicans are absent from the Senate floor attending the conference luncheons of their parties, Senator Percy, whose ambitions are very poorly disguised, introduced and secured passage of a Resolution on the floor of the Senate with only four other members of the Senate present, and then tied down the vote so that the action taken could not be reconsidered except by unanimous consent. He proposed that an independent prosecutor be appointed to deal with the Watergate episode. The Resolution was apparently hastily written without the knowledge of most other Republican members of the Senate, who did not see a copy of it until after it had been favorably voted upon by the five members of the Senate who were present.

Late in the afternoon Senator Curtis attempted, through the unanimous-consent route, to get permission to reconsider the action on Percy's Resolution, but was blocked by the Senator from Illinois himself. Later, Senator Percy, realizing that he may have been in error, made the same request for unanimous consent to reconsider the action that Senator Curtis had made, but since Senator Curtis had left the Senate, those few members who remained did not look kindly upon such a request, and Senator Percy was also blocked. I expressed myself in terms which some folks thought were too vigorous, with words too short. However, I did tell Senator Percy that if he made the same request the following morning I would have no objection to his doing so; in fact I would support it. But by Wednesday morning Senator Curtis and Senator Cotton took over the situation and told the Senator from Illinois, Nothing doing.

The Percy Resolution in itself had no binding effect upon the Ad-

NO. 1. *Governor Aiken, left, and his good friend Alf. Landon—former governor of Kansas and 1936 Republican Presidential candidate—in 1939 on one of their fishing trips in Vermont. (Author's collection)*

NO. 2. *Senators Hugh Scott and Hubert Humphrey, left, and J. William Fulbright, far right, greet eighty-four-year-old Alf. Landon at a Capitol luncheon given in the distinguished Kansan's honor by Senator Aiken, here seventy-eight (1971). (Author's collection)*

NO. 3. *President Harry S Truman signs the National School Lunch Act in June of 1946. Standing, left to right: Secretary of Agriculture Clinton P. Anderson, Congressman Malcolm C. Tarver, Senator Richard Russell, Senator Allen Ellender, Congressman Clifford R. Hope, Senator Aiken, and Congressman John W. Flannagan (U.S. Department of Agriculture, photo by Forsythe. Courtesy the Harry S. Truman Library)*

NO. 4. *Agriculture leaders in the nation's capital are interviewed by David Brinkley in April of 1950. Left to right: Secretary of Agriculture Clinton P. Anderson, Congressman Harold Cooley, Mr. Brinkley, Senator Aiken, and Gene Hamilton of the American Farm Bureau. (Author's collection)*

NO. 5. *President Dwight D. Eisenhower with Senator Aiken, 1955. Behind the Senator is James Haggerty, Presidential press secretary. (Official photograph, The White House)*

NO. 6. *Senate Republican leaders with Vice President Richard Nixon at the Capitol in 1960. Left to right: Everett Dirksen, Hugh Scott, Barry Goldwater, Mr. Nixon, George Aiken, and Thomas Kuchel. (Author's collection)*

NO. 7. *As a member of the Joint Committee on Atomic Energy visiting the* U.S.S. Enterprise, *Senator Aiken operates the Ahead throttle of one of the nuclear-powered aircraft carrier's main engines at sea off Guantanamo Bay, Cuba, in the spring of 1962. (Official photograph, U.S. Navy)*

NO. 8. *President John F. Kennedy, Secretary of the Interior Stewart Udall, and members of the New England Delegation discuss a project to harness power from the tides off the coast of Passamaquoddy, Maine, in July of 1963. Left to right: Mr. Udall, Senator Thomas McIntyre, Senator Edward Muskie, the President, Senator Aiken. (Official photograph, The White House, Abbie Rowe)*

NO. 9. *Five Vermonters in the statuary hall of the Capitol: Kay Casellini of Barre, Linda Waite of Bennington—the state's representatives to Girls' Nation in 1961—and George Aiken of Putney admire the heroic figure of Ethan Allen, a leader of the Green Mountain Boys during the Revolution. The great Mormon at the left was born in Whitingham, Vermont. (Author's collection)*

NO. 10. *Sargent Shriver, left, director of the Peace Corps, Senator Margaret Chase Smith, and Senator Aiken share a joke in the Capitol (1964). (Author's collection)*

NO. 11. *"The most efficient senatorial staff in the Congress"—and the smallest. "L.P.A.,"* *at George Aiken's left, was removed from the payroll by her husband when they were* *married June 30, 1967 (which coincided with the end of the fiscal year), but continued* *as office manager. Standing in back, left to right: Stephen Terry, Therese Lepine,* *Elizabeth Quinn, Charles Weaver, Maryann McKinney, Ellen Jones, Patricia Terpstra,* *and Marion Whitney (1971). (Author's collection)*

NO. 12. *Wearing his favorite sweater—its torn left elbow soon to be mended with a leather patch—George Aiken mulls a problem at his desk in the Senate Office Building (1970). (Mrs. Aiken's collection)*

NO. 13. *In 1963 on the plane to the Northwest to arrange with British Columbia for harnessing the Columbia River system. Left to right: Senators Wayne Morse, Howard Cannon, George Aiken, and Lee Metcalf, President Lyndon Johnson, and, facing the camera, Senator Michael Mansfield.* (*Author's collection*)

No. 14. *At a meeting of the Senate Committee on Foreign Relations in 1970: George Aiken, ranking Republican, Chairman J. William Fulbright, and John Sparkman, ranking Democrat. (Author's collection)*

NO. 15. *The seven members who worked the hardest to put the historic Civil Rights bill of 1964 in shape so that it could pass the Senate after cloture. Left to right: Warren Magnuson, Hubert Humphrey, Leverett Saltonstall, George Aiken, Michael Mansfield, Everett Dirksen, and Thomas Kuchel. (Author's collection)*

NO. 16. *Senator Edward Kennedy, left, meets Madame Ymelda Marcos, wife of the President of the Philippines, at a Senate luncheon in 1970. (Author's collection)*

NO. 17. *Members of the Joint Committee on Atomic Energy, 1974, left to right: Senator Wallace Bennett, Senator George Aiken, Congressman Chester Holifield (chairman), Congressman Craig Hosmer, and Senator Alan Bible. (Courtesy the United States Atomic Energy Commission, Office of Information Services, photograph by Westcott)*

NO. 18. *Confidants and breakfast companions for twenty-one years—Mike Mansfield and George Aiken. In the Senate dining room (here in 1970). (Author's collection)*

No. 19. *Breakfast at the White House, September of 1974. Facing the camera, right to left: Senator Michael Mansfield, President Gerald Ford, Senator George Aiken, Senator Hubert Humphrey, and, at the end of the table, William Timmons, liaison officer for the Senate; with their backs to the camera, right to left, are Congressman Thomas Morgan, Secretary of State Henry Kissinger, Senator Hugh Scott, and Congressman Leslie Arends. (Official photograph, The White House)*

NO. 20. *King Faisal, left, greets George Aiken at a state dinner in Washington in 1966. Ibrahim Al-Sowayel, Saudi Arabian Ambassador to the United States, is in the center. (Author's collection. Courtesy the City News Bureau, Washington, D.C.)*

NO. 21. *Senators at a breakfast meeting with Canadian Prime Minister Pierre Trudeau, December of 1974. Front row, left to right: Jacob Javits, George Aiken, the Prime Minister, Charles Mathias; in the back, left to right, are Adlai Stevenson III, Walter Mondale, and, behind Senator Mathias, Robert Stafford. (Author's collection)*

NO. 22. *A last handout for a Capitol pigeon before George Aiken retires from the Senate after thirty-four years' service. (Mrs. Aiken's collection)*

NO. 23. *Samuel Ervin and George Aiken, with the fishing poles they hope to use after their Senate service ends in January of 1975. (Author's collection)*

ministration since it merely advised the appointment of an outside prosecutor for the Watergate case instead of leaving the matter entirely in the hands of the Attorney General and the Department of Justice. Why Senator Percy was in such haste to get his own proposal approved in an unusual manner Tuesday noon came to light late in the afternoon, when it appeared that Senator Ed Brooke, who is also suspected of having designs on the 1976 election, had intended to oppose the Percy Resolution and sponsor one of his own. He actually did offer his own Resolution on Wednesday morning, and it is still pending before the Senate and will doubtless never be acted on.

If we could only find some way to rid some of our ultra-ambitious members of the Spirit of '76—1976—we could possibly get a sine die adjournment before Christmas, which right now looks to be a hopeless objective. I have always felt that the best qualification for a Presidential or Vice Presidential candidate is to do well the job to which he has already been assigned. I am also satisfied that President Nixon would say now that the price one has to pay for glory is too exorbitant, because I am already receiving telegrams and letters urging his impeachment, although I am satisfied that the senders of these communications never voted for him anyway.

¶ I MIGHT GET DISCOURAGED thinking about what happened during the week just ended, if history did not tell us that all the things going on today which serve to take away our appetites have been going on since the days of the first Continental Congress, the difference being that now the other fellow's sins get a great deal more publicity, with charges and denials occupying a bigger share of the space in newspapers and magazines than used to be the case.

As an instance, many supposedly reputable periodicals printed a story that six Republican members of the Senate had been to the White House and served notice on President Nixon that unless the Watergate case was satisfactorily cleared up, they would all refuse to run for re-election in 1974. Being one of the six Senators named, I knew the story was a complete fabrication, and so did the management of the publications which carried it. But this is one of the more harmless fabrications of the week, so I am not complaining.

The grand juries have been sitting, the Department of Justice has presumably been busy, and guilty parties have undoubtedly been thinking of alibis and defense procedures, so next week we can expect events and reports even smellier than those which have offended our olfactory senses so far.

Week ending May 12, 1973

AN EVENTFUL WEEK with some progress made on legislation.

The Committee on Agriculture and Forestry finally agreed upon a bill for a farm program to take the place of the present act, which will soon expire. My principal concern was with some twenty-plus dairy marketing proposals submitted by an organization called the Mid-America Dairymen, Inc., and not made available to the dairy co-operatives of the country until late last week—nor had the Department of Agriculture been asked to give its opinions on them. I decided that some of the proposed amendments would be very bad for our dairy people, and the committee rejected most of them. Unfortunately, some of the dairy organizations in the country appear to have succumbed to a political urge and, I fear, do not fully respect the actual needs of their producers.

The committee also decided to hold the price of wheat, feed grains and cotton at a profitable level for the producers, and therefore may have gone too far in insisting upon high-level supports for certain commodities. By recommending high levels of support, the Senate committee is assured of the bargaining power needed in dealing with the House, which is considered much less farm-minded than the Senate.

Legislation relating to the Rural Electrification Administration was finally accomplished. It had been tied up in Conference between the two Houses for some time, but the executive branch—possibly prompted by a desire to offset the Watergate debacle—worked with the conferees to an unusual extent. The bill with its compromises has now been approved by both Houses and sent to the President, who promptly signed it. It will provide for setting up a fund from which rural electric and telephone co-operatives can borrow, instead of depending on federal loans. This will undoubtedly put the co-operatives more on their own feet and make them less dependent upon the whims of the Congress and the Administration.

¶ THE FOREIGN RELATIONS COMMITTEE held hearings throughout most of the week on a bill sponsored by Senators Cranston and Taft which is designed to make the World Court more effective.

I do not question the motives of the sponsors, and agree that their objective is a good one, but the World Court up to now has been almost a total loss and under almost any sort of procedure cannot be effective unless some way is found to enforce the Court's findings against countries which disregard them. Only two cases are now before the Court, both involving Iceland and the fisheries industry. If and when a decision is reached, the loser will ignore the verdict.

¶ DURING THE WEEK the Watergate scandal continued to blossom in all its glory—or ignominy. The grand jury in Washington is still working up a list of people to face criminal charges in the near future; the grand jury in New York has produced indictments against two former Cabinet officials, Secretary Stans and Attorney General Mitchell. Also, a man named Robert Vesco was indicted under the charge that he delivered $200,000, in what used to be called a "black bag," to the Committee to Re-elect the President—a committee which should never have been organized in the first place and which later on, undoubtedly too late, is said to have returned the money. The Committee to Re-elect the President is now charged with all sorts of misdoings, and the only good it can be credited with is to make the National committees of the Democratic and Republican parties look much more respectable than folks have believed in the past.

Senator Ervin's committee is continuing its plans for open hearings to start next week on the Watergate affair. Since these hearings are to be televised, I expect they will be so popular that advertisers on the regular programs may complain that Sam Ervin's committee is hurting their business. I also fear that the televised Senate hearings may seriously affect the ability of the federal courts to carry on effectively.

¶ THURSDAY the House of Representatives slapped down the Administration by voting to prohibit the use or transfer of funds for the purpose of continuing the bombing of Cambodia. The Senate will agree with the House that bombing in Cambodia, as well as any other actions relating to warfare in Indochina, should be stopped. The House might not have taken this action except for the Watergate affair, which has lowered the prestige of the Administration to such an extent that even many Republicans do not care to be associated with it at this point. That the President recognizes this downgrading in the public mind is evidenced by the many changes he is making in the executive branch within a short time. Not only has he accepted resignations of his principal lieutenants, Haldeman and Ehrlichman, but he has asked for resignations of others, and is changing heads of departments so fast that it is difficult to keep up with him.

Secretary Rogers is personally very popular with the Congress, but on Friday a newsman asked me if I had heard the report that Mr. Kissinger was to be the new Secretary of State. I told him I hadn't heard the report, but it might be a good idea if Secretary Rogers is really getting out, as I strongly suspect he would like to do. Mr. Kissinger, in spite of all the difficulties of the Nixon Administration, seems to have retained his good standing with members of Congress, with the public, and with officials of foreign countries.

¶ JOHN CONNALLY, having transferred to the Republican Party, has been announced as a Presidential adviser without pay. He is a politician, and had he been running the campaign for the Republicans last year I am sure that the disgraceful Watergate episode would not have occurred. President Nixon can use a few experienced politicians in his establishment if he is to restore respect for the party and the White House. The trouble does not lie with our form of government, but with the operations of ignorant and foolish people who believe that dishonesty and lawbreaking are essential parts of a political campaign.

Week ending May 19, 1973

THIS WEEK was very much like the week when the circus comes to town. But even though the Big Show with its tightrope-walkers was put on by Sam Ervin's committee on Thursday and Friday, the Senate did find time to attend to some other business.

¶ THE AUTHORIZATION BILL for the State department itself will be delayed until after the Memorial Day recess. The Foreign Relations committee, by a one-sided vote, added an amendment prohibiting expenditure of funds for carrying on warfare in Indochina. The committee's action was prompted primarily by the Administration's persistence in bombing Cambodia. The President had stated previously that bombing would be carried out in Cambodia only for the protection of American military personnel operating in South Vietnam. With that personnel now being withdrawn, Congress expected the President to stick to his earlier statement. The attitude of opposition in both Houses of the Congress is overwhelming, and if the Administration persists in operations which could conceivably lead to another Indochina war, it will be seriously handicapped in having certain other restrictive recommendations agreed to by the House and Senate.

I do not know just what is behind our present intensive bombing in Cambodia, but I regard it as a very serious operation which should be stopped without further delay. The alibi used for it is that if we do not protect the present government of Cambodia the communists will take over. As a matter of fact, though, Cambodia under Prince Sihanouk was not pro-communist to any degree. The word *communist* is badly misused, and is frequently applied to those who do not have communistic leanings but who stand in the way of certain political or economic interests with which our government is in sympathy.

¶ IN ITS COLLABORATION with the rest of the world, the United States must make sure that its objectives are constructive and its practices fairly arrived at. How long we keep our position as the most powerful nation in the world is a matter for conjecture. Other countries are coming up fast, have tremendous natural resources, and people equally as intelligent and astute as the leadership of the United States. However, there is a tendency on the part of the larger, stronger nations to undertake to control the politics of less developed countries, even to the extent of undertaking to influence their elections and political policies.

It was on Tuesday that I had a visit from former Ambassador Ong, who represented Malaysia in Washington up to about a year ago. Mr. Ong is now president of the Malaysian Senate, and what prompted his visit to me and other members of the Senate was a proposal by our government to sell tremendous amounts of strategically important commodities which we have on hand and which are not likely to be needed by us in the foreseeable future.

Malaysia is the largest tin-producing country, and tin is its principal export. World production is only 162,000 tons of tin a year; the United States possesses about 200,000 tons of tin. Therefore if the United States offered its surplus holdings to the world market it would undoubtedly ruin the tin industry of Malaysia, upon which that country depends so largely.

I don't think the United States has any desire to wreck the economy of any other country by dumping our surplus holdings on the world market, but Mr. Ong was not taking any chances. He was always a good friend to the United States, and, while I believe that his fears are groundless, it is important that we do not contribute unthinkingly to the economic ruin of any small country.

¶ ON THURSDAY the Big Show started. Eight full-time television cameras covered the hearings of Sam Ervin's committee. Seats in the Caucus Room were at a premium. The audience was craving excitement. The news media were vying with each other in writing sensational reports. Millions of people in foreign countries are reported to have watched the televised programs transmitted by satellite.

Some people have already made up their minds as to who is guilty and what ought to be done about it. They can't wait for committee findings or court decisions. But then, the pages of history are replete with episodes in past centuries where innocents were unceremoniously executed and guilty parties escaped punishment. I think, however, that most people want to let our Constitutional processes take their course, make their findings and decisions, and mete out punishment for the guilty and acquittal for the innocent. It is the best system I know of, and yet it is not infallible, because almost anyone who has rightfully or wrongfully been accused of crime receives a degree of punishment for the rest of his days. Most of the world will likely forget his indictment, but he himself cannot escape the belief that some others are pointing their fingers at him.

¶ THE WATERGATE AFFAIR is saturated with politics, and there are those who say that because it was a Democratic headquarters which was broken into, the Republican Party is doomed in future elections. These people cannot wait to point out that the Teapot Dome scandal was perpetrated under a Republican administration in the 1920's, apparently forgetting that the next two federal elections following Teapot Dome resulted in overwhelming victories for the Republicans in the election of President Coolidge in 1924 and President Hoover in 1928. It was only after the public got short of spending money during the Hoover Administration that political sentiment changed, resulting in the election of President Roosevelt in 1932. This history convinces me that more votes are influenced by the amount of spending money in a voter's pocket than by the degree of sin that permeates the administration in power at that time.

[Putney, Vermont]

Week ending May 26, 1973

As FAR AS legislation and government operations go, it was not an impressive or world-shaking week. Committee meetings were held. Some legislation was enacted the first three days of the week. And Sam Ervin's Watergate committee had three days of hearings that were televised all over the United States and some other parts of the world—hearings that resolved themselves into a kind of TV-show entertainment, but which left only confusion and disgust in the minds of millions of Americans.

Not that I blame Sam and his associates for getting all the favorable publicity they can and performing what they consider to be a service to their country. But when they announced Thursday afternoon that further hearings would be postponed for two weeks, until June 5th, I could not blame people for regarding this as a move to prolong the show. It is a prime-time spectacular that becomes more and more indefinite and uncertain as time goes on and witness after witness takes the opportunity to put himself in as good a light as possible, and to insinuate that others are to blame for the sinful atmosphere which has permeated the District of Columbia and spread its fumes over the rest of the country. Certainly the Watergate situation smells bad. It is clearly evident that sins have been committed, but that is no reason for everybody to qualify himself as the person to throw the first stone. ¶ L.P.A. AND I CAME HOME to Putney on Wednesday and had four days of the most beautiful weather imaginable for the month of May. So we had a chance to clean up things at home, replant most of the garden seeds that had failed, and put in some fifty hills of squashes, pumpkins and cucumbers, to say nothing of short rows of corn and beans; blueberries and raspberries were doing wonderfully well. This garden, some sixty feet square, could produce enough food to serve a family for a full year if properly attended to.

[United States Senate]

Week ending June 2, 1973

TUESDAY AFTERNOON the Senate took up the USIA bill to authorize appropriations for U.S. publicity throughout the world. The principal issue on this bill was whether $16 million could be added to provide for relocating our radio transmitter from Okinawa to South Korea, where news about the United States could be beamed to Central Asia and eastern Russia. The proposed location in Korea of the new and larger transmitter was supposed to be a classified secret, but since the Washington *Post* had used this information on Monday, it was no longer a secret and probably never was anyway.

I supported the measure, but it was killed by the vote of those Senators from states which are about to lose certain military installations. It was simply a case of getting even with the executive branch of the government.

¶ DURING THE WEEK the Foreign Relations committee held hearings on the energy situation, since petroleum products are an important factor in foreign trade. Our witnesses have mostly been professors who know quite a lot of history but who are hardly in the same class as the hardheaded, ruthless petroleum interests when it comes to providing solutions to our energy problems. There is no question but what the major oil companies, who are still able to supply their customers, are seeking a monopoly in the field of energy; I believe, too, that they are being co-operated with by major financial institutions.

On Thursday the principal witness from the Ford Foundation told us what we needed energy for, stating that 15 percent was for heating, so much for industrial purposes, so much for this and so much for that, until he had allowed for 100 percent of all energy available. But unfortunately he had not allowed any energy whatsoever for agriculture.

When it came my turn to question him I asked him how long it had been since we stopped eating, because, according to my information, American agriculture—in producing commodities, processing them, and getting them to market—is still the largest consumer of petroleum products of any sector of our national economy. The witness hesitated and then said, "You are right." After I left the hearings I understand that Senator Humphrey came to the meeting and took the witness to task for the same error. Certainly, when supposedly important witnesses can overlook the value of agriculture, it is time for the people of this country to do a little worrying.

¶ THE MAJOR OIL COMPANIES are international in their outlook and ambitions, and in any country where there are prospects of undeveloped oil fields there is also the possibility of revolution and bloodshed. As an example of this I might point out that on Thursday the Senate voted overwhelmingly to cut off all funds that might be used for the continued bombing of Cambodia. Cambodia is not at present a great oil-producing country, and maybe never will be, but there is the possibility of discovery and development of oil fields in that general area, which also includes South Vietnam and Thailand. I had been trying for weeks to get the State department to tell our committee who held the rights to oil exploration in Cambodia. Finally we got the answer. All rights for inland and offshore exploration had been granted by the Cambodian government to a French company, but, Lo and behold, last year the Exxon Corporation of the United States bought 35 percent of the interests of the French company in offshore exploration. This may not be the reason why the United States continues bombing the area of Cambodia so long after our troops and POW's have been withdrawn from Indochina, but it is just possible that if our military is instructed to bomb that area long enough, the investment of the American oil company might be a bit more secure.

What bothers many people these days is the fact that, when our initial bombing of Cambodia started three years ago, the President declared it was for the purpose of protecting our military men in South Vietnam. But our military men have all left that area now, and people are wondering why it is necessary to continue bombing Cambodia long after the original purpose stated by the President had been achieved. These bombings, added to the Watergate scandal and the cutting-off of funds for important domestic programs, have caused the prestige of President Nixon to sink very low. I am sorry for this, because there are so many things to his credit, so many things that have been good for the people of the whole world.

At this point I am wondering if President Nixon would not be more than ever in favor of a single six-year term for the Presidency. Conceivably he might feel that a single four-year term would be even better.

Week ending June 9, 1973

A STUMBLING SENATE finally approved two bills which ought to have been acted on at least two months ago. The first one related to allocation of fuels among regions and among dealers. The petroleum war seems to be going full speed ahead, with the major oil companies making every effort to eliminate the smaller and so-called independent competitors, all of it in response to the inherent urge of man to get monopoly control of something.

On Tuesday I had a long visit with William Simon, Deputy Secretary of the Treasury, in my office. He apparently is the President's top man in trying to work out solutions to the threat of an energy crisis. His job is not easy, and while he predicted more refineries for New England I did not find his hopes and plans too re-assuring. Certainly he promised little increase in our supply of gas and oil before 1980 and no assurance that there would be no increase in costs.

From Tuesday night until Friday the Senate debated the new farm bill, with the usual conflict between the "city slickers" and the "greedy farmers" of the Senate. It was surprising how many members of our August Body found a way to get on both sides of the issue. The fact is, however, that there is no greater degree of interdependence among groups than there is between the city consumer and the rural food-producer. I have actually had very little complaint from the consumers themselves, although their representatives and lobbyists have been very vocal and seem to enjoy the support of much of the metropolitan press.

Week ending June 16, 1973

THERE HAS BEEN an apparent change in the attitude of the White House toward the Congress. Since the departure of such White House stalwarts as Haldeman, Ehrlichman and several others, co-operation between the executive branch and the Congress has shown considerable improvement, particularly as far as the House is concerned. With Mel Laird and Bryce Harlow coming back to aid the President after a considerable absence, Congress seems more optimistic for the future. The President's personal secretary, Rose Mary Woods, who has been under strain for the last four years, has been designated as an executive assistant to the President. Rose, who has showed an understanding of legislative practices, has remained loyal to the President and to the country through all the years of stress and strain and reported efforts of the Haldeman-Ehrlichman staff to get rid of her.

The President may have been successful in bringing our troops out of South Vietnam and making progress in our relations with the People's Republic of China, Russia and other countries, but he surely did not draw any high rating or applause for his selection of White House personnel during his first term of office. We hope things will be much better now. They couldn't get much worse than they were.

¶ HENRY KISSINGER came back from Paris and up to the Hill on Thursday to report on a new understanding with the factions of Vietnam, particularly North Vietnam, which I hope will result in a lessening of hostilities in that area. The decisions reached in Paris simply attempt to make the agreement reached on January 27th more effective. There may be a slight improvement in the situation over there, but people who have enjoyed fighting for power during the last several generations are not going to abandon that sport completely in the near future.

¶ GENERAL SECRETARY BREZHNEV of the U.S.S.R. is arriving in this country tonight and will begin meetings with the President on Monday. I sincerely hope that he won't be subjected to unwarranted embarrassments during his week-long stay in our country. But there are plenty of irresponsible people who feel that by condemning Russia and embarrassing her chief official they will be helping Israel. Nothing could be further from the truth. The economies of Russia and the United States bid fair to be much more interdependent in the future, and such a mutual dependence will play an important part in maintaining world peace and the security and prosperity of many smaller countries, particularly those bordering the eastern Mediterranean.

Of course Mainland China always keeps a watchful eye on Russia even though both countries claim, and pretend to embrace, the communist philosophy of government. As a matter of fact both these great nations are apparently deviating from that philosophy so fast as to make the future of their governments most uncertain.

Realizing that China will have qualms over the visit of Russian officials to the United States, the White House planned for a two-week visit to China by ten members of the Congress. Senator Magnuson apparently has insisted on being leader of the U.S. delegation, and a couple of days ago I heard that he is quite anxious that it be accompanied by reporters from the news media. Since "Maggie's" term in the Senate expires next year and he will undoubtedly be a candidate for re-election, his desire to be accompanied by news people is quite understandable.

¶ ON THURSDAY Senator Mansfield gave a luncheon for a few people, including the chief representative of the People's Republic of China and three of his assistants. Mr. Huang is, in effect, an ambassador to the United States, just as Mr. Bruce is our ambassador to Peking. These representatives from Peking lost no time in getting acquainted with us and are particularly interested in our methods of production and our trading practices, which indicates that the People's Republic will before long become one of the most important factors in world trade. World trade is increasing already at a tremendous rate, and with it has come inflation—not only in the United States but all over Western Europe and a good share of the rest of the world.

This inflation prompted the President on Wednesday night to take advantage of authority given him by the Congress and impose a sixty-day freeze on prices, during which time a practical method of controlling costs and prices is supposedly to be devised. Although he exempted raw farm produce from price controls, he also recommended export controls and a possible lowering of tariffs on goods imported into our country. I expect that the President will find that such a declared war against the law of supply and demand will be most difficult to wage and win.

Week ending June 23, 1973

THE WEEK STARTED with a brunch Sunday for Helen Smith, Mrs. Nixon's press secretary, given by the White House women correspondents at the Congressional Club, with quite a few well-known Washingtonians in attendance. This didn't wear me down so much that I wasn't able to work Monday on the first speech I have made in the Senate for some time. In it I tried to point out the tie-in between American agriculture, consumer costs of living, and foreign relations. I didn't expect all the members of the Senate press corps to understand what I was talking about; but immediate publicity was not my aim anyway.

The United States can be the world's greatest supplier of food for many years to come. And believe me, the world needs food: statisticians claim that 70 percent of the people of the world don't have enough decent food to eat. What I tried to point out was that if the United States is to become producer for the world we have to keep developers and others from gobbling up our best farmland and taking it out of use. We are already exporting billions of dollars worth of food, largely grain, each year, and these exports have naturally resulted in an increase in price for our own consumers. However, if our farmers can be assured of a continuing market they will plant more in the future. Big orders from Russia precipitated the present situation, and it looks as if Russia intends to continue with her purchases if we will continue with an excess of production. It also appears that Russia hopes eventually to repay us by the sale of natural gas and other commodities for which we have a growing need in this country.

But we must conserve our productive land. The Senate recognizes this fact, and during the week debated and ultimately approved a land-use policy sponsored primarily by Senator Jackson. This bill would provide federal assistance in the form of money for states that developed land-use plans on their own that met with federal approval. Senator Jackson also proposed an amendment which, by cutting down federal funds available for highway construction and airports, would penalize states that failed within five years to enact programs satisfactory to the Interior department. I opposed this amendment, which was defeated, although I supported the bill. At present, of all the fifty states, only Vermont and Hawaii have shown much concern over land use and have enacted legislation accordingly. But I don't think we should start out by threatening the other forty-eight states with punishment if they fail to go ahead as desired by the Interior department.

Anyway, thanks to the Russians, the country now recognizes the desirability of conserving our land resources, particularly productive agricultural land. It is safe to say that legislation will be passed by both Houses of the Congress before the end of this 93rd Session.

Also, coincidentally with consideration of a land-use policy by the Senate, the Russians descended upon us: General Secretary Brezhnev, members of his cabinet, and a hoard of reporters and photographers. On Monday, Mr. Brezhnev and President Nixon began discussions of mutual objectives and mutual problems. During the week several agreements between these two men were signed and, although no way has yet been developed which would prevent anyone from breaking an agreement, the fact is that the world will breathe somewhat easier as a result of the meetings.

¶ ON TUESDAY the Russians invited about twenty of us from the Congress to lunch at Blair House. After the lunch—which included five different kinds of wines and heaven knows how many courses—the General Secretary favored us with a two-hour discussion, which was extended for another half-hour after Senators Griffin and Javits had asked questions concerning the emigration policies of Russia. Mr. Brezhnev showed that he had been well coached as to the character of the people he would meet here and the problems they would present to him. He also showed himself to be an experienced actor. This was demonstrated more than ever on two occasions at the White House when he and President Nixon signed agreements. He did a lot of clowning and was noticeably superior to President Nixon in this field.

The Russian news media were really active, and I expect the people of the Soviet Union got more coverage of events taking place in Washington than they had ever seen before. I also suspect that Mr. Brezhnev was considering the political effect on his own constituents, for he certainly looked and acted as if he was really happy and everything was going his way. And, indeed, I do think that he accomplished about all he set out to when he came here. That doesn't mean that the United States got the short end of the stick all the time. It means that Russia and the United States demonstrated a cordiality that has not been known for a generation, and the agreements signed, whether enforceable or not, should have a beneficial and salutary effect not only on the people of our two countries but on those of other countries of the world as well. I don't think the Chinese need to worry over the improvement of U.S.–Soviet relations; some of the agreements reached, particularly those concerning the start of new wars, should be re-assuring to China as well as to all other countries.

¶ LATE THURSDAY AFTERNOON, Henry Kissinger met with nine members of the Foreign Relations committee at the invitation of Chairman Fulbright. I didn't think he did as well as usual: his comments on Cambodia, in particular, were not satisfactory to most members of the committee. We still don't see why it is necessary to continue bombing in that country. China, of course, is hopeful that Prince Sihanouk may return to the leadership of his country. Many people in the United States and other countries seem inclined to agree that this might be a good solution, even though Sihanouk himself was never over-friendly to the United States.

Tied to the whole situation is a bill which Hubert Humphrey proposed in the Senate for himself and me. This measure provides for continuation of the economic and technical assistance features of the old Foreign Economic Aid bill, and in itself is quite a radical departure from the programs we have been using in the past. It emphasizes strongly the use of private organizations in carrying out the work of aiding the poor people of smaller countries. It emphasizes our intention to aid people who are desperately in need, rather than to control or to direct their governments.

Although Senator Humphrey offered the bill just for the two of us, several members of the Foreign Relations committee have already indicated a desire to join as co-sponsors. There will be some who will oppose it, some who oppose any foreign aid programs at all, others who would like to have such programs written by and credited to themselves, and still others who would like to have any program benefit primarily our own manufacturers or our own financial institutions.

I believe the Nixon Administration would like to have our economic and technical aid bill tied to the military aid bill, but I have advised against this effort because action of this kind might result in our getting no legislation at all. And without legislation, we would have to resort to Continuing Resolutions to sustain operations—always an unsatisfactory way to carry on a long-range program.

¶ THE WATERGATE HEARINGS under Senator Ervin were suspended in order that Mr. Brezhnev's visit and other matters might get some coverage in the press during the week. On Friday the three men who had been in Skylab for twenty-eight days came home, landing in the Pacific some seven hundred miles off the California coast. The Skylab return was the real event of the week. It will do more to change the future than the nauseating Watergate affair, the visit of Mr. Brezhnev, and all the week's other happenings.

Next week Senator Ervin and his committee will start again holding hearings on the Watergate matter, with the public now in the mood to believe nothing anybody says. As Sam himself remarked to me the other day, it is now apparent that Ananias was a piker.

Week ending June 30, 1973

ON SUNDAY, Soviet General Secretary Brezhnev and President Nixon held a last powwow in San Clemente, and the Soviet leader took off for Washington to spend the night before leaving for Paris. There are folks who say that the Russians won't keep any agreement, and undoubtedly there are those in the U.S.S.R. or elsewhere in the world who say the United States won't keep any agreement. But it is much better to set world peace as an objective than it would have been to have Mr. Nixon and Mr. Brezhnev parting company under any other circumstances.

¶ SAM ERVIN'S WATERGATE COMMITTEE hearings continued throughout most of the week, with John Dean, who was fired by President Nixon, as a principal witness. His testimony has been largely and subtly directed against the President, which is understandable since no one really loves the boss who fired him. I feel that politics is the predominating motivation in some quarters of the committee, with certain Democrats trying to depict President Nixon as highly irresponsible, if not actually crooked; they are forgetting that he has terminated our involvement in the Vietnam war, and has done more to create an atmosphere of peace around the world than any other international leader. The Republicans are anxious to show that, even though there were crooked and illegal acts involved in the Watergate affair, such practices didn't originate with the Nixon Administration.

But one thing really stands out, as stressed by Senator Mansfield, and this is that none of the culprits in the Watergate break-in, and hardly any of the White House suspects appointed by President Nixon, had ever run for public office or had experience in government at any level. This simply emphasizes a claim that I have made for years: namely, that good government begins at the community level. Unless a person has performed his duties honestly and conscientiously at the lower levels of government, he certainly is not qualified for promotion toward the top.

As a matter of fact, I don't believe that politics is any more crooked in government now than it has been by spells over the last two hundred years. Dishonesty in government now receives a great deal more coverage by the news media, however. While such publicity can be sickening, it may also be helpful in the long run; and in the meantime it helps publishers to sell more newspapers and magazines.

¶ THE HOUSE APPROVED a supplemental appropriations bill which carried a proviso that no funds could be spent by the executive branch for the continued bombing of Cambodia; this proposal has now been accepted by the Senate.

On Wednesday the Senate took up the bill providing for a continuation of the federal debt ceiling, which passed the Senate easily and went to Conference with the House. Although efforts were made to complete the legislation last night, they were stymied by Senator Hartke of Indiana, who seemed far more anxious to get out a bill that President Nixon would be sure to veto than to get out legislation which, if properly written, could have brought early and more liberal aid to the needy people of this country.

I believe the President does at times exercise the veto power too much, but members of Congress who insist on sending to the White House legislation which they know will have to be vetoed are even more at fault than the President.

The outstanding bit of legislation during the week was the approval by the Congress of the supplemental appropriations bill which the President had vetoed a few days before because it carried a provision requiring the immediate stop to our bombing in Cambodia. The veto was upheld in the House by a substantial margin, well over the one-third necessary to prevent it from being overridden. Like the majority of the Senate, I believe that the bombing carried on after our military had all been withdrawn from South Vietnam was ill-advised and unwarranted, but when the House sustained the veto, there was little the Senate could do except to rewrite the legislation.

Thursday and Friday the Foreign Relations committee members worked out a compromise with the White House to the effect that the President would sign the very important and necessary supplemental appropriations bill, provided that the stipulation attached to it would only require the Cambodian bombing to stop not later than August 15.

Since the President didn't want any restrictions on the bombing at all, while the Senate wanted an immediate end to all bombing in Cambodia, the agreement reached was indeed a compromise.

Week ending July 7, 1973

[*Putney, Vermont*]

THE WEEK-LONG VACATION from Washington was taken up with getting federal help to repair flood damage in Vermont, with seeing friends and neighbors and working in the garden, and with assessing political news from the nation's capital.

The flood that had hit hard last Friday and Saturday caused great concern to the people of the state. While the Connecticut River and its tributaries did not create anywhere near the ruin suffered by Vermont in the 1927 flood, the damage left by the high waters was severe enough to warrant the President's designating the state a major disaster area, with the cost of reconstruction and repairs to be borne by the federal government.

¶ TOWARD THE END OF THE WEEK I was privileged to get my hands into real honest-to-goodness dirt, the kind that keeps people alive. The garden I had planted during our two earlier spring visits home was literally growing like weeds. The potatoes that I took a chance and planted prematurely at Easter time were two feet tall and in full bloom. Pumpkin seeds put in just before Memorial Day had not started any runners when we arrived last weekend, but by this evening, just one week later, had runners six feet long. The hot rainy weather that did so much for the pumpkins severely damaged the strawberry beds of the commercial growers in the area and destroyed about half the crop on my old homeplace; on the other hand, it brought a promise of better-than-usual blueberry and raspberry production.

On the roughly two acres of woodland that Bob Gray has cleared for us, we will sow buckwheat by July 16th—about two weeks later than normal here on the mountain. Even if the crop fails to mature, it will provide the neighborhood bees with the means of producing honey.

Bob, one of the leaders of the United States cross-country ski team, lives half a mile up the hill beyond us. He had made a pet of a fledgling hawk that was just learning to fly. There are seven youngsters in the neighborhood ranging from two to ten years old, and they are really learning about life and death in a way they would not have a chance to see in a city. Their mothers do not always appreciate the kids' bringing home young garter snakes and letting them out in the house. There is also an unusually good crop of toads this year.

On the Fourth of July it was my privilege to lead a parade in nearby Brattleboro. Despite a drizzling rain throughout most of the proceedings the parade was well attended.

¶ EXCEPT FOR THE PERIODS when the telephone was out of order as the result of flood damage, we were in close contact with Washington. The office called three times a day, and on Saturday I had calls from the White House, and talked with both Bryce Harlow and Mel Laird. The country is indeed fortunate that these two men were called back to take the places of the inexperienced persons who had previously been serving, theoretically at least, as top advisers to the President. Bryce and Mel know the Congress and they know the country, and so far as I know they are not overwhelmed by any personal ambitions.

Mel Laird told me the President was going to notify the Watergate committee that he would neither appear before it nor submit his personal Presidential papers. Mr. Nixon sent his message to Senator Ervin on Saturday and of course the violently anti-Nixon press expressed their feelings in a vitriolic manner, completely ignoring the facts, which were published in *The New York Times,* that since the days of George Washington, fourteen other Presidents had rejected subpoenas by the Congress or demands for information from their inside files. Time alone will tell who wins out in this controversy, but it is my impression that the Ervin committee will get a look at only such personal documents as the President may ultimately decide to give them.

¶ ANOTHER EVENT which occupied some of the press during the week was Teddy Kennedy's visit to George Wallace in Alabama, where he made a speech that praised Governor Wallace and irritated many of his own adherents. Even the Boston *Globe* lambasted Teddy for what seemed to them to be a case of sheer hypocrisy, since Senator Kennedy and Wallace have had virtually nothing in common except a yen for higher office. Assuming that Teddy has had an idea of running for the Presidency in 1976, the reactions to his visit to Alabama should serve to dampen any aspirations with which he may be affected. However, Teddy isn't the only one that has let ambition warp his judgment.

[*United States Senate*]
Week ending July 14, 1973

WEDNESDAY the Foreign Relations committee got down to business and listened to Bill Sullivan, who had been nominated to be Ambassador to the Philippines and who was opposed by some because of his close involvement with the Indochina situation over the past few years. He also acted as Henry Kissinger's righthand support during the meetings with the North Vietnamese in Paris. Sullivan is undoubtedly one of the more capable members of our Foreign Service, and was approved by the Senate committee by a 12 to 3 vote, with his name now waiting approval by the full Senate.

After approving Sullivan the committee, on motion of Senator Fulbright, voted to postpone indefinitely consideration of G. McMurtie Godley to be Assistant Secretary of State for East Asian Affairs. Godley had previously been Ambassador to Laos and was as heavily involved in Indochina maneuvering and manipulating as Sullivan had been. But the majority of the committee felt that anyone who had been as closely involved in the Vietnam war as Godley should not be confirmed as a high-ranking official of the State department itself. By recommending that he be given an embassy post in some other area, the committee in effect damned him with faint praise.

It is my opinion that the committee members, having approved the nomination of Bill Sullivan as Ambassador to the Philippines, a genuinely sensitive spot, felt that their honor and prestige could be preserved only by voting down Godley. Three Republicans Case, Javits and Percy supported the majority of the committee Democrats led by Chairman Fulbright. Hubert Humphrey valiantly supported both nominees, as did four Republican members of the committee, but it was not enough. It was reported that the President tore his hair and was highly uncomplimentary about the Foreign Relations committee for its action. I really don't know whether he did or not, because many newspaper reports involving President Nixon are usually predictable and always uncomplimentary to him. In contrast to such papers as the Washington *Post* and the Boston *Globe, The New York Times* still tries to present its news and comments fairly, although it evidently labors under a considerable strain in so doing.

¶ THURSDAY the Senate Foreign Relations committee started to mark up the economic aid bill, which was sponsored by Senator Humphrey and myself and which had nine out of the seventeen members of the committee as sponsors. When it seemed that the committee was about to report it favorably Senators McGovern and Fulbright offered amendments which could be interpreted only as expressions of distrust for the executive branch of government, or even as harassment of the President. Although I grant that the President has made serious mistakes during his term of office so far, I expressed quite plainly my opinion of moves that seem to be designed solely to embarrass the President. Apparently my remarks had some effect, because Chairman Fulbright did not offer his proposal at all, and Senator McGovern modified his until for all practical purposes it was meaningless. I have tried to make it plain that I would support all efforts of the Congress to recover Constitutional powers which have been taken away—or, in the early days, given away—to the executive branch. But I cannot for a moment co-operate in any effort to take from the executive branch those responsibilities and authorities which Constitutionally belong to it. Yet we are constantly faced with proposals to require the executive branch to report everything that goes on in the course of even informal agreements made by the State department or other agencies of the Executive.

There is too much tendency on the part of some of our members to regard any President who occupies the White House as the executive branch of government. It is true that he has a great deal of power and authority, some of which was not intended or contemplated by the framers of our Constitution and its amendments. But Presidents change and Congressional action should not be based on one's likes or dislikes for the current holder of that office. The intense dislike for President Nixon on the part of some members of Congress is such that they seemingly would be willing to take action which is not good for the country in order to gratify their dislike. President Nixon, as of today, may be regarded as an unpopular President. Besides those who would expatiate on their hatred for him we have others whose ambitions to succeed him know no bounds, and who feel that exhibiting their feelings towards Mr. Nixon in some way qualifies them to succeed him.

Week ending July 21, 1973

ON TUESDAY the Alaska oil pipeline controversy came to an end with an overwhelming vote of the Senate for approval. The bill had been amended in a manner which was intended to block court interference with immediate start of the construction. Although I was in favor of an early start of the pipeline I opposed the amendment, which was offered by Senators Gravel and Stevens of Alaska, because I have a feeling that approval of the amendment, if agreed to by the House, will open up a new avenue for litigation in the courts.

The opponents of the pipeline can, and probably will, question the Constitutional right of the legislative branch of government to interfere with the judicial branch in this manner. If the Congress votes to set aside the responsibility and the authority of the courts in this case, we will undoubtedly be requested to take similar action in other cases where the legality of private operations is in question.

Members of the Congress received considerable mail from environmentalists opposing the Alaska pipeline and requesting a review of a Canadian route which would bring oil from the Arctic south to the U.S.A. I don't think their reasoning was too good, for the Canadian pipeline would be at least twice as long as the all-Alaska pipeline, consequently increasing the risk of damage to the environment. Of course there is a risk that an oil tanker may slop over and pollute the shore of the North Pacific, but that risk is always with us, and certainly affects the Atlantic and Gulf coasts as well as the Pacific.

Most of the opposition to industrial development generally comes from those interests that are already well supplied with energy, or who finance generously some of the organizations dedicated to the preservation of a more primitive environment.

¶ FOLLOWING CONSIDERATION of the Alaska pipeline by the Senate, proposed amendments to the minimum-wage law were taken up. Debate on this issue was concluded on Thursday by a very substantial vote—almost two to one—favoring an increase in minimum wages, which, over a three-year period, would increase from $1.60 to $2.20 an hour. As might be expected, employers generally opposed the increase, while labor unions and others who felt that wages should be kept in line with increases both in salaries paid to corporation officials and in dividends to their stockholders, supported the increase.

The bill also aids domestic workers and people employed in the households and grounds of the more well-to-do. I doubt if it was the increase in wages that bothered well-to-do employers of domestic labor so much as it was the necessity for keeping records and making reports. However, if a rich family employs a person to the extent of less than $50 per quarter, reports are not required. And there are quite liberal exemptions for small business and strictly local business interests.

It is rumored strongly that the Congress will agree to increase substantially the pay of Congressional members and those connected with the judiciary and executive branches of government. The employees of Congressional offices seem to be strongly in favor of this, since a substantial increase for the boss would doubtless entail an increase for them also. At a time when inflation is the order of the day, I feel that Congress should set an example in trying to hold prices within bounds. However, what is going on here in the U.S.A. is a worldwide trend, and people who are traveling to other parts of the world for pleasure or business find that costs have increased even more in practically all of the other industrial nations.

My guess is that Congress will approve a substantial increase in salaries for everyone employed in the legislative, executive, and judicial branches on the grounds that it is necessary to raise salaries in order to compete with private industry for competent personnel. Fortunately consistency is not required of a member of Congress, and one can strongly deplore the condition of our economy while at the same time lamenting the advantages which business has over government in attracting employees.

¶ THE WAR POWERS BILL was approved on Friday by a 72-to-18 vote. In my opinion it would not do violence to the Constitutional authority of the President. Times have changed over the last two centuries to such an extent that the legislative branch has inevitably become more concerned with international affairs and quite properly feels that no President should have the right to involve our country in war without the approval of the Congress. It is true that incidents detrimental to the U.S.A. may occur in almost any part of the world at any time that would require prompt use of our military personnel for the protection of American lives or property. Provision for the President to meet such emergencies is made in the bill approved by the Senate.

The War Powers bill may not be perfect, but it will now go to Conference with the House and oversights and imperfections can be corrected by the conferees. It is reported that the President will veto the bill when it is presented for his signature. It is also probable that the House of Representatives would sustain such a veto, since to override would require a two-thirds vote, which supporters of the bill in the House apparently lack. The large majorities in the House and the Senate in favor of the bill, however, will serve notice on the world that the United States does not intend to engage in major warfare in the future simply because some President might feel like exercising his power to this end.

¶ DURING THE WEEK Senator Jackson started hearings intended to show that the United States was badly cheated, and that consumers were forced to pay higher prices for food because of the sale of wheat to Russia. Certainly the sale of wheat to Russia raised prices in the United States. I am glad that it did, because the producers of grain in the United States could not continue to exist on 85 cents a bushel for corn and less than $1.50 for wheat, which were the prices they got at harvest time in the fall of 1972. I have no doubt that the American farmer, if he can get reasonable pay for his work, can and will produce food enough not only for the United States, but also for people of other countries who are in want. Certainly speculators who bought grain in the fall of 1972 at a very low price and sold it in the spring at a high price made a lot of money, but that is nothing new. Dealers have always bought at the lowest possible price and sold for all they could get.

I wish I could believe that Scoop Jackson's hearings are designed solely to aid the consumers of the United States and to discourage speculators and their possible collaboration with officials of our government. I fear, however, that part of Scoop's motivation may be due to his very evident desire to continue at least a "cold war" with Russia, and possibly to get support for his very obvious desire to be the Democratic candidate for the Presidency in 1976. If the American people really want to maintain peace in the world they will go slow on supporting Scoop for the Presidency. I don't believe he has a chance anyway, but one can never tell.

Week ending July 28, 1973

As IN SO MANY WEEKS, the Foreign Relations committee had visits from heads of state from other countries. This week it was the Shah of Iran, who by the time he left for his home country on Friday surely must have been tired with all the dinners, luncheons, and coffees that he had to attend. Wednesday afternoon he came for coffee with the Senate committee for a little over an hour. During the time he was with us, the committee members had to break away three times to go to the Senate Chamber to vote. While this was not entirely respectful to a visiting dignitary, it was required of us as members of the Senate. Anyway, the Shah was very tolerant and seemed to understand our situation.

After meeting with Foreign Relations, he went over to meet with the House Foreign Affairs committee, but he evidently got back to the Iranian Embassy in time to attend a dinner given by the Ambassador from Iran for the President and Mrs. Nixon. I was tired, too, after an extremely busy day, but did enjoy the dinner and visiting with the people there. It was a comparatively small affair with only between sixty and seventy persons present.

Iran is one of the most important countries in the world, one of the biggest customers for our equipment exports (which they pay for) and one of the countries upon which the Western world depends for a considerable part of its oil supply. Since Iran lies between the Arab countries, Turkey and Russia, the Shah evidently believes that the maintenance of a very strong military force, particularly air force, is most instrumental in maintaining peace in that area, which might otherwise be consumed by the fires of war.

¶ ON TUESDAY we had another group of visitors, five members of the Canadian Senate and twelve members of the House, who in effect came down here to lobby us in favor of a Canadian pipeline for the transportation of Alaskan oil. They hope to find large deposits of petroleum in the Canadian Arctic, but up to now have not discovered enough to afford a pipeline of their own, and, naturally, would like to have the United States interests build a line which not only would carry Alaskan oil south through the Mackenzie River valley, but also would permit what Canadian oil has already been discovered to share in the transportation line.

However, our oil companies, who located the huge deposits in Alaska, are not especially interested in a Canadian line, and prefer a pipeline of less than half the distance from Prudhoe Bay, the site of the discovery, to the southern Alaskan coast where it would be loaded on tankers for shipment not only to the West Coast of the United States but to foreign ports as well. Japan is particularly interested in the possibilities of this route and, quite naturally, users of petroleum through the central part of the United States are apprehensive that Japan might get the lion's share of this production unless strict precautions are written into our law.

Legislation is necessary to authorize the Alaskan pipeline for the reason that much of it would traverse a federally owned area. Under present restrictions a right-of-way through federal lands is required to be so narrow, only 30 feet each side of the pipe, as to be prohibitive. However, legislation would also be necessary if it were decided to transport oil over a Canadian route, because Prudhoe Bay is something over 200 miles from the Canadian border.

I think it is not generally known that approximately half the oil used by Canada comes from other countries, principally Venezuela, to Portland, Maine, where it is transported by pipeline across Maine, New Hampshire, Vermont, and the Province of Quebec to Montreal, where its capacity of 500,000 barrels a day is delivered to six refineries. Although the Canadians profess to be very much concerned over a possible oil spill on the coast of the Pacific, they don't seem to show an equal concern over the possibility of an oil spill on the Atlantic.

¶ ON WEDNESDAY, House and Senate conferees began work on the new farm bill, which had quite different provisions approved by the House and the Senate. The House bill provides that food stamps could not be issued to people on strike who might suffer reduced incomes. Of course, the chambers of commerce and manufacturers' associations all favored this provision, while labor unions strongly opposed it. The Administration would accept the ban on food stamps for strikers, but the Senate conferees are opposed to this ban, since a great many people on strike are not responsible for the situation, but get hungry just the same.

¶ FOR THE LAST FOUR DAYS of the week the Senate gave its attention to what is called a Clean Elections bill, which on the surface purports to insure complete honesty at election time and even greater honesty in the giving of campaign contributions throughout the year. It is about the biggest farce that the Senate has so far attempted to stage. The Watergate episode has created within many members of the Senate a great urge to demonstrate their own purity of conscience and honesty in getting elected or re-elected.

One part of the bill allows for exempting labor unions and corporations from some of the provisions. This bill is a superb example of hypocrisy, and I seriously doubt that the House will have anything to do with it. Even if it became law, we would find the same evasion and cheating on the part of candidates that we have found in many past elections. Passing a law doesn't make people honest, although in some cases it may provide punishment for those that get caught. Passing a law won't erase the old saying that "to the victor belong the spoils," and the "victor" in our elections has come to mean the most generous campaign contributors. Of course we could pass a bill that would make the campaign-contribution route a bit more circuitous, but we can't enact any legislation that would imbue all our candidates and most of our voters with a high degree of piety and righteousness.

Week ending August 4, 1973

A BUSY WEEK filled with doubt and uncertainties.

In the matter of the farm bill, the House exercised common sense and acquiesced to the Senate decision not to withhold food stamps from strikers, and the bill has now gone to the President, who is expected to sign it. It was very important that there be no delay in enacting this legislation since it applies to the wheat crop, which, in the Southwestern states, is sown in the fall months, and it is necessary that the program become known before planting takes place.

¶ MONDAY saw passage by the Senate of what was popularly known as a Clean Elections bill. I was one of eight members of the Senate who voted against it. Admitting that the present law is not very effective in preventing cheating and a variety of sins committed by candidates and their friends at election time, the new bill makes things even worse. The existing law prohibits direct contributions to candidates by labor unions and government contractors, although it is common knowledge that such contributions are even now made in circumvention of the law. The bill approved by the Senate legalizes such contributions.

The new bill carries no prohibition against passing the hat at political rallies, one of the principal sources of income for candidates. It also places the wealthy candidate for Congress in a favorable position compared with less affluent opposition. Although the amount a candidate can spend in primary or general elections is limited by law, a well-to-do candidate could make unlimited contributions to the "do-good" societies and organizations with a hint that, should he be elected, he might do even better by them. In this way he could secure several times as many workers for his election as he would be permitted to hire under the proposed law. Not only could the recipient of his generosity work for him politically, but the candidate would also be entitled to tax deductions on the amounts given. It is obvious that a less affluent candidate would be at a disadvantage under such conditions. These are only a few of the loopholes contained in the bill, which passed the Senate by a vote of 82 to 8.

A common excuse for voting for the Clean Elections bill was that it was easier to vote for it than it was to explain why one did not vote for it.

What the House will do remains to be seen. That body could plug the loopholes left in or inserted new by the Senate and possibly make a respectable bill of it. But it seems to be the general impression that the House will not be very much interested in even touching it.

¶ THE WATERGATE HEARINGS went on through the week, developing more evidence of sin and filling the air with odors. Tempers are getting short among members of Sam Ervin's committee and even among one or two of the witnesses. Former candidates for the Presidency are becoming noticeably quiet and decorous, possibly wondering when some witness is going to divulge some of their suspected or proven sins. I never knew a President, or even a candidate for the job, who never did anything wrong with his life, but right now, with the country sin-conscious, erstwhile candidates have more to worry about than usual. And with conditions as they are now, it will take more than just voting for an ineffective elections bill to rid them of their apprehensions.

¶ THE SENATE also voted overwhelmingly for the elimination of price controls on beef, and this was done for good reason. Our beef animals are going in large numbers to Canada, where they are slaughtered; the meat can then be resold to the United States at a high price. Even in Vermont, I am told, dairy cows can be sold for beef at $40 per 100 pounds, which is several times the price that has prevailed in the past. We may have a shortage of milk before many months go by. The cost of milk production, plus the high price obtainable for beef, is likely to reduce our dairy herds materially. Already the President has had to lift the restrictions against imports of powdered skim milk in order to keep our cheese factories going. And, strange to say, the more we import—some 165 million pounds at this moment—the higher the price gets.

All this situation comes about as a result of too many people in government who don't even know what end of the cow gives milk. But the upshot of their operation proves only that it is primarily the farmer, the consumer, and the taxpayer who pay the price for their ignorance.

¶ WE ENDED THE WEEK on a good note. The Defense department representatives came to the Hill on Friday afternoon and met with the chairmen and ranking members of key committees, nine of us in all. They told us that they really aren't going to drop any more bombs on Cambodia after midnight of August 14th. They insisted that they aren't going to break the deal which the President made with the Congress a month ago. I am certain that this assurance comes as a big disappointment to some of the Administration's most bitter enemies, who had laid carefully thought-out plans to condemn the President for breaking his agreement not to drop any more bombs on Cambodia.

[*The Diary topics for the week ending August 11, 1973—the first portion of Senator and Mrs. Aiken's summer vacation at their home in Putney, Vermont—describe the progress of their vegetable garden, the busy tourist season, and their visit to the Addison County Fair.*]

[*Putney, Vermont*]

Week ending August 18, 1973

WEDNESDAY NIGHT we listened to President Nixon's nationwide TV speech. This received mixed reaction. The Nixon-haters had already made up their minds to condemn him even before they knew what he was going to say. And his supporters, with some difficulty, endorsed his message. The one thing he said which I think should receive full public consideration was that he didn't believe the President should be required to turn over to Congress, or even to the courts, confidential discussions taking place between the President, representatives of foreign countries, official members of the government, or even members of Congress. To be required to turn over such confidential and intimate discussions would make it extremely difficult for the President to carry out the duties of his office properly. The heads of foreign countries would certainly be reluctant to let their hair down and talk frankly if they felt that everything they said might someday be made public. It could have a disrupting effect on world affairs, beyond a doubt.

However, the Ervin committee says they wouldn't use any of this other material, but only the President's private discussions relating to the Watergate mess. Nevertheless, the committee would have all his private discussions from which to sort out the ones they felt pertained to the Watergate. If they could take over the records of all his private discussions in order to sift out those few pertaining to a special purpose, I fear that the leaks we have had from government so far would be small in comparison with what we might expect. Anyway the matter is now up to the courts. If our court system is to function as intended by the Constitution, this is a good time for it to show its merit.

¶ THURSDAY MORNING we drove up to Ludlow, Vermont, for the dedication of a small watershed project, where four reservoirs had been constructed on the Jewell Brook, a tributary of the Black River. I was really glad to attend this dedication because it was in 1954, at President Eisenhower's request, that Congressman Hope and myself, being the respective chairmen of the House and Senate Agriculture committees, introduced the legislation for projects like the one in Ludlow. Up to that time the executive branch of government had concentrated on the construction of large dams across main rivers. The effect of these dams was to destroy a large amount of productive agricultural land in the valleys. President Eisenhower, as well as Congressman Hope and myself, felt that the construction of more small dams on less productive land in the headwaters of tributary streams would accomplish the same purpose at less cost and afford more protection, not only for industrial enterprise but for agricultural land as well.

It was a proposal to construct a very large number (eighty in all) of dams on Vermont streams and tributaries that got me into politics in the first place. Of course these dams, ostensibly for the purpose of flood control, were really largely for the benefit of downriver power plants; and in those days [1930's] any dam site which could produce 500 kilowatts of power was considered feasible anyway. Those were the days when for rate-making purposes the value of dam sites was inflated many times over. That was when I felt that it was time for someone besides politicians to get into politics. The power companies didn't like it at all, and did the best they could thereafter to keep me from going to Washington.

Apparently the majority of the voters believed as I did, though, so I went to Washington without any intention at the time of staying thirty-four years. Everybody asks me now if I am going to try for another six years, but I tell them I am not going to make an announcement this week, or this year, but next spring, maybe, they will find out.

[*Putney, Vermont*]

Week ending August 25, 1973

ON MONDAY we attended the dedication of the maple-products laboratory at the University of Vermont. Secretary of Agriculture Butz, U.S. Chief Forester John McGuire, President Edward Andrews of the university, and a lot of other notables, including several members of my office staff and family, were present for the occasion. I learned that it was a surprise party for my birthday, and that the laboratory, which is really a pretty good building, had my name across the front of it. Oh well, we have to put up with surprise parties once in a while. What's worse, we have to put up with birthdays.

¶ SECRETARY OF STATE ROGERS called me Wednesday morning to say that his resignation would be announced that afternoon. President Nixon held his press conference at 2:30 and immediately after the President's conference ended, Henry Kissinger called to say that he was to be appointed Secretary of State to succeed Bill Rogers. Of course I knew that anyway, but Kissinger evidently was calling all members of the Foreign Relations committee to make sure that they don't give him trouble when his nomination is sent to the Senate. I told him I didn't think he would have much trouble, because members of the committee like Senators Fulbright and Symington and others who lose no opportunity to fire darts at the President, seem to like Henry Kissinger.

I was not too happy about one statement Kissinger made to the press, however, which was that when he became Secretary of State there would be closer co-operation between the State department and the Congress. This intimated that he would get along better than Bill Rogers had, when as a matter of fact Secretary Rogers was very well liked by the members of Congress, and at times had a great deal of sympathy from us because of our feeling that the White House staff was undertaking to downgrade him.

The White House press conference seemed to put President Nixon in somewhat better standing with the news media. There were some complaints that he didn't answer all the questions concerning the Watergate, but with fifty or more lawyers hired by the Ervin committee being paid to think up questions, it would seem to me that no President would be able to answer them all to the satisfaction of everyone.

¶ THURSDAY, while speaking at a Rotary Club meeting in Brattleboro, and throughout that afternoon, I received phone calls from Washington, mostly relating to the Vermont Yankee Nuclear plant and the prospect that the Atomic Energy Commission was likely to order a reduction in its power production. The AEC did issue an order at noon on Friday which probably could reduce production at the plant by about 20 percent from its supposed capacity. About a dozen plants—boiling-water plants made by the General Electric Company—in the United States are affected by this order. Whether GE will be able to correct the troubles which are recognized by the Atomic Energy Commission remains to be seen. If this can be done, the plants can operate at 100 percent capacity. It is certain that the country is going to need all the increased energy production capacity it is likely to get.

[*Putney, Vermont*]

Week ending September 1, 1973

AMONG THE PHONE CALLS from Washington this week was one from Henry Kissinger asking for an appointment with me, which is set for September 5th. I don't know just what he is worrying about, but I suspect he is looking ahead to some possibly hot and embarrassing questions when he comes before the Foreign Relations committee for approval as Secretary of State.

¶ FRIDAY AFTERNOON I had promised to speak at the 150th Anniversary of the Montpelier Center Church, which used to serve as the town hall for both the town and city until Montpelier got to a size where pride demanded that it build its own City Hall. The first of the messages I tried to give in my talk was that no matter how good an idea a person, or a group of persons, may have, we ought not to expect adoption of that idea without delay; nor should we expect perfection even when it is adopted. Most worthwhile programs are the result of compromises. A person is so likely to get carried away with his own ideas that he fails to see the problems and the drawbacks connected with them. Therefore I told them—as I have told a lot of people during the years of my public life—that if you can't get 100 percent of your ideas, take 90 or 80 or 70 or even 60 percent, and then work for the rest. Later on you may decide that the 100 percent that you asked for would not have been desirable anyway.

The second point I made was intended largely for our enthusiastic, well-meaning environmentalist individuals and societies. The idea which I tried to plant is that in seeking to make a few people happy we have to watch out that we don't create more trouble and hardships for the many. There are quite a few people who would not hesitate to close down an establishment giving employment to a large number of people in order to eliminate its stream or air pollution, even though such conditions may have existed in the area for two or three generations. Of course we have to do all we reasonably can do to eliminate hazards to health, particularly from increased air pollution. Yet many people derive their income from working in a plant which contributes to air or water pollution, or both. So when our environmental friends get overenthusiastic and insist on immediate correction of all the hazards that exist from the past, we have to tell them to slow down. On the other hand, if a plant operator objects to any correction at all in the methods used by his father or grandfather, then indeed we have to tell him to get a move on and catch up with the times.

¶ I HAD A ROUTINE CHECK-UP on my eyes and ears, and I suspect that the doctor was as disgusted as most doctors are who look me over for this or that, because my vision turned out to be 20/20 and my hearing was about the same as it was when I was in first grade in school. I hear plenty of low notes, but miss high ones like telephone bells. As a matter of fact, this sort of hearing turns out to be a convenience once in a while, because it lets me hear what I want to and not hear what I don't want to.

[*United States Senate*]

Week ending September 8, 1973

BACK TO WASHINGTON on Tuesday, catching up on accumulated mail.

Congress met on Wednesday to consider routine legislation, including the Treasury Appropriations bill. Visitors at the office during the week included Henry Kissinger, nominated to be Secretary of State, and representatives of the Department of Agriculture who came to discuss new proposals for administering the Rural Environmental Assistance Program, the origins of which go back to the late 1930's. This is a program which has done a great deal in preserving and improving the quality of our agricultural production acreage. The department feels that after thirty-five years some changes in its application are desirable, and, in truth, I have to agree with them.

¶ LATE THURSDAY AFTERNOON I had a visit from Bui Diem, who for a few years was Ambassador for South Vietnam in Washington. I was glad to see him again because, during the years he served as ambassador, I found the information received from him from time to time to be accurate. He now is worried for fear economic aid to South Vietnam will be cut off or reduced sharply. Actually, it appears to me that we should continue to help these people for whom we went to war for the last few years. The cost should be far less than the amount we spent in waging war in their country, and some 80 percent of the money spent there for economic and technical assistance will come back to the United States anyway.

¶ ON THURSDAY the Senate approved legislation authorizing an appropriation of some $50 million for continuing radio transmission in Germany and Eastern Europe. Frankly, I am agreeing more with Senator Mansfield that the time has come when Western Europe should bear more of the cost of its own security. I would not withdraw our support all at once, but would serve notice upon those countries that we do expect them to participate more fully in their own behalf than they have been doing.

¶ FRIDAY WAS A BIG DAY for the press and the TV boys and girls Henry Kissinger came before the Foreign Relations committee for questioning in regard to his nomination to be Secretary of State. Some seventy members of the news media were on hand. I did not even realize at the time that we were being covered by live television, but it wouldn't have made any difference if I had; if any committee member spends time playing to the TV cameras, he is not nearly as effective in his work for the committee and the Senate. Kissinger made a very good appearance and the critical questions fired at him by some members of the committee, noticeably by Senators Case and Symington, were in effect directed more at the President or other high officials of the executive department. Each member of the committee had ten minutes in which to ask questions or make statements concerning the Kissinger nomination.

Quite a few communications are being received opposing his nomination, but the fact is that President Nixon could not have nominated anyone for the job who would not have met with opposition. Hearings will continue Monday, and I hope may be concluded next week, since it is not good for our country to go without a Secretary of State for very long.

Week ending September 15, 1973

PRESIDENT NIXON's address to the nation on Sunday was partly an effort to turn attention away from Watergate and toward the necessity of getting down to business and meeting the problems which need prompt attention by both the legislative and executive branches of government.

He gave especial attention to the growing need for energy in this country and the necessity for finding and developing all our domestic sources of supply. I agree with him that we have been altogether too dependent on imported supplies of oil, largely from Venezuelan and Canadian sources. Meanwhile, the world's largest known supply of oil lies in the Middle East, particularly in the Arab states, and though we use only a small percentage of the exports from these countries, there are prospects that we might become much more dependent on them in the future because of the rapidly increasing use of petroleum products in our country.

Canada is a growing industrial country also, and already depends upon imported oil, largely from Venezuela, for half its needs. Canada has up to now permitted the export of oil from her Prairie provinces to the North Central United States, but how long this will continue is an unknown factor in the economy of North America. Canada at present depends on imported oil, and other oil-producing countries are quite understandably taking advantage of the situation to raise prices. The time may come before long when the Canadians will find it more to their advantage to slow down exports to our Central states and divert their production more to the eastern part of the Dominion.

Over the strong opposition of environmental organizations, Congress has now voted to authorize a pipeline from the large oil deposits of northern Alaska to the shipping points in the southern part of that state. But this supply will not become available for a few years and, when it does, it will undoubtedly be required to meet the needs of the Pacific states. In addition to this, Japan is very anxious to purchase a large percentage of the Alaskan production.

In the meantime, environmental organizations are opposing the production of electrical energy from the atom, concentrating their fire upon the Vermont Yankee plant in my home state. I don't know what really ails Vermont Yankee, but it seems to be jinxed both from Heaven and Earth, since it has been knocked out of commission twice by lightning and several other times by other causes.

It is not only the nuclear plants that are in difficulties. On Wednesday several hundred home-heating-oil distributors from New England descended upon the Congress expressing great apprehension that the supply of heating oil now in sight will not be adequate to meet the requirements of the Northeast during the coming winter. I have discussed the fuel situation with federal officials from the White House on down and believe that if we face a cold winter the federal government will, of necessity, have to find a supply of home heating oil from somewhere.

One reason for concern about the energy supply is that food for the world depends to a considerable extent upon the availability of enough energy to produce that food. In the old days grain was stored away in bins and left to dry out naturally. But now, with many mechanical drying facilities even on the farms, there is an exceptional demand for propane gas, and this demand has resulted in transferring to the grain-producing states of the West much of the supply that would ordinarily be available to the Northeast.

A further complication results from the fact that many people today are so insistent on eliminating pollution from our waterways and air that they impede efforts to facilitate the production of food supplies through the use of new sources of energy. Western states, particularly Montana, have tremendous deposits of coal, but the method of making that coal available arouses the wrath of many people whose dedication to purity runs ahead of their ability to realize that eating and keeping warm during the winter are still important. Complete control of stream pollution would mean that every leaf of the trees bordering such streams would have to be removed, because so long as there is life, either vegetable or animal, left on earth, there is bound to be some pollution.

¶ The Kissinger nomination came in for attention throughout the week. Attorney General Elliot Richardson and his assistant, William Ruckelshaus, came before the Foreign Relations committee on Monday to explain the part, if any, which Kissinger played in the wiretapping of the phones of seventeen persons—mostly federal employees, but also including four disciples of the news media. It was apparent that information which conceivably, but not inevitably, would have affected our national security had been leaked to *The New York Times,* which printed the names of the seventeen persons whose phones had been tapped. Actually, I felt that Dr. Kissinger had probably complained of the leaks; and anyway, the Attorney General— John Mitchell at that time—had authorized tapping the phones. I asked Ruckelshaus if they had found out who was the guilty party, and he said that although they did not have positive proof they had a pretty good idea as to who it was.

The upshot of this visit was that the members of the committee insisted that we be permitted to see the FBI report of its investigation in the case, and Senators Sparkman and Case were appointed a subcommittee to consult with the Attorney General. The result was that the Department of Justice agreed to let the subcommittee see the report, and they did see it a day or two later. I understand that the report did not seriously involve Dr. Kissinger, but Sparkman and Case will make a report to the full committee next Monday. It was quite interesting that, while Kissinger's part in the investigation caused considerable concern among some of our members, they didn't appear too interested in finding out who actually leaked the information to the press.

It looks now as if the committee will approve Kissinger by an almost unanimous vote early next week, although on Friday ten witnesses appeared in opposition to his approval. As the committee meeting neared its close yesterday I advised the members of the opposition that if Henry Kissinger was approved as Secretary of State I would still hold the President responsible for his actions. I said further that if he were not approved it was fairly certain that he would continue to exercise as much influence in formulating and carrying out international policies as he does now from his position as Presidential assistant.

¶ EARLY IN THE WEEK the government of Chile was overthrown, and President Allende reported killed. This came as no surprise, since Allende had been elected president by only 36 percent of those who voted in the election. Also, the economic situation of that country had been going from bad to worse during recent months.

Of course there were those who could not wait to blame the United States for this overthrow of government, and although I cannot help but feel that the wielders of political and economic power in the United States have little regret over the events in Chile, I think our government itself was not involved. It has been repeatedly reported to us that American corporations do undertake to interfere with the politics of other countries. I have no doubt that this is true, since American corporations participate in our own elections for the purpose of gaining advantages for themselves. Chile has been a significant case, since American copper companies were heavily involved there, and I have no doubt but what they encouraged their former employees to vote for the regime that would give them most favorable terms. But I do not believe that the United States government itself was particularly involved in either the election or the overthrow of Allende.

For a long time Chile was the leading democratic republic of South America, but after Allende's election by a plurality vote it adopted socialist practices, including the expropriation of industries, particularly the copper mines. There is no question but what the communist countries of the world were hoping for Allende's success. With his overthrow they have obviously received a setback, since almost the first act of the military government which took over was to order Cuban propagandists out of the country and to sever Chile's relations with Cuba.

¶ On Monday night a reception for John Connally was given by Texas Republicans who, of course, have in mind running him for the Republican nomination for President in 1976.

Wednesday night there was a reception in honor of the Italian actress Gina Lollobrigida which I had to attend because the reception was given by my friend Jack Valenti, and because L.P.A. would have been very difficult to get along with had I not gone. Gina was good-looking, all right, and I had a chance to visit with other people there, including Judge Sirica, who has become very well known because of his handling of the Watergate proceedings. Also, I learned from House members that the House has no intention of approving the so-called Fair Elections bill passed by the Senate in July. I still think that this bill would do anything *but* improve the chances of having honest elections.

Week ending September 22, 1973

Watergate is moving into the background. Only the sins alleged to have been committed by Republicans have been investigated so far, and it looks like a sure thing that Sam Ervin's committee isn't going to dig very deeply into the sins alleged to have been committed by the Democrats in the 1972 election campaign.

¶ Federal officials are going easy on recognition of the new government in Chile—a government which may, or may not, be lasting.

Thinking of Chile reminds me of the very bad earthquake which occurred in that country in 1960. In September of that year President Eisenhower asked the Congress to promote greater co-operation with the Latin American states and requested several hundred million dollars to get an organization started. The Chilean earthquake occurred before Congress concluded action on Ike's recommendation, and so $100 million more were added to assist the people of that country. Folks have forgotten how co-operation with the Latin states got its big start, and I notice now that some editors are giving the credit to President Jack Kennedy, who established the name "Alliance for Progress." As time goes on it becomes more and more apparent that President Eisenhower was a good administrator and that other candidates, past, present and future, are not loath to take credit for the good work he did.

¶ On Monday, Senators Sparkman and Case reported to the Foreign Relations committee that they had received good co-operation from

Richardson and Ruckelshaus relative to the possible involvement of Kissinger in the tapping of telephones, had been shown the FBI report, and had found nothing detrimental to approving the Kissinger nomination. That they were permitted to see the FBI report represented a considerable step forward in our effort to secure greater co-operation between the legislative and executive branches of government. Mr. Kissinger spent most of the day with us after 11:00 A.M., and was asked plenty of questions. He handled the questions very adroitly and left a good enough impression, so on Tuesday morning the committee voted to approve him 16 to 1, with Senator McGovern not actually opposing him, but voting No to show his objection to the Indochina war.

¶ MONDAY HAPPENED to be the 177th anniversary of George Washington's farewell address to the Congress. By scanning this address rather hurriedly I discovered that even as far back as 1796 rivalry existed between the different branches of government. Washington warned the country against letting any branch usurp the Constitutional powers of another, but said that if the Constitution was imperfect, it should be amended through the means provided for in that document itself. He warned against trying to run the affairs of other countries with whom we did business but with whose policies we disagreed. Applied to the present, President Washington's argument could be considered as opposition to Senator Jackson's proposal to restrict trade with the Russians because their country has been putting the squeeze on Jews who wish to emigrate.

Washington's address showed pretty clearly that human nature hasn't changed much since he ended his second term as President. And it was quite apparent to me that had telephones been in existence in Washington's time they would undoubtedly have been tapped just as surely as they have been in recent years.

¶ VICE PRESIDENT AGNEW is having difficulties with the press, which has intimated that because of charges against him relative to his service as Governor of Maryland and as a candidate for Vice President he might resign. I am not sure what prompted these charges, but feel that Vice President Agnew is no more guilty of wrongdoing during election campaigns than are those who would now condemn him. The big battle going on in Washington right now is the battle between the pots and the kettles.

¶ FRIDAY MORNING Kissinger was confirmed as Secretary of State by a 78-to-7 vote and was sworn in at the White House by Chief Justice Burger next morning. The ceremony was quite dramatic. Not only was he the first nationalized citizen, but also the first Jew, to take over this office. Secretary Kissinger was deadly serious and made a very deep impression on the two hundred and fifty persons gathered there. He remarked that in no other country could he be standing beside the President to accept the highest office in our Cabinet. That is indeed the truth, and I hope that the U.S.A. will maintain this honored status in the world for all the future. Former Secretary Bill Rogers was not there in person, but he was there in the minds of most of those who were in the room. Bill was highly respected and honored, but most of us felt that he never had a real chance, being completely overshadowed by Henry Kissinger's White House position.

The new Secretary of State is now definitely on trial and can have no alibi if he fails to carry out his pledge to co-operate with the Congress and keep our Foreign Relations committee fully informed at all times. We expect him to expand the area of peace in the world, to improve the world economic situation, and to bring about a greater degree of tolerance and understanding among people of all races. He has a terrific job on his hands. He will be watched by people the world over, especially by those who for racial or other reasons would like to see him fail. I believe he will succeed and will do all I can to help him, as I have done for his predecessors.

¶ ON MONDAY I received a letter addressed to "Jesus Christ c/o George David Aiken" and, boy, was I really set up! It was actually a pretty good letter about current affairs, but I am in no hurry to deliver it in person.

Week ending September 29, 1973

LATE SUNDAY AFTERNOON we flew to New York with Secretary Kissinger. Congressmen Morgan and Mailliard from the House and their wives went with us, as did the U.S. Ambassador to the United Nations, John Scali, and about a dozen aides, assistants, and security people. Monday morning after the Brazilian representative had spoken for an hour or more, Secretary Kissinger delivered his speech to the U.N. There was an excellent attendance in the General Assembly room, and the audience was so quiet one could almost hear a pin drop. He spoke for about forty minutes and, after a few generalities to start with, dealt with specifics relating to the political, economic, and social affairs of the world. It was an exceptionally good presentation of what I hope is, and will continue to be, the United States' position in the world.

Not far from where we were sitting with Kissinger's parents was the Syrian delegation. They had a full attendance that morning and sat quietly listening to everything he said, but they did not applaud when he concluded. I don't think some of the other Arab countries applauded either, for they would naturally expect him to favor Israel in any dispute with the Arabs. He has, however, pledged himself to be fair, and he has to be if he is to maintain the respect of the rest of the world.

I noted that Foreign Minister Gromyko and Ambassador Dobrynin of the U.S.S.R. came across the chamber to shake hands with Kissinger after his speech.

After we had listened to speakers from Peru and Equador for over an hour, during which time the Assembly room got very noisy, the Secretary of State took us across the street to have lunch with representatives of the African nations. So far as I could see, only representatives of the black nations were present; the Arab Moslems of North Africa were invited to attend a luncheon for countries of their faith on Tuesday.

The Foreign Minister of Mauritania sat between Secretary Kissinger and myself at the luncheon. He was leader and spokesman for the African guests, and he made it pretty plain that the African countries —particularly his own, which is suffering badly from a four-year drought—expected a great deal of economic assistance from the United States. Secretary Kissinger made it plain that our country couldn't do everything that every other country wanted us to do, that we had our limitations, too. The fact is that the United States has not gone overboard in helping African countries to the extent that it has in contributing to many countries on other continents. President Nixon has not visited Africa since he took office, and Secretary Kissinger has been there only once as a tourist.

Our failure, if it can be called a failure, to co-operate more completely with the black African nations may be due to the fact that most of them have in the past been colonies of the countries of Western Europe, and we naturally felt that their welfare, even after they became independent, was the responsibility of France, England, and Portugal. Portugal still retains colonial possessions on the African continent and is not at all popular among those who have achieved at least political independence.

¶ ON WEDNESDAY the Foreign Relations committee had a busy day with the War Powers legislation, which would restrict the President's powers and was, in effect, an attempt to amend the U.S. Constitution by Congressional Resolution. Senator Javits, with a remarkable versatility in using legal terms, had prepared wording for the Resolution which he urged the conferees to accept. The other Senate members of the Conference were quite nonchalant, however, while the House conferees apparently were united in opposition to his eloquent proposals. I suspect that if a conference agreement can be reached and is approved by both Houses the President would not hesitate to veto the measure, as indeed he ought to do, because you cannot amend the Constitution just by passing a Resolution through both Houses of Congress.

But even if such effort to bypass the Constitution were successful, it could at best only express the sentiment of the Congress, for I can see no way in which it would be binding upon the President.

¶ ABOUT NOON on Wednesday we were called to vote upon an amendment proposed by Senator Mansfield to an amendment proposed by Senator Cranston to the Military Procurement bill. Senator Mansfield has worked for a long time to secure a reduction of our troops in Europe. As I said on the floor, his proposal went too far too fast but I voted for it, primarily for the purpose of prodding the European countries to carry a bigger load of the cost of their own defense. It also gave me a chance to support Senator Mansfield, who has accommodated me so many times.

Much to the surprise of all of us his amendment was approved by a small majority of the Foreign Relations committee, and later in the day the Cranston amendment, as modified by Senator Mansfield's proposal, was voted upon by the Senate and was defeated. While I voted for the Mansfield perfecting amendment, I also voted against the Cranston amendment because I felt that its adoption might have a harmful effect upon the efforts of the countries of Eastern and Western Europe to reach an agreement looking to a substantial reduction in the military forces of both areas. Those countries seem to feel that, in the course of the next six months, they can reach some agreement to reduce their own forces which they now feel are necessary for their security. This would permit the United States to get a comparable reduction in the military personnel which we now have overseas. While I am skeptical of the chances of agreement among the European countries, I am willing to give them a chance to try.

The Administration deserves much credit for bringing the war in Indochina to an end, withdrawing about 650,000 American troops from foreign soil, and reducing the total number of all our military forces from about 3.5 million to 2.25 million, with the reduction of another 150,000 or so in the offing. For the first time in almost a generation the United States is not now using the draft to maintain the strength of the military.

¶ THURSDAY I was called to the White House with other ranking Republicans of the Congress to meet with the President and discuss the military situation in general. Secretary of State Kissinger was also there. The President seemed to be quite a bit on edge; the Vice President, who was with us at the start of the meeting, seemed more calm than the President, although considering the attacks now being made upon him, it was difficult to see why he should be calm. The discussion centered around the Military Procurement bill and the proposal of Senator Jackson to write into the trade bill an amendment prohibiting the granting of most-favored-nation status to Russia unless and until Russia guarantees free emigration of people without charging high rates for exit visas. The President insists that the Soviet Union has eased restrictions on the emigration of Jewish people, and, should we enact legislation that would give the Soviets a low level of consideration in trade, it could not help but make much worse the plight of Jews wishing to leave Russia. He intimated strongly that he would rather give up the whole trade bill pertaining to business and economic transactions the world over, than approve any legislation that the Soviet leadership could regard as hostile and insulting, which is the interpretation they would most certainly give to the Jackson amendment if it were approved. The fact is that other countries now enjoying the most-favored-nation status, such as Poland, are notoriously less considerate in their treatment of their Jews than Russia is at present.

As I view the situation, members of Congress closest to the military establishment and to the companies manufacturing munitions and other materials of war are not too unhappy with political differences between the United States and other countries, since these differences make business better for them.

¶ MONDAY the Senate will take up the Foreign Aid bill that is sponsored by Senator Humphrey and myself. Foreign aid isn't always the give-away program that a lot of people think it is: some 80 percent of the money spent for the purpose of helping what we call "undeveloped countries" will come back into the treasuries of American business firms. Anyway, these programs do help other smaller countries which, in turn, contribute to the economy, and to the welfare of all.

Week ending October 6, 1973

MONDAY STARTED OFF with a legislative bang. The Military Procurement bill was finished towards night and brought on criticism because of an increase of some $500 million for the Air Force. However, this bill is authorization only, and the amounts may be reduced when the appropriation bill comes up.

Sad to say, consideration of this procurement measure made apparent the rivalry between the Air Force and the Navy. After the Air Force got the $500 million increased authorization, members of the Senate whose states have big air bases or other air interests (such as the Air Force Academy in Colorado) tried to take some $885 million away from the Navy, which is planning a new nuclear submarine named the *Trident*. The *Trident* is expected to be far superior to any nuclear submarine we have at present and eventually could eliminate our need for bases in foreign countries, since it can go to sea for an indefinite period of time and could actually fire atomic missiles into any part of the world while lying comparatively close to our own shores. The nuclear submarine fleet we have now has probably been most instrumental in preventing a world war during recent years, since even under present conditions it could drop devastating bombs on any country which might feel inclined to go into a big war against us.

A lot of folks who charge that the U.S.A. is war-minded, and that the Nixon Administration is risky in this field, forget that our military personnel have been reduced over one-third in the last three years and that we now have, with the exception of about 60,000 men who came under the draft a year or so ago, an all-volunteer army. Of course we have an element in this country which has great faith in our being able to rule the world by force, but the public, just as it has been for a century, is more devoted to peace.

¶ ON TUESDAY we took up again the Foreign Aid Authorization bill, which produced a lot of arguments but was finally voted on favorably, 54–42, that night. The closeness of the vote does indicate the strong and growing opposition in this country to any foreign-aid program. To ignore the needs of people in other parts of the world would be a major mistake on our part, and even though we claim to be, and probably are, the most powerful nation on earth, we do need friends. It is aggravating to listen to folks who appear to have bleeding hearts for the plight of other people in other places and who yet oppose programs designed to help them.

Other amendments to the Foreign Aid bill were offered, one of which would have refused aid to any country which holds any political prisoners. Besides the difficulty in identifying political prisoners in any country, this amendment would have put us in the position of telling other countries how to run their own business and would have pushed us to refuse aid to about ninety different countries no matter how much they needed it. Ironically, the United States itself is listed as one country which has political prisoners locked up.

¶ CHAIRMAN FULBRIGHT is pretty friendly with Secretary of State Kissinger, and attended a dinner given by Kissinger Thursday night in New York, along with Senator Mansfield and a few others from the Congress. I was invited, but having spent Sunday evening and nearly all day Monday last week with the Secretary, I felt it best that Mansfield and Fulbright share the spotlight with him this time. Anyway, a party for five hundred people is not a good place to learn anything. Kissinger is unquestionably a worker and an effective operator, but whether he can sway members of our Foreign Relations committee who are so strongly opposed to the policies of the Nixon Administration remains to be seen. I would say that we do have an obligation to help the South Vietnamese for the next few years, but I would go along with the Fulbright-Church feeling that aid should be given by multilateral organizations as far as feasible. Indeed the bill sponsored by Senator Humphrey and myself points in this direction; nevertheless, we cannot safely give up bilateral co-operation at this point.

¶ LAST NIGHT L.P.A. and I went to the Saudi Arabian Embassy for a buffet dinner for about seventy-five people. The only other Senator there was Jim Abourezk of South Dakota, who is of Arabian descent; from the House, only Frank and Mrs. Horton were there. The Middle East seems likely to be the next source of serious trouble, with the feeling between the Jews and the Arabs intensifying. If Secretary Kissinger can prevent further outbreaks in that area, he will have done well. An actual outbreak of war between Israel and the Arab states would likely involve some of the great powers, including the United States and Russia. Most of the members of both Houses of Congress would be partial to Israel, and I fear that a few of them would not be adverse to stirring up more trouble with Russia.

¶ SHORTLY AFTER DICTATING the foregoing we heard that war had broken out between Egypt and Israel along the Suez Canal and between Jews and Syrians in the Golan Heights area. As the day progressed, we learned that each side charged the other with starting the fighting. Today is the Day of Atonement for the Jews, however, and it is unlikely that they would start a war on a Holy Day.

Later in the afternoon, Secretary Kissinger called me to report what he knew about the situation and what he was doing to bring an end to the new war through the United Nations and direct contact with both the parties involved, as well as with Russia and other concerned diplomatic sources. I believe he is pursuing the right course, and if his efforts are not impeded by intense partisanship on either side the situation will improve within the next few days. As a result of the present flare-up, it is possible that the long-range conditions will grow better sooner than we now think. The principal obstacle to ending the current fighting and to the promise of a longer era of peace is the activities of fanatical individuals or groups on either side whose judgment is warped by hatred.

On Monday the Halls of Congress will likely ring with advocacies of extreme measures to help out Israel, the Arabs in the U.S.A. will have little to say in the Congress. My advice to them all is to let Mr. Kissinger alone. He knows what he is doing, and the world will be safer and better off if all our candidates for election or re-election either next year or in 1976 keep still for the next few days.

Week ending October 13, 1973

MONDAY some of us had luncheon with four members of the South Vietnamese Parliament. Tuesday evening, I attended a small dinner for ten at the Belgian Embassy. The Belgians are fully aware of the fact that war in the Middle East could seriously affect their own economic situation. Wednesday, with Senator Humphrey as host, we had coffee with President Mobutu of Zaire (formerly the Congo). While we were meeting with him, L.P.A. was at a White House reception honoring the wife of the president of the Ivory Coast. Work on Thursday with the conferees on the Foreign Aid bill prevented my attending a reception at the White House for two hundred top businessmen interested in international trade and export expansion. On Friday another coffee hour with Foreign Minister Macovescu of Romania. Besides this I and a few other members of the Joint Committee on Atomic Energy met with Dr. Eklund of the International Atomic Energy Agency, which has its headquarters in Austria. Also, Senator Talmadge and I met with Roy Ash, Director of the Office of Management and Budget, and others from OMB, regarding future agriculture priorities.

After lunch with Mr. Ash I inadvertently dropped into another meeting to which I had not been invited and had dessert with Governor Love [of Colorado] and Senators greatly concerned with the oil and coal situation in our country, particularly in their states in the West. While the problems and desires of the Northeast are not identical with those of the Western states, we nevertheless have to consider all our energy problems on a national as well as international basis.

¶ THE MIDDLE EAST WAR continued almost unabated throughout the week. On Wednesday, President Nixon had the Congressional leadership at the White House to get a report and briefing, while Friday afternoon Secretary Kissinger came to the Foreign Relations committee room and gave a similar statement. My prediction of a week ago that the fighting would be quickly concluded by a truce—and which was really more of a hope than a prediction—did not come true. The United Nations and the Security Council had accomplished nothing towards bringing hostilities to an end or at least to a truce. However, I am still hopeful, and believe that there will be an easing of hostilities before long. This belief was bolstered by a short conference I had with Soviet Ambassador Dobrynin and Secretary of State Kissinger at the White House last night.

¶ THE BIG NEWS of the week, which wiped the Watergate hearings almost completely off the map and reduced the Middle East war to the middle pages of the newspapers, was the resignation of Vice President Agnew. Everyone was caught by surprise and shock when he appeared in court in Baltimore on Wednesday afternoon, admitted that he had not paid income tax on money received in earlier years, and announced that same day that he had resigned as Vice President of the United States. He took the only honorable course, and it took courage for him to do it. He could have dragged the matter out in the courts for a long period of time, but he knew that it would be harmful to our government and to the country to take this course of action. Although he may have accepted money from improper sources I very much doubt that Spiro Agnew is anywhere near a wealthy man today.

His resignation meant that President Nixon would have to nominate someone to fill the vacant seat of the Vice President, as is required by law. It is essential that such nomination be sent to the Congress, where it can be considered by both Houses as early as possible. Last Thursday afternoon, I had a call from the White House asking my opinion as to whether the President could send up any name he chose and have it approved by both Houses of the Congress. My answer was that if he submitted the name of any ambitious Republican who was looking for the Presidential nomination in 1976 it would be a near disaster, since others competing for the same position in both parties would be sure to make trouble.

Friday evening the President announced to a group of some two hundred people invited to the White House for the occasion that he was nominating the leader of the House Republicans, Gerald Ford of Michigan, for the position. Ford has been a member of the House for twenty-five years and seems to get along well with members of both political parties.

The nomination is to be considered by the Judiciary committee in the House and the Rules committee in the Senate. The Senate Democrats had a caucus on Friday and apparently had a real circus—which is not unusual for the Democrats. They finally voted 24 to 20 to ask the Senate to expand the Rules committee by six members (three from each party) This scheme was apparently aimed at securing a majority of Democrats on the Rules committee who could control the committee and at the same time keep conservative Democrats like Senators Allen of Alabama, Byrd of Virginia, and Cannon of Nevada in their places. The Republicans in Conference later didn't agree to this scheme at all, and with only three exceptions—Senators Javits, Case and Percy—voted to stand by the Rules committee as it was established at the beginning of this Session of Congress. After the vote was taken the three recalcitrants agreed to make it unanimous.

The experience of this week indicated to me that the Democratic party still has more friction within its ranks than does the Republican party. On the whole, we have a pretty good class of freshman Senators, but at least three of the new Democrats simply can't wait to become important, and delight in demonstrating their importance by undertaking to thwart the philosophy and the operations of those who have been here for a long time.

¶ TODAY THE CONGRESS decided to call it quits, with only *pro forma* meetings until October 29th.

[Putney, Vermont]

Week ending October 20, 1973

WE DELAYED starting for Vermont until Tuesday morning in order to attend the dinner which the President was giving for Bill Rogers at the White House. Since those in attendance were contemporaries of

Rogers (and myself) I knew nearly everyone there. I sat near Jerry Ford, who indicated a desire to come up to the office for consultation, but I told him we would be in Vermont for the rest of the month.

I think he is going to have trouble and a long delay in being approved by both Houses of the Congress. Politics are still taking a vicious turn, and the opposition to the Administration will move heaven and earth to find something wrong with Ford, or something he did in his younger days or even more recent days which, in the minds of the opposition, would justify delay or even refusal to approve him. I consider Jerry Ford politically a little to the right of center, but anyone else, particularly those with future political ambitions, would have been viciously and violently opposed for this position.

¶ I HAD HOPED, after talking with Kissinger and Ambassador Dobrynin on Friday evening, that there might be some progress to report on the Middle East war, but that hope was lessened when Mel Laird advised me that the situation was considerably worse as of Monday night. The news Thursday morning seemed a little better to me. It may be that the fighting, in which both the Arabs and the Jews are bound to sustain heavy losses, will give an incentive to reason and possibly hasten a cease-fire agreement. This hope was heightened when on Thursday morning the news reported that Kosygin was in Cairo and that it was believed Dobrynin had gone to join him there.

There is no doubt in my mind that if this war is brought to some kind of an end, and the spread to a wider area is prevented, Russia and the United States will have to do it. I don't believe the Administration of either country wants the war to spread, although both countries are supplying the combatants with war matériel and economic material in large quantities. I still recall the optimism expressed by Kissinger and Dobrynin when I talked with them at the White House on Friday evening, the 12th.

¶ GETTING BACK TO VERMONT on Tuesday evening I was somewhat surprised to find people who I had believed were ardent supporters of Israel now putting responsibility on that small country for the present conflict. It was in 1967 that Israeli armed forces caught the Arab countries by surprise and defeated them in the Seven Days' War, but in the process Israel took—and has since refused to give up—a considerable area of land which was claimed by the Arabs and which had not been assigned to Israel when the boundaries of that country were established by the United Nations in 1948. People who had been strong in their support of Israel and who had been equally strong in denouncing the war in Southeast Asia, now feel that Israel should give back the land which they took from Egypt, Syria, and Jordan in 1967. I feel that the Sinai Desert, being a very large territory, may not belong entirely to either the Arabs or to the Jews; and I feel the same about the Golan Heights area, which Israel considers necessary to protect her from attacks from the east. The settlement of these areas may have to be determined by major countries, particularly Russia and the United States.

¶ On WEDNESDAY MORNING President Nixon and Secretary Kissinger met with representatives of several oil-producing Arab states. The United States does not depend so heavily upon oil from the Arab states as all of Western Europe does. The oil-producing countries, according to reports, informed the President that they would reduce exports to the extent of 5 percent a month so long as the Middle East war continues. I understand that the Arab states also declared there would be a very substantial increase in the price they would charge for their oil—as much as 66 percent. It is safe to say that for every cent per gallon they increase their price for oil, the American consumer will find his costs for gasoline, heating oil and other petroleum products increased several cents a gallon—because that is the way business is done, not only with oil but with other natural products as well.

¶ WEDNESDAY AFTERNOON I received word that Javits and Humphrey are introducing a Resolution which, if I understood it correctly, would give any kind of aid to Israel which that small country might require. They wanted me to be a co-sponsor. I told them definitely not. The worst thing we could do for Israel at this point is for the Congress or even the Senate to try to take away from the executive branch, and particularly from Secretary of State Kissinger, full authority to deal with the war situation at this time. If Congress should go so far as some desire, it could eventually result in a widespread war and virtual obliteration of Israel itself.

It is commonly reported that President Nixon and the Administration will do for Israel anything that country may desire, including the contribution of arms and unlimited war matériel, and that the United States will fight for a victory for the Jews. What the President actually said, however, was that we would never agree to the destruction of Israel as a country, but neither would we agree to the destruction of the smaller Arab states around it. But prejudiced supporters of Israel fail to report that his statement, which I heard, applies to the other states of the Middle East as well.

There is also the impression held by some that the United States will fight to help Israel retain the area taken from the Arabs in the

1967 war. I have heard no such statement from the White House: what the Administration is aiming for now is a cease-fire and a return of both sides to the positions they held before the present conflict started, preparatory to bringing permanent—or anyway what is called permanent—peace to the Middle East.

¶ THURSDAY MORNING I was listening to the "Today Show" when it had as a guest Mrs. Helen Wise, the new president of the National Education Association. And was she vicious! She blamed Nixon and his Administration for everything that goes wrong in education today. She completely ignored the fact that federal aid to education has increased tremendously during his first term in office. She said that the trouble with education is that it is spoiled by politics. If any speaker was more political than Mrs. Wise, I just don't know who it is. She emphasized the fact that children were going without milk in schools, and put the whole blame on the President and the Administration, completely ignoring the fact that it was a Democratic Congress that held up the Agricultural Appropriations bill which carries the money for school milk and school lunch. A good share of the Agricultural Appropriations bill today carries funds for general welfare purposes. Only a part of it, possibly one-third, is for agriculture itself. Mrs. Wise's opinions won't carry much weight with me from now on, although it is possible that I will agree independently with some of the things she advocates.

¶ TODAY—Saturday—the political violence increased.

Tom Korologos called me from the White House to tell me that a compromise had been worked out between Senators Ervin and Baker whereby Senator Stennis would be permitted to read and listen to all White House records and tapes relating to the Watergate debacle and report his findings to the Senate Watergate committee. Late in the day any elation created by the compromise turned to gloom. Another call from Tom advised me the Watergate Special Prosecutor, Archibald Cox, had blown his top and refused to co-operate on any terms except his own. The President lost his cool, if indeed he still retained it: he ordered Attorney General Elliot Richardson to fire Cox. Then Richardson and his chief assistant, William Ruckelshaus, both resigned, and Cox was fired by Acting Attorney General Robert Bork.

The Senate can take much of the blame for this fiasco, since it held Richardson, then nominated to be Attorney General, hostage until he agreed to appoint an outside prosecutor for the Watergate affair, as well as to investigate the 1972 election campaign in general. Thus far he has concentrated only on discovering wrongdoing among Republicans, though in the course of time he might have paid some attention to the four candidates for the Democratic Presidential nomination. The four ambitious Democrats, by the way, are all members of the U.S. Senate.

[Putney, Vermont]

Week ending October 27, 1973

A WEEK of pretty wild excitement both in the Middle East and in the U.S.A.

The White House called Sunday afternoon saying that Kissinger and the Russians had agreed to a cease-fire resolution for the Middle East which they would submit to the U.N. Security Council that night. I told General Scowcroft, Kissinger's man at the White House, that the fact that the peace proposal was a day late did not make it any less welcome.

¶ MONDAY I had several phone calls from women in the state who were worried over the Washington situation and felt that the President should be impeached. After I explained to them that impeachment proceedings had to start in the House and that the Senate had to serve as a jury if impeachment was voted, they seemed to feel a little better about it. I did not detect any great enthusiasm for Speaker of the House Carl Albert, or for President Pro Tempore of the Senate Jim Eastland, to become President, as it appeared that the ruckus which had been caused by the Saturday night resignations would undoubtedly delay the approval of Jerry Ford to be Vice President.

I heard on the radio Monday that there was a demonstration of about 250 people before the State House in Montpelier, all demanding that something should be done about the situation in Washington. I was told that this demonstration had been organized by a man in Tunbridge named Robert O'Brien who came to Vermont some years ago, purchased a good-sized farm in Tunbridge, wired everything on the place for electricity, and then last year started a campaign to cut down on the use of electricity. I asked him where we should cut down on its use. One of his friends from out of the state recommended that farmers start cutting down.

Well, we have just a few of those folks in Vermont who want everything for themselves and not much for anybody else.

¶ AT ELEVEN O'CLOCK on Tuesday, Elliot Richardson went on nation-wide TV and made several points which I think should have helped clear the air somewhat, the first being that Special Prosecutor Cox wanted access to all records, tapes, and files of the White House and not just the Watergate records. This had convinced many people that he was on a fishing expedition, since neither Mr. Cox nor the Ervin committee has made the slightest motion towards the campaigns of the four Democratic candidates for the Presidency in 1972, all of whom were members of the Senate and supported the move to set up the special Watergate investigating committee.

The second point Elliot Richardson made was that the President had not defied any court order, since no court order had been served on him. I feel that a big percentage of the public felt he had already defied a court order, which was not the case.

Another point that the former Attorney General made was that he had confidence in Senator Stennis who, the Executive and Senators Ervin and Baker had agreed, would have access to all the tapes relating to the Watergate, and would then report his findings to the courts and, of course, to the Ervin committee.

But the point that Richardson made that impressed me most was his advice to people to get the facts before making their decisions. A lot of people simply hate to go through all the court procedure or presentation of evidence; they prefer to make up their minds as to the guilt or innocence of an accused party without listening to all the testimony—a procedure which, under our form of government, is not only permissible but is supposed to be required.

I had felt all along that the issue of the President's papers and tapes would have to have its final resolution in the Supreme Court. There was a considerable feeling that the President might be sustained by the Supreme Court, but I can easily imagine that had such been the case there would have been an immediate clamor to impeach the members of the Court. The usual demonstrators have made up their minds to this and that, and many will spend the rest of their lives trying to justify their early erroneous opinions.

Incidentally, there was a special election for a member of the Massachusetts legislature on Tuesday in a Democratic district and the Republican candidate won. So it is quite apparent that the furore and uproar of today is not along strict party lines.

Tuesday afternoon, the country was treated to a surprise when the President agreed to turn over the records and tapes relating to the Watergate mess to Judge Sirica, who had suggested a few weeks ago that this should be done, although no subpoena had been served on the President.

¶ THE NEWS MEDIA thrive on controversy. News writers have repeatedly agreed with me that good news doesn't sell papers and this is probably one reason why the Rutland *Herald* on Tuesday continued to misrepresent my position on some things. Their paper is selling wonderfully well and they get a lot of advertising, so I don't know that we can blame them too much. Certainly, I don't want to put the entire staff of any newspaper on welfare.

On Wednesday *The New York Times* had a story by Clifton Daniel which I think was pretty decent in explaining the clash between the President and Archibald Cox. He reported that he had been told that Mr. Cox had already hired eighty lawyers and that his first four appointments, outranking the others, were all given to Kennedy Democrats. Although I was reported to have said that the President did right to fire Mr. Cox, I didn't say any such thing. I said I was surprised that the Administration had agreed to him in the first place, since he represented the most hostile part of the country as far as the President was concerned.

¶ AN ANALYSIS of the three weeks' fighting between the Arabs and Israelis indicates that, although the Israelis were caught completely by surprise when the Arabs attacked, and suffered heavier losses than would have otherwise been the case, they were better skilled in maneuvering tactics and apparently are the victors in this present conflict. The real danger lay in the fact that, had the Arab states been made to suffer so extensively that they could have lost their entities as separate countries, Russia would have sent military strength in to take their part. Had they done this, the United States would undoubtedly have supplied military strength to Israel, thus involving a war between the two great atomic powers. The result of such action would have meant the almost total destruction of Israel and possibly some of the neighboring Arab states as well.

Of course, it will be a long time before Israel and the Arabs reach agreement as to territorial boundaries. Israel will undoubtedly insist on retaining part of the Golan Heights, from which area they have been subject to many attacks in the past.

If Secretary Kissinger and the Russians have done nothing else, they have got the United Nations to function as it should have been doing long ago. The People's Republic of China abstained from voting in the Security Council on the Middle East proposal, but the other fourteen members voted unanimously—and that is something of a miracle in international politics.

¶ PRESIDENT NIXON was on the air Friday night with a press conference attended largely by hostile members of the news media. He didn't mince matters and neither did some of the reporters present. But at least he showed he was human and not afraid of them. Actually, I thought he had gone too far in expressing his opinion of the news media, although he did make an excellent and encouraging presentation of the international situation. That evening he called me under the impression that he was returning a call from me, which was not so. I told him that I felt that he went a little too far on the domestic scene but did exceptionally well on the international.

It is too bad that the President cannot be on better terms with the press, and that the press can't be more decent and accurate in their reporting. Some weekly magazines seem to think their goal in life is to make the President of the United States unhappy, make him out to be a crook and a liar. They little realize that what they are doing will some day, if they keep it up, result in disaster to their country and themselves.

Two schools of thought seemed determined to make trouble for the President and Secretary Kissinger. One school has it that our objective as a nation should be to overthrow the government of Moscow, and the other group's mission is to overthrow the government in Washington. These two groups probably don't comprise over 2 percent of our total population, but they are organized. When even a comparatively small number, say 500,000 or maybe two million, which is only 1 percent, get organized they can do tremendous damage to their country and its form of government.

¶ THE MIDDLE EAST situation seems to be quieting down with the hostile forces actually observing the peace agreement reached earlier in the week. So not everything is bad, although there is more that is bad going on in this country and in the world than I would like.

[Putney, Vermont]

Week ending November 3, 1973

MR. ARCHIBALD COX, who was fired by the President under somewhat questionable circumstances, did more to justify his firing than all his opposition could possibly have done. He admitted before the Judiciary committee that he had leaked to Senators Hart and Kennedy information obtained from former Attorney General Kleindienst—

which was that the President had asked Kleindienst not to investigate any further the tax return of the International Telephone and Telegraph Corporation. The fact that Mr. Cox had apparently been consulting and confiding in Senators Hart and Kennedy really let the cat out of the bag, since these two gentlemen—Mr. Hart, who is very able, and Mr. Kennedy, who has a pretty complete and powerful organization—may be considered the most effective of the anti-Nixon forces in their attempts to keep the President from having a productive administration, and to expose all the things which he does wrong. And he has probably done more things wrong on the domestic scene than some other Presidents.

Cox's confession to the Judiciary committee seems to have started his old friends and allies worrying, for on Wednesday morning the Boston *Globe* lead editorial was pretty critical of him, and said he shouldn't have done what he did in confessing that he leaked information to Kennedy and Hart. What seemed to bother the *Globe* was that Cox confessed to it, rather than the fact that he did apparently confide in two of the worst political enemies the President could have had.

¶ BY MIDWEEK, efforts at restoring and keeping peace in the Middle East were going ahead full speed. Egypt's Foreign Minister, Ismail Fahmi, was in Washington talking with President Nixon and Secretary Kissinger. This was really exceptional, since the United States and Egypt do not have diplomatic relations. Golda Meir had set foot on Egyptian soil, the first time an Israeli leader has ever done that. Medicine, food, and supplies were being delivered to the 20,000 Egyptians cornered on the east bank of the Suez. Ambassador Dobrynin had spent Tuesday night at Camp David where he could talk with President Nixon, and Secretary Kissinger was already planning to leave for Egypt very shortly.

¶ THE ARAB STATES seem to be carrying out their threats to reduce the exports of oil to nations that have been favorable to the Israeli cause. Tuesday night they announced the embargo on exports of oil to Holland. They are continually raising the price of oil and this is not surprising since they can get more for their production with a shortage in the market. But they are overlooking one very important thing. By increasing the cost of the oil and creating shortages, they are going to force the large oil-consuming countries of Western Europe, and the United States, Japan, and others, to seek new sources of energy. President Nixon has already intimated that we should possibly direct our attention to developing nuclear energy by the so-called fusion method. There are also other sources of oil, untapped, throughout the world. So instead of strengthening their economic position in the world by using their oil production as a weapon, the Arabs may actually be reducing it.

¶ PRIME MINISTER GOLDA MEIR came over from Israel for visits in Washington with President Nixon and Secretary Kissinger. It looks very much as if they are trying to work out some deal whereby the Middle East warfare could come to an end. There are a lot of people who choose not to recognize progress made in the establishment of peace and a better understanding in the Middle East. They choose to continue their attacks on the President, particularly since the White House has admitted that two of the nine tapes supposedly to be given to Judge Sirica are missing.

This has started up the mail again from people urging impeachment of the President or demanding his resignation. One letter received the last of the week said that the public should decide on the President's guilt, completely ignoring the court system which has been in existence for over 175 years.

Probably the most sensible letter I got from Vermont said "Either impeach the President, or get off his back." And another letter said we ought to go back to the form of government established by our forebears nearly two hundred years ago, completely ignoring the fact that impeachment proceedings were provided for in our Constitution. This seems to be an age of emotions, with an awful lot of people thinking that their views are what are best for our country and our government and ought to be followed.

¶ SATURDAY we came back to Washington, to find a few stacks of mail waiting for us. Just what we are here for is anybody's guess. The town seems to be charged with political accusations and hearings bearing on the political situation. A few bits of legislation await action. Then there is some work which we should have attended to some months ago. The White House and the executive branch pulled many boners, but the Congress isn't going to let them get ahead of us in this respect.

I am convinced of one thing—that the Constitutional amendment limiting the President to a single six-year term, which has been offered by Senator Mansfield and myself for some years, should be approved, and I am inclined to think now that a single five-year term is about all any person could stand in that office.

[*United States Senate*]
Week ending November 10, 1973

AT NOON ON WEDNESDAY I spoke in the Senate for fifteen minutes urging the Congress not to duck its duty relative to the repeated charges which are being made against the President by those who are asking him to resign. I reminded the Congress that only the legislative branch of government can make the final determination as to the fitness of the President to continue in office.

So far the demand for the resignation of the President is largely the result of inspired emotionalism with very little, if any, evidence being produced which would warrant removal from office. I admitted to the Senate that the White House has handled its domestic troubles with such relentless incompetence that it has been very difficult for those of us who would like to help out in the administration of good government, but the question as to the fitness of the President to serve out his term is a matter which only the Congress itself can judge. Some members of Congress appear to be working overtime seeking escape routes from their duty. If the President could be forced to resign his position, then the Congress would be relieved of its responsibility to proceed on the evidence and find out if impeachment charges are warranted.

I advised the Senate that the politicians I have known are no greater or lesser sinners than the average person listed in the telephone book, and that the level of sin in public life is about the same as it is elsewhere. One thing that bothered me, I said, is the intensive campaign now going on to make people believe that Richard Nixon and his associates alone are the ones who corrupted America. People today have more money, more time for agitation and crusades, and through radio and television the news media have a greatly expanded means of dispensing information, some of which qualifies as almost pure propaganda. I wound up my speech to the Senate by advising the Congress to "either impeach him or get off his back."

¶ WEDNESDAY EVENING the President spoke to the country to the effect that the energy shortage—which last summer was deemed only a possibility—is now with us, with the Arab states, in an apparent effort to stop the United States or any other country from furnishing material or any kind of aid to Israel, announcing a progressive embargo on shipments of oil to other countries. With the exception of Holland, Western Europe buckled to its knees and West Germany, of all countries—which has depended upon the United States so much for the last twenty-five years—actually forbade us to move any material out of that country to Israel. Holland refused to knuckle under, and Portugal still permits the United States to use its Azores base as a way-station for delivering goods to Israel. At any rate, we found that the friendly nations of Western Europe weren't as friendly when the pinch came, and I have come to the conclusion that we should very substantially reduce our military aid to NATO countries.

Russia, of all countries, is for the time being apparently working with us to restore a more lasting peace in the Middle East. How long this effort will last remains to be seen, but I am satisfied that the Soviets do not relish the thought of any war which might involve that country itself in the fight.

¶ How SECRETARY KISSINGER stands the pace of his diplomatic work is a marvel to most people of our country. As a matter of fact, I think he enjoys the work and has the ability to carry it out. Now he will soon be on his way to China, where presumably he will undertake to further improve the relations between that country with its 800 million people and the United States. If he accomplishes his purpose it will be little less than a miracle. It is astounding to me that so many Americans who praise the work of Kissinger completely ignore the fact that he was selected for the job by President Nixon, and that the work he is doing has the full backing and approval of the President.

¶ ON THE WHOLE, this Congress has declined to override President Nixon's vetoes, until, on Wednesday, we had to consider his veto of what is known as the War Powers Resolution. I supported the Resolution as it progressed through both Houses of Congress and as it was approved by the Committee of Conference, but to tell the truth I felt very much like a hypocrite in doing so. One might say that I voted to override the veto for political reasons; and in a sense this is true, since my voting for it makes it quite likely that a few of my colleagues will vote with me on other, really worthwhile, measures.

The Resolution itself is supposed to prevent the President from carrying on a war without the consent of the Congress. This sounds awfully good, but the measure—which he vetoed and which was then enacted by a two-thirds vote of both Houses of Congress—permits a President to carry on a war for sixty days before he can be brought up short by Congressional action. Tom Eagleton, Senator from Missouri, who was ousted as the Democrat candidate for Vice President last year, opposed the Resolution and stuck by his guns until the veto was overridden by a vote of 75 to 18. But Tom was absolutely right.

If the United States gets involved in a major war of any kind within the foreseeable future, it will inevitably become a nuclear war because of the shortage of the energy required to carry on a war fought with air-power, tanks, factory production and other factors requiring the use of large amounts of power. In my opinion no war fought with atomic weapons would last anywhere near sixty days, for within a few days over one half the people of America and nearly as many of the people of Russia, our most likely opponents, would have been killed. So I consider the so-called War Powers Resolution as largely a political effort to claim glory, but a dud in a practical sense.

¶ AT A QUARTER TO TWO on Friday I got a call from the White House asking me to come down and meet with the President at two o'clock. This really didn't give me much notice, but I did get there at five minutes past two, and on my arrival the President came into the Cabinet Room and sat down with some of his own staff and six other Republicans from the Hill. These were Scott, Griffin and Tower from the Senate, and Ford, Rhodes and John Anderson from the House. For two hours we all sat there talking and listening, except for a period of fifteen minutes when the President had to leave to greet seven new foreign ambassadors.

I think the President gave us a clean story on his part in the Watergate affair. He expressed his willingness to make available to the court and to the public any and all information, including notes and tapes, pertaining to this rather ghastly political mess. The situation is complicated by the fact that all of the tapes subpoenaed are now in the legal possession of Judge Sirica and the court, but are in the physical possession of the White House, since the Judge is not yet ready to listen to them and make decisions based on their contents. The President appears to be perfectly willing to make the entire lot public, but should he do so now he could be held in contempt of court. Therefore his hands are tied until Judge Sirica makes a final decision. I feel that the Judge will make every effort to be fair in the matter.

I fear, though, that the President's bitterest opposition will try to delay a verdict as long as possible. They don't want the President impeached, nor do they want a court decision which would almost certainly put him in a more favorable light publicly. They want to use him as an example of all that is terrible and dishonest, even through the 1976 Presidential election campaign if they can work it out. It becomes more apparent every day that the President has been horribly inept politically, and that his bitter and ambitious opposition has taken an unscrupulous advantage of the fact.

¶ COME NEXT MONDAY the conferees will resume consideration of the foreign aid bills, and although this legislation is extremely important,

I do get some amusement out of watching some of my colleagues turn back-handsprings to get away from positions which they took only a short time ago before the outbreak of the Arab-Israeli war. Since Portugal was the only country in Western Europe that would really co-operate with us in getting aid to Israel, they now are anxious to take out of the legislation any wording which might be considered as a reflection on or condemnation of Portugal. This maneuvering simply proves, however, that we are all human and that willingness to acknowledge an error is one of the better traits of the human race.

Week ending November 17, 1973

THE COMMITTEE OF CONFERENCE took up the Foreign Aid Authorization bill and reached agreements on all the controversial provisions, so that it can be acted upon by the House as soon as that body ends its mid-November vacation. Some twenty-five members of the House have gone to the Middle East, regardless of the fact that the situation there is very sensitive. Another group is going to Korea and presumably other parts of Asia.

Dr. Morgan, Chairman of the House Foreign Affairs committee, has suggested to every one of his colleagues that they would do better to stop criticizing the President for taking what some think are unnecessary trips to California and Florida, while in a ten-day period the members of the House, including Mr. Nixon's critics, will use up enough gasoline to fly the President to his weekend resorts many, many times. Right now it is my guess that some columnists will take them to task not only for calling a recess and taking trips abroad at a time when we should all be busy, but also for using the fuel required for their journeys.

¶ TUESDAY NIGHT I was asked to come down to the White House again when the President met for a couple of hours with fifteen Republican members of the Senate. The other fourteen all had comments to make, and most of them pointed out to the President actions which he had taken or had not taken which many people throughout the country were disturbed about. The President didn't fly off the handle at any of the remarks, although he must have had some difficulty restraining himself. Some sections of the news media, being under no such restraint as the President, did not hesitate to color the reports of the meeting. Later in the week some of them insinuated, or actually stated, that the President had called former Attorney General Elliot Richardson a liar. Having been there, I know that the allegation by certain press units was incorrect. What the President said was that several weeks ago, when he had discussed the proposal for what became known as the Stennis Compromise, and also the dismissal of Archibald Cox as a Special Prosecutor, Elliot had apparently agreed with him until the last day, when he changed his mind, evidently in opposition to the firing of Cox.

I believe that Elliot Richardson himself must have planned the so-called compromise agreement whereby Senator Stennis would listen to all the tapes pertaining to the Watergate mess and then report through the special investigating committee of the Senate. This agreement appeared to me to be identical with the agreement which Attorney General Richardson had reached with the Senate Foreign Relations committee relative to letting members of the committee have access to FBI reports at the time when Henry Kissinger's nomination to be Secretary of State was being considered. Saying that a person has changed his mind is not exactly the same as calling him a liar, although there is no doubt in my mind that the President had thought that Richardson was going with him all the way and was surprised by his change of heart.

¶ THE DISCUSSION on the proposed energy bill in the Senate has convinced me that, regardless of what the final version of the act may be, rich people will get the most consideration and the poorer people will get the short end of the stick. This is nothing new, however, and even though low-income people and handicapped people and elderly people don't get the consideration the big shots do, they will still be much better off than they were in the past.

¶ THE WEEK WOUND UP with a television broadcast tonight of President Nixon meeting members of the Associated Press Managing Editors Association in Florida. For the first ten or fifteen minutes he appeared very nervous, but as the questioning went on and he found himself able to answer in good form, he seemed to recover his poise. Some of his answers and comments set critical members of the press back on their heels, which seemed to please him but not them. When he told the Washington *Post* representative that he enjoyed their sports section, the rest of the audience laughed.

In discussing energy, he tried to put the bee on the Congress. He did tell us at a White House meeting on April 18th that there was no energy crisis then but there would be one in a few years unless we did something about providing new sources of supply. He also stressed, as I have tried to do, that what actually caused the shortage of energy was the industrial and agricultural boom which took place not only in this country but throughout the world. After the Russians placed the large order for wheat with us in July 1972, more people got more jobs and more pay and bought more outdoor and indoor equipment than they had bought for years. Probably the safest thing for us to do is to blame the Russians for the shortage of energy at this time, because they started it with that order of wheat.

Week ending November 24, 1973

On Tuesday, Secretary Kissinger came to the Capitol to report to the Foreign Relations committee on his trip to the Middle East, to China, and Japan. It is almost a miracle that Henry Kissinger is on good terms with the Senate Foreign Relations committee while at the same time he enjoys the full confidence and support of the President. I am not sure that this degree of confidence extends fully to the National Security Council, however.

On the whole his report was optimistic, and it looks now as if the Jews and the Arabs will get together before Christmas to work out a longer-range deal which, in the long run, would cover location of boundaries and a common-sense attitude towards economic and military affairs. Both Israel and Egypt rely upon the United States to promote peace in this troubled area.

¶ President Nixon has made a few speeches in the South during the early part of the week, and he apparently made some gains in the field of public opinion, since for the first three days of the week, at least, communications in his favor outnumbered those that insisted upon throwing him out of office. There was some change in the tenor of the notes demanding his ouster, however. Instead of demanding impeachment, the opposition, which is well organized, is demanding his resignation from office, the reason being, apparently—as was pointed out by one of our communicants last week—that the President refuses to give up the evidence which they consider necessary in order to secure a verdict of guilty for the charges made against him. They seem to doubt their ability to impeach him.

¶ The *Wall Street Journal* has been printing some very good articles and editorials lately, and its reports are generally more factual than most of the other daily publications. Its lead editorial on Wednesday described the situation in which the Pilgrims found themselves in 1620 when they left the Old World to face the wilderness in America. There was another excellent article by Douglas Hallett that quoted from a communication which Daniel Patrick Moynihan, now Ambassador to India, wrote to the incoming President Nixon in early 1969:

> . . . Your task, then, is clear: to restore the authority of American institutions. . . . [Johnson] in a sense . . . was the first American President to be toppled by a mob. No matter that it was a mob of college professors, millionaires, flower children, and Radcliffe girls. . . . The leading cultural figures are going—or have gone—into opposition . . . they take with them a vastly more numerous following of educated middle-class persons. . . . It is their pleasure to cause trouble, to be against.

A large percentage of the big public demonstrations going on today are inspired and led by teachers in our colleges. Of course we might say that they do a lot of good, for many of the better things they advocate would never come to pass without agitation. But they also have an inclination to go so far at times that they defeat the purposes for which they work, by inspiring others even to the point of mob demonstrations which kick back more often than they succeed.

¶ WITH NOBODY IN THE OFFICE THURSDAY, mail piled up. Mail now is more likely to be concerned with fuel and gasoline than it is with Watergate. Watergate had a flare-up, however, when it was announced that one of the White House tapes which the Court had requested had a skip of eighteen minutes on it. Of course, I don't know what caused the skip, but I do know that, when I went to the White House to meet with the President on November 9th, he left us for about fifteen minutes to go out and meet with some new ambassadors from foreign countries—and maybe something like this occurred on the tape. Well, what happens now is up to Judge Sirica. In our meeting on the 9th, General Haig told us that the Judge didn't want the tapes for at least two weeks and it would then require three weeks to read and analyze them. Maybe we will get some opinion from the Judge by Christmas, but anyway the mess is now in his lap and we will just wait and see.

Week ending December 1, 1973

IN A BROADCAST Sunday evening the President discussed the energy shortage, with particular reference to heating oil and gasoline, and this lost no time in stirring up the country. The ski areas of Vermont got excited, for not only does the major part of their patronage come from people who arrive in automobiles, but some of the resorts use energy to make artificial snow. Filling-station operators in some towns did not realize that their supply of gasoline was allocated on a monthly basis by the wholesale dealers, and sold out their entire supply before the end of the month.

Industrial plants here and there about Vermont found themselves running short of chemicals necessary to continue their operations. So far as I know, none of them has had to actually close down, but the supply of material on hand was so low that they were plenty scared. Fortunately, we were able to contact the federal officials quickly enough to avert a necessity for a shutdown at this time.

¶ WITHIN THE NEXT FEW DAYS, Secretary Kissinger will be meeting with our NATO partners in Europe. He made it quite evident that he is displeased with the attitude of the European countries who knuckled under to the Arab threat to reduce the oil supplies upon which most countries of Europe depend. It is clearly evident that if these small oil-producing countries can whip all of Europe into line on the Israeli controversy, they will most certainly use this same threat to whip Europe into line in the future whenever it suits their purpose to do so. One result of the European countries' sliding out from under when we needed them has been to force the economies and the politics of Canada and the United States closer together. Not many months ago we were told that this is "the year of Europe," but those who told us so have changed their minds appreciably in the last six weeks. The United States has also held that the larger countries of the world could not prosper economically without giving due consideration to Japan. Apparently the countries of Western Europe disagree.

¶ THE MAJOR ITEM OF LEGISLATION coming before the Senate was the Social Security bill, to which a host of amendments were proposed, many of which were adopted by the Senate. Some are good, more are no good, and it is presumed that in Conference with the House the whole bill will be strengthened. Every would-be candidate for higher office felt the urge to offer amendments which could give him added publicity, and some of my colleagues go to ridiculous extremes in this respect. However, the main purpose was to provide an 11 percent increase in Social Security benefits to people who qualify for them.

The so-called Debt Ceiling bill, approved by the Senate early this week, was encumbered with ridiculous non-germane and damaging amendments. The majority of the Senators who claim to be liberals (although that qualification is subject to question) went all-out to force the House and the White House to accept amendments which would have been disastrous to our election system. These folks, largely supported by the news media, are constantly crying for election reforms. I would like election reforms, too—reforms that would make candidates more honest and strengthen both the legislative and the executive branches of government. The reforms which they supported this time, however, would have made elections more dishonest and would have encouraged more unqualified persons to try for their party's nomination to the Congress or even the Presidency.

Under the amendments now proposed for the Debt Ceiling bill, candidates would be given large handouts of federal money provided by the taxpayers. In Vermont, for instance, a candidate for the Senate would get $175,000 towards his election campaign, and in the larger states much, much, much more; and an opponent would also get a similar amount. Theoretically, federal financing of election campaigns would do away with the sin of accepting contributions from corporations, labor unions, and millionaires seeking political appointments. Actually it would do no such thing. It simply would mean that a candidate for the Congress or the White House could dip into the federal treasury up to his elbows, and the labor unions, corporations, professional organizations and others would carry on as usual, but probably in a somewhat different manner, since their direct cash contributions would be restricted under the law.

¶ THE CHRISTMAS SPIRIT is supposed to pervade the atmosphere from now on, but if it doesn't hurry up, it is likely to be too late. Right now a lot of people are trying to get even with someone, and this doesn't mate up well with the Christmas spirit. Congress will certainly be in session for another two or three weeks and maybe longer, and this is not conducive to gaiety and happiness among many of its members, especially myself. Yet if we would only stop to think of it, the people of our country have better living, more luxuries, better health, better education and, temporarily at least, more peace in the world than we ever had before. These aren't bad Christmas presents, if we would only take time to think of them.

Week ending December 8, 1973

SUNDAY STARTED OFF with a political bang. The Senate was called into session at ten o'clock to vote on a cloture motion to stop debate on the Debt Ceiling bill with its ultra-generous amendments providing handouts of federal money to political candidates. The promoters of this scheme know what they're up to. They think they are giving more power to labor unions and so-called non-profit organizations and taking political power away from the corporations. Fortunately, the cloture vote didn't carry on Sunday.

On Monday the Senate went at it again. The second cloture vote failed by a vote of 49 to 39, and then Jim Allen moved that the Senate recede from the controversial amendments which aroused so much hostility in the House. House members opposed public financing of candidates because such action would undoubtedly bring forth opposition to every one of them in future elections. In each Congressional district there would be someone who would be a candidate just to get a good big slice of the taxpayers' contribution. The motion to recede from the amendments failed by a vote of 42 to 43, indicating what seemed to be a permanent deadlock.

I finally yielded to the urging of some of my colleagues to take a hand in the matter. By asking a few questions of Senator Long, chairman of the Finance committee, I received answers for the record which put the whole deplorable and strictly political affair before the entire Senate. The result was that Senators Scott and Mansfield, leaders of the Republican and Democratic parties in the Senate, both of whom had favored public financing of political candidates, agreed to the Senate's receding from its position with the understanding that the Rules committee would take the matter up early in the next session. So the Debt Ceiling bill, unencumbered by amendments, was approved by the Senate and sent to the President, who signed it immediately Tuesday night.

¶ THE FOREIGN AID CONFERENCE REPORT was approved by a small margin on Wednesday. A good many of the Senators are getting fed up with foreign aid, but didn't feel that this was the time to give it up completely, and so 44 voted in favor of the current proposal and 41 voted against it. I supported the conference report and spoke for it on the floor. The new arrangement stresses more multilateral aid through international financing agencies, with particular reference to Southeast Asia. It also tends to encourage greater effort by private organizations in rendering assistance to the people of less affluent countries.

¶ ON THURSDAY Jerry Ford, Republican leader of the House, was sworn in as Vice President to take the place of Spiro Agnew. Jerry made a good impression at the swearing-in ceremony and also in his short speech given in the Senate after he became Vice President and, consequently, president of the Senate.

¶ WATERGATE REPORTS and testimony still drag on and many people, including myself, are sick of it. Although the House appropriated one million dollars to consider impeachment proceedings against the President, little progress has been made, and to all appearances House members are reluctant to bring specific charges against Richard Nixon While the President has been deluged with charges, evidence necessary to bring impeachment proceedings against him has not been forthcoming in sufficient quantity. The effect of this deluge is showing up in his personal physical appearance.

One result of the large number of charges against him has been to divert charges which might be made against many other officials of government, including members of the Congress. So long as public concern is directed at the President, others may escape the attention which they might otherwise receive.

¶ ON FRIDAY, General Moshe Dayan, now Minister of Defense for Israel, met with the Senate Foreign Relations committee and several other Senators to discuss the Middle East situation from Israel's viewpoint. I found his comments to be rather re-assuring, since he agreed that Israel would discuss almost anything that promised to lead to a long period of peace in that area. He also said he believed that the countries most seriously involved all wanted to get things straightened out so that they could live together more amicably. And while General Dayan was visiting with the members of the Senate here on the Hill, Secretary Kissinger was talking with a representative of Egypt at the State department.

¶ I AM HOPING that we can all get home for Christmas and stay away from Washington for at least a month. Visitors to Washington find it a beautiful city, but some of us who are required to stay here in performance of our elective duties are prone to get other ideas.

Week ending December 15, 1973

PRESIDENT NIXON and the U.S. Government now declare our intention of becoming independent from the rest of the world for energy, but once let the supply of oil imports become adequate again and people may find this new declaration of independence has become weakened. The world has become just one big community, with squabbles among its nations just as there used to be squabbles among the people of our home communities.

There is a little better understanding between the executive and legislative branches of government than there was only a year ago. While Elliot Richardson was Attorney General, a *détente* was worked out between the Senate Foreign Relations committee and the Justice department relative to the exchange of information. This seed has since grown until the White House seems willing to meet, as far as it can do so, all the requests of the courts for information relating to the Watergate. I doubt if it is the Christmas spirit which prompts this better relationship. Certainly the sound of Santa's sleighbells has not deterred our ambitious Presidential candidates from making the most of every opportunity to disparage the President and to weaken other candidates in their own party, as well as discrediting potential Presidential aspirants of the opposition. The old saying credited to Alben Barkley or Teddy Roosevelt, that "once a Presidential bug gets into one's blood the only way to get rid of it is with embalming fluid," was never more evident than it is today.

Ambitious Democrats have made it plain that they want to eliminate Hubert Humphrey and others who might be considered formidable in the nominating convention of 1976. The news media seem to show a preference for Teddy Kennedy and Chuck Percy. They boost Teddy because the Kennedys have always been good to the reporters, and they are boosting Chuck because they think he would be the easiest Republican for Teddy to beat, just as the Republicans boosted George McGovern as the 1972 Democratic candidate.

¶ IT APPEARS NOW that next week Israel and the Arab states, escorted by the United States, the U.S.S.R., and the United Nations, will have a conference in Geneva. Yesterday it was announced that my Vermont neighbor, Ellsworth Bunker, would head up the U.S. delegation to the conference as representative of the President, subject to the leadership of Secretary Kissinger. On Friday, Ellsworth and his wife, Carol, came up to lunch with L.P.A. and me. It is difficult to imagine that anyone living only a couple of miles from us at home can be so influential in world affairs, but I am glad that my neighbor qualifies in this respect. ¶ NEXT WEEK I expect that the Congress will appropriate something like $2 billion to assist Israel in recovering from the losses in military equipment incurred during the October war. Saudi Arabia, Kuwait, and other Arab states have already assisted Syria and Egypt to the amount of some $2 billion to recoup their losses. Since these same Arab oil-producing states have raised the price of oil to an unheard-of height, it would appear that we in the United States are, in effect, financing both sides. And who gets the profit? Russia, of course, because the Arab states will use the American dollars which we have paid for oil to purchase the needed military equipment from the Soviet Union. Theoretically the Russians will spend this money in purchasing supplies, equipment and grain from the United States—but to what extent remains to be seen.

Week ending December 22, 1973

THE AUCTION for the purchase of Jewish influence went merrily on in the Senate, with the Foreign Aid bill up for action. Senator Fong proposed an increase of $36.5 million to aid Jewish refugees coming out of Russia. Israel had not indicated a need for this money. The State department said they didn't want this money because so much was left over from the previous year's appropriation that it was not needed. Nevertheless, the Senate voted for the amendment.

Not to be outdone, Senator Humphrey then proposed that, of the $2.2 billion which the Administration has asked for aid (primarily military) to Israel, the $1 billion of it that is authorized as grants should be raised to $1.5 billion. Of course this amount was accepted without any trouble, also.

Teddy Kennedy then rose to offer an amendment, and quite naturally I thought that he would probably try to outbid Hubert for the political support of Israel and of the American Jewish population. Teddy, however, didn't undertake to outbid Senator Humphrey, but instead offered an amendment taking a slap at the new Chilean government. The deposed government had expropriated hundreds of millions of dollars worth of American investments, and the new government is bargaining with American companies over compensation for their expropriated plants and industries. It is a safe bet that if the

U.S. Congress should take a good hard slap at the present government of Chile, the prospects for private industry's recovering full value for the property taken over by the previous Chilean government would be very slim indeed.

A couple of years ago we authorized by legislation the establishment of OPIC [Overseas Private Investment Corporation] to insure the investments of American corporations in other countries. If Chile now refuses to compensate adequately for the expropriated American investments, it could mean that OPIC will go on the rocks. I doubt that Teddy Kennedy was aware of this when he offered his Resolution, but I am sure that Senator Javits, a staunch advocate of OPIC, is fully aware of the hazard. Anyway, the conferees threw the Kennedy amendment out of the bill, an action which I felt was desirable.

¶ DURING THE COMMITTEE CONSIDERATION of the Foreign Aid Authorization bill, Senator Pell proposed an amendment denying credit for Greece until Greece complies with all the rules and regulations laid down by NATO. Although a quorum of the Foreign Relations committee was not present at the time, a roll-call vote was taken, and Senator Pell won by reason of proxy votes being cast for members who were not there. Of course the whole thing was irregular and contrary to the rules of the Senate, so I doubt that it will get anywhere, though it will probably get good advertising in areas which will irritate the present Greek government.

[Putney, Vermont]

Week ending December 29, 1973

THERE IS STILL TALK of rationing gasoline here in the United States. In my opinion, this talk is partly political and partly in preparation for a possible later emergency—political, because if the Administration goes in for rationing the result would be wholesale cheating for which the executive branch would get the blame. There is dirty work enough going on right now, but on the whole, the gas stations—at least in this locality—seem to be abiding by rules.

¶ VERMONT POLITICS are beginning to boil up. I am advised that the Republican State Committee has hired a pollster to determine whether I should be a candidate for re-election or not next year, and what my prospects would be if I decided to seek another term in the

Senate. I could tell them right now that the results of the poll won't have the slightest effect on my decision, which in fact was made a long time ago. But they also want to find out what Republicans would run best for both state and federal offices. I well recall the results of the polls in 1936 which indicated that Alfred Landon would be elected President by a great majority. And, again in 1948, the pollsters indicated that Harry Truman didn't stand a ghost of a chance against Tom Dewey. How wrong they proved to be!

1974

Week ending January 5, 1974

TUESDAY I received a call from President Nixon, at San Clemente, California. He wanted to wish us a happy New Year, and then qualified it somewhat by saying a *happier* New Year. Well, the year 1973 was not altogether happy for him, although his accomplishments in the field of international affairs were indeed quite remarkable. Of course Secretary of State Henry Kissinger gets the lion's share of the credit from the people who inherently dislike the President. But when I ask them who appointed Henry Kissinger and who is it that backs him up whenever he needs backing, all they say is "We don't like Richard Nixon."

This type of reaction is exemplified by a sign we saw at an occasional gas station which isn't finding everything just as it wants it to be. The sign says "Don't blame us, blame Washington." L.P.A. took after one of the people who pointed this sign out to us and said, "Why blame Washington for your troubles?" The reply she got was, "Well, we have to blame someone."

¶ THE CHRISTMAS SPIRIT did not reduce the attacks on the President materially, and soon after the first of the year, they went at him again, accusing him of conspiracy with the ITT and the dairy co-operatives of the Southwest. Undoubtedly ITT did promise a substantial sum to the Republicans last year if they would hold their nominating convention in San Diego, because the ITT had constructed a huge hotel in that city. If I am not mistaken the big hotels in any city are expected to make substantial contributions to either political party that is holding its convention there. As far as the Southwest dairy co-operative is concerned—and I have never regarded this co-operative as the finest of our dairy organizations—it is my understanding that they were ready and willing to contribute to candidates of both parties, although to read the papers one would think they were only prejudiced in favor of Republicans. I think they made a rather generous contribution to the candidacies of some of my good Democratic friends, as well as to President Nixon's campaign.

¶ EARLY IN THE WEEK we got news that Senator Hubert Humphrey was in the hospital. Hubert and I have worked together on a lot of good objectives ever since he was first elected to the Senate—the Food Stamp plan, school lunches, feeding of needy people and so on. So on Friday I called him at the hospital in Washington—and he was pretty encouraging. I hope that he will be able to snap out of his illness and get back to work in the Senate at an early date.

[Putney, Vermont]

Week ending January 12, 1974

THIS WEEK STARTED OFF with the change from Standard to Daylight Saving Time, which is supposed to result in a considerable saving of electric energy. So far as I can learn, though, the principal effect up to now has been to increase the sale of reflectors to pin on school children because their mothers are worried about their going to school in the dark. However, in a couple of weeks more the sun will be getting up considerably higher, and Daylight Saving may come into its own and be respected and admired once more.

On Monday we got word that the Vermont Yankee Nuclear Power plant in Vernon would be permitted to operate at full capacity. Presumably some of the environmentalists who opposed its operation are dependent upon electric energy for their own comfort. And Vermont Yankee has finally complied with all the rules and regulations of the Atomic Energy Commission.

Also on Monday, L.P.A. and I went to Brattleboro, where I got my first haircut in six weeks and she had her first hairdo in six days. I have noticed for some time that when women get discontented or sad or something, a trip to the hairdresser does much to put them back into a generous mood.

Tuesday at noon I had promised to speak to the Barre Lions Club. Since it was their annual Ladies Day, they had a full house for the luncheon. I spoke from notes and at one point shuffled my notes around somewhat, which prompted a reporter for the Rutland *Herald* to put in his otherwise pretty good story next morning a statement that, although I was pretty well received, I did appear to be fuzzy, which might react against me should I run for re-election. However, Bob Mitchell, principal owner of the *Herald,* straightened things out next day in the lead editorial by saying that I always was like that; having known Bob since he was a cub reporter I realized that he knew me pretty well, too.

L.P.A. says I ramble. Of course I ramble. It is my nature to ramble when I get to speaking, but it isn't always a question of fuzziness or uncertainty, because sometimes a speaker can fend off a more difficult situation by diverging from the subject. But then, she enjoys telling me when I make a mistake, even though I do it on purpose, and delights in kicking me under the table if she is near enough. Well, I talked with Bob Thursday and we had a good laugh. I told him to tell his man not to worry over his story at all because it was, on the whole, a pretty good one. And anyway I don't have much use for news reporters that couldn't make mistakes—deliberate or otherwise—from time to time.

¶ There have been some complaints that certain ski areas in Vermont have put in gas stations to make sure that those who come up to ski at these resorts are able to get gas enough to go back to New York or southern Connecticut or wherever they come from. As a matter of fact, I am quite certain that the gasoline and oil furnished by our recreation areas to down-country skiers is not charged to the Vermont allocation; instead, the supply has been arranged by oil-company executives who are also mightily concerned with Vermont ski areas through investment and otherwise, and the fuel with which they supply their visitors is charged to Connecticut and Massachusetts rather than to Vermont. However, we don't advertise this fact right now, because there are other interests in our southern neighboring states who would raise a considerable howl.

¶ Thursday was a memorable day in that it was thirty-three years ago that I took the oath of office as a United States Senator. L.P.A. and I are about the only ones of the initial group left to celebrate that event; and quite a lot has happened since. On that day I recall that L.P.A. [then Lola Pierotti], going down with some of the rest of us, lost her hatbox at Newark airport, and one of the aides had to run halfway across the field to get it for her. Well anyway that's what I remember about that day except that I was sworn in by Vice President John N. Garner of Texas.

¶ Saturday—today—is about the most beautiful winter day one ever saw. About sixteen inches of pure white snow on the ground. Mount

Monadnock and a lot of New Hampshire landscape, including lights in the evening, showing up fine.

The corn popped extremely well and the fireplace keeps us warm with wood I cut myself and L.P.A. piled up in the cellar and garage. Who could want more?

[Putney, Vermont]

Week ending January 19, 1974

BUSINESS KEPT ON as usual. Tuesday the new regulations for petroleum products, particularly gasoline and heating oil, went into effect. Much of the responsibility has been turned over to the states, but there are still a lot of users that don't understand all the regulations, and during the latter part of the week we got calls from people who had problems they wanted cleared up. The big oil companies are undoubtedly undertaking to gobble up the business which heretofore has been the stronghold of independent dealers. But then, if the little fellows were in the position of the big fellows, they would probably do the same thing. As I have said before, the only trouble with the world is that it is run by people.

¶ THE FIRST OF THE WEEK David Aiken, my grandson, presented me with a framed copy of the front page of *The New York Times* dated August 20, 1892, which happens to be my birthday. I took some comfort in copying excerpts and reading them to the annual meeting of the Brattleboro Chamber of Commerce. The conditions were almost identical with those that are with us today. Beef went up 2 cents a pound wholesale and 5 cents a pound retail. The black people of Georgia surprised the Republicans by adhering to the Democrat candidate of that year. Transportation problems affected the New York Central and other rails running out of Buffalo, due to a strike of the switchmen. And so on.

When I concluded reading the excerpts, I relieved the guests' feelings by telling them that the issue of the *Times* was dated in 1892. And, if anyone happened to ask them what else was new, they could answer, "Skylab."

¶ OF COURSE, the Watergate tapes came into the picture during the week. This situation was played up by the news media as a great exposure. As far as I could see, nothing was exposed that was not already pretty well known. But with the Department of Justice, the U.S. House of Representatives and the special Senate committee now employing as many as two hundred lawyers and investigators, we seem to have a bear by the tail. And all these people hired at good salaries are not going to give them up easily, or without a lot of maneuvering and political byplay.

¶ PROBABLY THE BEST NEWS of the week was transmitted to me Thursday forenoon by Tom Korologos from the White House, who told me that at noon the President would announce an agreement reached by Israel and Egypt. The White House gives us anywhere from ten minutes' to two hours' notice of such announcements so that we can be prepared to comment when called by representatives of the news media. The news was very gratifying, although I had had full confidence that some progress towards Middle East peace would be made.

[*United States Senate*]
Week ending January 26, 1974

LAST WEEK I suggested that the Vermont State Republican Committee wasn't showing good judgment in inviting [California] Governor Reagan to speak at a fund-raising dinner on the 20th: weather could be bad, folks wouldn't want to go, and all the other handicaps typical of that time of year. But the weather was fine, the hall in Barre was crowded—thirteen hundred people bought dinner tickets at fifty dollars apiece—and Reagan made a pretty good speech. Whether he will be a candidate for President or not remains to be seen, but he sure had the earmarks of being a potential number.

¶ ABOUT THE ONLY good news of the week was the announcement Saturday afternoon that Chairman Ervin had called off hearings on the Watergate which were slated to begin within the next few days. The committee to investigate the 1972 election, called the Watergate committee, has about run its course, and the longer it continues the worse it will look. This committee made the same mistake that other committees do and the same mistake that President Nixon made in the White House: it hired a manager and gave him too much authority. And like other lawyers hired by some other committees, he became so impressed with his own importance, that the Watergate committee members themselves were soon relegated to the background. Apparently—I hope—Sam will get rid of him and his numerous and expensive staff. The life of this special committee expires in a little over a month and if it is not renewed, I for one will say good riddance. Investigations are one thing, but when investigators feel that they are charged with getting convictions rather than facts and become unbearably impressed with their own importance, then they don't do the Congress or the country any good.

The pigeons were glad to see us back and lost no time in making that fact known.

The weather is too warm for this time of year. I certainly hope that having warm weather throughout most of January doesn't mean a short crop of maple syrup this spring. We simply have to have maple syrup in this office, because I found out many years ago that a quart of maple syrup wields more influence among my colleagues and friends in Washington than money could ever be expected to do.

Week ending February 2, 1974

WEDNESDAY EVENING President Nixon gave his annual address to the joint session of Congress. Although I was supposed to be one of his escorts to the rostrum of the House, discretion proved the better part of valor, and I stayed in bed with a cold and listened to him on television, leaving the honor to Senator Young of North Dakota. The President's address was pretty good on the whole. For the main part of it he didn't argue much with the Congress, advocating most of the programs which many Democratic members of Congress are supporting or promoting anyway.

But at the end of his address he extemporized on the Watergate mess and efforts made by political antagonists to get something on him. If he hasn't done wrong he is the first President I have known that didn't commit any sin, but I agree with him that one year of harassment over the Watergate situation should be punishment enough, and that the country would be better off if we now settled down to work, leaving the charges against the President to be handled by the judicial branch and the courts and the Judiciary committee of the House, which will determine whether impeachment charges are justified or not.

¶ ON FRIDAY the so-called Genocide Treaty was laid down before the Senate. This treaty, which is a convention that has been signed by about two-thirds of the members of the United Nations, including all the communist countries of the world, provides for the trial and punishment of persons, governmental and otherwise, who have tried to destroy people because of their race. The treaty itself is thoroughly unworkable, but it has been held up as a symbol of sympathy for the Jewish race. It was, indeed, the treatment of Jews by Germany in previous years that inspired the United Nations to adopt and promote this new style of punishment for crime on a worldwide scale. However, from the beginning the proposal has had its drawbacks. The questions arose: How could we undertake to enforce the law in other countries? And how could the United States permit other countries to undertake to enforce the genocide law in the United States? The treaty has dragged on now for twenty-five years or more.

Although the Senate Foreign Relations committee, by a voice vote, has favorably reported the treaty to the whole Senate, it did so with so many reservations as to make the treaty virtually inoperative. Senators Church and Javits will now offer another reservation which in effect would require that any American charged with violation of the genocide treaty in a foreign country be entitled to be tried under the rules and privileges provided by the United States Constitution. If approved, the Church-Javits amendment would simply make the genocide treaty more completely inoperative than it is already. Senators Church and Javits are both up for re-election next fall, and approval of the treaty would undoubtedly help them. Each of these Senators has great ability in his field, but apparently both are caught in the middle. Most of the communications to members of Congress are strongly opposed to the treaty's adoption.

¶ THE JOINT COMMITTEE ON ATOMIC ENERGY has been considering new legislation to succeed the Price-Anderson Act of 1957, which insures nuclear power plants against damage claims from radiation releases, and which expires in the very near future. In the seventeen years of operation, no payments have had to be made by reason of injury from radiation, and although a total insurance value of $525 million has been carried, the total payments for damages of any kind have amounted to only $3,500. Environmentalists insist on making production of electric energy from the atom as costly as possible. In spite of their efforts, however, the producers of nuclear energy plants now have on hand orders far exceeding any which they have had in the past. The use of energy from all sources has increased to such an extent, not only in this country but in the whole world, that new sources must be found.

Week ending February 9, 1974

A BUSY WEEK, but not exactly fruitful.

The genocide convention has apparently gone out the window for the Session. With all the reservations which had been added by committee and proposed on the floor of the Senate, it wouldn't have amounted to anything more than an expression of sympathy for the Jews.

¶ THE ERRATIC METHODS of selling gasoline to automobile owners has made most everybody fit to be tied. Monkey business seems to be the order of the day with everyone from the biggest wholesaler to the little retailer trying to get all the profit he can while the getting is good, and every country that has a surplus of oil trying to gouge the consuming countries to the utmost.

President Nixon has called a meeting of the oil-consuming nations of the world to meet in Washington beginning Monday, February 11, and while the matter of price may enter into the purpose of this meeting, the important feature will be to develop sources of energy supply so that countries which now have a deficiency will never again have to depend upon the Arab states or any other countries that are rolling in wealth because of present advantages. Already, we are told that some producing states are having difficulty in getting bids at anywhere near the price which they obtained only a month or two ago.

¶ CONGRESS FINALLY got a bill reported by the conferees of both Houses which would give the President greater authority in controlling and regulating the supply and distribution of oil products. The agreement reached by the conferees calls for a cutback in the price of oil produced in the United States. Senators from the oil states heartily oppose this provision, and indicated that, if necessary, they would filibuster on the legislation to block it. Efforts to postpone action until February 18th were not agreed to, so on Thursday and Friday the Senate proceeded to consideration of the conference report in a desultory manner.

Members of the Congress then started out to make the most of the ten-day vacation, basking in the sun of warmer climates or going home to campaign for re-election. I advised the Senate that taking a ten-day vacation and making no serious legislative effort to cope with the energy situation would not set well with at least 205 million inhabitants of the U.S.A.

Just what we need a ten-day vacation for now is unclear to me, since we reconvened only on January 21st and haven't done work enough yet to warrant any vacation at all.

¶ THE JOINT COMMITTEE ON ATOMIC ENERGY has had several hearings this week and will have more next week. It is generally understood that the most likely way to make the United States independent of other nations for energy, particularly electric energy, will be the construction of many more nuclear power plants.

The FEO [Federal Energy Office], under the leadership of Mr. Simon and his assistant, Mr. Sawhill, has been trying to put into effect rules and regulations calculated to make the distribution of oil and its distillates fair and equitable. They are having a hard time. The people whom they have hired to carry out this work have, for the most part, very little knowledge of the business. Also, the number who are trying to make fortunes overnight and evade rules and regulations faster than they can be made might be called legion. However, the FEO seems to think that in another month they will have the situation better in hand, and if they do many of us will be very grateful.

¶ GOVERNOR TOM SALMON of Vermont dropped in Wednesday afternoon. He didn't have any special issue on his mind, and folks in my outer office said he was dropping in to look me over to see if I might be healthy enough to run for re-election. Tom is having trouble enough with his legislature in the state, and while he undoubtedly has further political ambition, he seems a bit uncertain as to what to do about it at this time.

¶ IN THE FIELD OF FOREIGN AFFAIRS the committees on Agriculture and Foreign Relations have both decided not to oppose a new agreement which this country has made with India relative to the repayment of $3.2 billion worth of rupees which India owes us. Ambassador Moynihan briefly met with both committees explaining the deal being proposed, which would allow India to use $2 billion worth of rupees to promote its own economy in manners approved by the United States through a U.S. commission, of which I am a member. The other $1 billion worth of rupees would be paid to us gradually over the coming years, with the money being used to finance the expenses of our embassy at New Delhi, plus the transportation costs for weary members of Congress who like to travel around the world for various purposes. Not only members of our State department and the Foreign Relations committees of both Houses, but also other members of government and of the Congress, can use rupees for traveling expenses so long as they stop over in India on their way going or coming. This is just one way of enjoying the beneficence of the taxpayer in a manner unknown to the general public.

¶ HENRY KISSINGER went to Panama and signed an agreement with Panamanian officials relative to the future of the Canal. The agreement is not very far-reaching, but does make the Panamanians feel good and may develop into a better understanding between the governments of Panama and the United States.

Had the United States not seized that area over seventy years ago and constructed the Canal, there wouldn't be any country of Panama at all today. We simply took the area from Colombia and established a small nation according to our liking. Now Panama thinks they should own the Canal Zone, which has been in our hands for so long. It is my opinion that within the next decade or two we will make arrangements to turn the Canal Zone over to them, subject to such arrangements relating to the operation of the Canal itself as may be agreed to. I expect a furor here, sparked by members of Congress and others who will insist that our country continue to hold that territory, by force if need be.

¶ ON FRIDAY occurred what may be the most important event of the decade. Our three astronauts, Carr, Gibson, and Pogue, after spending eighty-four days in Skylab, landed almost on their destination point in the Pacific. The people of this country were not interested enough for any local television station to go to the bother of broadcasting this most important event: the stations just continued on with programs already scheduled and paid for by advertisers—programs that, in my book, consist of a very high percentage of hogwash. Yet a hundred years from now, if history continues, and I guess it will, the landing of astronauts in the Pacific Ocean after eighty-four days outside the earth's atmosphere will be regarded as an event comparable to the discovery of America by Christopher Columbus.

Week ending February 16, 1974

As I PREDICTED, the public wasn't too well pleased with the Congress taking a vacation when it really hadn't earned it. Although I don't have too much confidence in polls I was pleased to see the Harris Poll report that while the President's popularity has dropped to 30 percent, the public admiration for the Congress has dropped to 21 percent.

Some newspapers took the Congress to task for leaving its job at this time, but on the whole the news media were very kind and didn't say much about it.

We didn't run out of work in my office, however. On Sunday L.P.A. and I attended a brunch for Lady Bird Johnson, being almost the only Republicans there. I like Lady Bird, and President Johnson did splendid service in working for the Rural Water program and other phases of rural development which I either sponsored or strongly supported. Under the 1965 Act, the first local rural water program, costing nearly $3 million, was started in Addison County, Vermont, and L.B.J. went to Vermont, coincidentally on my birthday, August 20th, to help them get started right.

Monday night I went to a stag dinner at the White House which President Nixon gave for the visiting representatives of some thirteen countries who depend upon other nations, particularly the Arab states, for gas and oil. Some of my Canadian friends, including Canadian Minister Mitchell Sharp, were in attendance, and I found the occasion interesting.

¶ THE CONFERENCE of the oil-deficient nations lasted until Wednesday and, although no direct beneficial results were evident, all but one of them agreed to continue their efforts to insure adequate energy supplies for the economy of all. The representative of France kicked up his heels and refused to go along with the others. France has been giving the international community a lot of trouble in the last few years. Whether or not this is due to a natural disposition and increased prosperity of France, I cannot say. Personally, I feel that France has never recovered from the loss of the empire which she once controlled, including some nine colonies in Africa and others in other parts of the world. I think the French people actually became more prosperous when they lost their colonies. But there seems to be a matter of pride involved, or at least I think there is.

Anyway, all of the energy-deficient countries are now facing a major problem and are looking for additional sources of energy so they will not have to depend upon the Arabs in future emergencies. The Western Hemisphere, particularly the United States and Canada, is more fortunate in this respect, although we are buying more and more Middle East oil each year. The Arabs have more than doubled the price of their oil, and we have more than doubled the price of the wheat we sell them, and the cost of living has gone up all over the world. In the U.S.A., folks are burning more wood and coal to keep their homes warm. Environmentalists, who in some instances oppose the generation of power from other sources, say that if we burn coal a lot more people will die at an early age. I am sure many of these idealists have a wonderful time taking their anti-energy positions and making their dire predictions.

¶ IT SO HAPPENED that the second man in command at the Federal Energy Office, John Sawhill, had a press conference at 9:30 A.M. on Thursday and announced they were investigating the situation in nineteen states that had complained bitterly about the gasoline situation. One of these states was Vermont, where state authorities insist that we are 31 percent short of what gas and oil we used in February 1972, whereas our allocation from the federal government was based on a 17.8 percent shortage. Wednesday night I talked with Sawhill and told him that if they didn't do something about it we were going to have a revolution up our way and would probably get Ethan Allen and the Green Mountain Boys back to lead it. He promised me that they would check the situation immediately and not announce new allocations until they had fully accurate information.

Of course getting accurate information from the oil dealers, big and little, will be about as easy as it would be to learn what seat each of us will occupy in the Promised Land.

But Friday morning representatives of the Washington FEO office landed at the Montpelier airport. The Boston regional office has already accepted figures submitted by the state. Sawhill tells me that he expects a more favorable allocation within a matter of a few days. What the federal people apparently overlooked was the very rapid economic growth of the state, which had started in 1972 but increased even faster during 1973. All industrial and manufacturing plants were going full blast by the fall of 1973, and the influx of people from out of state had also increased. Vermont apparently showed the greatest increase in its economy of any New England state.

¶ ON THURSDAY morning I gave out the only news that had come out of Washington for a long time without being leaked. I announced that I would not be a candidate for re-election next fall. This happened about 10:30 in the forenoon and the rest of the day was spent answering the telephone and sitting in the office in the glare of TV lights and cameras. The news media were a little short of material that day, so my announcement came in handy. As a matter of fact, I could have made the announcement months ago, but felt it best to wait awhile, though not too long.

On Friday we had more telegrams relative to next fall's election, and letters began to arrive. Most of the communicants said they didn't blame me for not running again, but wished I would, anyway. I told them it seemed to be the only way that we could get any time off, that I left a lot of unfinished work when I came to Washington, and haven't had a chance to go fishing for the last five or six years. I think most of them understand my position. A few will claim that they scared me out, but I understand confidential polls taken by both parties in Vermont indicate that I might have had about 70 percent of the vote had I chosen to continue in the field of public service.

¶ A RECORD NUMBER of experienced legislators are voluntarily leaving the Congress after this year, and a record number of unqualified members of the Senate seem to have the idea that each of them would make the best President that the United States ever had. Their desire is one of the reasons why the poll shows that only 21 percent of the people think Congress is doing its work properly. Too many candidates for promotion simply constitute a costly nuisance and impede the work of those who want to serve their state and country well.

Added to the unquenchable desire of the candidates, we have a multiplicity of overstaffed subcommittees which contribute to smothering the important work of Congress.

Week ending February 23, 1974

THE SENATE CAME BACK into session Monday noon but accomplished little until Tuesday, when the so-called energy bill, reported out by Senator Jackson's Committee on the Interior, was acted upon late in the afternoon. In my opinion this was not a good bill, and played into the hands of foreign oil operators.

To make an appeal to the domestic users of gasoline and fuel oil, the bill cut back on the price of domestically produced oil. This would have had the effect of discouraging the use of low-production wells and the search for new producing wells in the United States. After voting for three amendments that would have given encouragement to United States producers, I finally voted to send the bill over to the House in the hopes that that body could make many desirable corrections in it. What I didn't like about the bill was that the Interior committee had pre-empted many functions of the Congress which belong to other committees. This was undoubtedly done to boost Senator Jackson's prospects for securing the Democrat nomination for President in 1976.

If the House doesn't make the corrections needed in this bill, and it is sent to the White House, I certainly hope that President Nixon will veto it. And I, for one, would sustain such a veto.

¶ SECRETARY KISSINGER is still flying high, wide, and handsome, traveling here and there around the world. He passes through Washington once in a while, and on Wednesday afternoon left for Mexico accompanied by some twenty people, including Senators Scott, Mansfield, and McGee. The purpose of the meeting is to impress upon the Latin American countries the importance of all working together under the implied leadership of the United States. If the Secretary thinks he is going to get all the countries of the Western Hemisphere working together under his leadership, he is overly optimistic. Secretary Kissinger shows signs of being rather too ambitious, and in the minds of many people is assuming credit which properly belongs to others. I suppose, however, that he is human after all, and his apparent desire to be the most important man in history may be fully justified. At least the work that he has done so far in bringing about an understanding between Israel and Egypt and, I hope, other Arab countries, has been praiseworthy. Only time will tell whether Mr. Kissinger is undertaking to go too far too fast. I hope that I am wrong in feeling that there may be a kickback to his widespread diversification of effort.

¶ EARLY IN THE WEEK the special Senate committee known commonly as the Watergate committee decided to hold no more hearings, and asked for another $300,000 with which to pay part of their employees for preparing a report to the Senate. I still feel that this committee was considerably out of place in undertaking work which could have been more properly carried out by the Justice department.

A committee of the House of Representatives is preparing a report on the advisability of impeaching President Nixon. Their chief of staff seems to feel that if a President becomes so unpopular that the public wants him ousted, he could be impeached without having committed a crime or having violated his oath of office. If the House does vote to impeach President Nixon the vote will be almost fully drawn along party lines. If such proves to be the case, it could be a severe blow to the structure of our government itself, in that a President elected by the overwhelming vote of the people could be removed from office, or at least brought to trial, by the party which lost the Presidential election but which controls the Congress.

The situation doesn't look very good, but I have to say that the President and his White House associates have not contributed very much to restoring a lot of lost confidence on the part of the people.

"What is a man profited, if he shall gain the whole world, and lose his own soul?" Perhaps the President feels that if a general era of peace in the world can be restored this year, he can recover the good will of many people disillusioned over the last two years of his second term of office. I hope this turns out to be the case, but I am very doubtful.

Week ending March 2, 1974

A RAFT OF APPROPRIATIONS BILLS providing funds for the many committees of the Senate was approved Friday by the Senate. Most of the amounts have been cut down by the Rules committee well below what had been asked for; but this doesn't mean too much, since about three times a year Congress enacts what are called supplemental appropriations bills, and any committees running short of the amount requested in the main appropriation bill can usually get what they want in supplemental acts.

Practically every committee in the Senate asks for more of the taxpayers' money than it ought to have. Some of them get as much as $2 million to carry on the ventures and the research of the committee and the many subcommittees created within it. These subcommittees have become so numerous and hire so much personnel that they come pretty close to obstructing the work of the Congress. Many of them are, in fact, conducting political campaigns under the guise of seeking economy and righteousness. But the party in control of the Congress almost inevitably looks out for its own and this year is no different from other years, except for being more expansive and more expensive.

¶ THERE WAS SOME GOOD NEWS during the week when the President announced at noon Thursday that formal relations with Egypt would be renewed, and on Friday the renewal took place. Secretary Kissinger is in the Middle East now, running from Egypt to Syria to Israel and back again to all these places. Foreign Minister Gromyko of the U.S.S.R. is also covering a lot of mileage, and it appears from this vantage point that he is actually co-operating with the United States in an effort to forestall the threat of any new wars in the Middle East. Syria and Israel are at last making proposals which purport to prevent future military clashes between the two countries. I certainly hope the effort is successful.

¶ SOCIAL EVENTS FOR THE WEEK were held to a minimum. Wednesday evening we went to Drew Pearson's old home where a party was being put on by Jack Anderson, with Drew's widow, and her son and daughter-in-law. We saw a lot of folks we knew there that we hadn't seen in a long time. I understand that the party was to celebrate the publication of Drew's diary for 1949–59, and that everybody mentioned in his diary was invited. I used to see quite a lot of Drew, both at his home and elsewhere. And although he was not noted for writing a column complimentary to a lot of people, he was always pretty decent to me, as his successor, Jack Anderson, has been.

I don't see how all the columnists can keep up their work day after day without driving either themselves or their readers nuts. If they write columns that are very decent to people, apparently the newspapers are not interested, because good news and kind remarks don't seem to sell newspapers.

On Thursday night L.P.A. and I went to the White House at the invitation of President Nixon for an informal dinner followed by a bloodcurdling movie comedy called *The Sting*. It was right down L.P.A.'s alley, because she loves the kind of picture that would have caused most of the women to faint dead away when I was a kid. But now it appears that any picture that is replete with crime makes the most money for the producer, and *The Sting* was no exception.

There were ten members of the Senate and about the same number from the House with their wives at the dinner, and enough people connected with the White House to make fifty in all. President Nixon toasted me as representing the members of Congress present and I toasted him because that is required at all dinners where the President is present. My response was about two or three minutes long and I kept it very light, which seemed to meet with the approval of the guests present. I told the President that I was glad he was having a light gathering instead of one of those deep dismal occasions when everyone is expected to consider profoundly all the ills and issues of the day.

¶ WHILE PRESIDENT NIXON had a couple of light parties Thursday and Friday nights, any enjoyment he might have gotten out of them was dampened by Judge Sirica's grand jury, which returned indictments against seven people who had been closely associated with the President, including his chief aides, Haldeman and Ehrlichman. The President was quick to point out, however, that indictments don't mean convictions, and expressed hope for early decisions by the court. A lot of folks seem to think that when a person is brought to trial he has already been found guilty.

The action of Judge Sirica's grand jury bore out what I have insisted upon from the very beginning of the Watergate scandal: that the work of deciding who may be guilty and who may be innocent belongs to the judicial branch of government and not to the Congress, unless the President himself becomes involved in possible lawbreaking and crime. In such case, it is up to the House of Representatives to make an investigation and decide whether impeachment proceedings are warranted or not. The House is now making such an investigation, although—I would say—without too much enthusiasm except on the part of a few members who find that making charges against prominent parties is a pretty sure way to front-page news coverage, whether the parties will ultimately be found guilty or not.

Week ending March 9, 1974

THIS WEEK the pots and kettles were really throwing things, with the Democrats throwing charges of sin and more sin against the President and the White House, while at the same time some of them seemed to be shivering for fear that the charges might boomerang.

In the spotlight this week were the criminal trials against former Attorney General Mitchell and former Secretary of Commerce Stans, who had charge of much of the financing of President Nixon's last campaign and who were charged with having accepted $200,000 from a man named [Robert] Vesco, supposedly in return for getting him special favors from the Securities and Exchange Commission. The chief witness against these men is one named Scars [Harry L. Sears, formerly majority leader of the New Jersey legislature], who says he handed over the money to Mr. Stans. The unfortunate factor from Mr. Vesco's standpoint is that while he made the contribution of $200,000 to the Nixon campaign, he was not repaid with special favors.

It appears that Attorney General Mitchell did get Vesco an appointment to meet with the Securities and Exchange Commission, but did not attempt to make a case for him. The fact is that probably every member of the Senate makes appointments with government officials for people who think they can get more favorable consideration if a Senator makes the appointment. This goes for Cabinet members, too. But making an appointment for a constituent doesn't mean that his case will get favorable consideration. It simply saves time for the constituent or claimant or the seeker of special favors who otherwise, even though he has a perfectly just reason, might spend two weeks in Washington without getting to see the right party.

As the week comes to a close it looks to me as if Attorney General

Mitchell and Secretary Stans might not be convicted of wrongdoing in the Vesco case, but then one never can tell what juries may do. This is particularly true of grand juries, which seem inclined to follow the suggestions of the prosecuting officer and render indictments if they are in any doubt.

¶ A BILL now creating quite a lot of discussion would prevent the recommendation of a special commission on Congressional salaries from taking effect. Previous to 1968, when this special commission was established by Congress itself, the pay of all members of Congress and staff employees had been fixed by the Congress, as was also the pay for judges and other politically appointed officials of government. At the time this new commission was established—to be headed by my good friend Bernard Segal—it appeared that Congress wanted to duck the issue of raising its own salaries even though it favored a good-sized increase.

There are some members of the Congress, I am sure, who are thinking in terms of annuities even more than salaries. Some members who have to rent homes in Washington and have sizable families actually find it difficult to get along. But I take the position that members of Congress should face the issue themselves rather than transferring responsibility—which is a polite way of saying "passing the buck."

The proposal to raise salaries again at this time was soundly defeated. Members of the judiciary didn't seem to be happy in the least, since most of the encouragement for salary raises came from them and other highly paid non-members of Congress. With an election coming up next fall, however, it appears that every member of the Senate who is a candidate for re-election (except one) voted against the pay raise. I voted against it because I felt that, with the strong inflationary trend under way, any action by the Congress relating to those who are already getting salaries of $36,000 a year and up would only encourage more inflation.

One of my wisecracking colleagues stated that the reason this proposal was defeated was because one-third of the members of the Senate are millionaires, one-third of them statesmen, and one-third cowards. This was indeed a dirty crack, and on the whole it was not true, although there may have been an occasional instance where it could be applied.

¶ THE CAPITOL ENJOYED, or some might say suffered, an influx of very important people throughout the week. Bankers came in force. The American Legion arrived for its annual meeting and banquet. Mayors and community officials numbered in the hundreds. Finally the governors of the fifty states showed up. All organizations had dinners to which members of Congress were invited. All members of Congress received plentiful advice as to what action to take on pending legislation.

The governors had a reception for members of Congress Wednesday evening. I noticed not too many members of Congress went, however, and some of the governors themselves seemed to have other items of business or pleasure in mind, so they didn't show either. A few bedraggled members of Congress attended both the governors' reception and the Legion dinner and got to their offices late on Thursday.

One of my colleagues, Senator Packwood of Oregon, is reported to have had his Governor, McCall, to dinner and after the dinner, the Governor confided in him that he intended to run against him next fall. This surely was an exaggerated case of adding insult to injury, but it brought out a lot of hilarity among Senator Packwood's colleagues the following day.

Thursday night the governors went to the White House, and I understand had a genuinely delirious time, with Pearl Bailey taking over the show by getting President Nixon to play the piano for her.

¶ THURSDAY, too, I found myself drafted into being host at a table where luncheon was provided for members of the Western European Union. This was one of those luncheons where representatives of Germany, the United Kingdom, France, the Netherlands and Italy came over to sit down and practice the good neighbor policy with Americans. I think the fact that the U.S. Congress may be reluctant to contribute as much to Western European security as has been done in the past may have had something to do with their visit at this time. Anyway, I enjoyed visiting with them.

A year ago only eight members of the Western European Union came to visit Washington. This year there were thirty-one, and next year nobody knows. While it took a lot of roast beef to feed them, in all probability there will be two or three times that number of Americans who will repay the visit through the European countries. Actually, I think it is a good idea for members of Congress to talk with officials from other countries. Whatever it costs them to feed each other roast beef is rather small compared with the costs of war.

Week ending March 16, 1974

THE SENATE stayed in session three days, and on Wednesday away they went.

The most important piece of legislation was a vote to restore the death penalty for certain crimes, such as hijacking and kidnapping. The bill was sent to the House for further consideration. It will probably pass the House and be signed by the President, but I am doubtful that it will reduce the crime rate much. Maybe some, in certain cases in certain states. But if a few convicted criminals are executed, particularly if they are black, there will undoubtedly be another uproar around the country. Since the Supreme Court invalidated capital punishment laws some twenty states have re-enacted them. I don't know of any executions that have taken place yet, however.

I also believe that some judges and juries will be reluctant to find accused parties guilty when such a verdict requires the death penalty. I feel that better enforcement of the laws we now have would be more effective; but as it is now, there are a lot of people who seem to think that anyone committing a crime and being found guilty is being treated unfairly. So they go to work and hire lawyers to get the guilty party set free so he can go out and commit another crime. I don't say that every accused person should not have his day in court and a fair trial, but some persons who have committed outrageous crimes have been permitted to escape punishment.

I do believe that many convicted criminals can reform and become good citizens, possibly most of them can, and I know some who have done this. However, there are many people who seem to feel that all criminals are good at heart and the trouble they get into may be the fault of society or of the law-enforcement officers. Only recently certain persons, including former U.S. Attorney General Ramsey Clark, have made charges against the late J. Edgar Hoover to the effect that he did wrong in planting undercover men in the midst of gangs suspected of criminal activities. Such critics simply make it more difficult to maintain law and order in this land, and their attitude gives encouragement to lawbreakers and gangsters.

Certainly our laws are full of inequities which permit the criminal, high or low, to escape justice, and sometimes they inflict punishment upon milder offenders who cannot afford the cost of adequate representation in the courts. That is no excuse, however, for saying that the lawbreaker is always right and the law is always wrong.

¶ THURSDAY WAS A BUSY DAY with the diplomats. L.P.A. had invited the new German Ambassador, Berndt von Staden, and his wife up to lunch. Frau von Staden is a farmer at heart, and was good company. They left us about 1:30, and then I went into the Foreign Relations committee room as Senator Sparkman was giving a luncheon for King Hussein of Jordan. While we contribute heavily to Jordan, it may be worthwhile since it serves as a buffer state between Israel and Syria.

At three o'clock Secretary Kissinger came before our committee to tell us how things are going in the Middle East, and especially in our relations with Western European countries. I felt that he was not as optimistic as on previous occasions, although the situation still could be worse. Syria insists on Israel giving up the land which was taken from them a few years ago. Unless an agreement can be reached on this score, the threat of war is likely to remain for a long time. Israel wants to control the land because in the past and even now it is a source of raids upon the Jewish people and the Jewish communities.

It is probable that Russia could exert influence on Syria if we did the same on Israel, so that an agreement could be reached. However, Russia and particularly Foreign Minister Gromyko, seem to be somewhat out of sorts these days. The U.S.S.R. apparently is not at present working for an early understanding among the Middle East states. There is some justification for the new Russian attitude.

Last November, when I talked with Ambassador Dobrynin and Secretary Kissinger at the White House, they were very optimistic that between them our two countries could establish peace in the Middle East. It was assumed at that time that the Soviet Union and the United States would be equal partners in this effort. However, the strong support of Egypt and certain other Arab states for Secretary Kissinger has resulted in a downgrading of the Russian position. The fact is that the Arabs never really liked Russia at all, and it was only to get military assistance that they worked together. Now it seems that only Iraq and Syria are strongly dependent on and quite close to the U.S.S.R.

It appears, too, that Kissinger has taken over the negotiations to the extent that Russia feels left out and humiliated. So long as this condition prevails, reaching agreements in the Middle East is going to be more difficult.

And trouble is still brewing in Western Europe. France in particular seems highly emotional and jealous of the success our Secretary of State has had in wielding influence with Egypt and some other countries. At present it is highly uncertain whether the co-operation in defense and other matters which has existed between the United States and the European community will continue to exist. There is no question but what Henry Kissinger is a climber, and his outstanding successes as a representative of the United States in world affairs may have inflated his ego to the danger point. His successes in China, Russia, and the Middle East have been remarkable, but these successes in themselves have created suspicion and jealousy among many countries. The next few months will doubtless tell the story as to whether we are making permanent progress in that important area of the world or not.

To complicate our problem in this area the General Accounting Office has directed that credit to Eastern European countries—Czechoslovakia, Romania, and Poland—be shut off. These three countries have a strong tendency to emulate the Western states, and I am sure they much prefer our attitudes to those of the Russians. The matter of destroying much of the trade between the United States and these countries is crucial: it most certainly would have a damaging effect upon our own economy, and could conceivably become a prelude to another cold war.

There is no doubt that the United States is the strongest nation in the world today, both economically and militarily, but we have to watch out lest under Secretary Kissinger's leadership we get too big for our britches.

During the week the Atomic Energy committee heard testimony on the arms control conferences now going on in Geneva and the efforts being made to reach another SALT agreement with Russia. However, until the problems in the Middle East and with Western Europe are stilled, it will be very difficult to reach any further agreement with Russia relative to arms control.

L.P.A. and I attended a dinner in our honor at the Republic of China embassy on Thursday evening. Sixteen people were present, including both American and Asian friends and acquaintances. Taiwan, which we used to know as Formosa, lost its position on the Security Council of the United Nations when mainland China, officially known as the People's Republic of China, was accepted by the United Nations and established full diplomatic relations with the United States. Nevertheless, the small island of Taiwan, intensely populated with some fifteen million people, seems to have been remarkably successful in its economic development. Although the People's Republic of China will probably continue to claim Taiwan as part of their land, it is doubtful that any strenuous measures will be taken to enforce this claim. In the course of time, agreement and settlements may be reached. The Asians don't mind taking time and don't expect problems to be settled as fast as we do here in America.

In South Vietnam, Cambodia, and Laos the tension seems to be caused not by what is happening now but by what might happen in the future. All of which simply proves that countries are run by people, and the traits of people are generally reflected by their governments.

[Putney, Vermont]

Week ending March 23, 1974

THE WEEK STARTED OFF with L.P.A. and me attending religious services at the White House at the invitation of the President. The speaker was Norman Vincent Peale, whom L.P.A. took a shine to after hearing him a year or two ago. The sermon was pretty good and the audience was pretty high-level, with Chief Justice Burger and Mrs. Burger and other distinguished servants of the government on hand, along with special folks from around the country.

Monday we tried to catch up on the work at the office so that we could take the five o'clock train on the AMTRAK system for Montreal. We didn't get out of Washington until about a quarter past six but the time was made up before we got to Montpelier Tuesday morning. This train has been in operation something like a year and a half, and could have a lot of business if it had equipment. The two sleeping cars which it is allowed are pretty well booked up two or three months in advance. The AMTRAK management doesn't seem too concerned over their lack of equipment, though. I think it is high time that we put some railroad people to running our railroads. There is apparently great interest in getting railroads under the charge of lobbyists who feel that the right way to run a road is to get as much money as possible out of the Congress for subsidies. I am satisfied that there could be a large and profitable passenger business for railroads in the country if the right people were put in charge of them.

¶ IN VERMONT we met winter head-on with a foot or more of new snow—the kind of winter we should have had a month or two ago. Tuesday morning, as we were getting out of a rented car by Harold Roop's filling station in Montpelier, L.P.A. announced that she had broken a leg. Well, if she had to do it, it was a good location, because in just a few minutes we had an ambulance for her that took her to the hospital four or five miles away, where the doctor set her leg, put it in a cast, and put her in bed for four days.

¶ I DON'T THINK MUCH of the proposed legislation which is before the Senate at this time. A new system for handling the budget was taken up by the Senate on Tuesday and ran through until Friday, when it was passed and sent to the House. Congress now has plenty of authority to make sensible appropriations for sensible programs if it had the courage to do so, but I suppose they will say that enactment of this legislation would show the executive branch of government who is running this country. However, there is some question in my mind whether the House will agree to the Senate bill in anywhere near its present form. The whole thing looked to me as if it was an effort to gain credit for the Congress, while at the same time ducking the issue.

¶ THE ATTACKS ON THE PRESIDENT still continue vigorously and viciously. His critics are getting so vehement that they are probably helping him more than they are hurting him. Even Senator Buckley, the arch-conservative from New York, jumped on him and said he should resign. This was indeed base ingratitude, because the White House has been very kind to Jim Buckley. I guess he wasn't getting enough publicity in the news media. But if his statement asking President Nixon to resign was expected to help his standing, it apparently has a pretty vigorous kickback, because even Senator Javits, who cannot be considered a close Nixon friend by any means, disagreed sharply with his colleague from New York.

Of course resigning from the Presidency would be the worst thing that Mr. Nixon could do, because it would mean that we had abandoned government by law and were resorting to government by demonstration. Time will tell what comes out of this battle, but I still am not willing to abandon government by law or discard the United States Constitution.

[Putney, Vermont]

Week ending March 30, 1974

THE WEEK ENDING MARCH 30TH was spent in Montpelier, where L.P.A. was paroled from the hospital on Saturday. She spent most of the time bending over a red-hot telephone, one of the early callers being Richard Nixon. He didn't seem to care about talking to me, but the call really set her up for quite a while. Later in the week she had calls from a lot of other important people, including Admiral Rickover, who asked if she would like to take a submarine trip. Meanwhile I took calls from the office and listened to all the troubles that people had been reporting there.

¶ NEWS ON RADIO and in the newspapers on Tuesday was all about the centennial of Robert Frost's birthday. His daughter, who I never thought was too close to her father, made a big occasion of it. She lives in Derry, New Hampshire, where the memorial stamp issued in Frost's honor was first released. I didn't know Robert Frost until in late years of his life. I well recall visiting with him on his last trip to Washington, where, with parties at the Library of Congress and elsewhere, they kept him pretty busy although he was then over eighty years of age. At that time he told me that he supposed several states claimed him as their citizen, but, since he had been living in Vermont for forty-three years, he felt that he had a right to call himself a Vermonter. However, his daughter over in New Hampshire seemed to want all the glory for celebrating the issuance of the new stamp.

I recall that on my last visit with Frost he remarked that people were crowding him this way and that way all the time, and he said that someday he was going to sneak away and come to Washington without telling anyone so that we could sit down and have a good visit in our own language.

¶ TUESDAY I got calls from the press relative to the proposed Dickey-Lincoln power plant, a major hydroelectric project to be built in Maine. The plant would produce over 800,000 kilowatts of electric power on a part time basis. There have been efforts made to get this power plant constructed in recent years, and I have supported them. The proposal was strongly opposed by the private power companies, who were successful in defeating it in the House, although we did manage to get it through the Senate every year since 1967.

Now, with the price of oil being as high as it is, the power companies are changing their position, and it is possible—in fact, probable—that steps will be taken looking to the construction of this important addition to the electric power supply of New England. I always did have trouble with the power companies, and it was largely their opposition which prompted me to run for the United States Senate in the first place. They were inveterate grabbers of power and wealth even before I got into politics at all. I used to think that the next generation of utility people would be broader-minded, but they weren't. Now that the shoe pinches and they need whatever power they can get from any and all sources, they're very happy to come to Uncle Sam and ask him to spend a lot of money which they are sure will benefit them. I don't mind public funds being spent to develop electricity but I do insist that public power companies and co-operative distribution systems have equal chances at whatever power is developed with public money.

¶ THE FIRST OF THE WEEK Secretary Kissinger got to Moscow. Apparently he was feeling pretty cocky when he got there, and had stopped in Germany to talk with officials there while on the way. He evidently got a warm reception from Mr. Brezhnev and other top Russian officials, but by Thursday he acknowledged that he hadn't made much progress in making a disarmament deal with the Soviets. Only a couple of weeks ago it became quite apparent that Kissinger felt the glory for restoring peace in the Middle East largely belonged to him. I recall last November talking with Kissinger and Ambassador Dobrynin of the U.S.S.R. in the White House, and I gathered from the discussion which I shared that night that Russia and the United States would work together to restore peace in the Middle East and ultimately in the rest of the world. I strongly suspect that the reason our Secretary of State was not able to announce more progress in the field of disarmament this week was because the Russian top officials were showing their discontent with being in effect downgraded by Kissinger's diplomatic successes. Also, some of the European countries apparently are not as keen about our Secretary as they were a few months ago. I certainly hope that, whatever worthwhile accomplishments he can make, he lets some other folks have a share of the credit.

¶ I JOINED WITH SENATOR PASTORE in introducing a bill to establish a new Joint Committee on Energy to take the place of the Joint Committee on Atomic Energy. Scoop Jackson didn't like it, and made that plain. If there is one thing Scoop doesn't like at all, it is sharing credit or publicity with anyone else. His fantastic effort to take jurisdiction away from other committees and put it all in his own Interior committee is knocking his Presidential ambitions for a loop.

¶ SOME OF THE NEWS that leaked out during the week must have been a shock to some people, mostly Democrats. It developed that big business had contributed generously to Democrat candidates during the 1972 campaign. This scanty news didn't shock me a bit, because it is common knowledge in political circles that big corporations and their officials nearly all contribute to candidates of both parties, giving the most, of course, to candidates of the party they expect to win. In the aggregate, I am sure that millions and millions of dollars were put into the campaigns of Muskie, McGovern, Humphrey, and other Democrats, though not as much as went into the Nixon coffers, since it was foreordained that he would win over the Democratic candidates.

Before we lament too much over the skulduggery going on in our elections, we should consider what goes on in elections in other countries or in those foreign states where there are no elections at all. Perhaps the publicity being given here to law evasion and cheating will help to make some slight addition to our credibility as a nation. At least I hope so.

¶ AFTER NEARLY TWO WEEKS in Vermont with L.P.A.'s broken ankle on the mend, we hope to get back to Washington early next week where plenty of work is waiting for us.

[United States Senate]
Weeks ending April 6 and 13, 1974

No RECORD WAS MADE of the week ending April 6th because we simply had so much on our hands after returning to the office in Washington that it was impossible to find time for the extra work of dictating.

¶ ON FRIDAY EVENING, April 5th, the nurserymen and landscape people gave a reception for me. It was a real spread, with some five hundred people in attendance coming from all parts of the country—California, Florida, Rhode Island, and Vermont. I appreciated it, but I hate to think what the cost must have been. Even nurserymen and landscape architects, in spite of the fact that they are doing better than they used to, should be careful of the dollar.

The next evening the Gridiron Club had its annual swanky dinner, and I attended as a guest of Roscoe Drummond of the *Christian Science Monitor*. Probably I wouldn't have gone except in my early political days the *Monitor* was very decent to me, in contrast to many other newspapers. Something of a precedent was made this year with the attendance of some fifteen or sixteen women. Previously the Gridiron Club, which is comprised of fifty newsgatherers throughout the country, had been severely criticized because of its exclusion of women, not only from its ranks but from its parties as well. But the women at last achieved the break-through just as they have in many other fortresses considered invulnerable, and I guess from now on they will probably increase in influence and numbers until they take over the club itself—maybe.

¶ ON THURSDAY, the 11th, we had a bill before the Senate to provide disaster aid to those people whose homes and property were destroyed by a series of tornadoes which swept through the Central states, doing a tremendous amount of damage. I voted for the bill, as I felt these people should have some federal aid, although I kicked about it because it applied only to those who had suffered great loss after April 1st of this year. Even the people of a town in Louisiana which had been destroyed by a tornado in late March are not eligible for any assistance under the bill as it passed the Senate. And when I offered an amendment to extend comparable aid to those people in some thirty-five or thirty-six other states who had suffered equally great loss during the past months, my amendment was defeated 49 to 40.

What griped me particularly was the fact that in 1947 I had sponsored a provision in the Congress which was the beginning of general federal assistance to victims of floods and other forms of disaster. My reasons for pushing the proposal at that time were that the city of Ottumwa, Iowa, was receiving excessive damage from floods, and Port Arthur, Texas, had been largely destroyed by a tremendous explosion. Sad to say, the Senators from Texas and Iowa voted against my proposal of last Thursday to aid victims in other states. I don't suppose they knew that I had gone to bat for their own communities in a previous session of the Congress. But the bill is now in Conference with the House, and we hope that better judgment will prevail among the conference committee members.

¶ Too many of the proposals coming before Congress these days are in the form of what is called "comprehensive legislation," which means that although a proposal involves a good idea the committees handling it are so anxious to get full credit for everything pertaining to it that they undertake to include in the bills reported to the Houses of Congress provisions for meeting any possible matter which may be involved in the application of the law at a later date, sometimes well into the future.

I told some of them if they really want to make progress they should follow the advice of the old Vermonter who said, "If you have a hundred problems to deal with, you'll make more progress if you take them up one by one." And so it is with legislation. Everyone wants to be very important, and that applies to the groups that comprise our legislative committees, so they overdo it and sometimes it takes a long time to get things straightened out.

[The entry for the week ending April 20, 1974, recounts springtime planting of the vegetable garden at the Aikens' home in Putney, Vermont, during a brief vacation from Washington.]

[*United States Senate*]

Week ending April 27, 1974

A WEEK OF COMMITTEE HEARINGS and a little action on the Senate floor.

It was rather difficult for me to attend all the hearings, since so many of them are called for the same hour of the same day. With Agriculture, Foreign Relations, and Atomic Energy being of importance at this time, I simply had to move from one hearing to another in an effort to keep up with testimony which was being presented.

I did get in considerable time at the Atomic Energy committee hearings, where things coming under the jurisdiction of this committee have become rather uncertain and messy. I was particularly interested in the new efforts of the private power companies to get out from under the antitrust law. It was something of a miracle that I was able to get the committee to make this law applicable to the utility interests in 1970. Most certainly, if these companies had their way and were not subject to the antitrust laws, I fear they would take as great advantage of the public as the big oil companies are doing today.

¶ WEDNESDAY, the President called about sixteen of us from both Houses to the White House to explain his new proposals for foreign aid. Like most White House meetings it was not for the purpose of consulting with or receiving advice from members of Congress, but to tell us what the executive branch had already planned to do. This attitude is not restricted to the present Administration; it has been practiced by other Presidents ever since I have been in Washington.

The President asked for very large foreign aid appropriations. Israel would be the major beneficiary, but $250 million would be available for assistance to Egypt, including the clearing of the Suez Canal and making it subject to navigation again; there was also $100 million for Jordan, and $100 million which could be used in other parts of the Middle East, provided that their co-operation in restoring peace to the area is agreed to.

The turn of these countries to the United States is due primarily to their distrust of European countries, as well as Russia. Even that former large French colony of Algeria is now showing an indication of wanting to work more closely, and to restore relations, with the United States. At the present time it appears that the French government is likely to gain the title of the world's greatest troublemaker. I would not apply this name to the French people, but, as in so many other countries, governments do not fully and adequately represent their constituencies. Anyway, the prospects are better than ever that we will succeed in the job of intermediary between the countries of the Middle East.

¶ A BIT OF LEGISLATION that turned out satisfactorily to me was the bill providing federal disaster assistance to a few states which had suffered during the first week of April from an epidemic of tornadoes. Obviously the proviso making federal assistance available to disaster areas only after April 1 of this year was unfair to all those regions that had been declared disaster areas during previous months, extending back to April 1973. There were only a few members of the Senate on hand when I explained why I thought the situation unfair, and a motion to table my amendment was agreed to. Almost immediately, though, some of those who had voted against me realized the unfairness of their position and sought to make amends for their action. The only opportunity to make a fair correction came in Conference with the House. The Senate conferees, led, I understand, by Senator Baker of Tennessee, persuaded the House members to agree to set the effective date for eligibility back to April 1973, so that communities in some thirty-seven states, including Vermont, could qualify for federal disaster assistance. It was a good example of members of the Senate making a mistake and seeking to correct it as fast as possible. And of course Vermont, like many other states, is very grateful for the results.

¶ ANOTHER BIT OF SATISFACTORY LEGISLATION was a bill establishing certain wilderness areas in the Eastern states. The Senate Agriculture committee had reported legislation establishing these areas last February, but the chairman of the Interior committee of the Senate had prevented the legislation from coming up for consideration for fourteen months until his committee could bring out a bill of its own, which included some undesirable provisions. Had his bill prevailed, the Agriculture department would have gone too far in surrendering jurisdiction over the Forest Service to the Interior department.

In order to maintain peace as much as possible between the Senate Agriculture and Interior committees, our respective staffs had been working on a new bill which would eliminate the undesirable provisions of the Interior bill and include those which promised to be helpful from both bills. It has been just another example of some government agencies and Congressional committees trying to raid the jurisdiction of others. The fact is that of all the land affected by the bill which will be reported to the Senate, 95 percent of the area has been under the authority of the Agriculture department, while only 5 percent represented the authority of the Interior department.

¶ ALL IN ALL I consider it a pretty good week, but not everything was sweet. Demands for impeachment of the President continued. Senator Jackson pursued his own cold war against Russia, which, if successful, could lead to a hot war devastating to the whole world. Senator Kennedy was over in Russia, with the success of his apparent aim to be a world leader subject to question. The Washington *Star* stated editorially that apparently he was not yet dry behind the ears. I suppose his visit was to offset Senator Jackson's political ambitions. If they would both settle down and do the work they are supposed to do, the prospect of promotion to higher federal office would be better for each than it seems to be right now. But politics is politics, and a lot of office-holders, including members of Congress, are becoming very nervous, since the tide of public opinion seems to be running against those who hold office, with resulting benefits to those who never have, but who express a willingness—even an eagerness—to do so.

Week ending May 4, 1974

THE MAJOR BILL passed this week which had application to the whole country was the No Fault Auto Insurance bill. Although I supported its passage, I am somewhat skeptical as to its value. However, as Senator Magnuson told me after its passage by the Senate, we have to make a start sometime, and I agree that we have to have uniform liability legislation protecting all people from monetary loss due to automobile injuries and accidents as far as possible and, I might add, practicable.

The bill has now gone to the House, where I feel that its reception will be somewhat less than enthusiastic. The 435 members of the House, all of them up for re-election this fall, are not too happy when the Senate sends them controversial legislation. The No-Fault Insurance bill is controversial, with lawyers almost unanimously against it, hospital and medical practitioners apparently divided, and the so-called left-wing advocates of government almost unanimously for it. While about twenty states have already enacted no-fault legislation of their own, their action has been so recent that the results are not readily discernible at this time. Only Massachusetts has a record of no-fault insurance long enough to get a fair analysis of the results. But it is apparent that if no-fault legislation spreads to many other states, it will be essential to have a uniform application of it so that persons from one state incurring accident damage in other states won't become hopelessly involved in legal entanglements.

¶ THE SENATE was also involved during the early part of the week with a bill providing for a continuation of the International Economic Policy Act of 1972. The bill itself was not particularly in dispute but the commotion and dissension which prolonged the debate were created by an amendment offered by Senator Muskie and others which would re-establish wage and price controls. For the most part I considered this a political action, since the proposed amendment itself would invest so much authority and responsibility in the White House that the President could be held responsible for all the public dissatisfaction over most anything that might go wrong. It was a great departure from recent activities of the same Democratic Senators who have been trying to divest the President of authority which had been previously put upon him by the Congress.

It is not only members of the Majority Party in Congress that seek to put the President at a serious disadvantage: this week the President himself may have contributed substantially to their crusade. On Monday night he addressed the country by nationwide television and radio and announced that he would make public the conversations and discussions he had held with members of his staff which had been requested, demanded, and subpoenaed by the House Judiciary committee. He told the public that the release of the material contained on the tapes which recorded these discussions with staff members and associates would be, perhaps, confusing and contradictory in spots. He also stated that he would not deliver to the House Judiciary committee the tapes themselves, but would deliver a transcript of them to the committee and to the public as well, with the understanding that two members of this committee—supposedly Chairman Rodino and ranking Republican Hutchinson—could listen to all the tape recordings to make sure that the transcripts were accurate.

After listening to the President's broadcast I was called by a White House staff member to see what I thought of it. I told him that I thought the war on the President would be intensified; that the President had attempted to put his adversaries on the defensive, and they would probably try harder than ever to justify the charges which had been made against him. I also told some of the news media at home that, while I felt that release of the taped material might help the President in a legal sense, I didn't think he would personally benefit from it, since foul language which had been deleted from his discussion with his associates and staff members would come as a shock to many people. Even though the bad words he used had been deleted, readers of the transcripts could fill in the spaces themselves. And I doubt that this will enhance the President's popularity.

Just why he spent so much time consulting with John Dean, who was substantially discredited by the New York jury which found secretaries Stans and Mitchell innocent of all charges made against them, is a mystery. Eventually, John Dean turned against the President and testified about as the President's adversaries wanted. I have suspected that he did so for fear of receiving a long term of imprisonment for himself if he did not turn on the President. Of course we are all entitled to our individual opinions as to whether this was blackmail or not, but if it was, it is not the only case in history, because the fear of God and the fear of going to jail have probably been responsible for the positions taken by more than one federal official or employee.

On Thursday afternoon the House Judiciary committee decided that the President's attorney, Mr. James St. Clair, could sit in on the impeachment hearings which are presumed to start within the next two weeks or so. This concession on the part of the committee was apparently made to prevent a split along partisan lines. The committee also agreed to televising at least parts of the hearings. If that is done, it appears to me that the corporation sponsors of other radio and television programs who find their time usurped by the House Judiciary committee will not be too happy. But then, that may be qualified as a political risk, and when one becomes a member of Congress he must expect to encounter political risks. So many members of the public are now in political turmoil that the prospects for a considerable change of the makeup of the next Congress seem very good, depending on how one looks at it. Incumbents in office today are worrying more than they have done for years, regardless of their party membership.

¶ On Tuesday six New England Senators plus Senator Javits of New York met with Secretary of Transportation Brinegar. The concern of the Senators related to the recommendation of the Transportation department that much of the railroad trackage in the country, and particularly in the Northeast, should be abandoned. Secretary Brinegar and Undersecretary Barnum weren't very enthusiastic about continuing adequate rail service in rural areas. They showed little interest in passenger service on the railroads, and seemed to feel that truck service and, of course, air service could handle most of the increased freight and other traffic which would result from abandonment of a lot of our railroad lines. Their opinion seemed to be in sharp contrast to those federal officials who have been urging the conservation of energy during the past few months. Secretary Brinegar didn't seem to worry at all about the increased use of gasoline and oil which their recommendations would necessitate. I came to the conclusion that when the Secretary finished his work for the federal government, the oil industry will again have a good place for him among their ranks. [Brinegar had been associated with the Union Oil Company of California before becoming Secretary of Transportation].

And speaking of energy, the private power interests are still wriggling under the antitrust laws, and are determined to get out from under if they possibly can. The Justice department, as well as municipal and co-operative power systems, which helped me get the private power industry under the antitrust law in 1970, assure me that they will go to bat if necessary to keep them from rescinding the law.

¶ WEDNESDAY, L.P.A. and I went to a black-tie dinner given in our honor by Patrick Munroe [news reporter and representative of a book publisher]. This was a pretty high-level occasion, with ambassadors from seven foreign countries, the leadership of the Senate, Senators Mansfield and Scott, and high-ranking dignitaries of official and private life in attendance. Included, of course, were my neighbors Arthur Burns [Chairman of the Board of Governors of the Federal Reserve System], and his wife, Helen. Arthur, who carries a whale of a lot of influence nationally and internationally, bought a 150-acre farm in Vermont in the 1930's, thereby demonstrating his good judgment during that depression era. Carol Laise Bunker, whose home is a couple of miles from us in Putney, was on hand, too, although her husband, Ellsworth Bunker, had to be over in the Holy Land with Secretary Kissinger at the time. Admiral Rickover and his very attractive wife, Eleanor, were there. As of course was Mary Munroe, who, it develops, is president of the District of Columbia Democratic Women's Club, with its eighteen hundred members; until recently I didn't even know she was a Democrat.

Short speeches were delivered by Ambassador Cadieux of Canada, Arthur Burns, and Senators Scott and Mansfield. The speeches were very complimentary to the Aikens but I fear that my response was not up to par, since the Senate had worked until after seven o'clock and we had had one of the busiest days of the whole Session. Anyway, we appreciated what Pat and Mary had done and the fact that seventy of our oldest and closest friends were in attendance.

Week ending May 11, 1974

IT'S GETTING so appropriations bills don't mean too much, because departments and agencies of government are constantly asking for additional funds. These agencies of government usually ask for more than they need, expecting that Congress will cut the amount substantially—which, as a rule, Congress does. Then the agencies come back later with one, two, or sometimes three requests for more money, and they usually get it.

¶ TESTIMONY before the Joint Committee on Atomic Energy this week related to development of solar energy and wind power, that is, power generated by windmills such as our ancestors used, particularly in the Prairie states. Witnesses representing the National Science Foundation, National Aeronautics and Space Administration and the Ford Foundation came before us. The principal impression they made on me was that they desired to keep control of research work within their jurisdictions rather than have it transferred to any other agency of government.

The Ford Foundation of course is always interested. This foundation seems favorably inclined to the oil companies, and its testimony indicates to me that it must have considerable investment in the petroleum industry.

The NSF and NASA thought it would be the year 2020 before we had very substantial supplies of energy generated from the sun or the winds. They talked in terms of energy necessary to supply the country or some of our greater centers of population. I told them they reminded me of some folks who believe that all good government originates in Washington, whereas I have always felt that good government originates in the thousands of communities in our country. I suggested that they go out into the farm country and find out how to develop solar energy or wind power for individual homes and farms in an economic manner before undertaking to develop a means of supplying the whole country.

¶ THE BIG NEWS of the week internationally was the tumbling of the Trudeau government in Canada. Trudeau never had a majority of

Parliament with him anyway, but he got along fairly well until prices began to go up so high in Canada that our neighbor to the north had to blame someone for it. And so they blamed him. Elections will have to be held there on July 8th, and then we will see what the Dominion's new government looks like.

What happened in Canada this week is only one example of what has been happening in the world. In the last few weeks the governments of six other countries have been thrown out of office: in Britain, France, Germany, Portugal, Iceland, and Israel. I am satisfied that there is a list of as many more countries, large and small, that are waiting for their top officials to get bounced. I doubt if as many governments have ever been toppled in the same length of time as we have seen go out of office in the last few weeks. The whole world seems afflicted with an epidemic created by inflationary prices and an unholy greed for power on the part of those who are presently on the outside looking in.

The United States is no exception, and whether President Nixon weathers the storm or not remains to be seen. Certainly the news media are having a field day and a rich harvest from the sale of services. The voice of the individual is heard louder than ever, not only in the United States but throughout the world. While the clamor of individuals is probably responsible for the toppling of governments, big industry is really taking over. It is a paradox if I ever saw one. While the individual is exercising his freedom of speech and his voting power the world over, the same giant enterprises and conglomerates which he condemns are making even faster gains. We talk about enforcing antitrust laws, but when our big international industries get crowded too much, they can simply move their operations to other parts of the world. Nevertheless, I think the United States is today better off economically than most other countries.

The situation has reached the point now where labor leaders and some others would like to stop imports of manufactured goods into the United States, while others, representing what they choose to call consumer interests, would like to stop exports from our country. If either side had its way, it would just be too bad for America.

¶ LEGISLATIVE DISCUSSIONS came to an end in the Senate Thursday when the bill to continue the Council on International Economic Policy was put down the drain by a one-sided vote, and we recessed until Monday.

This result was largely due to a week of partisan and political chicanery. Still, we have so many government agencies already that we probably won't miss this outfit.

¶ ON THURSDAY, the House Judiciary committee's thirty-eight members began meeting to consider the advisability of impeaching the President. After a one-day meeting, further consideration was put over until next week. It looks as if this matter would be continued until midsummer and possibly later than that. That means that a hundred or so employees of the committee working on the job will be sure of being kept on for a few months more, to say the least. Whether the committee will ultimately recommend impeachment proceedings is unclear, but with elections coming up in November the political panic is increasing in volume. If a Republican Senator makes a statement derogatory to the President, he gets more news coverage than all the others who tend to business. But whether that will help him or not remains to be seen.

Week ending May 18, 1974

THE SENATE met on Monday, and Senators Byrd and Mansfield, speaking for the Democratic Party, urged members of Congress to let the House of Representatives act under its Constitutional authority to handle the charges made against President Nixon and decide whether impeachment charges are warranted. In asking the Congress and the people to follow our Constitutional procedure, they reiterated what I had said a year ago. The difference is that they got fairly good newspaper coverage, compared to practically nothing that I received. But that didn't make me feel bad at all.

Almost immediately after the start of the hearings in the House on impeachment proceedings, leaks developed from the House Judiciary committee. There is something about leaking confidential information that makes some members of Congress or their staffs feel very important. But the early leaks dripping from the House hearings were apparently intended to discredit the President, and had little connection with the Watergate affair itself. This situation prompted Mr. St. Clair, the President's lawyer, who has been permitted to attend the hearings, to ask that all proceedings be open to the public. Of course if this were done, the leaks would have little value for the perpetrator. I doubt that Chairman Rodino [of the Judiciary committee] will agree to the open hearings which the President's counsel has requested.

¶ ON MONDAY, too, a large number of members from the House and Senate in Mexico came to make their biennial visit to their U.S. counterparts. It is quite apparent that political difficulties may be brewing in our neighbor to the south, although a serious situation may not develop for some years yet. The main difficulty seems to be that, despite efforts to control the situation, the spread between the "haves" and the "have nots" in Mexico has not narrowed, but because of inflation has probably grown wider. This, coupled with the fact that the entire government is pretty much controlled and run by a single political party, is a sure formula for discontent.

The high point of the visit at the White House with the Mexicans seemed to be President Nixon's autographing the cast on L.P.A.'s leg. Two days later she received a batch of photographs which I assume she will put to good use. So far as I know, this was the only time that a President of the United States has ever been photographed putting his autograph on anybody's hind leg, but then anything can happen in the world today.

¶ OTHER COUNTRIES concerned with the financial situation and economic development of the world, and particularly with the IDA [International Development Association], are meeting in a few days to announce their position and the amount of contributions they will make to this agency. Unless the United States is ready to announce our own position, it means that this agency concerned with world development will be pretty well messed up. Politics are heavily involved, with some members of the Congress, particularly in the Senate, stating their opposition to the United States making contributions to international organizations of this kind, while others are concerned with the desires of internationalist organizations of this country, and the desire of industrial plants in their home states, to get orders for material necessary to world development.

Food producers and exporters naturally want a big export trade on our part, a business which will probably amount to $20 billion this year, if we permit it. On the other hand, labor unions are taking positions against the importation of manufactured products from other countries, which would go to pay for the huge export of farm commodities that we sell.

I doubt that there ever was a time in Congress when it was so difficult for a member seeking re-election to vote in such a manner that re-election would not be jeopardized. On Friday morning I told Senator Mansfield that I would not be surprised if there were twenty new members of the United States Senate next year due to the fact that most every vote we cast carries a conflict of interest. At this time I would estimate that the Republican party in the next Senate may sustain a net loss of three of four members.

¶ ALTHOUGH there is a lot of talk about cutting down the costs of elections, my observations are that, with the exception of the 1972 national election, more money is being spent this year to influence political elections than ever before. And the "dirty tricks department" seems to be working overtime. In Florida, Senator Ed Gurney was indicted by a grand jury on the charge that he had previously accepted campaign contributions before he had appointed a treasurer for his campaign. Yesterday the judge presiding at the trial angrily dismissed the case. It appears that the Democrat dirty trickster who had made the charge against Senator Gurney had quoted a law which was no longer on the books, and had, in effect, lied to the grand jury that made the indictment. Frankly I don't see why the trickster who lied to the grand jury shouldn't go to jail, but that is not likely in this day and age when most anything goes.

Somebody made a suggestion this week that persons making large political contributions should be prohibited from receiving federal appointments. This suggestion represents almost the ultimate in public stupidity, for persons elected to high positions in government have always favored those who made their election possible and, regardless of party, this political trait isn't going to change. The old saying that "to the victor belongs the spoils" still stands.

It is apparent, however, that all the commotion, justifiable and otherwise, has put the fear of God and of the U.S. court system in the souls of many candidates, as evidenced by the almost complete compliance with the law enacted recently which requires candidates to make disclosures of political contributions and income received from speaking engagements and from writing articles. The salary of a Senator is $42,500 a year, but some of my distinguished colleagues have made considerably more than that amount by giving speeches probably worth about $50 to groups and organizations that are willing to pay up to $10,000 a speech. These high amounts paid for speeches simply represent a desire on the part of some to repay political office-holders for services rendered, or to contribute to the next campaign for re-election, and still keep within the law.

Week ending May 25, 1974

THE WEEK STARTED OUT with a meeting with eight members of the Soviet government who represented what we would call four Senators and four Representatives of the House. Russia has a pretty good-reading Constitution, with one House representing areas and the other representing population. The members have to run for election and re-election just as they do in the U.S.A., but when they once get their seats the Communist Party takes over, and they all seem to vote alike.

They were very well received in the United States by members of the Senate and House, by the State department, and by the White House. Before leaving for New York late in the week, the Soviet representatives were wined and dined generously.

It was about twenty years ago that members of the Union of Soviet Socialist Republics indicated a desire to exchange conferences with members of our Congress, but at that time they would not have been very graciously received in this country. In fact they would have been demonstrated against and probably mistreated. Not until four or five years ago would it have been advisable to have them in this country as our guests. President Nixon's visit to Moscow a couple of years ago broke the cold-war barrier, and we are now witnessing an increase in business as well as better diplomatic and cultural relations with Russia.

I realize that Soviet officials have felt let down by not being able to play a more important part in efforts to settle the Middle East conflict. But since Egypt and other Arab states as well as Israel want that settlement to be handled by a one-man, one-country intermediary—namely, Kissinger and the United States—Russia has not been able to play the part which she had hoped to.

In the meantime the press and commentators in the states here are getting pretty critical of Secretary Kissinger for being away from the State department so long. And the State department itself seems to be getting a bit rickety, due largely to his absence. However, so long as there is hope for a Middle East settlement, I think it will be wise for him to stay on that job until some kind of a settlement has been reached, if a settlement is possible.

¶ ON TUESDAY I spoke for ten minutes in the Senate on the importance of President Nixon making his trip to Moscow next month. I pointed out that some critics of the Russian government felt he should not do so, though in my view the trip is very important, not only for the purpose of increasing trade between our two great countries, but also in developing co-operation in other ways. I pointed out that the door to continuance of the SALT talks must be kept open for the purpose of reaching an agreement looking to a halt, or at least a reduction, in the increase in preparations for war by our two countries. The hostility to the Soviets and the opposition to increasing trade with them and other communist countries is dying down somewhat, but it is still present to a dangerous degree.

¶ JUST TO KEEP diplomatic relations cooking, the Foreign Relations committee had the Deputy Prime Minister of Poland, Mr. Jan Mitrega, to lunch on Wednesday. I had not expected to attend but at the last minute found time to drop in and visit briefly. One of his aides, named Chowaniec, told me that he had spent two summers in Putney, Vermont, on an exchange with the Experiment in International Living. It is really surprising how many people in the world know all about my home town and have spent some time there. This exchange of visitors and students has indeed worked to our advantage, and apparently to the advantage of those who exchange with us as well.

¶ LATE WEDNESDAY FORENOON Senator Sam Ervin and I were asked to go down to the Reflecting Pool to meet with the officials of the American League of Anglers, a new super-organization made up of representatives of those who are concerned primarily with hunting, fishing, and wildlife. Sam and I were invited because some months ago, when we were asked what we expected to do after quitting the Congress, we both said we hoped to get a chance to go fishing. The result was that we had our picture taken with beautiful little fishing rods which were presented to us. And the picture was apparently reproduced in almost every newspaper in the United States. Whether we get a chance to use these fishing rods remains to be seen.

Week ending June 1, 1974

ON WEDNESDAY, the Senate concluded work on the International Development Association bill, approving it by a 2-to-1 vote. The records show that the more the affluent countries, particularly the United States, give in financial assistance to what we call the underdeveloped countries, the more business they build for themselves. I pointed out on the Senate floor that when we enacted *Public Law 480* to help feed the hungry people of the world back in President Eisenhower's first term the cost of providing food for hungry people in other countries was $800 million, and this increased to nearly $2 billion by 1957. In that year our exports of agricultural commodities for cash totaled only $2.8 billion. By 1973, however, the costs of providing food, either free or at a cut rate, to other countries had dropped to $1 billion while the sales for cash had reached a total of almost $12 billion. And this year, 1974, it is anticipated that we will export agricultural commodities to the amount of $20 billion or more.

It appears that people who are well fed are better customers for our export products, since 80 percent of the cost of contributing to the programs for the development of the poorest nations comes right back to the United States in the form of more business for our industries.

¶ JUST BEFORE NOON on Wednesday I received a call from the White House advising me that a cease-fire agreement had been reached between Syria and Israel, and that the President would make the announcement at one o'clock.

The despondency of last week over the Middle East took a decided reverse turn. For the first time Syria had recognized Israel as a state with its own government. Secretary Kissinger, although rather considerably discouraged last week, had stayed on a couple of days the early part of this week to make one last effort towards establishing tolerable relations between these two countries. Egypt and Jordan had been co-operative with the Secretary throughout his efforts to restore better relations, but Syria had just held up until the middle of this week.

The Secretary got home Thursday night, and on Friday morning some of us whom they call Congressional leaders were asked to come to the White House to get a report from the President and Secretary Kissinger. In the afternoon the Secretary came before members of the Senate Foreign Relations committee. What was a mystery to some of us was how he could look so healthy after having worked day and night for weeks on what was considered to be a long-shot effort. It seems that the Arabs have no hesitation at all in carrying on discussions until five o'clock in the morning. Nevertheless, Secretary Kissinger had evidently kept up with them and if he was any worse for the wear after eighty days of diplomatic struggle, he didn't show it.

Possibly, the major problem in the Middle East now is what can be done about a settlement for the Palestinians, whose land was taken from them at the time the country of Israel was formed by the United Nations nearly a generation ago. The situation may seem insoluble at this time, but as one of my old banker friends used to tell me when I was governor of Vermont, if a thing is worth doing, there is a way to do it.

Week ending June 8, 1974

THE SENATE has been debating the Military Procurement Authorization bill all the week and is not through with it yet. A close vote was had on Senator Mansfield's proposed amendment to reduce American military forces in other countries, but Mike lost by a vote of 44 to 46. I voted with him, although normally I would have supported the committee and the Administration. However, the terms of this bill seem to have developed not so much out of consideration for the security of the United States as out of a domestic war between the manufacturers of military equipment and supplies (munitions makers, they used to be called), and the producers of exportable goods and equipment for peaceful uses.

The executive branch, from White House assistants down through the State and Defense departments, lobbied strongly against any proposal to reduce our troops in Europe. The argument was that such action at this time would weaken President Nixon's position when he meets with Brezhnev in Moscow late this month. They put up a good argument for opposing the Mansfield proposal, but I felt that the Western European countries should be expected to stand on their own feet a little more than they are now doing, and therefore I voted with Mike. However, the close vote indicates that the situation may be changed after the election next November.

Probably the most glaring proposal to put the affairs of the United States in the hands of the military was Senator Jackson's amendment, which would have placed control of all exports from the United States to Russia and other communist countries under the jurisdiction of the Defense department, taking this authority away from the President and the Commerce department, where licensing for export now rests. Jackson's amendment was proposed out of a blue sky with only a few members of the Senate present. It had not been printed and apparently was in the nature of a surprise attack on the Soviet government and other nations that are favorable to the communist cause. While there may be some question as to Senator Jackson's motivation, it appears to me beyond any doubt that his principal purpose was to make it impossible for President Nixon to meet on anywhere near cordial and co-operative terms with the Russians in Moscow. I don't believe that Scoop actually wants war with Russia, but keeping alive the constant threat of war means good business for certain industries that manufacture materials needed in times of actual warfare.

While the Jackson proposal was undoubtedly intended to please some of this country's makers of war supplies, it was assumed that his amendment was aimed at curtailing exports by manufacturers of computers, which would play an increasingly important role in any future war, particularly a nuclear war. With the internationalizing of American industrial concerns, however, it would be futile to expect that any such export restrictions would be effective. Only a few years ago one of our leading makers of computers is reported to have sold or given its latest designs to a French affiliate, with the result, as I understand, that types similar to ours are now being produced in France, where they are for sale to other countries. Be that as it may, the Jackson amendment was so written that the Department of Defense could have vetoed our export of food, machines—even hand tools—such as are now being sent all over the world, and are thus helping us to maintain a more nearly favorable balance of trade with other countries.

This proposed sleight-of-hand legislation failed for the time being at the insistence of Senator Mansfield, and final action was put over until Tuesday of next week. I have never questioned the necessity for maintaining a strong military defense for the United States, but when it comes to letting the military and its suppliers control our economic fortunes, that is going just too far.

¶ CATTLE PRODUCERS at present are not doing so well. The price for beef went so high last summer that the people stopped buying it, and they still haven't returned to consuming the amounts which were sold before the price skyrocketed.

To complicate the picture further, there is a demand now that imports of beef from other countries be prohibited, at least for a while. But since much of the meat produced in other countries is grown on the grains which we export, the interests of our grain-growers and our meat-producers are in conflict.

The sad part of the present meat situation seems to be that retail stores have not reduced prices in proportion to the lower prices paid to farmers. Instead, many retail stores are apparently devoting much of their increased profits to carrying full-page advertisements in the newspapers, and so long as this is kept up, the farmer isn't going to get too much help from the metropolitan press.

¶ No HOLDS ARE BARRED in the domestic political struggle. Yesterday reports were prevalent that the President is making his visit to six countries in the Middle East and later in the month to Moscow for the purpose of diverting attention from the charges made against him as a result of the Watergate fiasco. President Nixon visited China and Moscow quite some time before his political adversaries even heard of the Watergate break-in, but facts and figures don't bother our over-ambitious candidates for higher office.

Week ending June 15, 1974

ON THURSDAY morning it was announced that Scoop Jackson would go to China the first week in July on invitation of the government of the People's Republic of China. I hope that his visit does not result in an increase in the trend of hostilities between China and Russia, even though that could lead to an increase in business for the producers of war materials here in the United States. While I realize that each country in the world, including our own, must have enough military strength to insure its own security, yet the major business of the world should be the production and exchange of commodities and material used for peaceful purposes.

¶ TUESDAY FORENOON a political bombshell exploded with the report of a press conference which Secretary Kissinger had held in Austria. The news media at the conference did not restrict their questioning to the work which he had done in the interest of a more peaceful world. One reporter, who takes delight in irritating the important people he interviews, made an inquiry concerning tapping the telephones of people working in the National Security Council, of which Dr. Kissinger was formerly the head. With this questioning our good Secretary of State apparently lost his cool and did not get over it even after he landed with the President in Austria. After the conferences here last week, Secretary Kissinger had breakfast with Senator Mansfield and suggested he thought he should resign if he is to be criticized by the news media. While in Salzburg, Austria, he called another press conference and displayed his feelings to an even greater extent than before he had left our country. The Secretary stated that he had written a letter to Chairman Fulbright of the Foreign Relations committee asking for a further study of his part in the bugging of government employees who had access to confidential material relating to the security of the United States. It so happens that last September, when his name had been submitted for confirmation as Secretary of State, the Senate Foreign Relations committee made a pretty thorough investigation of the situation and gave Dr. Kissinger a clean bill of health, which resulted in his being approved by the committee and by the Senate.

As the committee was meeting Tuesday morning it turned out that Senator Fulbright had not yet received Kissinger's original letter, but I had in my pocket a copy of it which I made available to the committee. I couldn't for the life of me figure out why one who had been

so thoroughly investigated and cleared of any wrongdoing would ask
to be investigated again. I do believe that as head of the National
Security Council Dr. Kissinger did what any responsible person would
have done when he found that confidential material was being leaked
to the news media, and indirectly to the rest of the world: that was to
try to find the culprits and get rid of them.

Of course Dr. Kissinger himself has given the news media much firsthand information of the harmless variety. This practice built him up
with the press and radio until, from reading columnists and the reporters' stories, one would naturally come to the conclusion that he
could do no wrong and was doing a perfect job. So I realized what a
shock it was to him when any member of the press had the temerity to
suggest that his work was not perfect in every way. But Secretary Kissinger's demand for a retrial, and his threat to resign unless given
complete exoneration, were a bit too much for me, and I suppose I was
somewhat sarcastic in commenting on the situation; at least, the press
said I was. I probably agree too much with President Truman's saying
that if you can't stand the heat you'd better get out of the kitchen.

¶ THE ACTION OF OUR SECRETARY OF STATE provided a golden opportunity for the adversaries of President Nixon. My friend Senator Allen
of Alabama, aided by Senators Thurmond, Jackson, and others, who
are not regarded as the world's greatest pacifists, lost no time in preparing a Senate Resolution expressing the utmost confidence in Secretary Kissinger, and apparently no confidence at all in the President of
the United States, without whose backing Dr. Kissinger could not have
achieved such worthwhile successes. In fact, it has been President
Nixon all the time who has given the directions and made the decisions for which the anti-Nixon forces would now give full credit to his
Secretary of State. But when Senators Scott, Griffin, and other Republican leaders joined in promoting a Resolution which so obviously was
intended to downgrade our own President, I was a bit bewildered.
Also, when other Senators who were not at all enthusiastic about withdrawing our military forces from Indochina praised Kissinger to the
skies as a disciple of peace, I felt I was justified in being still more
bewildered.

The Resolution, which was finally endorsed by over half the members of the Senate, was referred to the Senate Foreign Relations committee. The over-all effect of it is to say that the Senate has made a
finding of complete innocence for Secretary Kissinger, even before the
Foreign Relations committee can conduct the investigation which was
requested by the Secretary himself. If this is the way to do business, it

seems to me that the Senate might also adopt a Resolution finding the President innocent of any impeachment charges which may be brought against him by the Judiciary committee of the House. What a furor there will be if representatives of the press now succeed in finding something wrong with which to charge the Secretary!

¶ DURING THE WEEK one piece of legislation relating to expenditures of government was amended to put a ceiling on the total amount which could be appropriated by the Congress. This amendment, by Senator Proxmire, cleared the Senate by a vote of 74 to 12. I was one of the twelve against it, but some of those who voted for the ceiling assured me that they fully expected that such a provision would be deleted in Conference with the House.

Fixing a ceiling in dollars for expenditures in the future is sheer foolishness. We don't know what a dollar will be worth even six months from now as inflation continues. But I do know that, should this proviso become law, and should appropriations for various programs supported by those who voted for an over-all ceiling exceed that amount by, shall we say, $10 billion, the Congress would then find itself in a situation whereby funds already appropriated would have to be reduced. That would create an intolerable situation, since some would reduce the military, some would reduce welfare, some would reduce foreign aid, and so on. And the war and the arguments would start all over again.

However, we can be thankful that we have two Houses of Congress, and when one passes the buck to the other the conference committees simply get together and straighten things out. Then every member of Congress can tell his constituents that he voted for the things they wanted and against the things they opposed, and they will never know the difference.

¶ As IF THE KISSINGER OUTBURST on Tuesday morning was not enough excitement for the week, we got a bit more on Friday when it was reported that President Nixon had reached an agreement with Egypt whereby we would furnish them with the plans for a commercial-sized nuclear power plant, and also sell them the fuel necessary to operate it. Of course the United States is to reserve the right of inspection of this plant to make sure that it would not be used for military purposes.

The news media descended on me asking for details. Well, I could tell them honestly that details of the agreement had not yet been worked out, but will be by the end of this month. I could tell them honestly that Secretary Kissinger had not talked with me about it, nor had the White House, but that I was not surprised that the deal was being arranged, and that I would be very much surprised if a similar arrangement is not reached with Israel. In the middle of the afternoon a reporter for the Chicago *Tribune* called me and said that he understood that Governor Holton [Virginia], now the State department's principal contact with the Congress, had briefed a few members on the matter. All I could say was, "You may be right." Of course he was right. I feel that it was perfectly proper that the report pertaining to Israel also came out on Friday, otherwise there would have been a hullabaloo over our doing business with Egypt over the weekend.

Israel does not need much advice as to the construction of a nuclear power plant, but she will require economic help. What is not commonly known to the public is that throughout the world several hundred nuclear power plants are being planned, with many of them already under construction. Nearly all countries are short of energy, and it seems to me that a country which has the ability to produce food, household equipment, and the power needed for civic and domestic purposes, is far less likely to become involved in war than one inhabited by desperate people who lack the advantages which the people of more affluent nations enjoy.

¶ A LITTLE BAD NEWS popped up on Thursday when a Presidential message to the Congress indicated that the Eastern Wild Areas bill, which had taken almost two years to get prepared and through the Senate, was "inadequate." My humble opinion is that the bill was too adequate, in that it set aside a relatively small area of the country east of the 100th Meridian for the preservation of wilderness conditions without retaining special benefits for the vested interests. I may have something to say about this next week, but my present opinion is that the industrialists—power, mining and lumbering—have a bigger clout in the executive branch of government than have the more idealistic environmental organizations.

Week ending June 22, 1974

THE FIRST HALF OF THE WEEK in the Senate was devoted largely to politics, which became smellier and smellier. Ostensibly we were working on the debt ceiling limitation and extension. Actually our ambitious Presidential candidates were making a political mess of it.

Senator Kennedy and his friends offered as an amendment to the

Debt Ceiling bill now pending a whole new tax bill, which was intended to please a lot of voters even if it wouldn't help the United States much. Teddy, like some of the other brilliant young members of the United States Senate, seems to have quite an organization preparing political legislative proposals for him. Senator Jim Allen, classed as one of the greater conservatives of the Senate, seems to have the ability to make Kennedy's more brilliant young colleagues look like monkeys from time to time. And so the political campaign continues in full force without much regard for the future of our country and its government.

¶ As EXPECTED, the President promised Israel a similar deal on a nuclear power reactor to the deal offered Egypt last week. Israel does not need such a reactor quite as badly as Egypt does, because France had aided the Israelies in getting one of fairly good size a few years ago. Israel was reported to have begun the production of plutonium some fourteen years ago, and I always felt that the product had been sold to France. Nobody seems to know, or at least nobody is willing to tell, whether there was a deal of this nature or not.

Egypt has a many times greater population and only a small 2-megawatt reactor, which they acquired with Russian help. Egypt is in a far more desperate position as far as energy is concerned than is Israel; but as I see it now, Israel is in a far greater need of Egyptian friendship, or at least tolerance.

Apparently Egypt, Israel and Jordan could get along with each other and eventually expand their economies to the benefit of all. Nevertheless there are people in this country who say that we should not help Egypt at all in any way. For the most part they are those who have been the recipients of sizable campaign support from Jewish citizens in this country in past elections.

¶ HAVING JUST RETURNED from the Middle East, the President is planning to go to Moscow on the 27th to meet with Brezhnev and other top Soviet officials. There is not too much optimism here concerning any improvement in Soviet–United States relations, but from Moscow we get more optimistic predictions, which I hope will come true.

American industry, including American bankers, seemingly find the U.S.S.R. a most fertile field for investment. Now in the works is a contract for a $200 million fertilizer plant there, for which the U.S. Export-Import Bank will put up 45 percent and the international bankers another 45 percent, leaving the remaining 10 percent to be supplied by the Soviets. There is little question but what the world needs more crop fertilizer if the standard of living for another two billion people is to be raised. The phosphate rock which the plant will need is expected to come largely from Florida, although I understand that Morocco has an enormous supply that could be used.

I did not succeed in finding out from Mr. William Casey, president/chairman of the Export-Import Bank, just what interest American banks who already have established branches in Moscow will receive for their part of the loan. He only told me that it would be ¾ of 1 percent above the prime rate. I didn't tell him that I didn't even know what the prime rate for American money in Russia would be, but I believe it is in the neighborhood of 11 percent. Knowing some of our bankers pretty well, I guarantee they won't lose on the deal.

The news yesterday informed us that Russia is also undertaking to make a deal with Boeing Aircraft, not only for planes but also for the establishment of a manufacturing plant in Russia. How this news will affect the government of the People's Republic of China remains to be seen. And how it will effect Senator Scoop Jackson's trip to China, already announced for the first week in July, is unpredictable. I have been disturbed that Scoop might undertake to increase the friction already existing between China and Russia, but since Boeing Aircraft headquarters are in his home state of Washington, he might encounter complications.

[Putney, Vermont]

Week ending June 29, 1974

THE FEATURE EVENT of the first half of the week was the manner in which the so-called liberal element of the Senate, led by Teddy Kennedy and Hubert Humphrey, got set back on their heels. They were trying, and very improperly I thought, to annex a lot of politically promising amendments to the Debt Ceiling bill—a bill which we had already spent over a week on. Under the opposition leadership of Jim Allen and others who are more interested in getting necessary legislation passed this week, they had to throw in the sponge. After three votes, each of which set them back a little bit further, Hubert and Teddy decided they had had enough, and permitted the Debt Ceiling bill to go through as it should have done two weeks ago. Even so, a lot of conservative votes were cast against it because of the substantial increase which the Administration had to have in order to meet the requirements of government.

¶ PRESIDENT NIXON and Secretary Kissinger took off again for foreign fields on Tuesday, stopping in Belgium to assure the NATO countries that just because the President was headed for a visit in Moscow did not mean that we plan to neglect support for Western Europe. It is rather ironic that when the United States was undertaking to prevent complete defeat for Israel in October 1973, and had to meet the challenge of the oil embargo imposed by the Arab nations, virtually every one of the Western European countries refused to assist us—that is, all but Holland. I suppose they ran out on us because they were more completely dependent on oil for the production of energy than we are, but it did make me unhappy to see how quickly they skedaddled when we could have used their assistance to the advantage of all.

¶ LOBBYISTS AND TOURISTS were more prevalent than usual during the last part of the week and it was a relief to head north on Thursday. We had hardly reached our house in Putney before the State department called to find out what I thought of furnishing several nuclear reactors to Iran. I had not read the morning papers, but it appeared they carried the story that Iran had ordered $5 billion worth of nuclear reactors from France to be delivered over the next few years, and had paid France $1 billion to start with. It was and is my opinion that if Iran will purchase nuclear reactors from us on the same terms that she used in dealing with France, we might as well sell them, since if we do not she will order the rest from France or some other country.

¶ SATURDAY, Governor Holton of the State department called. This time State wanted to know what I thought of giving Israel $1 billion as a grant rather than a loan. The Congress last year made $2.2 billion available to help out Israel as a loan. Of course the news media forget this $2.2 billion, so most of the country thinks that all we help Israel with is $450 million. I told him that in all probability a loan of an extra $1 billion might not be repaid anyway, and I felt that if the money was given outright to Israel there wouldn't be too much complaint, since the principal adversaries of the White House, like Senators McGovern, Kennedy, Church and others, are very devoted friends of Israel.

¶ ON SATURDAY I got word from the Foreign Relations committee asking my approval for hiring a staff member for $35,000 a year to aid Senator Javits. Probably the money will be granted, along with another $100,000 or so for a computer and people to run it, in the next few weeks. But I do believe that we are heading into more difficulty in the political and ideological fields than we realize. Whereas our staff on Foreign Relations had only about twenty members a few years ago, it will now have nearer seventy, and the end is not in sight.

And that goes for other committees, too. In my opinion and in the minds of most of the public, Congress is as bad as the White House. New agencies of government are set up at all levels, local, state and federal, and consultants are hired at all levels. This is really a make-job program because there just aren't enough job opportunities available otherwise.

[Putney, Vermont]

Week ending July 6, 1974

ON TUESDAY we got our local tax bills and, while I haven't checked them carefully as yet, I would say that there has been an increase of about 15 percent in taxes at the community level. This is probably true of most of the towns in Vermont—as well as other states—and is at least partly the result of revenue-sharing by the federal government. When the communities and the states found out that they had a substantial amount of federal money handed to them, they promptly went to work to get started on a lot of facilities and conveniences which they had always wanted. And some found out that it not only took all the revenue-sharing money but an increase in local taxes as well to meet the costs.

¶ TUESDAY NOON we listened to President Nixon's radio address to the Russian people. He told them outright—and of course what he said was meant for us also—that there had been no major disarmament agreements. Before he left for Moscow, the President and Secretary Kissinger had advised us not to expect major agreements for disarmament. Furthermore, neither the United States nor Russia is likely to lessen efforts to develop more deadly weapons for use in case of war at this time. With other countries, especially France and China, as well as other lesser countries, bending every effort to develop atomic weapons as well as improved reactors for power development, we can't expect either Russia or the United States to make agreements in this field that would greatly minimize their own power.

The President announced that there had been an agreement on the ABM [anti-ballistic missile], but this simply recalls the prediction of four or five years ago that the United States was developing the anti-ballistic missile so that when we met with Russia, as the President has been doing, we could trade them something of ours that wouldn't work for something they had that wouldn't work. And the effectiveness of the ABM for protecting any country against ballistic missiles has always been in doubt.

¶ AMBASSADOR BILL MACOMBER was recalled from Turkey for consultation regarding Turkey's decision to continue the production of opium poppies regardless of the agreement made with the United States a couple of years ago whereby we would pay them some $30 million not to raise opium poppies. Just another case of what happens when the United States undertakes to regulate the customs and habits of other countries in return for a cash handout.

¶ SCOOP JACKSON has spent some time in China this week and the assumption by many people is that he is trying to convince the Chinese leaders that we are great friends of theirs but not of the Russians.

GEORGE MCGOVERN and HUBERT HUMPHREY are both coming under attack on account of last election's political contributions and so on. Looks to me as if the Democrats are trying to reduce the number of candidates for the Presidency in the 1976 election.

[United States Senate]

Week ending July 13, 1974

HENRY KISSINGER got back from overseas Tuesday, and the Congressional leadership met with him and the President at the White House on Wednesday morning. Kissinger was very affable towards me, and the meeting was one of the best White House meetings I have ever attended. In fact, I found almost nothing to disagree with in the manner in which the President and Secretary Kissinger had been handling our relations with other countries.

It is apparent that we can expect no new SALT agreement in the near future. I brought up the question of France making so much progress in the nuclear field, and wondered whether, if France could produce and sell reactors successfully, she could not also produce and sell nuclear weapons. Both the President and Secretary Kissinger assured us that in the course of several years France could not develop any more destructive weapons than could be found in a tiny portion of our own supply. Of course Russia and the United States are not going to start any nuclear war that would guarantee the almost complete destruction of both countries. But I had to point out that it would only take one or two nuclear missiles in the hands of a small country to get a worldwide nuclear war started. Probably there is no immediate danger of this, but we do have to remember that the wars of this century have had their starts in small countries.

¶ THE MOST CLASSIC EXAMPLE of political hypocrisy I have seen for a long time, maybe ever, occurred on Thursday when a bill purporting to regulate the sale and use of drugs came before the Senate. Senator Walt Mondale offered an amendment which would have prohibited any military or economic aid to Turkey unless that country would cut out the production of opium from poppies. Of course, with only Turkey and Greece now permitting our military forces to occupy bases in their countries, bases important to the defense of the Middle East, Walt's proposal created some consternation among the most earnest advocates of support for Israel.

The result was that Walt changed his amendment to include all opium-producing countries. Although Turkey undoubtedly reduced its production of poppies from which opium is derived at the request of the United States last year, the business quite naturally diverted to other areas of the world. Many countries throughout Asia and elsewhere produce large quantities of opium-poppy seed, and are also dependent on economic or military aid from the United States. Some of them couldn't even begin to control the illegal drug traffic unless we supported them. And in this respect the Mondale amendment would be self-defeating.

Having gotten themselves into a box, the members of the Senate who felt that their prospects for political advancement or re-election would be enhanced by battling against the illegal drug traffic, figured the usual way out and amended the proposal so as to put the final responsibility on the President of the United States. Heaven knows how many times, in order to duck an issue, members of Congress have passed the buck to the President so that if something goes wrong they can claim the glory and blame the President.

After opposing the crippling and hypocritical amendments, I did vote for the bill, in the belief that the House would either put a little sense into it or that the President would veto it. If the bill goes to the President in the form that it passed the Senate, I feel confident that he will veto it, and that I will sustain his veto.

How do we expect to gain the respect and friendship of other countries in the world if we are insistent on telling them that they have to run all the affairs of their country in accordance with our desires? I admit that this policy has worked from time to time, but I feel that we are going much too far in this direction.

¶ ON THURSDAY we also had what is called the Legal Services bill up for action. This bill had been passed by both Houses, and changes had been agreed to by the conferees. The changes, however, did not meet with the approval of the White House, which had frankly promised a veto unless certain provisions were changed. Knowing full well that Congress would not pass the bill over the President's veto, it was re-committed and an agreement was reached to bring it up before the Senate again next Tuesday.

This bill would provide legal counsel for poor people at government expense, and also provide clients for a good many lawyers who otherwise might have difficulty in making both ends meet. To say that a good deal of politics was involved in the handling of this bill would be an understatement.

¶ THURSDAY MORNING we had a hearing on a bill which was originally sponsored by Senators Humphrey, Young, McGee and myself, although a dozen more of our colleagues climbed aboard as soon as they could. This bill related to the food supply of the world. Even though the United States has done more to keep people from going hungry in this world than any other country or combination of countries, there are those who continually condemn us for not doing more.

Of all the efforts of international organizations to feed hungry people in the world, the United States provided 32 percent of the cost. Millions of people, particularly in Asia, owe their existence today to the generosity of Uncle Sam. I call it generosity, but *Public Law 480,* as it is known around the world—or "Food for Peace," as some politically-minded Americans choose to call it—was enacted partly as a means of getting rid of our farm surpluses. Anyway, people of the world are living infinitely better today than they were when the bill was introduced by Senator Schoeppel of Kansas—I was a co-sponsor—in 1953. To hear some of our ambitious colleagues talk about it today, one would never guess that Republicans had anything to do with this splendid bit of legislation.

Week ending July 20, 1974

MEMBERS OF THE SENATE are getting somewhat impatient. Some have developed an itch to get home and start campaigning; others want to travel here, there and everywhere all over the world, with the tax-payers picking up the tab. I have had to approve foreign travel for almost every member of the Foreign Relations committee, with some of them making their third and fourth trips outside of this country. I think that travel to other countries really does quite a lot of good, but this business has been overdone. Yesterday I told Art Kuhl of the Foreign Relations staff to remind these folks that they are all supposed to give the committee written reports on their travel, although in many cases such reminders will doubtless prove futile. The excessive number of trips abroad, frequently with members of the family and staff, is partly my fault, because Bill Fulbright and I could have kept them in check had we started to do so in the beginning. But it is too late now, and I only hope the total result will be a much better understanding between our country and other countries of the five continents. Most of these trips do have a legitimate excuse, since they pertain to international organizations of which the U.S.A. is a member.

¶ THE IMPEACHMENT FEVER has been rising again and assuming a more partisan appearance every day. The House Judiciary committee has completed its hearings, and indicates its intention to start acting officially next week on the evidence of wrongdoing on the part of President Nixon. My personal opinion is that 90 percent of the members of the House would rather not vote on impeachment findings. However, the House Judiciary committee wants to get the mess off its hands and I suspect it will recommend, largely on a party-line basis, that the house vote for impeachment proceedings. Then the full House will have to take action. I am sure that most of them would rather be home in bed than have to vote on this issue, since no matter how they vote they will arouse resentment among a certain number of their constituents. The fact remains that the House has to get rid of this matter some way, and right now I have a rather strong feeling that the majority of the members will vote for impeachment in order to get the issue off their backs and unload the responsibility onto the backs of one hundred Senators. The whole mess is pretty sordid, and will likely resolve itself into an act of ingenious buck-passing.

¶ NOT EVERYTHING THAT HAPPENED during the week was bad. Thursday night President Nixon authorized two of his top aides, Tom Korologos and Pat O'Donnell, to take the President's yacht, the *Sequoia*, for the evening. L.P.A. and I were invited to go on this boat trip, which lasted from about six to nine in the evening. White House and other government officials and members of the Senate, eighteen in all, enjoyed a welcome change from the smelly messes we have to contend with on Capitol Hill.

Somebody will probably get the bright idea that the President permitted his aides to take us on this trip and give us dinner in order to influence our votes. I can truthfully say that no votes were influenced, but I would have enjoyed the dinner more had my dentist not operated on six of my teeth earlier in the day.

Week ending July 27, 1974

INFLATION IS GOING FULL TILT AHEAD towards an inevitable national crisis of one kind or another. The period we are going through resembles the years of the late 1920's when business was good and the bankers were all happy, predicting that there never would be another depression. But we got our comeuppance then, with the longest depression in our history, and with legislation by a one sided Democratic Congress under President Roosevelt which virtually changed the character of our government.

¶ UP TO THE END OF THE WEEK things appeared to be going smoothly in the Mediterranean, looking towards an avoidance of any armed conflict over the current Cyprus affair. It is rather ironic that if Turkey and Greece should engage in war over Cyprus, both would be using military equipment furnished by the United States. At present, however, our country is adopting a hands-off position. England is playing a greater part, in co-operation with both Greece and Turkey. The United Nations is acting a bit more effectively in restoring peaceful understanding, and once more Secretary Kissinger and his supporters, particularly Joe Sisco, have done a good job. By the end of the week the situation got more shaky, with Turkey and Greece shaking their fists, but right now I doubt that a real war will develop in this area.

¶ THE MOST SENSATIONAL NEWS of the week was the decision of the Supreme Court that President Nixon should turn over to Judge Sirica's court about sixty-four tapes, some of which may be related to the Watergate affair and the charges made against the President and other Executive officials. The President promptly agreed to comply with the decision of the court, and now Judge Sirica will have his hands full for the next few weeks in deciding what part of these tapes relate to the charges made against those implicated in the Watergate affair.

The House Judiciary committee, headed by Congressman Rodino of New Jersey, but supposedly influenced greatly by House leader Tip O'Neill, started arguments Wednesday evening as they began looking into charges against President Nixon which might warrant impeachment. The last act of the committee on Saturday night was to vote 27 to 11 in favor of one charge against the President. Live television coverage assures the members of the committee that they will get considerable public attention.

It looks now as if the committee will report in favor of other impeachment charges; and the matter will then be considered by the whole House, probably in about three weeks. The matter is assuming a more partisan nature—and that is not good.

Week ending August 3, 1974

THE BIGGEST ITEM OF INTEREST during the week is the House Judiciary committee's voting to recommend a bill of impeachment against President Nixon, based on mismanagement of government affairs and attempting to cover up wrongdoing and law violations by White House employees and associates.

¶ DURING THE EARLY PART OF THE WEEK the Senate considered the so-called Consumer Protection bill, which looks good on the face of it but which would put the U.S. Department of Agriculture's operations in an almost intolerable position, since consumer representatives could intervene in almost any decision made by the Secretary of Agriculture. While the passage of the bill might mean additional income for thousands of lawyers, in my opinion it would most certainly mean a general reduction in food production in the United States. The USDA now has jurisdiction over food programs such as school lunch, school milk, food for infants and mothers, and the Food Stamp program. Whereas the Food Stamp program cost only $350 million a year some five years ago, the appropriation will amount to about $4 billion this year.

¶ CONGRESS is becoming increasingly aware of the need for more nearly balancing our federal expenditures, but so far has done nothing about it. Next year a new committee will decide at the beginning of the Congressional Session what the total amount of appropriations should be. If the total amount exceeds the ceiling, then the Budget committee would undertake to recommend the cuts to be made for each department. This is a flagrant—and I believe vain—attempt on the part of members of Congress to vote for whatever appropriations their constituents demand, and then, when the amount has to be cut, to claim credit for voting for the larger amount and put the blame for the reductions on the Budget committee. In my opinion this system is not going to work, but it may help some of the members get some votes from their constituents who are not aware of the ultimate consequences.

¶ At 5:00 p.m. Thursday afternoon, L.P.A. and I boarded the Amtrak Montreal train for a brief trip home. We got to Montpelier Junction early Friday morning. The weather was pretty hot and the air conditioning in our car didn't work, so we didn't get a very good night's sleep. Apparently, the railroad powers that be don't like the idea of running a passenger train from Washington to Montreal anyway, though the employees on the train are very enthusiastic, accommodating and hopeful for the future.

Week ending August 10, 1974

After staying in Putney long enough to go over to Ellsworth Bunker's eightieth birthday party late Monday afternoon, we drove to Montpelier, where at 10 p.m. we boarded the Montreal-to-Washington train, which was right on time. Whereas on our northbound trip the air conditioner in the car had failed, on the southbound journey the water gave out shortly after we boarded the train.

Later in the week the bill for the support of the railroads, particularly Amtrak, came before the Senate. After expressing my opinion of the way certain lines, particularly in the Northeast corridor running from Washington to Boston, hogged most everything which Congress appropriates for all of the lines in the country, I finally voted for the bill. Senator Hartke, in charge of the bill on the floor, agreed with me that something had to be done to prevent certain vested interests from grabbing everything, and expressed the opinion that a new member of the Amtrak board, Joe MacDonald, would be helpful in getting more equality into the Amtrak operations. Joe is already making a nuisance of himself to the old-line boys.

One morning while listening to the radio at 6 a.m., I heard a voice encouraging people to travel by Amtrak to New York or Boston and telling the world that they didn't need any reservations—just come to the station and get on the train. This advertisement had something to do with my expressing a candid observation on the Senate floor that if one is traveling from Washington to Montreal, or going to Vermont or New Hampshire, he is required to make a reservation in advance, and can't even get standing room unless he has a reservation.

¶ THE FOREIGN RELATIONS COMMITTEE spent considerable time from day to day trying to write a bill authorizing foreign aid for the fiscal year 1975. It is not easy to do this. People like myself want to help those people in other countries who desperately need assistance, but we are faced with a situation in which a large percentage of aid given by the United States is gobbled up by greedy interests or political leaders in the recipient countries. Those people who run the affairs of small foreign countries constantly threaten, by implication at least, to make trouble for the United States if we don't come through and give them what they want.

¶ OF COURSE the big news of the week—the big sensation—was the resignation of Richard M. Nixon as President of the United States. Although I had constantly opposed resignation on the President's part, preferring the impeachment process if he were found guilty of the charges made against him, my position collapsed on Monday when it came out that the statements he had been making for the last two years were not true, and that he was aware of the Watergate break-in scandal soon after it occurred. It was then obvious to me that he had tried to protect the guilty parties. When he made this admission his support in the Congress rapidly dissolved, until by Thursday he had decided that it would be best for the country if he resigned.

Thursday night the President called about fifteen members from each House of Congress, including myself, down to the White House to state his position. The President told us that personally he would prefer to fight the charges made against him to the end, that he did not like to be a quitter, but in view of the many domestic and international situations that require full-time Presidential attention, he had decided that this country could not properly meet its problems with a part-time President. If he were required to spend some months in defending himself against impeachment charges, rather than devoting his time to the critical issues which lie before us, the effect could be very hard on our nation. No one could disagree with this line of reasoning, and so the situation has been well accepted by most of the members of Congress, so far as I can see.

It was an extremely sorry and emotional occasion with many tears being shed, including those of the President himself, who had difficulty in starting his story to us, and finally left the Cabinet Room in a highly emotional and tearful condition.

At nine o'clock that night the President went on the air to tell his story to the public. How he recovered his poise enough to speak on

TV a half-hour after meeting with us was a surprise to me, but he did go through with it and announced that he would cease to be the President at noon on Friday.

L.P.A. happened to be the only woman who was privileged to watch the President's TV address from within the White House. She had driven me down at about 7:30, and was sitting outside in the car when White House aides discovered she was there and brought her in to sit with members of Congress until after the President had spoken to the world.

Those people who are either overcome with hatred and desire for revenge, or who are antagonistic to our democratic form of government, have been sending telegrams urging fullest punishment for Richard Nixon, but I think that most of the members of Congress and most of the people living back home are relieved that this crisis in American history has been met; what they want now is for our government—all three branches—to perform honestly and successfully the responsibilities placed upon us by our own Constitution.

Friday noon, Jerry Ford took the oath of office as the thirty-eighth President of the United States. He will not have an easy time, but he will have a better understanding of the necessity for the executive and legislative branches to work together for the good of the country, and I think he will have very good co-operation from leaders of both the House and Senate in this regard.

The new President will address the Congress next Monday night, and I believe that what he has to say will be very well received.

Week ending August 17, 1974

CONGRESS IS GETTING NERVOUS. The change in the occupancy of the White House has brought about a change in the plans of the Democratic leadership. Business has speeded up. The Congress is showing a greater desire to co-operate with the new President. Conference reports are being hustled through for final action by both Houses, and the last of the regular appropriations will soon be before both Houses for action.

President Ford insists that expenditures and receipts of government be more nearly in balance, and the Congress will accept insistence from him that it would not from President Nixon. Jerry Ford has gotten off to a pretty good start. His address Monday evening before a joint session of Congress was well received, although members of the Senate and the House disagreed with some parts of it. His speech included some humorous references, in contrast with President Nixon's very earnest, very pointed, and usually very dry discussions. President Ford announced his intention to veto legislation which he felt was unsound and unwise, and has already declined to approve some legislation.

¶ SECRETARY OF THE TREASURY BILL SIMON, and Assistant Secretary of State Joe Sisco reported on the goings-on in the Mediterranean to the Foreign Relations committee. Turkey has taken part of Cyprus by force, and the Greeks are apparently irate with the United States for not having prevented this. Although there are more Greeks than Turks living in our country, and they are far better organized, I believe that the United States has followed a right course of non-intervention, at least in the military sense. The Greeks decided they couldn't defeat the Turks by themselves, and therefore yielded to military pressure. Between the Israeli-Arab situation and the Greek-Turk-Cypriot warfare, conditions in the eastern Mediterranean are naturally very tense, with each small country hoping, expecting—and even demanding—that the United States take its part in the difficulties with its neighbors.

¶ LAST NIGHT PRESIDENT FORD gave a dinner in honor of King Hussein and his wife and official family to which L.P.A. and I were invited. The change in atmosphere was almost miraculous, particularly among representatives of the news media whose assignments cover the White House. Some of them were invited to the dinner and many more to the dancing which followed.

If President Ford can keep a sense of humor and a willingness for co-operation, he stands an excellent chance of being Republican candidate for the Presidency in 1976. The most recent polls indicate that he would most likely be elected. However, he does not have an easy road to follow. He has to nominate a Vice President to fill the position he has recently vacated. He cannot meet the demands of all the small countries of the world; nor, without making enemies, can he lead in an effort to control the inflationary practices which are now sweeping the country and the world.

[*Putney, Vermont*]

Week ending August 24, 1974

ON TUESDAY PRESIDENT FORD sent to the Congress the nomination of Nelson Rockefeller for the Vice Presidency. Congress accepted this nomination with seemingly almost full approval. Although it may be some weeks or months before Governor Rockefeller is approved, the apparently full approval given his nomination by leading Democrats is somewhat disturbing to me. They seem to be altogether too happy that he was nominated, which indicates that he may be in for considerable trouble before he is approved. I suspect that he may have difficulties with members of Congress representing both the far right and the far left.

¶ THE SENATE went ahead with legislation approving appropriations bills for major government departments. The Interior department appropriation carries $1.5 million for purchase of land in Vermont by the National Forest system, and another $1.5 million for construction work on a salmon hatchery to be located on Vermont's White River, the largest tributary of the Connecticut River. The Federal Power Commission has assured me that it will not extend the licenses of the power companies having dams on the Connecticut River except on a temporary year-to-year basis until these companies construct fishways which will enable the salmon to reach the headwaters of the Connecticut River system. It is my understanding that construction has begun on these fishways—or ladders, as some call them—at Holyoke, and will begin next year at Turners Falls, both in Massachusetts. That will leave the dams at Vernon and at Bellows Falls, Vermont, with this work to be done before the salmon can go back to their spawning places in the White River at Bethel.

People in Vermont are very much interested in the prospects both for salmon-fishing by 1980 and for extension of the Green Mountain National Forest. What will happen remains to be seen, since Government is sometimes fickle, and a new Congress will be coming into the Capitol next January.

¶ WELL, these things happened before L.P.A. and I got home to Putney Friday morning. That afternoon and Saturday we found plenty of work to do in cleaning up around the house, chopping some sod out of the edge of the garden and eating the products of our own enterprise. L.P.A. purchased meat, bread and other exotic foodstuffs at a store in Putney, but on Sunday I figured out that what we had had to eat and drink—including blueberries, raspberries, second-crop peas, and so forth—and which had cost a total of $18, would have cost approximately $180.00 had we bought the same products and services at a Washington restaurant.

[*During the week ending August 31, 1974, the Aikens harvested vegetables and fruit from their garden, were honored guests at the Champlain Valley Fair, and the Senator arranged to give to the University of Vermont the material of public and historical interest from among his private papers accumulated over nearly thirty-four years in the United States Senate.*]

[*United States Senate*]

Week ending September 7, 1974

I HAVE LEARNED not to let the work of today be controlled by memories. The good old days are gone, but, except that we miss old friends, hardly anyone wants them back. People talk about depression, inflation, and all the things they don't like, forgetting that no generation ever enjoyed the standard of living the American people have today. Yet they keep reaching into the future and demanding more, just as they have been doing since the days of Adam and Eve.

¶ WASHINGTON seems to be in a different mood since ex-President Nixon left office and President Ford took over. How long this will last nobody knows, but certainly members of the news media seem delighted to think that the President will now welcome them cordially. Gerald Ford has been very active since being sworn into office, and I sincerely hope that he will be able to carry the burdens of his new job.

¶ ON WEDNESDAY the Senate accomplished very little except to pass a bill requiring that 20 percent of the oil imported into this country must be carried by American crewmen on American-made tankers. This precipitated a conflict between Senators from the Northeast, including all from New England except Hathaway [Maine, Democrat], those from states which look forward to the construction of more American tankers, and members from states where labor unions are strong. It was felt that the requirements for higher-cost importation of petroleum would certainly increase costs to consumers in New England and other Northeastern states. However, the labor interests and the shipbuilding centers carried the day, even though it was estimated that the costs of new shipbuilding facilities would reach at least $500 million. It is obvious that the end of inflation is not yet, but the debate on this shipping bill reminded me of the "good old days," since virtually everybody cast his vote in favor of his own area of the country and made no apologies for it.

¶ PRESIDENT FORD on Thursday called in leading economists from around the country to discuss means of handling the inflationary economic situation. No doubt many of these economists are well qualified to advise the President, but I have a feeling that some of them would have difficulty in producing food for their families if worst came to worst. Some twenty-five members of the Senate were not present at all during the week and it is quite obvious that President Ford is going to have a rough road ahead.

Some increase in unemployment and a heavy increase in prices prevail already, and I see no end to this situation without encountering more serious difficulties than we have seen to date. I certainly hope that the period which we are now going through does not end, as the Depression of the 1930's ended, in another world war. I don't think it will, because no major country would risk such a hazard today.

Week ending September 14, 1974

ONE OF THE MOST UNHAPPY WEEKS of the year, with the honeymoon between President Ford and the Congress and the public getting rather badly damaged.

After I had been given about an hour's notice on Sunday, President Ford announced a complete pardon for ex-President Nixon covering any sentence which Mr. Nixon might receive later on if found guilty of participating in the Watergate mess through illegal action. Since the ex-President had not been found guilty of any charges which had been made against him, I was naturally somewhat surprised, as were a lot of other people in Congress and throughout the country. There is no question but what the President had the Constitutional authority to grant such complete pardon, but whether such granting was premature or not is a matter for individual opinion.

When called by numerous members of the press asking my opinion, I stated that the President showed a good deal of courage in granting a full pardon, since he must have known full well that he would come under very vigorous attack for his action.

It was also reported that Special Prosecutor Jaworski, Archibald Cox's successor in prosecuting Watergate offenses, knew nothing about the President's plan to pardon Richard Nixon. This proved to be false, since it appeared that the Special Prosecutor was aware of what was going on at all times and may even have had a part in working out the plans. However, there is no question that if the ex-President is guilty of any of the charges made against him, he has already received a stiffer punishment than any of the participants in the Watergate break-in who have already served time or are serving time in prison.

An announcement by the Justice department on Monday indicated that all the evidence received would not warrant a grand jury even in making an indictment against the ex-President on the charges which had been made against him, except for one. There still remains, though, the charge that he undertook to cover up and protect some of those who have been found guilty in the Watergate affair or in the Ellsberg case [in which it was charged that medical-psychiatric records of Daniel Ellsberg, a critic of the Vietnam war and defendant in a pending federal court case, were the object of an illegal entry and search instigated by certain White House aides in July 1971].

President Ford has received comparatively little public support for issuing the pardon, and has been liberally condemned by those who evidently prefer torture to punishment. The pardon disturbed Senators Cranston, Byrd and Brooke, who introduced a Resolution to the effect that the President should not issue any more pardons unless the person charged had been tried and convicted. Since the Resolution was restricted only to those who had participated in the election campaign of 1972, it was such an obviously political slap at the President that I could not vote for it, and my judgment was shared by such outstanding liberals as Senators Hughes of Iowa and Case of New Jersey. The Republican leadership, Scott and Griffin, however, voted for the Resolution, much to my surprise.

A by-product of the approval of the Senate action on this Resolution lies in the fact that, since the Senate, in effect, is demanding separate trials for each of those charged with wrongdoing in the 1972 campaign, the President should also apply the same rule to granting amnesty to those who deserted the United States in time of war. I do not know what President Ford may have in mind relative to granting amnesty to deserters, but certainly the action of the Senate can only be interpreted as requiring that each deserter must be given individual attention before amnesty is granted.

¶ AMBASSADOR ZAHEDI of Iran puts on about the highest-level party in Washington, and the one Tuesday night in honor of L.P.A. and myself was no exception. A lot of important people, including Mel Laird, Bill Rogers and Arthur Burns attended. It was an enjoyable evening and the Ambassador presented me with a trowel with which to work in the garden after my retirement from the Senate. It looked like a pretty good trowel, and then I discovered it was made by Tiffany's. I did not know that Tiffany's made garden tools, but apparently they will make anything out of solid silver.

¶ NEXT WEEK the Senate resumes legislating with the Labor-HEW [Department of Health, Education, and Welfare] Appropriation bill the major subject. Believe me, there will be a lot of arguments, for many a member will try to see how much he can gain for his state, and everybody will have great sympathy for the lame, the halt, the blind, and the poor. And while urging an increase in appropriations, each will also be demanding a balanced budget for the executive branch of government.

The Senate will also vote again on Thursday on whether to invoke cloture on S. 707, the Consumer Protection Agency bill. Three previous efforts at invoking cloture have been defeated. The bill already has a substantial majority of the Senators in support, but lacks the two-thirds necessary to invoke cloture. We already have at least ten agencies of government which are supposed to protect consumer interests but I have to agree with the sponsors of S. 707 that none of them has completely met its responsibility. Now they want another agency of government to do what the ten federal agencies and innumerable state agencies have failed to do.

Senators Javits and Ribicoff and Congressman Holifield, chairman of the committee in the House which handled the bill, have been urging co-operation on my part and agreeing to amend the proposed legislation in most any way which will make it acceptable to me. They have an idea that I could change enough votes so that cloture would be invoked. I think their idea is exaggerated, but I will look at this legislation to see what can be done to meet my previous objections.

There is no question but that consumers are getting soaked today, and that the spread between the farm producers of food and the consumers has widened to an unwarranted degree. The Administration is opposed to the bill but so far has not raised a hand to help me in any way.

Week ending September 21, 1974

MONDAY MORNING President Ford announced the terms of conditional amnesty for draft evaders and deserters, again demonstrating courage to make decisions. At a press conference in the evening he handled himself very well answering questions thrown at him by members of the news media.

The subject at the press conference then turned to the charge, made by the staff of the Senate Subcommittee on Multinational Corporations, that Secretary of State Kissinger and the CIA connived to upset the Allende government of Chile, and used money for this purpose. President Ford told the press that the United States is indeed concerned in maintaining foreign governments which are favorable to and friendly with the United States. He pointed out that the communist organization uses the same practices in other countries for the purpose of electing public officials who will be favorable to the communist cause. The CIA is supposed to be an agency which gathers confidential and secret information in other parts of the world, but apparently we have in this country those who believe that every act and every finding of the CIA should be made public.

The report of this subcommittee—whose chairman is Senator Church —and its recommendations had been leaked to *The New York Times* and the Washington *Post,* and consequently was getting spread all over the country. The recommendations, if agreed to and carried out, would have created another Watergate situation. They included re-opening hearings in public session to question Secretary Kissinger and also re-opening the hearings on the Chilean election and the part which the United States might have played in attempting to influence that election. The third point recommended was that perjury proceedings be brought against Charles Meyer and Dick Helms, head of the CIA at the time. A fourth recommendation was for contempt proceedings against Ambassador Korry, who represented us in Chile for a while. A fifth recommendation would bring contempt proceedings against John Hennessy, Assistant Secretary of the Treasury. The report wound up with recommending that contempt proceedings be brought against Charles Meyer, Korry and Helms.

All in all, the actions recommended could cause worldwide harm to the United States and its government. I hope that was not the purpose. But certainly Senator Church is going pretty far out in his bid for re-election to the Senate.

The Foreign Relations committee took no definite action on the subcommittee report other than to ask other committees of the Congress for any evidence they might have to sustain the charges against our own government. I am satisfied that there is an organization in this country dedicated to the overthrow of our own government, and that it may be sustained by the governments of other countries. This situation has existed ever since I can remember.

Although all information being leaked to the news media indicates that our undertaking to influence the Chilean election began only two or three years ago, according to Secretary Kissinger it actually was started under the administration of President Kennedy and continued on through the administration of President Johnson. Personally, I think the leak is just another effort on the part of the Democrats to make President Nixon's administration look fully responsible for the effort to influence the Chilean election. Undoubtedly the Republican leadership will, as usual, let the Democrats get away with this political propaganda. When it comes to monkey business and sharp political tactics, I still say the Republicans are rank amateurs.

¶ ALSO ON TUESDAY the Foreign Relations committee rejected, by a 9-to-7 vote, a proposal that the United States claim jurisdiction over the sea for two hundred miles offshore. Our action was only advisory, however, since the bill had already been reported favorably by the Senate Commerce committee. The plea for favorable action on the bill was supposedly in the interest of our fishermen, but there is a very strong feeling that the oil companies were back of it. Nothing would surprise me: with the election only a few weeks away, the desires for campaign supporters have become pretty potent.

¶ THURSDAY we had further demonstrations of political maneuvering. First, we had a vote on invoking cloture for consideration of the Senate's so-called Consumer Protection bill. The measure is an effort on the part of the Democratic majority in Congress, aided by a few Republicans, to post itself as the champion for all American consumers—some 200 million of them, a very great number of whom are eligible to vote at election time. Although the sponsors had a majority in the Senate, they were blocked from coming to a vote by Senators Allen, Taft, and others who felt that the promoters of the bill were mainly looking for power and prestige; by using all the time in debate, these opponents kept the Senate from coming to a vote.

For many years I have refused to vote for cloture until discussion and debate on an important measure has been carried on for at least two weeks. However, the debate on the Consumer Protection bill had gone on for well over two weeks, so on the fourth time around I finally voted for cloture even though I was still skeptical as to the value of the bill. Senators Ribicoff and Javits had agreed to accept certain amendments which I would propose that would make it more palatable. Nevertheless the votes they could raise for the bill were not enough to offset the votes against it. Two members who did not vote on the measure were Senator Kennedy and Senator Fulbright, although both could have voted had they so desired. I think Senator Fulbright simply didn't want to take a position on the bill; and undoubtedly Senator Kennedy had his reasons for arriving at the Senate Chamber just as the vote was being announced.

¶ THE MAIN PIECE OF LEGISLATION considered on Thursday was a bill to continue the Export-Import Bank operations. This bill got involved in politics to the extent that peace in the world could be rudely shattered unless the amendments approved by the Senate are thrown out when it comes to Conference with the House. One of these amendments in effect would end economic assistance or the sale of military supplies to Turkey until issues between Turkey and Greece in Cyprus are settled to the satisfaction of the Greeks. This sentiment is very easy to interpret, since the Greek-Americans are exceptionally good political allies at election time—at least I have found them so. I could not vote for this amendment because only a few days ago at the White House, Secretary Kissinger had told some of us in confidence that he felt an agreement between Greece and Turkey on the Cyprus situation was near at hand. A slap at the Turks by Congress could not fail to disrupt the progress that is being made toward the restoration of peace, or at least a better understanding, over the Cyprus matter. Because the information which he had given us was called confidential, no one could explain to the members of the Senate just how much was involved in the proposed amendment.

¶ ON TUESDAY a big party for the Aikens and the Sam Ervins was given at the Washington Club by Dale and Scooter Miller. Because of working late in the Senate, the Aikens and Ervins arrived a half-hour late, and when we got there we found the place crowded. Instead of the twenty-five or thirty guests I thought would attend there were over two hundred, including fifteen ambassadors, Cabinet members, socialites, and others. We had a good time, although the Aikens might as well get used to going without such high-level treatment after the first of the year.

Week ending September 28, 1974

THE WEEK WAS ROUTINE until Wednesday night, when L.P.A. and I attended a dinner given in our honor at the Canadian Embassy by Ambassador Marcel Cadieux and his wife, Anita. Marcel was a member of the International Control Commission in North Vietnam after the French were ousted from that country; the other two member nations were Poland and India, whose representatives did exactly what Russia told them to do, so the commission wasn't very effective. There was so much persecution and actual killing of the Catholic population at that time that the United States finally sent ships to move close to one million persons to South Vietnam. Of course when they got there we felt responsible for their welfare, and that responsibility led to our involvement in the Vietnam war, which lasted for ten years. Just another example of the saying that "the road to Hell is paved with good intentions."

¶ THURSDAY MORNING I was one of the five members of the Senate and four of the House invited to the White House for breakfast with President Ford and Secretary of State Kissinger, where the Cyprus matter was discussed for nearly two hours. The leadership of the Greek-Americans in the United States seems to feel that our government should be responsible for effecting a settlement of the situation favorable to Greece. That isn't the easiest thing in the world to do, because we have furnished both Turkey and Greece with a lot of military equipment. Should we do what some are asking us to do and block further aid to Turkey until that country agrees to a settlement favorable to Greece, there is a strong belief that Turkey would withdraw from NATO and possibly give its powerful support to Syria, a move which could spell disaster for Israel. The people of Greece and the Greeks in this country apparently are not fully informed as to the situation, but are told only that if the United States puts enough pressure on Turkey a decision favorable to Greece will be the result. The new Premier of Greece, Karamanlis, seems to have the faculty of saying one thing publicly and something quite different to the United States officials— that is, according to Secretary Kissinger.

We were told at the White House that there would be a new election in Greece early in November, but by all means keep that secret! I kept it secret until on Friday I received copies of small Vermont newspapers and found that they had the news two days before we got it at the White House. That's the way it goes. The maneuvering which is really being carried on to bring about a peaceful settlement between Greece and Turkey and the Cypriots must not be divulged to the public, so our Greek friends and political supporters here in the United States are led to believe that the United States is culpable in not using its influence to bring about a better arrangement in Cyprus.

¶ A NEW TRADE BILL has been held up for almost two years because Senator Jackson, whose heart is set on being President of the United States, has so far insisted on attaching to it an amendment which would mortally offend Russia. Russia seems anxious to comply with his demands that Jewish people be given full freedom to leave the country, but cannot get down on its knees before us and beg for mercy. Scoop never got over the fact that we left Indochina without winning a military victory over the North Vietnamese, nor can he forget that he was virtually ignored at the Miami Democratic Convention in 1972.

¶ AFTER LEAVING THE WHITE HOUSE, I got back to the Hill late for a Foreign Relations committee meeting but went to a lunch given by the committee for President Leone of Italy. Next was a session of the Joint Committee on Atomic Energy, which was interrupted by a call for a vote on a wine tax amendment to the Daylight Saving Time bill. A "way-out" political amendment which had no relationship to the bill under consideration.

Late in the afternoon Senator Curtis handed me Richard Nixon's telephone number in the San Clemente, California, hospital where he has been confined for a blood clot in the leg the last few days. He said he was told that a call from me to the former President might cheer him up. I called the hospital about five o'clock, which was two o'clock Pacific time, and was told that Mr. Nixon was asleep at the time; they would give him the message. Friday he called back. I told him that I simply wanted him to know that we were thinking of him, and after two or three minutes' discussion, we hung up. He didn't sound very good to me, and I got the feeling that he might be more seriously ill than the reports we are getting indicate. That doesn't deter some people who simply want to persecute him to death. Again I say he made plenty of mistakes, but he also did a lot of good in restoring peace to the world and a better understanding among the nations, for which his political enemies give him no credit at all.

¶ FRIDAY NIGHT the staff of the Foreign Relations committee gave a two-hour reception for Chairman Fulbright and me and presented us with placards signed by all the members of the committee. There was a big crowd, including present and past officials of the government,

Secretary of State Kissinger, and many members of the Senate.

Senators Javits and Pell were not with us because they were on their way to Cuba to visit Premier Castro tomorrow. They were also accompanied by twenty-five or thirty newsgatherers, and will undoubtedly receive a lot of coverage in the press. Senator Javits apparently is taking no chances on his re-election this fall. In accordance with our committee rules, I approved their trip to Cuba, but only on condition that our State department would also approve it. The news this Saturday morning tells us that State department disapproved their trip. I don't believe the news story, because Secretary Kissinger would not disappoint Senator Javits at any price.

Week ending October 5, 1974

IN WASHINGTON, the first part of this week was devoted to work on the Agriculture and the Foreign Relations committees. Agriculture has always been the more satisfactory committee—better handled and far more sensible in its decisions.

After a hearing, I introduced on Wednesday a Resolution calling on the Department of Agriculture to base its price support of milk—a minimum of 80 percent of parity—on the estimated parity as of October 1st, instead of the April 1st date that could not reflect the sharply increased costs of feed and production during the past six months. The Resolution was endorsed unanimously by the committee, and I reported it to the Senate Wednesday night.

When we see dividend payments of big corporations increasing, it is aggravating to see the net income of food producers take a sharp reduction.

¶ ON THE SENATE FLOOR, the business was consideration of a Continuing Resolution for the foreign aid program. Some Senators went hog-wild, particularly those who are facing re-election contests. An amendment by Senator Eagleton requiring a cut-off of all aid to Turkey was approved, and, if it is retained by the conferees, could conceivably lead to the occupation of all of Cyprus by the Turks and the downfall of the present Greek government. The Greek government itself was privately opposed to the adoption of the Eagleton amendment, fearing that more trouble with Turkey at this time would result in the overthrow of Karamanlis and his government at the election to be held in early November. Nevertheless, the attitude of the Karamanlis government, which is of middle-ground politics, was not made public and, consequently, loyal Greek political supporters in this country urged the adoption of the Eagleton amendment. It is expected that the House and Senate conferees will be informed of the situation, and will handle it discreetly.

Tuesday afternoon the Greek Foreign Minister, Mavros, met with a few of us and confirmed my belief that the action of the Senate was ill-advised.

The Foreign Aid Authorization bill was loaded with so many harmful amendments that the Senate finally recommitted it to the committee by a narrow margin. It will undoubtedly remain dormant for the rest of this Session of Congress, and it ought to. The amendments of Senator Eagleton and others clearly carried the seeds of war, which, if they should germinate, could spell disaster for Greece, Israel, and perhaps much of the whole world. Turkey now has several times the military equipment of Greece, particularly in nuclear weapons, but all this seems to make no impression on those who apparently feel that the most important thing in the world today is to secure their own re-election regardless of what happens in the international field.

¶ THURSDAY EVENING we attended a dinner at the White House which President Ford was giving for retiring members of the House and Senate. The event was cheerfully informal, as it should have been: no receiving line, with the President coming into the group almost unnoticed and visiting in a quite informal manner. At present there are fifty-two members of the House and Senate who will not return to Congress. When I was asked to make some remarks I told the President he was very lucky to have the dinner on the 3rd of October rather than after the 5th of November because there might be twice the number of retiring members by that time.

We left at daylight Friday for Putney. When the Senate met during the day, they passed my dairy-price-support Resolution without debate. Evidently the best way to get approval of a measure in the Senate is to introduce it and then leave town.

Week ending October 12, 1974

I MISSED about twenty-five roll-call votes during the first part of the week, when I was in Vermont. Many of the votes were on amendments to what they called the Clean Election bill. This finally cleared both

Houses, and has been sent to the President for his signature. As I have said, this bill won't make many candidates for office more honest, but it may make them be more subtle. Fortunately the House adamantly refused to include members of Congress in the category of those eligible for government handouts for campaign expenses. How ridiculous it would be to enact legislation that would literally reward people to be candidates against sitting members of the Congress who have the general support of their constituents! The bill finally wound up providing $20 million contributions to the Presidential nominee of each leading party.

¶ WEDNESDAY MORNING the Senate had approved legislation carrying the Eagleton amendment, which would have prohibited any arms supplied for Turkey until that country had, in effect, surrendered to the desire of the Greeks over the Cyprus issue. But late in the afternoon Senator Mansfield put before the Senate a Resolution postponing this crackdown on Turkey until December 15th. The Mansfield proposal was approved by the Senate because so many Senators felt that the Eagleton amendment, supported by Scoop Jackson and other advocates of military supremacy in the world, would be so damaging that they changed their opinions and voted to support Mansfield. Eagleton admitted that he had had no consultation with the Greek government in any way, as some of the rest of us had. It was fortunate that the Mansfield proposal carried. Otherwise, I feel it would have been inevitable that the middle-of-the-road Greek government would have been toppled and the seeds of war sown generally throughout the eastern Mediterranean.

¶ ON FRIDAY legislative procedure and politics got worse. The House by a small margin refused the Mansfield Resolution, which would have given until December 15th to work out a settlement of the Cyprus dispute between Greece and Turkey. The Continuing Resolution carrying the Eagleton amendment was approved, and the bill authorizing money for foreign aid was sent to the President for his signature. President Ford sent word that he would veto the bill, and that meant that Congressional adjournment on Friday was out. The Congress will go back into session next Tuesday. If the veto is sustained, it will mean that a new bill will have to be proposed, and if it is overridden, I predict a serious crisis in the Mediterranean.

With Senators like Eagleton and Jackson leading what I feel could develop into a United States war party, I am at present apprehensive as to whether or not the world can avoid a widespread conflict within the next few years. I do not believe that either Jackson or Eagleton wants another war—but the manufacturers of war matériel have a powerful political influence, and the threat of war makes their business good.

Week ending October 19, 1974

THE SENATE THIS WEEK was primarily concerned with the Eagleton amendment, which was aimed against Turkey. The pro-Greek, anti-Turk element of the Senate finally won the day, and another bill was passed, still carrying an amendment which would have had the same effect as Eagleton's. The vote came on Wednesday. Thursday morning the President again vetoed this legislation because of the amendment.

On Thursday, the House sustained the veto by two votes, so the Senate did not have to pass on this matter again. The leadership of the two Houses finally succeeded in writing a compromise which would prohibit Turkey from transmitting to Cyprus any war matériel received from the U.S.A., and providing that if there is no progress toward the settlement of Cyprus by the 10th of December, then all military aid to Turkey should be suspended.

[Putney, Vermont]

Week ending October 26, 1974

SUNDAY THROUGH TUESDAY around the edges of reading and signing the mail and getting calls from the office, L.P.A. worked at arranging furniture and so forth sent up from Washington, and I went down to the orchard and picked a couple of bushels of apples. Cold weather had frozen some of them, but the Rhode Island Greenings—still the best pie apple in the world—hadn't frozen at all; the Delicious were small and nubby this year, but L.P.A. likes them, so I got about a bushel for her.

Around noon on Wednesday a girl in the NBC office in New York called with the crazy idea of finding out how all the members of the Senate would vote on about a dozen different issues after the Congress re-convenes in November. She wanted to know how I would vote on Social Security, abortion, taxes, and everything else. I simply kidded her along, for no member of the Senate knows how he is going to vote on legislation until he sees it in final form. He may be sure he intends to vote for the objective of the original bill, but when a bill gets amended in the Congress so that it has only slight resemblance to the original and, perhaps, may mean almost the direct opposite, then of course he can't vote for it unless he is a born hypocrite.

But this gal said, "What is the most important matter before our government today in the Congress?" Without hesitation I told her it is to keep out of another world war. Then she said, "What's next, or second most important?" I said to get a leveling-off between wages, prices and incomes so that more people will be treated fairly.

Of course we have been trying to do that for generations, and there never was yet a fair relationship between prices and wages for all people.

¶ IT SEEMS GOOD to get away from Washington and world affairs to the extent that we did, but it is hard to get away from the telephone and the news media. Secretary Kissinger is on the move. He is also coming under attack more and more by those people who succeeded in getting President Nixon out of office and into the hospital and who now seem to be devoting their attention to the next victim—which could be President Ford, or Secretary Kissinger, or both.

[*During the week ending November 2, 1974, the Aikens worked to prepare their home in Putney for the Senator's retirement in January and attended Farm Bureau and Chamber of Commerce dinners, where he was guest of honor. In the diary entry for the week ending November 9, Senator Aiken deplored the light voting nation-wide in the November 5th elections, attributing voter apathy to the difficulty in getting "really qualified people to run for office" at all levels, and declared: "Ever since I have been in politics, I have observed that Democrats are professional politicians tearing into each other and eliminating each other from the running for higher office—until election time, when they unite as a party. The Republicans, on the other hand, are rank amateurs, led largely by successful businessmen who know more about business than they do about politics, and who will not go out with wild-eyed promises as so many Democrats do. They will set an objective and say, 'That is what we want—we will have this at any price,' with the result that they don't achieve their objective and lose elections unnecessarily. I have always felt that if one has a worthy objective and can't possibly achieve it at 100 percent, he'd better take what he can get for the time being and try again next time."*]

[*United States Senate*]

Week ending November 16, 1974

NOT THE HAPPIEST WEEK OF THE YEAR. The International Food Conference is going on in Rome and Senators McGovern, Humphrey, and Dick Clark are all over there giving the world the impression that the United States isn't doing nearly enough to feed the hungry people of other countries. As a matter of fact, the United States has done more to eliminate famine, hunger, and disease in other countries than all the rest of the world put together. Possibly my ultra-ambitious colleagues are simply willing to put the U.S.A. in a bad light so they can tell the grain-growers of their respective states that "we tried hard to get you a higher price for your corn and soybeans." And possibly they are posing as self-anointed champions of the poor.

The American farmer is being played up as a greedy miscreant altogether too much, both at home and abroad. Sometimes his critics even say that the people on welfare are being gouged by farm prices. Actually, though, over 50 percent of the appropriations for the Department of Agriculture are now made for the benefit of the low-income consumer. The appropriation for food stamps alone has increased over 1100 percent in the last four years, until it now has reached $3.9 billion a year. There is no need for people going hungry in this country today if they are willing to take advantage of prevailing federal programs. Of course, there is a lot of abuse of these programs. Even in my own town in Vermont I find that food stamps are being used for the purchase of such food commodities as the beneficiary may choose for his diet, while he spends cash for high-priced wines and similar delicacies.

On the domestic scene we are confronted with an increase in consumer prices every month, but again I must point out that the prices of cattle, hogs, butter and other farm produce have dropped materially from what they were a year ago. However, speculators have been having a field day with the price of sugar, which has increased 500 percent within a year.

¶ MR. ANDREW GIBSON has asked President Ford to withdraw his nomination to succeed John Sawhill as administrator of the Federal Energy Administration. He actually never stood a prayer of being confirmed, since the Senate would not approve him for this office while he admittedly would be receiving $80,000 a year from the oil company for which he works, and which would come under his jurisdiction as a government official. The report is, though, that the President was unaware of Gibson's connection with the oil interests, and that the nomination was handled by a subordinate who succeeded in getting the usual FBI investigation bypassed.

¶ THE SENATE RULES COMMITTEE has had Nelson Rockefeller back for further inquisition relative to his fitness to be approved as Vice President. I never was a particular admirer of Rockefeller when he was governor of New York, but I will say now that he has made Senator Cannon's committee look rather inept and so politically biased that some of the members seem unable to recognize how necessary it is to fill the office of the Vice President of the United States, which has been vacant for three months. As has been pointed out by a prominent columnist, none of the members of this committee would be willing to answer the questions which they put to Rockefeller if these questions were directed at themselves. After the new Congress convenes on January 3, we will find out how many of the new members of the Congress are willing to put the need of the country ahead of their own desires for personal publicity.

Week ending November 23, 1974

THERE ARE STILL authorization and appropriation bills which ought to be enacted before the Congress adjourns sine die. I have an idea now that the Majority Party will put much legislation over until the next Congress, when it will have a considerably larger majority, especially in the House.

¶ DURING THE LATTER PART OF THE WEEK the Senate concerned itself with proposed legislation with which many of us were not very familiar. Much of the discussion on Friday was devoted to a bill relating to criminal proceedings that was considerably out of my line of work. The bill as reported from the Judiciary committee provided that when a person was charged with a crime his past connection with certain felonies could be reviewed and used in trying to determine his veracity or the veracity of witnesses. Senator John McClellan proposed that past history of the accused as related to any and all felonies might also be used, and his amendment finally prevailed. Although I voted against it, I am still not sure but what he might have been right.

This was one occasion where I had to rely upon the advice of some of my colleagues who are versed in the law. Our constituency at home would probably be amazed to learn how little we members of the Senate know about the fine points of some highly specialized legislation which we pass upon. It has always been like this. And so we simply have to depend on the expertise of someone well versed in the proposals that come before us.

As the Session of the 93rd Congress nears its close, more unwise legislation will be approved by Congress, since bills which we have not known about or have had little time to study will be brought up on short notice and sometimes no notice at all.

¶ DURING THE WEEK Attorney General William Saxbe announced that the Justice department is going after the American Telephone and Telegraph Company with full force, charging violation of the antitrust laws. Here is a case which will undoubtedly not be concluded for possibly several years to come, for AT&T is a pretty powerful organization, and apparently controls not only the telephone system, but also the manufacture of instruments to make the system work.

¶ ON SUNDAY MORNING President Ford took off to visit the top officials of Japan, Korea, and Russia. He will meet with Mr. Brezhnev in Vladivostok and then return to the United States. There is quite a lot of criticism because of his absenting himself from the country at this time, but his commitment to make the trip was made some time ago, and failure to meet a commitment with a foreign top official would also be subject to criticism.

During his absence two of his vetoes were overridden by both the House and Senate, and the vetoed bills will become law in spite of the objection of the executive branch. If the White House had made clear its position on these measures—one, the Freedom of Information Act, and the other, the Vocational Rehabilitation Act—well before they had been passed by both Houses and sent to the President, it might not have made any difference; but it would have created a better feeling had there been a closer understanding between President Ford and his assistants, and the leadership of the Congress.

¶ CONGRESS is still working to get back all the excess authority which has been given to the executive branch over the last forty years. I am virtually certain that if the Congress has its way it will not only recover all of the powers which have been so recklessly handed over to the Executive, but will also insist on authority which never belonged to it in the first place. The changes in our government likely to take place over the next few years are hardly predictable at this time, but I am certain that they will be far-reaching.

¶ WE STILL HAVE FORTY DAYS TO GO before my contract to represent the people of Vermont in the Senate is ended. It will be some change to get back to Vermont after the many social events being given in our honor, but right now I can't say that I am depressed by the prospect. Meanwhile I shall continue to do the work here as well as I can until January 2nd.

Week ending November 30, 1974

A LOT OF BUSINESS came up this week. President Ford got back from his trip to Japan and Russia Sunday night, and seemed to think that his principal accomplishment was an oral agreement reached with Mr. Brezhnev and the Soviet government to limit the construction of nuclear weapons.

It is a certainty that any proposal to limit the manufacture of war planes, nuclear missiles, or other matériel will meet with much opposition, even in the United States Congress. The large manufacturers of war planes will certainly downgrade the efforts of the peacemakers. Of course they don't really want war, but they don't have to have a real war in order to provide employment and profits. They call it "insuring national security," and an adequate supply of military equipment is indeed necessary for this purpose. However, an over-extended build-up of war matériel by competing nations can lead to a genuine war, one resulting in the loss of several hundred million lives and destruction of unbelievable proportions.

In spite of the efforts of Russia and the U.S.A., the danger is still very great, because a re-opening of armed conflict between smaller countries of the Middle East could lead to a genuine holocaust. Yet there are days when there seems to be progress towards a more peaceful understanding in this area, and we are hoping that peaceful arrangements can be made, not only as regards Cyprus, but also affecting the issues which exist between Israel and the Arab states. The United Nations, which seems to have lost nearly all its influence as a peacemaking body, has given overwhelming support to the Palestinian claim to a land which is also claimed by Israel under the agreement established by the United Nations itself over twenty-five years ago.

¶ TUESDAY MORNING, President Ford called the leadership of House and Senate to the White House. The report on his Asian trip was very well received and created considerable optimism among the twenty-two members of the House and Senate who were present. But after giving his Asian report, the President took up the matter of bringing the budget into line. He stated bluntly that he planned to veto the Veterans' Education bill, which would cost several hundred million dollars more than he felt advisable. He also called for reductions in expenditures for welfare, agriculture, military appropriations, and other programs for which he felt that the Congress is being too generous. I don't know who advises him to veto these bills, but all these vetoes mean an increase in the degree of unemployment in our country. It is a safe bet that the Congress will override most, if not all, of his vetoes.

We were advised at the White House that the interest alone on our national debt will amount to $33 billion this year. This reminded me of the time when the Democrat Party under President Roosevelt soundly condemned President Hoover for letting our national debt reach $22 billion. We are a country involved up to our ears in debt, all the way from town and state up to federal government. I don't know what the answer is going to be.

¶ THE NEWLY ELECTED MEMBERS of the Congress, both House and Senate, began to arrive during the week. Some of them seem to have pretty high ambitions. Others may turn out to be capable and conscientious members who are willing to deal with realities.

One of the twenty or more aspirants for the Democratic nomination for President in 1976, Senator Walter Mondale, announced that he was withdrawing from the field. Actually he was perhaps the best qualified of the lot, having a better understanding of human nature and human problems.

It has been announced that Congress will adjourn sine die not later than December 20 or 21 and that the opening of the next Congress will be postponed from January 3 to January 14. The 93rd Congress still has a lot of work to do and only three weeks to do it in. I hope we make good.

Week ending December 7, 1974

A RATHER UNSETTLING WEEK, although under the able leadership of Senator Humphrey the Foreign Aid bill passed the Senate by a vote of 46 to 45. It still has to go to Conference with the House and be signed by the President before this program can be extended.

¶ FRESHMAN DEMOCRATS in the House, apparently feeling their oats, have decided to take over and run things their way. Of course they have an exceptionally large freshman class, and, like other newcomers, seem to feel that seniority is wrong. Sometimes they are right, but when they have been re-elected a few times they will find the seniority system is fine. Personally, I have never found experience to be a handicap in my work.

¶ THE PRESIDENT'S VETO of the Veterans' Education bill was overridden almost unanimously by both Houses. This was not unexpected. The President keeps urging a balanced budget for this fiscal year, knowing full well that he is not going to get one. But by vetoing Congressional appropriations which he claims to be excessive, he can, and undoubtedly will, put the blame on the Congress for our national financial difficulties.

¶ TWO IMPORTANT FOREIGN VISITORS this week. Prime Minister Pierre Trudeau, who has been returned to leadership in Canada, was in town Wednesday and Thursday. Certain American oil refineries, particularly in Minnesota, have been protesting loudly at the announcement that oil exports from the Dominion to the United States will be lessened each year and finally terminated by 1982. The Province of Alberta, which produces much of the Canadian oil that is exported to the United States, doesn't like the proposal either. However, the Canadian government is under pressure, probably from the majority of Canadian people, not to take any chances on selling Canada short.

At a meeting which ten of us had with Prime Minister Trudeau on Thursday morning, I summed up the situation by saying that the trouble with Canadians lies in the fact that they act just like us: when they have something to sell, they like to get the highest price for it; when they have to buy, they want to buy as cheaply as they can.

The other foreign visitor was Chancellor Schmidt of West Germany. He was over here to meet with President Ford, but on Thursday afternoon also came to the Capitol to meet with about a dozen members of the Senate. He seems to be pretty capable and down to earth. West Germany today is probably the force which maintains a semblance of equilibrium in Western Europe. The other countries, particularly Spain, France and Italy, are so uncertain that no one can tell today what will happen tomorrow.

¶ ON THURSDAY, the waitresses of the Capitol Senate restaurant gave a luncheon for seven of us who are retiring from the Senate this year. They really made an occasion of it, the only unfortunate part being that they had it at the same hour that Chancellor Schmidt was meeting with some of us in the Foreign Relations committee room. Fortunately, the two rooms were so near together that I was able to divide my time between them.

¶ SENATOR MANSFIELD and party left for Mainland China on Friday morning. I think he is pretty well fed up with what is going on in the Congress and within his own party, and I understand just how he feels.

No session of the Senate on Friday. Some of the Democrats are heading for Kansas City, where a big mid-term convention is being held. They talk about achieving unity within the party and devising a program which will cut expenses, balance the budget, and make this a sane and sound nation. This reminds me of the 1932 Democrat platform, which was pure hogwash.

Week ending December 14, 1974

WITH THE RATE OF UNEMPLOYMENT increasing, the Senate devoted special attention to the Export-Import Bank and the Foreign Trade bill. The Export-Import Bank arranges for loans and insured credit to our industries and also our agricultural producers. The trade bill undertakes to improve trade relations with the rest of the world.

The labor organizations, under the leadership of George Meany, are very much opposed to imports from other countries which compete with American production. If it were not for imports, though, we would not be able to sell abroad the tremendous amounts of farm products and industrial production, which now add up to nearly $100 billion a year. Efforts were made to filibuster the trade bill, and labor organizations around the country were told to advise their members of Congress to block its passage.

For almost the first time in my life, I signed a cloture petition, this time for the purpose of bringing the trade bill to a vote in the Senate, and on Friday cloture was approved by a lopsided vote of 71 to 19. Mr. Meany had gone too far, and the union leadership took the worst defeat it has sustained in years. The trade bill—which had been held up for over a year by Senator Jackson and the amendment he proposed which would have had the effect of blocking trade with Russia— passed the Senate within hours after cloture had been invoked. Senator Jackson's amendment, which I felt contained the seeds of ultimate war, was modified to the extent that hardly anyone had any further objection to it. Even the Russians seemed to consider it harmless from their viewpoint.

Some of the forces in the U.S.A. would like to isolate this nation. It is becoming more and more apparent that they cannot do this. Trade has indeed become international, and industry favors the areas of low-cost production, particularly those where labor is cheap. There was a time when the textile industry moved from New England to the Southern states and then to the Southwest, for the simple reason that labor costs in those regions were comparatively low. That situation has changed, and the textile, shoe, and other industries are producing heavily in foreign countries where working people receive very small pay compared with our own. However, if the trend continues we will find costs of production increasing in those areas too, until there is a more equitable distribution of incomes throughout the world. The decisive cloture vote on the trade bill indicates that the people of this country and the Congress realize that the world is getting smaller and that operations on an international scale are inevitable.

¶ On Wednesday morning I spoke to the Senate about government salaries, with the recommendation that the highest-paid officials volunteer to accept small cuts in their salaries. Otherwise they cannot expect the low income people of the nation to give full co-operation in an effort to get government expenditures in balance with receipts again. I think it very unfortunate that members of Congress, now being paid $42,500 a year and having an extremely liberal expense allowance, are asking for higher salaries. I would like to see the most highly paid officials, from President Ford, who receives $200,000 a year, down to the Cabinet members and the judiciary branch of government, set an example. I don't expect that their effort would produce a balanced budget, but it would result in greater co-operation from many people who understandably say, "If these big shots at the top won't do their part, how can they expect us to carry the load?" Some folks agreed with what I said and some didn't

Week ending December 21, 1974

A tremendous week, which may have made a major contribution to history. As in the last week of any session, members of Congress wanted to get through legislation that would be pleasing and helpful to their friends and constituents. I was no exception, and finally succeeded, with the help of Senator Floyd Haskell of Colorado, in getting the Eastern Wild Areas bill through the Senate.

The Senate finally approved the Foreign Trade bill, which had been hung up for nearly two years, and although the final version carried some rather uncomplimentary gestures towards the Soviet Union, I do not feel that the result will be very damaging. The bill as a whole should be helpful to the interchange of commerce between the United States and the rest of the world.

¶ ON THURSDAY EVENING Nelson Rockefeller was approved by the House as the next Vice President of the United States, and later in the evening he was sworn in to office. He thereby becomes the presiding officer over the Senate. I have not seen him since he took the oath of office Thursday night, but I will say that his appearance before the investigating committees of the House and Senate pointed him up in my estimation, and in the minds of the American public.

Early Friday evening the Senate adjourned sine die. When the 94th Congress convenes on January 14th there will be eleven new members of the Senate and some ninety-two new members of the House. A lot of folks seem to think that they will be pretty wild-eyed and radical and insist upon removing the senior members of the Congress from important positions. I have seen this happen so many times that I am not particularly worried.

¶ I AM VERY GLAD to be winding up my own Senatorial career with the successful completion of nearly every project with which I have been substantially involved. There have been a lot of eulogies for departing members of the Senate spoken on the floor. Perhaps I should not call them eulogies, for I hope that leaving the Senate will not mean the end of my career. About seventy members of the Senate took the time to speak of the work I have done and the position which L.P.A. and I hold with the people of Washington, particularly those with whom we have worked.

Going back to Vermont will not be as difficult as they seem to think it ought to be.

Week ending December 28, 1974

A LOT OF ASTONISHING EVENTS have occurred during the past three years, the effect of which will be felt around the world for generations.

After maintaining American troops and other military forces in Vietnam for ten years an agreement was finally reached by the parties concerned to end the war there. The more militant element of our public felt that we should have continued to fight until a military victory was achieved and North Vietnam should be on her knees asking for mercy. Others soundly condemned President Nixon because it had taken four years to terminate our involvement. I know that President Nixon had hoped to get our troops out of South Vietnam in two years. The job should have been done several years before while President Johnson was in the White House.

The growing sensitiveness between the People's Republic of China and Russia had undoubtedly convinced both those major countries that continuation of the Indochina war was not in their best interest, and they evidently made this known to the North Vietnamese. The darkening skies of the Middle East and the Mediterranean must also have had their effect upon the Russians. Anyway our relationship with these two countries warmed up. In 1973 we renewed diplomatic relations with the People's Republic of China, and also engaged in *détente* with Russia. I believe that Russia and the United States are doing what they can to block another outright war, but only time can tell what the outcome will be. I don't think it will be very long before either better arrangements will be made or the situation will become decidedly worse.

The United States is almost the only country that is supporting Israel both militarily and economically. But whether the United States government and the Congress would extend our full military strength to the defense of Israel is still a momentous and uncertain question. It is virtually certain that, should we extend full military support to this small country in time of war, Russia would do the same for the surrounding Arab nations, and most likely be joined by Turkey and Iran in the effort. Certainly raids and minor conflicts will continue for some time to come, but unless the major countries have lost their senses completely another full-scale war will be prevented.

Our country is also working for better relations with other parts of the world, and has restored diplomatic relations with East Germany, Egypt and Algeria. Our trade and foreign aid bills have finally been approved by the Congress, and, much to my joy and surprise, some of foreign aid's erstwhile opponents fell into line and approved a reasonably workable program.

¶ ONE OVERRIDING PROBLEM has been the demonstration of political power by the oil-producing states, instigating far-reaching efforts to find new sources of energy not dependent on their petroleum supply. This effort will doubtless result in some rather remarkable discoveries in the coming years.

¶ WHILE THE CHANGES which have taken place on the international scene during the last three years have been almost radical in their effect, the changes in our domestic situation have been hardly less far-reaching. For almost forty years the farmers of the United States have been largely dependent upon federal support to provide income enough to keep them in business. During the last three years the situation has been almost reversed, for instead of having mandatory cuts in agricultural production with the price of the crops supported by government payments, the American farmer is now being encouraged to plant his maximum acreage available, especially for grain crops. The reason for this is that the whole world now looks to the United States to keep it from going hungry.

When in the spring of 1972 Russia placed orders with private grain dealers in the United States for large quantities of wheat and other grains, it seemed that the dam impeding international trade in agricultural products broke, and every country everywhere looked to us to augment their own food supplies. Only a few commodities are now grown on allotted acreage, and government payments to farmers for not growing crops have dropped way down. Almost all the countries in the world, it appears, want us to share with them our production of wheat, corn, soybeans and other lesser crops at substantial increases in prices. Wheat, for instance, which used to sell for $1.80 to $2.00 a bushel, shot up to $6.00, and soybeans went from $3 to $8 a bushel. Only cotton has shown a substantial decrease in price during the last two years. This big increase in the export of agricultural commodities, estimated to amount to $21 billion for fiscal 1974, has been a lifesaver for the international trade of our country.

Politically, the last three years have been no less shocking, with the resignation of Vice President Agnew in the fall of 1973, the appointment of Congressman Jerry Ford of Michigan as Vice President by President Nixon, the resignation of President Nixon himself on August 9, 1974, the accession of Vice President Ford to the Presidency, and his appointment of former Governor Nelson Rockefeller of New York to succeed him as Vice President. Thus, within a twelve-month period, the United States government acquired both a President and a Vice President who had not been elected to these positions.

All this commotion in the high circles of government was precipitated by the foolish efforts of certain Republicans to break into the Democrat headquarters at the Watergate building in Washington in the summer of 1972. It all seems so ridiculous and so unnecessary.

Partly as a result of the Watergate scandal, the Congressional election of November 5, 1974, showed a drop-off in the percentage of those qualified to vote who exercised this right. It is my opinion that both major political parties have been seriously affected. This view was emphasized strongly in the November 1974 election, when the State of Maine elected a non-partisan governor. I believe that what happened in Maine is going to spread considerably in local and state elections in 1976. The time has probably not arrived when an independent candidate would stand a chance of being President, but the time is here when we may expect very definite and decided changes in the makeup and control of our two major political parties.

[Putney, Vermont]

Week ending January 2, 1975

AT THE END OF THIS WEEK, L.P.A. and I left Washington for good after having been there thirty-four years, lacking one week. My retirement income amounts to more than my paycheck for the last few years. I could have added 7.4 percent to this by resigning before midnight on December 31st. I did not choose to do so, because I have always felt I should carry out contracts in full. When I came to Washington, I lost a week in the Senate because I insisted on completing my term as governor of Vermont. I have never been sorry that I did this.

When we got to the house on the mountain in Putney we found that the neighbors had cleaned the snow off the steps. Now, instead of looking out of the window and seeing the Capitol and the Washington Monument, we see Mt. Monadnock and the New Hampshire hills in the near distance, and the nearby hills of Vermont covered with one to two feet of snow. There are no deer in our yard, since they have all gone back to their own yard in the woods, but the chickadees and blue jays were on hand to meet us. Although we miss our many friends in Washington, Vermont is a welcome relief from the atmosphere in our nation's capital for the last few years.

It is good to be home.

Chronology

1892 George David Aiken born at Dummerston, Vermont, August 20, son of Edward W. and Myra A. (Cook) Aiken.

1909 Graduated from Brattleboro (Vermont) High School.

1910 Became Master of the Putney (Vermont) Grange.

1913 Helped organize the Windham County Farm Bureau, the second farm bureau in Vermont.

1914 Married Beatrice Howard (deceased).
Children: Dorothy Aiken Morse, Marjorie Aiken Cleverly, Howard Aiken (deceased), Barbara Aiken Jones.

1917 Elected president of the Vermont Horticultural Society, marking his contribution to gardening and to preservation and propagation of native plants, especially wildflowers.

1920 School Director, Town of Putney; served until 1937.

1930 Elected to the Vermont House of Representatives as the Member from Putney; served until 1935.

1933 Began a two-year term as Speaker of the Vermont House of Representatives.
His *Pioneering with Wildflowers* published (revised edition, 1968).

1935 Elected Lieutenant Governor of Vermont, served two years. G.D.A. was instrumental in bringing rural electric co-operatives into Vermont; secured passage of enabling legislation in the Vermont legislature that brought REA benefits to the state.
President of the Windham County Farm Bureau.

1936 His *Pioneering with Fruits and Berries* was published.

1937 Elected Governor of Vermont. For four years in office, he successfully resisted the federal government's claim to jurisdiction over Vermont streams and watersheds. He also initiated action to establish the Connecticut River Flood Control Compact (finally approved when he introduced the bill as a U.S. Senator in 1953).
G.D.A. the first governor to sign the Interstate Parole and Probation Compact.

1938 Received national attention for his call to end the "hate-Roosevelt campaign."
His *Speaking from Vermont* published.

1940 Elected (November 5) to fill the unexpired term (ending January 1945) of U.S. Senator Ernest W. Gibson, Sr., who died in office; at that time G.D.A. was one of the youngest men ever elected to the U.S. Senate. Re-elected November 7, 1944; November 7, 1950; November 6, 1956; November 6, 1962; and November 5, 1968.

George D. Aiken's Senate Committees

Aeronautical and Space Sciences 1965–67.

Agriculture and Forestry 1941–75; chairman 1953–55. Ranking member of the subcommittee on Agricultural Credit and Rural Electrification; member of subcommittees on Environment, Soil Conservation and Forestry, and on Agriculture Appropriations.

Joint Committee on Atomic Energy 1959–75. Became ranking Senate member of the committee, and of five subcommittees—on Communities, on Legislation, on Research, Development and Radiation, on Energy, and on Licensing and Regulation.

Civil Service 1941–47.

Education and Labor (since 1946 Labor and Public Welfare) 1941–46.

Expenditures in the Executive Departments (later Government Operations) 1941–49; chairman 1947–48.

Foreign Relations 1954–75. Chairman of Senate Delegation of Canada–United States Interparliamentary Group for ten years; chairman, subcommittee on Canada 1958–69. Became ranking member of four subcommittees—on U.S. Security Agreements Abroad, on Far Eastern Affairs, on Western Hemisphere Affairs, on Near Eastern Affairs.

Labor and Public Welfare 1947–54; chairman, subcommittee on Education 1947–48.

Pensions 1941–47.

1941 Opposed Lend Lease to Great Britain in his first major speech before the U.S. Senate. He saw Lend Lease as vesting unlimited authority in the hands of the executive branch to make international arrangements, bypassing Congress in the process.

1943 Introduced his first bill for the construction of the St. Lawrence Seaway, a major project that would involve dams, locks and canals to allow ocean-going ships access to the Great Lakes; also, at the international rapids, a hydroelectric project capable of producing 1.5 million kilowatt hours was planned. Opposition to the St. Lawrence Seaway came from railroads, utilities and seaboard harbor interests, all of whom feared economic disadvantage from the Seaway. G.D.A. and other Seaway proponents continued to work for implementation of the project every year for eleven years, at the end of which time the necessary legislation was finally passed.

Also in 1943 G.D.A. introduced the first Food Allotment bill to distribute surplus agricultural commodities among low-income people.

1944 Spoke of consumer co-operatives as the "greatest single force for effectively regulating private industry."

He opposed Congressional delegation of power to the President: "Congress has given the President enough power to do about anything he wants."

1945 Called on Republican Senators to support the legislative program proposed by President Truman.

Co-sponsored a dental aid bill that would give federal aid to non-profit private groups for dental studies and demonstration programs.

With Senator Robert LaFollette of Wisconsin, proposed a food-coupon program for low-income families, and a hot-lunch program for schools.

Re-introduced the St. Lawrence Seaway bill, which was again defeated.

1946 Criticized a speech by Winston Churchill in Fulton, Missouri, in which Churchill proposed a United States–Great Britain military alliance. G.D.A. said, "I am not prepared to enter a military alliance with anyone. England, the United States and the Union of Soviet Socialist Republics should work together for assuring the efficiency of the United Nations Organization"; also queried why the United States should support British foreign policy, pointing out that Britain and Russia had been at odds for two hundred years, and that the U.S.A. should "steer clear of this conflict and work instead to bring the two nations together."

On the United Nations, G.D.A. said "With public opinion as it is, we've got to take one step at a time toward an orderly world. The U.N. may not be working very smoothly or making much of a splash right now, but it's working better than our own government did in the first year of its existence."

Was instrumental in enacting the Farmers Home Administration law.

In November became eligible for the chairmanship of the Senate Labor and Welfare committee, but he was opposed by conservative Republican Senator Robert Taft because of his frequent support for labor and opposition to strike-control legislation.

1947 In a Senate speech, said that there was no mandate "for this Congress to block the development of atomic energy for industrial purposes, or to turn the benefits of such development over to a little group of ruthless men who would control all the sources of power of the United States and the world if possible."

In another speech he called for an extension of food shipments to Greece and other European countries, calling food "our most potent weapon" against totalitarianism.

As Acting Chairman of the Agriculture committee, guided the first pesticide bill through the Senate—the Federal Insecticide, Fungicide and Rodenticide Act.

Questioned a Navy requisition for $97,252.50 worth of silver-plated finger-bowls and matching plates; Secretary of the Navy Forrestal said such purchases would be reviewed in the future.

In an article about G.D.A. in *The New York Times*, Arthur Krock said that many of the Senator's colleagues thought his roll-call record placed him with New Deal Democrats: of 123 roll calls in the 79th Congress, G.D.A. voted with Republican majorities 21 times, against them 82 times, and was paired or did not vote 20 times.

Was appointed to the Commission on Organization of the Executive Branch, also known as the Hoover Commission, which was formed to study ways to simplify the structure of the federal government, and to define and limit "executive functions, services and activities."

1948 Co-sponsored the permanent Crop Insurance Act; also sponsored the Agricultural Act, which established price supports for basic farm commodities and laid the foundation for dairy-price supports.

Co-sponsored the St. Lawrence Seaway project.

1950 Proposed a dairy-support plan, including easier credit for low-income farmers and expanded consumption of dairy products through public education, school-lunch programs, and food coupons.

Joined Henry Cabot Lodge, Jr., in trying to strengthen the Republican platform on civil rights by including a pledge to enact civil rights legislation in the current Session and to break a filibuster if necessary; this effort overruled.

Received the annual award of the American Parents Committee for his outstanding service to the nation's children.

1951 Co-sponsored a voluntary medical insurance bill in which states would get federal grants to provide care to the poor.

Served as a member of the Douglas Committee to study ethics in government.

1953 Was author of the Farm Credit Act, the first in a series of new laws allowing the farm credit system to be farmer-owned.

1954 Co-sponsored *Public Law 480*, widely known as "Food for Peace," one of the major instruments of on-going United States foreign policy.

The St. Lawrence Seaway and Power Project, which he had sponsored since 1943, was signed into law on May 13.

Sponsored the Water Facilities Act, which extended loans for the development of water facilities to all areas, not just arid and semi-arid regions; also sponsored the Aiken-Hope Small Watershed Act, which provided for flood prevention and watershed management on smaller streams.

1955 Received the Distinguished Service Award from the American Farm Bureau Federation for meritorious service to American agriculture.

1957 Member of a study mission to the Caribbean as a member of the Consultative Subcommittee on the American Republics.

1958 As chairman of the Subcommittee on Canada of the Foreign Relations committee, he inaugurated the Canada–United States Interparliamentary Group to establish a forum for discussion of mutual problems between lawmakers of each country.

1959 Visited Latin America as a member of the Foreign Relations committee.

1960 Appointed by President Eisenhower as a representative of the United States to the fifteenth session of the General Assembly of the United Nations: was assigned to Committee V, Administration and Budgetary Matters.

In a speech in Boston, G.D.A. said the primary task of the United States in the 1960's "is to protect the nationalist revolution, with its subsidiary social and economic aspects, from scavengers, whether of the communist left or the totalitarian right."

1961 Received the Congressional Distinguished Service Award of the American Political Science Association.

1962 Aiken-Talmadge bill enacted, authorizing co-operation between state departments of agriculture and the federal government in the administration and enforcement of federal meat and poultry regulations.

Opposed President Kennedy's request for United States' purchase of $100 million in United Nations bonds, saying the U.N. already owed the United States $32 million, and urged that U.N. finances be scrutinized "in order to bring home to all members of the United Nations that their relationships with that organization itself are to be financially responsible."

Was appointed to the President's Commission on the Status of Women.

Helped defeat the Northeast Water and Related Land Resources Compact, which would have given southern New England utilities control over Vermont streams and adjacent lands.

1963 Appointed by President Kennedy as a member of the United States delegation to Moscow to witness the signing of the Nuclear Test Ban Treaty.

Co-sponsored the Land and Water Conservation Fund bills to improve rural recreational facilities (the bills authorized establishment of the Bureau of Outdoor Recreation in the Department of the Interior) .

1964 The historic Civil Rights bill of 1964 passed Congress as a result of intensive revision work and support by a bipartisan committee of seven Senators—Aiken, Dirksen, Humphrey, Kuchel, Magnuson, Mansfield and Saltonstall—cooperating with the office of Attorney General Robert F. Kennedy.

Sponsored legislation requiring registration of all pesticide chemicals.

1965 Joined Senator Mansfield and three other Senators on a special study mission to Europe and Asia, the mission including a period in Vietnam. Their report, published on January 6, 1966, was called "The Vietnam Conflict: The Substance and the Shadow." The report warned that Vietnam was an "open-ended" conflict and that the war's end was not in sight, either through negotiation or through increased military pressure.

The Aiken Rural Water and Sewer Act, providing for improvement of rural water and sewer systems, enacted.

Was a principal co-sponsor of the bill authorizing the Corps of Engineers to construct, operate and maintain a tide-harnessing power project at Passamaquoddy, Maine (subsequent appropriations bills blocked, but the project remains under study) .

1966 By October, he concluded (in a statement called "Vietnam Analysis—Present and Future") that the time had come for the United States to begin a withdrawal program. His plan for ending the war became known as the Aiken Formula: "Declare ourselves winners and get out."

Sponsored a bill to establish national recreation areas in the Connecticut River Valley.

1967 Married Lola Pierotti on June 30.

1968 The Aiken Fair Practices Act was passed, protecting farm co-operatives from coercion by urban processors of perishable farm commodities.

Drafted legislation to protect small utilities against regional monopoly of the generation and distribution of electricity by the nuclear-power plants of private utilities; bill redrafted and passed in 1970 as *Public Law 560*.

Named an honorary member of the Soil Conservation Society of America, one of the most coveted honors in American conservatism.

In an interview in *U.S. News and World Report,* he said: "There has been too much tendency on the part of the public to look to government to solve all its problems—including its morals."

1969 Co-sponsored, with Senator Alan Cranston of California, *Senate Resolution 205,* which stated that recognition of a foreign government does not necessarily imply that the U.S. approves the character of that government.

Helped stop Senate approval of the Foreign Aid Appropriations bill because it contained an unauthorized $54.4 million item for jet aircraft for Nationalist China.

Received the distinguished service citation from the Experiment in International Living.

Persuaded the Department of Agriculture to establish in Vermont one of five pilot programs for feeding infants and expectant mothers.

1970 The Senate adopted on June 30 the Cooper-Church-Aiken-Mansfield amendment to the Foreign Aid Military Sales bill, which said, in effect, that the executive branch could not wage further war in Cambodia without consent of Congress. This was the first legislative move against the widening of the Indochina war; the first time in nearly twenty years that the Senate reasserted its foreign policy authority under the Constitution.

He guided the first egg inspection act through the Senate.

Was ranked number three on a list of twenty-one legislators who have led in promoting conservation.

1971 With Senator Mansfield, re-introduced a Constitutional amendment providing for a single Presidential term of six years. The move sparked national debate.

Early in the year he suggested that the United States convene an Indochina peace conference that would include the United States, the People's Republic of China, the Soviet Union, and other nations.

In a Senate speech urging Asian nations to do more to promote peace in Indochina, he declared he was "convinced that neither the Senate nor the American people are of an isolationist mind, for we all know that the self-righteousness of isolationism is as dangerous to our security and prosperity as is the self-righteousness of misguided intervention."

1972 Secured passage of the Federal Environmental Pesticide Control Act, which set up new regulations for pesticide use in interstate and intrastate commerce.

Had a leading role in formulating and writing the Rural Development Act, which he called "the single most important piece of domestic legislation approved by the 92nd Congress." The law provided loans and grants for developing small rural business enterprises.

Initiated a drive that led, in 1974, to the Eastern Wild Areas legislation, which established sixteen wilderness areas and seventeen wilderness study areas east of the 100th Meridian.

1973 Worked for successful enactment of the Agriculture and Consumer Protection Act of 1973, which established the "target price" concept for agricultural commodities, a major change in farm policy.

Worked closely with Senator Humphrey in enacting *Public Law 93–189*, which directed foreign aid programs to concentrate on improving the health, education, and agricultural development of poor countries.

In a Senate speech about the Presidency and Watergate, he declared that Congress should "either impeach President Nixon or get off his back." In another speech to the Senate he spoke of the need for bipartisan foreign policy in the Senate to make the President accountable. He warned that if the President ignores Congress, "instead of accountability he will get partisan investigation; instead of consultation, he will have confrontation."

Sponsored legislation to revise the Rural Electrification Act, which insured that rural areas and small co-operatives would be able to obtain loans to expand their facilities to meet energy demands.

The George D. Aiken Sugar Maple Laboratory was dedicated in South Burlington, Vermont, making Vermont the maple research center of the United States.

1974 In a critique of Congress published in *U.S. News and World Report,* he said, "We duck too many issues. Somebody said we should take the eagle off the seal and put the duck on instead."

On Valentine's Day he announced he had much unfinished business at home and would not be a candidate for re-election to the United States Senate.

Index of Persons

Abbreviations: In addition to common abbreviations for the states, the indexes use the following: Sen., *U.S. Senator;* MC, *member of the House of Representatives;* R, *Republican;* D, *Democrat;* Ind., *Independent;* Adm., *Admiral;* Gen., *General of the Army;* Pres., *President of the United States.*

Subject Index

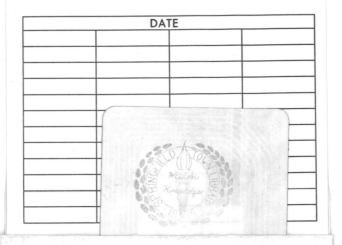